DATA SECURITY & ANALYTICS IN MODERN CYBER DEFENSE

From Data to Defense: Smarter Cybersecurity

Sai Ratna Prasad Dandamudi

Nageshwar Masakapalli

Rohith Vodapally

Amit Khanna

EXCELLER BOOKS®

A GLOBAL PRESS

Data Security and Analytics in Modern Cyber Defense
From Data to Defense: Smarter Cybersecurity

Cover by Exceller Books

ISBN: 978-93-47397-02-8

First published in India in 2025 by Exceller Books,
An imprint of GE Group

Address: G1, Dream Apartment, Degree College Road, Belgharia,
Kolkata, 700056, India
www.excellerbooks.com

EXCELLER BOOKS®
A GLOBAL PRESS

DATA SECURITY & ANALYTICS
IN MODERN CYBER DEFENSE

Dedication

This book is dedicated to the pioneers of cybersecurity and data science, whose vision and perseverance laid the foundation for a safer digital world.

To the students, researchers, and practitioners who will carry this mission forward, may these pages inspire your pursuit of knowledge, innovation, and resilience in the face of evolving challenges.

And to our families and loved ones— for your patience, encouragement, and unwavering belief in us. Your support has been the quiet strength behind every chapter of this work.

Acknowledgments

We owe a deep debt of gratitude to the many individuals and institutions whose support, guidance, and encouragement made the completion of this book, *Data Security and Analytics in Modern Cyber Defense*, possible.

First and foremost, we wish to thank our academic mentors and colleagues, whose insights and constructive feedback have shaped the ideas presented in this work. Their contributions, both direct and indirect, enriched the depth and rigor of the chapters that follow.

We are grateful to the institutions and research communities in the fields of cybersecurity, data science, and information technology that provided access to resources, publications, and discussions, which broadened our perspectives. Special acknowledgment is extended to professional associations and conferences that foster collaboration and knowledge-sharing among scholars and practitioners.

We extend our sincere appreciation to our students and peers, whose questions, debates, and curiosity constantly challenged us to think critically and refine our approach. This book is, in many ways, a reflection of our shared learning journey.

On a more personal note, we are profoundly thankful to our families and friends for their unwavering support throughout the long process of research and writing. Their patience, encouragement, and understanding sustained us through moments of challenge and inspired us to persevere.

Finally, we wish to acknowledge the countless cybersecurity professionals worldwide whose tireless work in defending our digital infrastructure serves as both the inspiration and the practical foundation for this book.

Preface

The twenty-first century has ushered in an era where data serves as the lifeblood of economies, institutions, and societies. Organizations no longer simply manage information; they rely on it as a strategic asset that underpins decision-making, innovation, and global competitiveness. Yet, this unprecedented dependence on data has also introduced profound vulnerabilities. As cyber threats grow in sophistication, scale, and persistence, safeguarding and intelligent data analysis have emerged as central pillars of modern cyber defence.

This textbook, *Data Security and Analytics in Modern Cyber Defense*, is designed to provide readers with a comprehensive framework that bridges the two critical domains of information protection and analytical intelligence. On one hand, the data security discipline ensures confidentiality, integrity, and availability through encryption, access control, and compliance frameworks. On the other hand, data analytics leverages computational power, statistical models, and machine learning to transform raw information into actionable insights, enabling defenders to detect anomalies, predict threats, and orchestrate proactive countermeasures.

Our intent as authors is not only to introduce the foundational principles of these domains but also to highlight their convergence in real-world applications. Cyber defense today is no longer a static process of building walls against intrusion; it is a dynamic, intelligence-driven practice that depends on understanding patterns hidden within massive data streams. In this book, readers will encounter case studies of high-profile breaches, explorations of cutting-edge technologies such as artificial intelligence in threat detection, and discussions of ethical and legal considerations shaping the field.

The work has been written with a diverse audience in mind—students seeking a structured introduction, practitioners aiming to deepen their expertise, and policymakers navigating the complexities of digital trust. Each chapter balances theoretical rigor with practical relevance, ensuring that the material is accessible while maintaining scholarly depth.

In an age where adversaries adapt quickly and attack surfaces expand relentlessly, the synergy between data security and analytics will define the resilience of future cyber infrastructures. We hope this text equips its readers not merely with knowledge but with the mindset to anticipate, innovate, and lead in the ongoing effort to secure our digital world.

Table of Contents

INTRODUCTION

The Digital Age and Its Reliance on Data

The dawn of the digital age has transformed the role of information in human society. Knowledge, which was once confined to physical repositories such as libraries or institutional archives, today flows seamlessly across interconnected networks, devices, and platforms. This transformation has elevated data to a status unprecedented in history. Economists, policymakers, and technologists alike often describe data as the "new oil" of the twenty-first century, emphasizing its role as a critical driver of innovation, productivity, and global competitiveness. Much like oil fueled the industrial age, data now fuels the digital economy, empowering decision-making processes, shaping social interactions, and enabling technological breakthroughs. Unlike oil, however, data is not finite; it grows exponentially, expanding in scope and volume with every interaction conducted in digital environments. The proliferation of smart devices, cloud computing, artificial intelligence, and the Internet of Things has created an ecosystem where billions of data points are generated each second, forming the foundation upon which modern life rests.

The reliance on data is evident across virtually every sector of society. In finance, data analytics governs trading algorithms, fraud detection systems, and digital payment infrastructures, ensuring both efficiency and security in global markets. In healthcare, patient records, diagnostic imaging, and genetic information are digitized and shared across networks to enable personalized medicine and evidence-based treatment. Education has also undergone a digital revolution, with online platforms, adaptive learning systems, and digital libraries enabling access to knowledge at unprecedented scales. Governments, too, have embraced data-driven governance, employing digital identification systems, e-governance platforms, and predictive analytics for policy-making and public service delivery.

Perhaps most critically, the military and defence sectors increasingly depend on vast streams of intelligence data to guide operations, enhance situational awareness, and anticipate adversarial actions. Each of these examples illustrates not only the ubiquity of data but also its indispensability in sustaining the functions of modern civilization.

Figure 1: Digital Transformation Across Industries Relies On Secure And Trusted Data Flows.

Yet this extraordinary dependence on data introduces a profound paradox. The same digital interconnectedness that allows for innovation and global collaboration also creates pathways for exploitation, disruption, and conflict. Every system that relies on digital information becomes, by necessity, a potential target for malicious actors. The interconnected infrastructures that enable instantaneous financial transactions can also be manipulated by cybercriminals to launder money or conduct fraudulent schemes. Healthcare systems, while empowered by digitization, are increasingly vulnerable to ransomware attacks that can paralyze hospitals and jeopardize patient safety. Educational institutions, while embracing online learning, must contend with data breaches and intellectual property theft. Government databases and election systems face threats from both state-sponsored actors and non-state cybercriminals, undermining trust in democratic institutions.

Similarly, the military's growing reliance on digital command-and-control systems makes them susceptible to cyber espionage, sabotage, and even offensive cyber warfare.

This paradox highlights the double-edged nature of technological progress. Connectivity, which brings efficiency, transparency, and global reach, simultaneously expands the attack surface of individuals, organizations, and nations. The once-clear boundaries between the physical and digital realms have blurred, creating an environment where a vulnerability in cyberspace can yield tangible consequences in the real world. A simple misconfiguration in a cloud server, a stolen credential, or an undetected vulnerability in a widely used application can have cascading effects across critical infrastructures and societies. The interconnectedness of modern systems means that local vulnerabilities often escalate into global crises. The COVID-19 pandemic demonstrated this vividly: as organizations shifted rapidly to remote work and online operations, adversaries exploited the expanded digital landscape, leading to a surge in cyberattacks that targeted healthcare systems, supply chains, and remote communication platforms.

Thus, while the digital age is characterized by unprecedented opportunity, it is equally defined by unprecedented risk. The reliance on data is not merely a matter of convenience or efficiency but a fundamental characteristic of modern existence. It is both the engine of innovation and the Achilles' heel of contemporary society. The challenge, therefore, lies not in questioning whether reliance on data will persist—it undoubtedly will—but in determining how societies, institutions, and individuals can secure, govern, and analyze this resource to mitigate vulnerabilities while maximizing its potential. This realization forms the foundation for exploring the intersection of data security and analytics within the broader context of modern cyber defense, where the stakes are nothing less than the resilience of the digital foundations upon which civilization increasingly depends.

Defining Core Concepts

To properly understand the significance of data security and analytics within modern cyber defence, it is necessary to establish conceptual clarity. The digital revolution has introduced terms and frameworks that are sometimes used interchangeably in casual discourse but carry precise meanings in academic and professional contexts. Three concepts in particular—data security, data analytics, and cyber defense—form the foundation of this discussion. By examining their definitions, scope, and interrelationships, we can appreciate how they converge to address the challenges of securing the contemporary digital landscape.

Data security refers to the discipline dedicated to protecting digital information from unauthorized access, alteration, or destruction. It encompasses a spectrum of practices, technologies, and policies that collectively ensure that data remains trustworthy and usable. At the heart of data security lies the well-established **CIA triad**: confidentiality, integrity, and availability. Confidentiality guarantees that sensitive information is accessible only to authorized individuals and entities, thereby preventing disclosure to adversaries. Integrity assures that data remains accurate and uncorrupted, free from unauthorized modification that can compromise its value or reliability. Availability ensures that data is accessible to legitimate users when needed, sustaining the continuity of operations in both critical and everyday functions. Together, these three principles establish a framework for evaluating and implementing protective measures across diverse digital environments. Data security thus extends beyond technical tools such as encryption or firewalls; it includes regulatory compliance, risk management, and organizational policies that collectively form the governance architecture of information protection.

While data security emphasizes protection, data analytics focuses on extracting knowledge and insights from information. At its core, data analytics is the systematic examination of datasets to uncover patterns, correlations, and trends that inform decision-making. In the context of cybersecurity, analytics has evolved into a cornerstone of threat detection and response. Analysts distinguish between different forms of analytics depending on their orientation: descriptive analytics provides an account of what has already occurred by summarizing historical data; diagnostic analytics seeks to understand why specific events happened, often by tracing anomalies or vulnerabilities; predictive analytics projects future risks or behaviors based on statistical modeling and machine learning; and prescriptive analytics offers recommendations for action, guiding organizations toward optimal strategies for prevention or remediation. These categories demonstrate the expanding power of analytics, moving from simple record-keeping to complex systems capable of anticipating and mitigating potential threats in real time.

The third pillar, **cyber defense**, encapsulates the strategies and mechanisms designed to safeguard digital assets, networks, and infrastructures against malicious activity. Unlike the narrower focus of cybersecurity, which is often defined as the protection of systems from attack, cyber defense implies a broader, more dynamic approach. It recognizes that modern adversaries are adaptive and persistent, requiring defenders not only to shield systems but also to actively detect, analyze, and counter threats as they unfold. Modern cyber defense integrates prevention, detection, response, and recovery into a continuous cycle, embodying resilience as much as protection. Where traditional security approaches were largely reactive—waiting for an attack to occur before responding—contemporary cyber defense emphasizes intelligence-driven operations, real-time monitoring, and proactive threat hunting.

What unites these three domains is their convergence in practice. Data security provides the protective foundation that ensures information is preserved and governed responsibly. Data analytics, in turn, enhances visibility and understanding of complex environments, enabling defenders to move beyond blind protection toward informed decision-making. Cyber defense ties these together, applying security measures and analytic insights to protect the integrity of digital infrastructures in a contested environment. This convergence reflects a shift in paradigm: effective defense in the digital era cannot rely solely on building barriers, nor can it succeed through analysis without protective measures. Instead, it requires an integrated strategy where security and analytics reinforce one another in the service of resilience.

In establishing these core definitions, we gain a conceptual map of the terrain this textbook will explore. Each domain—data security, analytics, and cyber defense—has a rich body of scholarship and practice in its own right. Yet their intersection is where some of the most pressing challenges and innovative solutions of our time emerge. As the chapters that follow will demonstrate, the interplay of these concepts defines the future of digital trust, resilience, and strategic advantage in a world increasingly shaped by data.

Historical Evolution

The evolution of data security and analytics within cyber defense cannot be understood in isolation; it must be traced alongside the broader history of computing and networking. Each stage of technological development not only introduced new capabilities, but also new vulnerabilities that demanded novel forms of protection and analysis. From the earliest days of stand-alone machines to the present era of globally interconnected digital ecosystems, the trajectory of cyber defense reflects a constant interplay between innovation and exploitation, defense and attack.

Figure 2: A Hacked System Exemplifying the Vulnerabilities That Have Driven the Historical Development of Modern Cybersecurity Practices

In the early decades of computing, the primary focus was not security but functionality. Computers were large, expensive, and limited in scope, often confined to government or research laboratories. Security, where considered at all, was largely physical—restricted access to mainframes or punched cards rather than protection of digital data itself. With the advent of personal computing in the 1970s and 1980s, however, the landscape began to shift. Systems became more widely available, and along with their accessibility came the first wave of malicious software. Viruses such as "Brain" (1986) and "Morris Worm" (1988) highlighted the vulnerabilities of increasingly networked environments. The defensive measures of this period—antivirus software and firewalls—were reactive by nature, designed to block or remove known threats based on signatures. These tools, though effective within their limits, marked the infancy of organized cyber defense.

The 1990s and early 2000s witnessed an explosion of connectivity with the growth of the Internet. Businesses, governments, and individuals migrated online, generating unprecedented volumes of digital information. This shift created both opportunities and risks. While digital infrastructures enabled e-commerce, online education, and global collaboration, adversaries, on the other hand, quickly recognized the potential of exploiting networks for financial gain, espionage, and disruption. Attacks grew more sophisticated, moving beyond simple viruses to encompass phishing campaigns, distributed denial-of-service (DDoS) attacks, and large-scale worms such as "ILOVEYOU" (2000) and "Code Red" (2001). Security professionals responded by deploying intrusion detection systems, patch management protocols, and more advanced firewalls. Still, the defensive philosophy of this era remained predominantly reactive, focusing on responding to threats after they materialized rather than anticipating them.

As the 2000s progressed, the scale and complexity of both data and threats expanded dramatically. The rise of **big data**—massive, heterogeneous datasets generated by sensors, mobile devices, and online interactions—posed new challenges for traditional security models. Organizations faced not only the task of storing and managing these volumes of information but also the difficulty of protecting them against unauthorized access and tampering. Cybercriminals adapted by exploiting this complexity, leveraging automation, polymorphic malware, and zero-day vulnerabilities. High-profile breaches such as the theft of millions of credit card records from Target (2013) and the compromise of personal data from Equifax (2017) underscored the insufficiency of conventional defenses.

It was during this period that **data analytics began to merge with cyber defense**, marking a pivotal turning point. Security Information and Event Management (SIEM) systems emerged, providing centralized platforms to collect and correlate log data from across networks. These tools enabled security teams to move beyond isolated incident response and instead analyze patterns across diverse data sources. Over time, analytics-driven approaches expanded to include anomaly detection, machine learning, and artificial intelligence, offering the possibility of identifying threats not only after they occurred but as they unfolded. The integration of analytics into cyber defense signaled the beginning of a proactive era, where defenders could predict, model, and anticipate adversarial behavior.

The past decade has further accelerated this convergence. Cloud computing, mobile applications, and the Internet of Things have exponentially increased the scale of data while simultaneously expanding the attack surface. Adversaries have become more organized, with nation-state actors, cyberterrorists, and criminal syndicates conducting highly targeted campaigns. In response, cyber defense has adopted new paradigms such as ***threat intelligence sharing, behavioral analytics,*** *and* ***extended detection and response (XDR).*** These approaches depend heavily on the ability to process and interpret vast quantities of data in near real time, underscoring the centrality of analytics in modern defense.

Thus, the history of cyber defense illustrates a progression from reactive measures based on signatures and static defenses to proactive, analytics-driven strategies. Each stage of this evolution reflects a dialectic between attackers and defenders, where innovations in offense prompt counter-innovations in defense, and vice versa. What remains constant throughout this trajectory is the recognition that as digital systems evolve so too must the methods of securing them. In the contemporary context, where the volume, velocity, and value of data are greater than ever before, the integration of analytics with data security represents not merely an advancement but a necessity for survival in the digital age.

Importance of Data Security in the Current Era

The centrality of data in contemporary society makes its protection not only a technical necessity but also a social, economic, and political imperative. In previous decades, the consequences of a breach might have been limited to isolated systems or small-scale financial loss. Today, however, the compromise of digital information can destabilize critical infrastructures, undermine public trust, and even threaten national security. The importance of data security in the present era is therefore multifaceted, encompassing dimensions of infrastructure resilience, regulatory compliance, economic stability, and the preservation of digital trust.

One of the most pressing areas where data security has become indispensable is in the protection of **critical infrastructures**. Modern societies depend on complex digital networks to manage essential services such as energy distribution, water supply, healthcare, transportation, and financial transactions. These systems are increasingly interlinked and automated, not only enabling efficiency but also magnifying vulnerability. A successful cyberattack on a power grid, for example, can disrupt entire regions, while breaches in hospital networks can jeopardize patient safety and interrupt life-saving treatments. Incidents such as the 2021 ransomware attack on Colonial Pipeline in the United States demonstrated that cyberattacks can have cascading effects that extend far beyond the digital realm, disrupting fuel supplies, triggering economic ripple effects, and raising concerns about national preparedness. The reliance on digital infrastructures thus makes their protection against cyber threats a matter of public safety and national resilience.

In parallel, the growing emphasis on **privacy and regulatory compliance** highlights the societal expectation that personal data must be safeguarded. Over the last two decades, governments across the globe have enacted robust data protection frameworks to ensure accountability in how organizations handle sensitive information. The European Union's **General Data Protection Regulation (GDPR),** introduced in 2018, set a global benchmark for privacy legislation, requiring organizations to uphold principles of transparency, consent, and data minimization. Similarly, laws such as the **Health Insurance Portability and Accountability Act (HIPAA)** in the United States and the **California Consumer Privacy Act (CCPA)** reflect efforts to protect personal information in healthcare and consumer contexts. Compliance with these regulations is not optional; failure to adhere can result in severe financial penalties, reputational damage, and legal liabilities. Data security, in this sense, is not merely a matter of technical defense but an obligation to uphold legal and ethical standards in a data-driven society.

The **economic implications of data breaches** further underscore the critical importance of security. Cyber incidents can cost organizations millions of dollars in direct remediation, legal settlements, and compensation to affected individuals. Beyond these immediate costs, the long-term consequences of reputational damage can erode consumer confidence and investor trust. For multinational corporations, breaches can disrupt supply chains, trigger regulatory investigations across jurisdictions, and weaken competitive advantage. Research by industry analysts consistently shows that the financial impact of data breaches is rising, fueled by factors such as ransomware demands, prolonged downtime, and the complexity of restoring compromised systems. In sectors such as finance and healthcare, where trust is paramount, a single incident can permanently alter the trajectory of an organization. Thus, investment in robust data security measures has become not only a defensive strategy but also an economic imperative for organizational survival and competitiveness.

Equally significant is the role of data security in maintaining **trust in digital ecosystems**. The proliferation of digital interactions—from online shopping and banking to remote work and education—depends fundamentally on the confidence of users that their information will be protected. Without trust, individuals may be reluctant to adopt digital services, thereby slowing innovation and economic growth. Trust is especially critical in emerging domains such as cloud computing, artificial intelligence, and digital identity systems, where the promise of innovation is accompanied by concerns about surveillance, manipulation, and loss of autonomy. For governments, sustaining public trust in digital governance platforms is essential to the legitimacy of e-services and electoral processes. In the absence of strong data security, skepticism and resistance may undermine the adoption of technologies that can otherwise enhance efficiency, inclusivity, and transparency.

The importance of data security in the current era can, therefore, be summarized as both foundational and transformative. It is foundational in the sense that without it, the digital infrastructures upon which society depends will be unsustainable, vulnerable to collapse under the weight of adversarial threats. At the same time, it is transformative, shaping the very ways in which organizations design systems, governments craft policies, and individuals engage with technology. Far from being a narrow technical issue, data security is a cornerstone of digital civilization, shaping trust, resilience, and progress in an interconnected world.

The Role of Data Analytics in Cyber Defense

As the volume, velocity, and variety of digital data continue to expand, traditional approaches to cybersecurity that rely solely on signature-based detection or manual oversight have become insufficient. The rapid evolution of cyber threats requires equally dynamic defense mechanisms that can process massive amounts of information in real time and extract actionable insights. This necessity has elevated **data analytics** to the forefront of modern cyber defense, transforming raw information into a powerful weapon against adversarial activity. Data analytics is not merely an adjunct to cybersecurity but an essential enabler that enhances situational awareness, predictive capability, and resilience in the face of ever-changing threats.

At its core, data analytics in cyber defense involves the **systematic collection, processing, and interpretation of digital traces** generated by networks, applications, users, and devices. Every interaction within a digital environment produces data—log files, system alerts, transaction histories, access patterns, and communication metadata. On their own, these fragments of information may appear insignificant. However, when aggregated and analyzed, they reveal patterns that can distinguish normal behavior from anomalies that signal malicious intent. For example, a sudden surge of login attempts from an unusual geographic location may indicate a brute-force attack, while subtle deviations in database queries may suggest insider threats. Through advanced analytic techniques, organizations are able to uncover these hidden signals and respond before damage escalates.

The integration of **machine learning and artificial intelligence (AI)** has revolutionized the role of data analytics in cybersecurity. Unlike traditional rule-based systems, machine learning models can adapt to new and evolving threats without requiring explicit programming. By training on vast datasets, these systems learn to identify complex patterns and make probabilistic judgments about potential risks. In intrusion detection, for instance, supervised learning models can classify traffic as benign or malicious based on labeled data, while unsupervised approaches can flag previously unseen anomalies. AI-powered analytics also support automation, reducing the burden on human analysts who would otherwise be overwhelmed by the scale of modern cyber environments. In effect, machine learning allows defenders to move beyond reactive strategies and toward **proactive, intelligence-driven security.**

A key dimension of data analytics in cyber defense is its role in **threat intelligence and predictive modeling.** Instead of waiting for an attack to occur, organizations can analyze global threat data, malware signatures, phishing trends, and dark web activities to anticipate potential risks. Predictive analytics enables security teams to model likely attack vectors, assess vulnerabilities, and prioritize defenses accordingly. For example, analyzing ransomware attack patterns can help organizations identify sectors at greatest risk and implement targeted countermeasures. Similarly, predictive insights can guide patch management by highlighting the vulnerabilities most likely to be exploited. This shift from reactive to predictive defense represents a fundamental reorientation of cybersecurity strategy, where foresight and preparation become as critical as immediate response.

Another critical contribution of data analytics lies in **incident response and forensic investigation.** When a breach occurs, the ability to quickly trace the origin, scope, and impact of the intrusion is essential for containment and recovery. Analytics tools can reconstruct timelines, identify compromised accounts, and map the spread of malicious code through a system. This forensic capability not only aids in immediate recovery but also provides valuable lessons for strengthening defenses against future attacks. In highly regulated industries, robust analytic systems also ensure compliance by documenting evidence of due diligence and reporting requirements to regulators.

Data analytics also enhances **strategic decision-making at the organizational and national levels.** Executives and policymakers increasingly rely on dashboards and analytic reports to evaluate cyber risks in the context of broader business or national security objectives. Quantitative insights allow leaders to allocate resources more effectively, balancing investment in prevention, detection, and response. At the governmental level, analytics supports national cyber defense strategies by integrating intelligence from multiple sectors—public infrastructure, private enterprises, and international partners—into a cohesive understanding of the threat landscape. This collaborative analytic framework ensures that no single entity is left to defend against globalized cyber threats in isolation.

Equally important is the recognition that data analytics in cyber defense must grapple with its **own challenges and limitations**. While advanced algorithms can uncover patterns invisible to human analysts, they are also vulnerable to adversarial manipulation, such as data poisoning attacks that skew results. Furthermore, the reliance on large datasets raises ethical concerns about surveillance, privacy, and bias. Organizations must therefore balance the power of analytics with strong governance frameworks that ensure responsible use of data. The success of analytic systems ultimately depends not only on technical sophistication but also on ethical stewardship and public trust.

Convergence of Data Security and Analytics

The landscape of modern cyber defense is not defined by isolated practices but by the integration of complementary disciplines. Among the most important of these is the **convergence of data security and data analytics.** While data security traditionally focuses on protecting the confidentiality, integrity, and availability of information, data analytics provides the intelligence needed to understand, predict, and counter evolving threats. Their integration creates a holistic defense strategy in which protective measures and analytic insights reinforce one another, yielding security systems that are not only resilient but adaptive.

To appreciate this convergence, it is necessary to understand how each component functions independently and then in tandem. **Data security** encompasses the technical and procedural safeguards—encryption, access control, authentication, and secure architecture—that protect data from unauthorized access or corruption. These are the frontline defenses that establish a perimeter and enforce rules of trust within digital environments. **Data analytics**, by contrast, does not focus on building barriers but on interpreting the activity occurring within and around those barriers. It identifies anomalies, extracts meaning from log files, and anticipates vulnerabilities that static defenses alone may not address. When combined, security mechanisms and analytic systems create a feedback loop: the stronger the data security measures, the cleaner and more reliable the data for analytics; the sharper the analytics, the more intelligently security policies can be enforced.

Consider, for example, the relationship between **encryption** and **anomaly detection**. Encryption ensures that sensitive information not only remains unreadable to unauthorized actors, but it also generates metadata that can be analyzed for irregularities. If an encrypted database is suddenly accessed at unusual hours or by unfamiliar credentials, analytic systems can detect the anomaly and trigger an investigation before the encryption itself is bypassed. Similarly, **access control systems** generate logs that, when analyzed, reveal usage trends and highlight suspicious deviations, such as privilege escalation or lateral movement within a network. In this way, security mechanisms generate the raw material—structured and unstructured data—that analytics transforms into actionable intelligence.

The convergence also extends to the realm of **real-time response and adaptive defense**. Static security controls, such as firewalls and intrusion prevention systems, have traditionally relied on pre-defined rules that attackers can eventually circumvent. When enhanced by analytics, however, these systems become dynamic and adaptive. For instance, machine learning models integrated into intrusion prevention can continuously refine their detection parameters based on newly observed patterns, creating a moving target that frustrates attackers. Likewise, secure identity systems, when linked to behavioral analytics, can transition from simple password-based authentication to **risk-based authentication** that adjusts its stringency according to context—tightening access for unusual behavior while remaining seamless for legitimate users. The result is a layered defense that is both secure and user-centric.

A further dimension of this convergence is found in **threat intelligence sharing**. Secure environments generate vast quantities of defensive data, yet this information achieves its full potential only when aggregated and analyzed at scale. Collaborative platforms allow organizations to contribute anonymized attack data, which analytics systems can then process to identify trends across industries and geographies. Data security ensures that shared information does not compromise the privacy or competitive position of individual organizations, while analytics turns collective intelligence into predictive insights. In this manner, security and analytics together foster not only organizational defense but also **ecosystem resilience**.

However, convergence also introduces new **tensions and responsibilities**. The reliance on analytics requires the collection and storage of massive datasets, often containing sensitive personal or organizational information. Without strong security safeguards, these very datasets can become high-value targets for adversaries. Similarly, overreliance on analytic outputs may lead to false positives or misplaced trust in algorithmic decisions. Ethical considerations, such as avoiding bias in automated threat detection or ensuring transparency in AI-driven security measures, become central to responsible practice. Therefore, organizations must balance the technical promise of convergence with careful governance, oversight, and ethical reflection.

Ultimately, the fusion of data security and analytics reflects a deeper shift in the philosophy of cyber defense. No longer can organizations rely solely on **static fortifications**; nor can they depend exclusively on **reactive detection**. Instead, security must be both **proactive and adaptive**, blending strong protective measures with intelligent analysis that evolves alongside the threat environment. The synergy between security and analytics transforms cyber defense from a fragmented practice into a **cohesive ecosystem of protection, intelligence, and resilience**. It equips organizations not only to withstand today's attacks but also to anticipate and prepare for the challenges of tomorrow.

The Human Dimension of Cyber Defense

While technology forms the visible infrastructure of modern cybersecurity, it is ultimately the **human element** that defines its effectiveness. Every encryption protocol, analytic model, or intrusion detection system is designed, configured, monitored, and refined by people. Conversely, nearly every breach, regardless of its technical sophistication, exploits a human weakness—whether through social engineering, insider negligence, or lapses in organizational oversight. This dual reality underscores the indispensable role of human agency in both the strength and vulnerability of cyber defense systems.

At the most fundamental level, **cybersecurity professionals** are the architects and stewards of digital safety. Their expertise spans a wide spectrum: from system administrators who configure secure networks, to threat analysts who decode attacker behavior, to incident responders who contain breaches in real time. These roles require not only technical knowledge but also critical thinking, creativity, and adaptability. Cyber threats evolve rapidly, often outpacing pre-defined rules or automated defenses. It is the human analyst who recognizes patterns that machines overlook, who questions assumptions, and who makes nuanced decisions under pressure. No matter how advanced the algorithms become, they cannot replicate the contextual judgment and ethical reasoning that experienced professionals bring to the defense ecosystem.

At the same time, the human dimension is also the **Achilles' heel** of cyber defense. Attackers routinely exploit psychological and behavioral vulnerabilities through techniques such as phishing, spear-phishing, and social engineering. A cleverly crafted email, exploiting curiosity or urgency, can bypass even the strongest firewalls if a user clicks on a malicious link. Similarly, the misuse of weak passwords, failure to update software, or improper handling of sensitive data often result in breaches that no machine can prevent. These human errors remind us that cyber defense cannot be reduced to technical controls alone; it must incorporate education, culture, and accountability.

This is why **cybersecurity awareness and training** have become essential pillars of organizational defense. Training initiatives must extend beyond one-time workshops or compliance checklists. Instead, they should foster an enduring culture of security, where every employee—from executives to interns—understands their role in safeguarding data. Effective programs use scenario-based simulations, such as mock phishing campaigns, to develop practical vigilance. They also emphasize the "why" of security, helping individuals internalize the broader consequences of their actions, rather than treating protocols as arbitrary rules. When employees perceive themselves as active participants in defense, the likelihood of breaches caused by negligence is significantly reduced.

The human dimension also manifests in the form of **insider threats**, which remain among the most difficult challenges in cybersecurity. Unlike external adversaries, insiders already possess legitimate access to systems and often a deep understanding of organizational workflows. Insider threats may be malicious—driven by personal gain, grievance, or coercion—or unintentional, resulting from carelessness or lack of awareness. Addressing this risk requires a combination of technical monitoring and human sensitivity. Behavioral analytics can detect unusual activity, such as mass data downloads or unauthorized access attempts, but organizations must also cultivate trust and accountability to discourage malicious intent. The convergence of human judgment and analytic vigilance is key to mitigating insider risks without eroding workplace morale.

Another critical aspect of the human dimension is **collaboration between humans and analytics systems**. Advanced tools—ranging from machine learning models to automated threat intelligence platforms—are designed to augment human decision-making, not replace it. Analysts rely on these tools to process vast quantities of data, filter irrelevant noise, and surface potential threats. Yet, the final interpretation often rests with humans, who assess context, weigh risks, and decide on the most appropriate response. This **symbiotic relationship** ensures that defenses are both scalable and nuanced: machines excel at speed and volume, while humans contribute judgment and adaptability. Over time, this collaboration is expected to deepen, with human expertise guiding the ethical design of AI-driven security and AI, in turn, amplifying human capabilities.

Finally, the human dimension emphasizes the importance of **leadership and policy** in cyber defense. Executives and policymakers set the tone for organizational priorities, resource allocation, and compliance with legal and ethical standards. Without leadership commitment, even the most advanced technical defenses may falter due to underfunding, poor enforcement, or misaligned incentives. Leaders must view cybersecurity not as an IT issue but as a strategic imperative, integral to reputation, trust, and national security. This recognition ensures that the human element—at all levels, from frontline employees to boardrooms—is harmonized with technological defenses in the pursuit of resilience.

In sum, the human dimension is both the **strongest defense and the greatest vulnerability** in modern cyber systems. The effectiveness of data security and analytics ultimately depends on how people design, implement, interpret, and adhere to them. By investing in education, fostering a culture of accountability, addressing insider risks, and promoting collaboration between humans and analytic tools, organizations can transform the human element from a point of weakness into a pillar of strength. In an era where cyber conflict is as much psychological as it is technical, the central role of people cannot be overstated.

Emerging Trends in Data Security and Analytics

The landscape of cyber defense is never static. As adversaries adopt new tools and tactics, defenders must continuously innovate to stay ahead. In recent years, several transformative trends have emerged at the intersection of **data security** and **analytics**, reshaping how organizations anticipate, detect, and respond to threats. These trends are not isolated developments but rather part of a broader paradigm shift in which data-driven intelligence forms the backbone of defense strategies. Among the most notable are artificial intelligence–driven security, predictive analytics, zero-trust architectures, and the looming challenge of quantum computing. Together, these developments point toward a future in which resilience depends not merely on static defenses but on dynamic, adaptive systems capable of evolving in real time.

One of the most profound shifts is the rise of **artificial intelligence (AI) and machine learning (ML) in security operations.** Traditional rule-based systems, while effective against known threats, struggle with novel attack vectors and the sheer scale of modern networks. AI, by contrast, thrives in environments rich with complex, high-volume data. Machine learning models can process logs, network traffic, and behavioral patterns to identify anomalies that might indicate intrusions. For example, unsupervised learning algorithms are increasingly used to detect zero-day attacks by flagging activities that deviate from established norms, even if no signature exists. At the same time, natural language processing tools enable analysts to mine vast repositories of threat intelligence reports, dark web chatter, and open-source data to generate actionable insights. Yet the adoption of AI in cybersecurity also raises new concerns: adversaries are themselves weaponizing AI, developing malware that adapts to evade detection or deploying automated phishing campaigns that mimic human communication with alarming realism. The "AI vs. AI" battlefield is thus a defining feature of the emerging security era.

Closely tied to AI is the expanding role of **predictive analytics**, which shifts the emphasis of cyber defense from reaction to anticipation. Predictive analytics employs statistical modeling, big data analysis, and machine learning to forecast potential threats before they manifest. For instance, by analyzing historical breach data, patterns of attacker behavior, and global threat intelligence feeds, organizations can identify which assets are most likely to be targeted and when. This enables proactive measures such as patching vulnerabilities before they are exploited, reallocating resources to at-risk systems, or simulating likely attack scenarios to strengthen resilience. Predictive models also enhance incident response by offering probability-based forecasts of how an intrusion might unfold, allowing teams to preemptively contain risks. While still an emerging discipline, predictive analytics reflects a strategic shift toward preemption rather than mere response, underscoring the value of analytics as a force multiplier in defense.

Another trend redefining cybersecurity architectures is the widespread adoption of the **Zero Trust model.** For decades, networks operated on the principle of perimeter-based defense: once a user or device gained entry, they were implicitly trusted. In today's hyperconnected environment, characterized by cloud computing, mobile devices, and remote work, this approach is dangerously outdated. Zero Trust flips the paradigm by assuming that no user, device, or application should ever be trusted by default, regardless of whether they are inside or outside the organizational perimeter. Instead, access is continuously verified based on identity, context, and behavioral analytics. This granular approach reduces the risk of lateral movement within networks, a common tactic in advanced persistent threats. Analytics plays a critical role here by monitoring behavior in real time, detecting anomalies, and enforcing dynamic access policies. The growing momentum behind Zero Trust reflects not just a technical shift but also a cultural one: from implicit trust to constant verification.

On the horizon, the development of **quantum computing** poses both opportunities and existential challenges for data security. Quantum computers, with their capacity to perform calculations exponentially faster than classical systems, hold the potential to revolutionize cryptography. On one hand, quantum algorithms, such as Shor's algorithm, can render much of today's encryption—RSA, ECC, and other widely used standards—obsolete, as they can factor large prime numbers or compute discrete logarithms with unprecedented efficiency. On the other hand, quantum technologies also open new possibilities for cryptographic resilience, particularly through quantum key distribution (QKD), which leverages the principles of quantum mechanics to enable secure communication resistant to interception. In anticipation of this dual-edged future, researchers and governments worldwide are racing to develop **post-quantum cryptography**—algorithms designed to withstand quantum attacks. This area exemplifies the foresight required in modern cyber defense: preparing today for threats that may only materialize in the coming decades.

Beyond these headline trends, there are other noteworthy developments shaping the future of cyber defense. **Blockchain technologies** are increasingly being explored as tools for secure data integrity, particularly in contexts where trust and immutability are paramount, such as supply chain verification or secure identity management. Similarly, the growing importance of **privacy-enhancing technologies (PETs)** reflects society's demand for solutions that safeguard not only systems but also individual rights. Techniques such as homomorphic encryption, secure multi-party computation, and federated learning allow organizations to analyze data collaboratively without compromising confidentiality—an innovation that balances the twin imperatives of security and privacy.

Taken together, these emerging trends illustrate a cyber-defense ecosystem in flux, characterized by rapid innovation and escalating adversarial tactics. AI and predictive analytics enhance detection and foresight; Zero Trust architectures reshape access and trust models; quantum computing challenges the very foundations of encryption; and blockchain and PETs introduce new paradigms for integrity and privacy. For students, practitioners, and policymakers, the critical lesson is that **stagnation is the greatest vulnerability**. Cyber defense in the twenty-first century is not about erecting permanent fortifications but about cultivating adaptive, intelligent systems capable of evolving alongside threats. The emerging trends explored here are not distant possibilities—they are the unfolding reality that will define the next generation of data security and analytics.

Structure of the Book

This textbook is organized into four major parts, each building upon the last to provide readers with a progressive and comprehensive understanding of data security and analytics in the context of modern cyber defense. The structure is intentional: it begins with conceptual foundations, moves into practical mechanisms, expands into analytical frameworks, and concludes with applied practices and forward-looking perspectives. In this way, both students and practitioners are guided from fundamental knowledge to advanced strategies, while maintaining a clear sense of how each domain contributes to the broader landscape of cybersecurity.

Part I: Data Foundations in Security establishes the conceptual and regulatory groundwork necessary for understanding data-centric security. It opens by examining the critical role of data in shaping security decisions and illustrates how diverse sources—ranging from system logs to cloud services—inform defensive strategies. The part then shifts to governance and compliance, addressing the policies, legal frameworks, and auditing practices that underpin responsible data handling. Readers are introduced to the principles that ensure data is not only technically protected but also ethically and legally managed in accordance with global standards.

Part II: Data-Centric Security Controls explores the technical safeguards designed to secure data in motion and at rest. Beginning with encryption and related cryptographic mechanisms, this section emphasizes the practical means by which confidentiality and integrity are preserved. The subsequent chapters address authentication, authorization, and identity management models, offering insight into the structures that control access to sensitive data. The discussion culminates with an exploration of data protection in complex digital ecosystems, particularly multi-cloud environments and API-driven infrastructures, where the challenges of scale and interoperability become central.

Part III: Security Analytics and Threat Intelligence marks the transition from control mechanisms to analytical capabilities. Here, the emphasis is on using data not only as an asset to be protected but as a tool for generating actionable security intelligence. Readers are introduced to monitoring practices through SIEM and SOAR platforms, followed by a focused treatment of machine learning in anomaly detection and predictive threat modeling. This section also addresses the emerging frontier of automated, data-driven incident response, highlighting how analytics can accelerate forensic investigations and streamline the containment of breaches. By situating analytics within real-world case studies, these chapters demonstrate the transformative power of data in enabling proactive cyber defense.

Part IV: Practical Implementations brings the theoretical and technical elements of the book into applied contexts. It explores risk assessment methodologies that prioritize vulnerabilities based on both technical severity and business impact, integrating data-centric approaches into organizational lifecycles. The final chapter looks to the horizon of cybersecurity practice, examining innovations such as privacy-enhancing computation, zero-trust architectures, and continuous monitoring. Importantly, it also considers the human dimension, outlining the emerging career pathways for professionals working at the intersection of data science and cybersecurity.

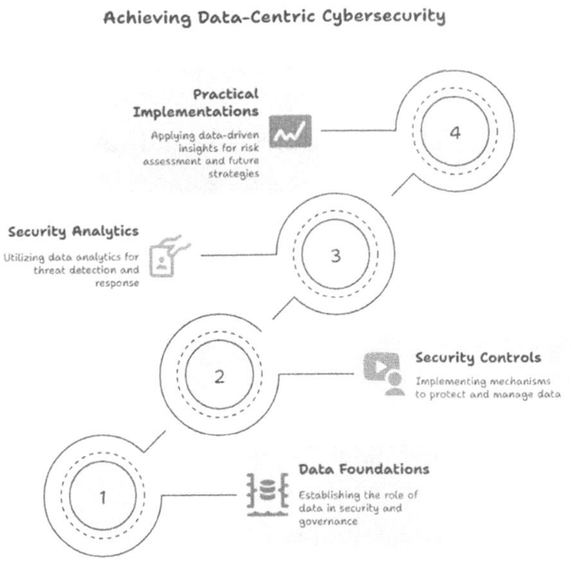

Figure 1.3: Roadmap of the Book Structure Showing the Four Main Parts and Their Corresponding Areas

Taken together, these four parts provide a logical and interconnected framework for mastering the subject. While the chapters can be read sequentially, each is written to stand on its own, allowing readers to consult specific topics as needed for study, research, or professional application. This structure ensures that the book can serve simultaneously as a teaching resource, a reference manual, and a practical guide for those engaged in defending digital systems in an era defined by data.

The story of modern cyber defense is, at its core, the story of data. Data fuels economies, informs policy, drives innovation, and underpins the very fabric of social and political life. Yet the same data that empowers progress also attracts adversaries who seek to exploit, disrupt, or weaponize it. In this paradox lies the central tension of our age: the more deeply societies embed digital technologies into their operations, the more vulnerable they become to those who would undermine them. This textbook begins from that tension, situating data security and analytics as not merely technical disciplines but as existential pillars of twenty-first-century civilization.

Throughout the preceding discussion, it has become evident that the evolution of cyber defense cannot be understood in isolation. The opening context revealed how the digital transformation has made data indispensable across sectors as diverse as healthcare, finance, government, and national defense. The rise of cyber threats showed the sheer sophistication of adversaries, from ransomware groups operating as global enterprises to state-sponsored campaigns targeting critical infrastructure. In response, analytics has emerged not as an optional tool but as the very foundation of modern defense, enabling detection, attribution, and foresight at a scale that human operators alone can never achieve. Legal frameworks, regulatory mandates, and international standards reinforce this defense ecosystem, illustrating that cybersecurity is as much about governance and accountability as it is about code and firewalls.

Equally important is the recognition that **security is not static but dynamic**. The emerging trends explored—artificial intelligence, predictive analytics, Zero Trust architectures, and quantum-resilient cryptography—underscore the imperative of adaptation. A defense model that was sufficient yesterday may already be obsolete today. The proliferation of connected devices, the rise of cloud-native infrastructures, and the globalization of cyber conflict all demand that organizations think ahead, not merely react. In this environment, analytics becomes more than a means of observing threats; it becomes a strategy for shaping resilient futures. By predicting risks, automating responses, and guiding policy decisions, analytics transforms the field of cybersecurity from a reactive posture to a proactive discipline.

For students encountering this material for the first time, the chapters that follow will provide both conceptual grounding and practical insight. They will trace the historical development of data security, examine the technical mechanisms of encryption, access control and monitoring, and explore the analytical tools that power modern security operations centers. For practitioners, the text aims to bridge the gap between theory and practice, highlighting not only the technologies themselves but also the human, organizational, and geopolitical dimensions that influence cyber defense strategies.

Ultimately, the central message of this introduction is clear: **data is the battleground of our era, and analytics is the compass by which we navigate it.** To defend data is to defend the integrity of digital society; to harness analytics is to transform overwhelming complexity into actionable intelligence. The road ahead is fraught with challenges—adversaries will continue to innovate, technologies will continue to evolve, and ethical dilemmas will continue to arise. Yet, within these challenges lies opportunity: the chance to build systems that are not only secure but also trustworthy, resilient, and equitable.

This textbook invites its readers to step into that ongoing journey. Whether as researchers, professionals, or policymakers, you are part of a collective effort to shape the future of cyber defense. By understanding the interplay between data security and analytics, by critically examining both the technical and societal dimensions, and by remaining vigilant in the face of emerging threats, you will be better prepared to safeguard the digital foundations upon which our world now depends.

PART I

DATA FOUNDATIONS IN SECURITY

INTRODUCTION

In the digital age, data has become both the lifeblood of organizations and the prime target of adversaries. Every transaction, message, medical record, financial exchange, and industrial process generates digital traces that can be harnessed for innovation or exploited for harm. The foundations of cybersecurity, therefore, are inseparable from the principles of data management: knowing what data exists, where it resides, who controls it, and how it is protected. Without these foundations, even the most advanced security technologies are reduced to reactive defenses rather than proactive safeguards.

At its core, data security is about control—ensuring that information maintains its confidentiality, integrity, and availability across its entire lifecycle. From the moment data is created or collected, through its storage, transmission, and eventual disposal, it must be governed by rules that preserve its value while minimizing risks. These rules are not only technical but also legal and organizational. Modern security frameworks recognize that protecting networks and systems is insufficient unless the data flowing through them is properly classified, governed, and monitored.

This foundational perspective explains why breaches are so costly and disruptive. When attackers compromise a network, their ultimate prize is almost always data be it personal records that can be sold on black markets, financial credentials used for fraud, or intellectual property that can shift the balance of global competition. The discipline of cybersecurity, therefore, must be understood as fundamentally data-centric.

The first two chapters of this part explore these foundations in detail. Chapter 1 examines the role of data in cybersecurity, highlighting its centrality to modern economies, its attractiveness as a target, and its implications for trust, risk, and national security.

Chapter 2 addresses the frameworks of governance and compliance that shape how organizations manage and protect data, from classification policies to global regulatory regimes and auditing practices. Together, these chapters establish the intellectual and practical scaffolding upon which more advanced technical mechanisms—such as encryption, access control, and incident response—are built.

By mastering the concepts in this section, students gain not only an understanding of why data lies at the heart of cybersecurity but also a framework for thinking critically about its protection in an era of exponential growth, cross-border flows, and evolving threats.

CHAPTER 1

The Role of Data in Cybersecurity

Learning Objectives

By the end of this chapter, students will be able to:

- Define and contextualize data in cybersecurity, recognizing why it is often referred to as the "new oil" of the digital economy.
- Explain the relationship between data and cyber threats, including how data attracts attackers and influences the scope of breaches.
- Differentiate between types of data (personal, financial, health, intellectual property, operational) and assess their varying levels of sensitivity and risk.
- Analyze real-world case studies of data breaches to understand the role of poor data protection in organizational failures.
- Evaluate the economic, reputational, and legal impacts of data loss or compromise on individuals, corporations, and governments.
- Discuss the strategic importance of data protection as both a regulatory requirement and a driver of customer trust.
- Identify emerging challenges in securing data in cloud, mobile, and IoT environments.
- Critically assess the role of cybersecurity as a discipline in safeguarding data across its entire lifecycle, from creation and storage to transmission and disposal.
- Connect data protection with national security and geopolitics, understanding how cyber espionage and data sovereignty debates influence international relations.

- Formulate arguments for data-centric security models that treat information itself—not just networks or devices—as the primary object of protection.

Overview

This chapter establishes why data is the backbone of every credible cybersecurity practice and how it powers security decisions from the boardroom to the Security Operations Center (SOC). It explains what we mean by "security data," traces how that data is generated across modern digital estates, and shows how defenders transform raw telemetry into evidence, insight, and action. Because contemporary environments are increasingly API-first and cloud-centric, the chapter devotes sustained attention to logs, APIs, and cloud systems as principal sources of security-relevant information. Along the way, it develops a practical "security data lifecycle," examines quality and integrity requirements for trustworthy analytics, and highlights the ethical and regulatory constraints that shape responsible collection and use. Three grounded case studies close the chapter, illustrating how data enables early detection, investigation, and response. The chapter concludes with a summary, key terms, and review prompts to consolidate learning.

Data as the Backbone of Security Decisions

Cybersecurity is often framed as a contest of tools and tactics, yet its essence is decisional: defenders must continually decide what to trust, whom to authorize, which events to escalate, where to focus finite attention, and how to respond under uncertainty. Each decision draws on data. Identity and access management relies on attributes and context to adjudicate requests. Detection depends on observations of behavior that departs from a baseline. Incident response is a sequence of evidentiary judgments grounded in logs, forensics artifacts, and correlated signals. Even strategic choices—how to invest a limited budget, which risks to accept—are best made with data: frequencies of control failures, distributions of dwell time, mean time to detect and respond, and the materiality of past incidents.

Data gives defenders reach across time and space. It records what happened when nobody was watching, allows hypotheses to be tested after the fact, and supports automation that would be impossible if each judgment required human inspection. Data also enables measurement. Without instrumentation, programs cannot demonstrate effectiveness or improve. With it, teams can track alert quality, false-positive rates, control coverage, and the lag between exposure and remediation. Put differently, data underwrites both the epistemology (how we know) and the governance (how we steer) of cybersecurity.

A consequence follows. Security programs that treat data as an afterthought—collecting "whatever the tool emits" with no plan for quality, structure, or use—will struggle to scale, to automate, and to earn trust. Programs that treat data as a first-class product—designed, owned, modeled, and governed—can move from reactive firefighting to proactive, evidence-based defense.

Decisions, Uncertainty, and the Security Data Loop

Every SOC lives inside a feedback loop that can be summarized as observe, orient, decide, and act. Observation is the acquisition of signals: events, metrics, traces, and states. Orientation is context: mapping signals to assets, identities, business processes, and known threats. Decision is selection: triage, escalation, suppression, or containment. Action is effect: blocking, isolating, resetting credentials, patching, or communicating. The loop's speed and reliability are limited by data: if events arrive late, without context, or in inconsistent formats, orientation lags and decisions degrade; if actions are not recorded as data, learning stalls because the system cannot evaluate outcomes.

Uncertainty is inherent. Attackers adapt, base rates for malicious events are low compared with benign activity, and environments are heterogeneous and dynamic. Good security data reduces uncertainty by increasing the signal-to-noise ratio and by supporting probabilistic reasoning. For example, combining failed logins, new device fingerprints, and an impossible-travel pattern increases confidence that a session is compromised. Conversely, poor or partial data invites the base-rate fallacy, where extremely rare malicious events trigger broad controls that overwhelm analysts with false positives. The craft of data-driven security is therefore as much about curation and context as it is about collection.

Sources of Security Data

Security data is any information that, when observed, stored, or analyzed, can improve the confidentiality, integrity, availability, safety, or trustworthiness of systems and information. Some of this data is obviously "security-ish"—firewall logs, endpoint detections, authentication events. Much is not obviously security-specific but becomes so in context: changes to a payroll table, a spike in storage egress, a new administrative API token for a build system. To reason about this landscape, it helps to group sources by the kinds of questions they help answer.

Identity and access telemetry answers who did what, when, from where, and with which privileges. Network and DNS data answers who talked to whom and how often, revealing command-and-control patterns, exfiltration, lateral movement, and service misuse. Endpoint and workload telemetry answers what processes executed, what modules loaded, what files changed, and which containers or functions spun up. Application and database logs answer how business operations behaved and whether requests matched expected workflows. Cloud and SaaS audit trails answer which control-plane actions modified infrastructure or data stores, and by whom. Configuration, vulnerability, and posture data answer what exists, where it lives, how it is configured, and what can go wrong even before an attacker shows up. Finally, external intelligence—from published indicators to behavioral TTPs—answers what the adversary is doing globally and how that might intersect with local exposures.

Security data is most effective when teams adopt a lifecycle mindset. Generation occurs at endpoints, services, networks, identities, and control planes as they operate. Collection happens by agents, forwarders, or API pulls and webhooks. Transport moves events reliably via protocols and queues, preserving order and timestamps. Storage persists records in structures optimized for search, correlation, and long-term retention, often tiered into hot, warm, and cold paths depending on query latency and cost. Normalization maps heterogeneous schemas into a common model, with careful preservation of original fields to avoid information loss. Enrichment attaches context—asset ownership, business criticality, geolocation, threat intelligence, or identity attributes—transforming raw events into situationally aware records. Analysis ranges from simple rules to complex machine learning models and from real-time streaming detections to slower batch analytics. Action closes the loop through automated or guided response, ticketing, and communication. Archiving and retirement fulfil legal retention requirements and enforce data minimization, including secure deletion. Throughout the lifecycle, governance defines ownership, access, quality controls, and evidentiary integrity (signing, hashing, chain of custody) to ensure data can support audits, legal proceedings, and post-incident reviews.

Logs

Logs are the diary entries of machines and services. They encode events—successes and failures, starts and stops, denials and approvals—with timestamps that allow reconstruction of causality. Because logs emerge from every layer of the stack, they provide the most diverse and ubiquitous security signals.

Operating system logs on servers and workstations record account activity, privilege use, process creation, driver loading, service state changes, and policy enforcement. Network infrastructure produces logs for ACL decisions, routing changes, VPN sessions, and wireless associations. Web servers record client addresses, HTTP verbs, status codes, user agents, and referrers. Authentication and authorization components issue records on successful and failed logins, token issuance and validation, multi-factor challenges, and role or group membership changes. Databases generate audit trails for connections, queries, schema changes, and access to sensitive tables or columns. Messaging and email systems reveal senders, recipients, attachments, and policy actions such as quarantine or rejection. Developer platforms log build pipeline steps, artifact signatures, secret detections, and deployment activity.

For logs to serve as evidence, they require rigor. Clocks must be synchronized so events from different systems can be ordered reliably; timestamps should include time zones or be normalized to UTC with precision sufficient for the expected analysis. Hostnames and IPs should resolve to stable asset identifiers. Message formats should be documented and ideally converted into a common schema while retaining the raw original. Where privacy is a concern, sensitive fields should be tokenized or masked at the source or during collection, with a reversible process for authorized forensic users.

Network and DNS Telemetry

While logs narrate discrete events, network telemetry captures relationships and flows. Flow records—summaries of connections that include source, destination, ports, protocols, byte and packet counts, and durations—enable coarse but scalable visibility. They can expose command-and-control beacons, lateral movement, and unusual egress. DNS query and response logs are equally powerful: malware relies on names, and misconfigured or abused systems often reveal themselves through anomalous query volumes, non-existent domains, DNS tunneling patterns, or sudden shifts in resolver behavior.

Deep packet inspection has become more complex as encryption has proliferated, but even encrypted sessions emit metadata. Certificates, cipher suites, Server Name Indication (SNI) values, and JA3/JA4 TLS fingerprints can characterize clients and servers without decrypting payloads. Combined with reputational or threat intelligence data, network metadata supports high-confidence triage while respecting confidentiality. In sensitive environments, defenders may implement selective decryption with consent and legal review for specific egress points, balancing visibility with privacy and regulatory obligations.

Endpoint and Workload Telemetry

Endpoints—laptops, servers, containers, and serverless functions—execute code, and code manifests intent. Endpoint detection and response (EDR) and workload protection platforms instrument process creation, module loading, memory allocation patterns, registry or configuration changes, filesystem operations, and inter-process communications. Containers and orchestrators add another dimension: pod lifecycle events, image provenance, runtime policy violations, and network policies enforced at the overlay. Serverless platforms emit invocation logs, execution durations, and permission use, which combine with cloud audit trails to illustrate least-privilege gaps.

Telemetry at this layer supports rich behavioral detections that are hard to express with network data alone. Examples include unusual parent-child process chains, LOLBins (living-off-the-land binaries) used in unexpected contexts, credential dumping tools, or scripts that touch sensitive registry hives. It also supports rapid scoping during incidents: answering which hosts executed a hash or contacted a domain in the last hour is often decisive.

Identity, Authentication, and Authorization Data

As applications moved to the cloud and users moved to the Internet, identity became the new perimeter. Authentication logs, federated single sign-on events, conditional access decisions, token minting and validation traces, privilege escalations, and group membership changes form a detailed ledger of who gained access to what and why. Context is everything: device posture, geo and network context, historical behavior, and the sensitivity of the requested resource combine to yield risk-based decisions. When stitched together with application and data-store audit trails, identity telemetry allows defenders to detect account takeover, privilege abuse, and insider activity with fewer false positives than network-only approaches.

Identity data is unusually sensitive. It demands careful governance: clear retention rules, separation of duties for those who can view raw identifiers, and auditable controls on any capability to de-anonymize tokenized fields. The same data that enables adaptive authentication can become invasive surveillance if used without policy, oversight, and transparency.

Application and Database Audit Trails

Attacks succeed when they move business value—money, personal data, intellectual property—or when they degrade the availability of business processes. Application logs and database audits, therefore, sit closest to the organization's mission. They reveal whether requests conform to expected workflows, whether records were read or modified in ways that violate purpose limitation, and whether controls such as rate limiting, input validation, and authorization checks behaved as intended.

Modern applications often span microservices, message buses, and third-party APIs. Observability practices—correlating logs, metrics, and traces with consistent request IDs—pay enormous dividends in security because they allow end-to-end reconstruction of user journeys or automated processes. When a fraud pattern emerges, for instance, traces show which internal services participated, which external calls were made, and which inputs triggered the behavior, targeted controls are needed that disrupt adversaries without degrading legitimate users' experience.

Cloud and SaaS Audit Trails

Cloud providers and enterprise SaaS platforms expose rich audit trails for control-plane actions: account and identity changes, network and storage configuration modifications, key management actions, policy updates, and data access. Because a single control-plane API call can reconfigure entire swaths of infrastructure, these trails are security-critical. They reveal misconfigurations before they are exploited, detect misuse of long-lived credentials, and document who modified what in environments where infrastructure is code and change is continuous.

Multi-cloud realities complicate life. Each platform uses its own nomenclature, event structure, and delivery mechanisms. Effective programs harmonize these differences into a common data model while preserving provider-specific detail for forensics. They also plan for scale: high-volume services can emit millions of events per hour, and naive centralization can incur both financial and performance costs. Event routing, edge filtering, sampling with care, and tiered storage strategies become essential.

APIs as First-Class Security Data Sources

APIs increasingly mediate everything from authentication to payments to device management. They are both an attack surface and a telemetry source. On the surface side, defenders scrutinize API gateways, authentication flows, rate limits, schema validation, payload inspection, and authorization checks. On the telemetry side, APIs expose exactly the kinds of structured, contextual data that analytics thrives on: who called which method, with what parameters, under which identity, from which environment, and with what result. Webhooks and event subscriptions allow security platforms to receive low-latency signals when critical actions occur—a repository is made public, an administrative token is minted, or a storage bucket's policy changes.

Working with APIs as data sources introduces practical concerns. Pagination and rate limits require robust collectors; authentication and authorization to the source must be strongly controlled and rotated; schemas evolve and must be versioned; failures should degrade gracefully and alert operators; and sensitive fields may need to be masked or tokenized in transit and at rest. Treated well, APIs offer high-fidelity, high-context streams that compress the mean time to detect and clarify root cause in minutes rather than hours.

Asset, Configuration, Vulnerability, and Posture Data

Before an incident ever occurs, posture data describes the terrain. Asset inventories answer what exists and who owns it. Configuration baselines and drift detections answer how systems are built and whether they deviate from secure states. Vulnerability scans and software bill of materials (SBOM) records identify known weaknesses and component dependencies, while exploitability intelligence helps teams prioritize. Control validation and attack-simulation results connect configuration to effect, indicating whether defenses actually work as designed. When combined with business context—criticality, data classification, regulatory scope, posture and vulnerability data drive risk-based prioritization and provide an essential counterweight to the cognitive pull of "whatever paged at 3 AM."

External and Threat Intelligence

No organization defends in isolation. External intelligence complements local telemetry with global context: indicators of compromise, toolmarks and tradecraft (tactics, techniques, and procedures), adversary infrastructure, and sector-specific warnings. Mature programs privilege behavior and tradecraft over raw indicators, because behaviors generalize beyond an adversary's current infrastructure and because indicator half-lives are short. Intelligence also informs hypothesis-driven threat hunting, tabletop scenarios, and red-team focus areas, ensuring that detection content evolves with the threat landscape.

Quality, Integrity, and Trustworthiness of Security Data

Not all data is created equal. For analytic conclusions to be reliable and for evidence to stand scrutiny, security data must satisfy quality properties. Timeliness ensures events arrive fast enough to act; accuracy ensures fields mean what they claim; completeness ensures coverage across relevant systems and that pipelines do not silently drop records; consistency ensures formatting and semantics remain stable across sources and time; and lineage records where data came from and how it was transformed so that analysts can reproduce results and auditors can evaluate process integrity.

Two additional properties matter uniquely in security. First, immutability: copies of evidentiary data should be written to storage that prevents modification (e.g., write-once or logically immutable tiers); with cryptographic digests allowing verification that records have not been tampered with. Second, clock discipline: without synchronized time, cross-system correlation becomes guesswork. Even millisecond differences can complicate causality in high-throughput systems; thus, time synchronization and explicit timezone management are operational imperatives.

Quality does not emerge by accident. It requires monitoring of the pipelines themselves: health checks on collectors, back-pressure and queue depth metrics, schema validation, drop-rate alarms, and sampling to verify that what arrives centrally matches what sources emitted. It also requires design choices, such as preferring structured logs with stable keys over unstructured text, and including durable identifiers (request IDs, user IDs, asset IDs) in every record to support correlation.

Privacy, Ethics, and Compliance in Data-Driven Defense

Security teams are entrusted with unusually powerful visibility. The same data that enables early detection of account takeover or insider misuse can expose individuals' movements, communications, and habits. Responsible collection and use depend on purpose limitation (collect only what is necessary for clearly defined security purposes), minimization (avoid collecting or storing sensitive fields when less invasive proxies suffice), transparency (document what is collected and why), and access control (strictly limit who can view raw data and under what justification). Techniques such as tokenization and pseudonymization reduce exposure by replacing sensitive tokens with resolvable surrogates, while differential retention policies ensure that highly sensitive data ages out quickly unless retained for a specific case.

Regulatory frameworks amplify these expectations. Security programs must reconcile obligations to detect and investigate with rights to privacy, data access, correction, and erasure where applicable. Employee monitoring requires additional scrutiny and consultation with legal and labor stakeholders. Cross-border data flows may trigger localization or adequacy concerns, so encryption and key management architectures should reflect those realities. Ethics and compliance are not constraints to be "worked around" but design inputs that shape sustainable, trustworthy programs.

Architecting the Security Data Platform

A security data platform is the nervous system of defense. At the edge, agents, forwarders, and collectors acquire events from hosts, applications, clouds, and SaaS. Where agents are not feasible, platforms use agentless methods—Windows event forwarding, syslog, cloud-native sinks, webhooks, and API polling. Message buses and queues decouple producers and consumers, smoothing bursts and enabling independent scaling. Central pipelines handle parsing and enrichment, mapping raw records into a common model and attaching asset, identity, and threat context. Storage subsystems balance hot search for the last few days (or hours) with slower but cheaper storage for months or years. Search and correlation layers expose query languages and APIs to analysts, detection engineers, and automation. Finally, response layers—ticketing, orchestration, and control systems—close the loop by enforcing decisions and recording outcomes.

Design trade-offs recur. Centralization simplifies correlation but can be cost-intensive and create single points of failure; distributed or "edge analytics" reduces latency and egress cost but complicates governance and incident reconstruction. Schema-on-write improves query performance and consistency but demands up-front modeling; schema-on-read preserves flexibility at the cost of per-query work. Multi-tenant designs support large enterprises and managed security providers but require fine-grained access control to segregate customers, teams, and data classes.

The guiding principle is product thinking: treat security data assets like products with roadmaps, service-level objectives, customers (such as analysts, incident responders, auditors, and leadership), and feedback loops. Assign ownership, document contracts, budget for lifecycle maintenance.

From Data to Detections to Decisions

Once pipelines are in place, the work turns to content: the rules, analytics, models, and playbooks that convert events into decisions. Rule-based detections remain powerful when built from strong domain knowledge and tuned against local behavior. Behavioral analytics and statistical models capture subtler changes and can adapt as adversaries shift infrastructure. Detection engineering treats these artefacts like code: versioned, reviewed, tested against simulated attacks or historical incidents, measured for precision and recall, and retired when they no longer earn their keep.

Decisions are not binary. A high-confidence detection might immediately isolate a host; a medium-confidence one might trigger stepped-up authentication or prompt a human review; a low-confidence one might merely raise risk scores. Feedback is essential. Every action should emit data—what was blocked, who was notified, what the outcome was—so the system can learn. Post-incident reviews should update content, enrich playbooks, and refine data requirements so that similar events are handled faster and with less disruption next time.

Cost, Performance, and the Physics of Scale

Security data can overwhelm budgets and teams if collected indiscriminately. Thoughtful programs are instruments for utility, not maximalism. They sample high-volume sources where statistical sufficiency permits, filter duplicates and noise at the edge, and prioritize fields known to drive analytic value. They archive raw data for evidentiary preservation but index only the slices required for operational search. They adopt compression and partitioning strategies that align storage to query patterns. They bring computation to the data when egress would be costly and place detections near the source when milliseconds matter.

Measuring the value of data helps make these trade-offs explicit. If a source contributes little to detections, investigations, or governance outcomes, it may not merit hot storage or immediate collection. Conversely, sources that consistently accelerate triage or reduce false positives deserve investment in reliability and depth.

Case Study A: Catching Ransomware in the Prelude

A mid-size healthcare provider experienced sporadic spikes in failed logins to clinical systems outside of typical shift changes. Identity telemetry flagged the failures but did not escalate them because each individual user's rate was modest. When the organization correlated those events with DNS telemetry, analysts noticed clusters of queries to algorithmically generated domains, interleaved with successful authentications from remote desktop sessions that used previously unseen device fingerprints. Endpoint telemetry on two radiology workstations recorded the launch of a built-in archiving utility invoked with atypical parameters. The combined picture suggested the reconnaissance and staging phases of a ransomware campaign: credential stuffing to find weak accounts, malware beaconing for command-and-control, and preparation of bulk file operations.

Because the data platform supported low-latency correlation across identity, DNS, and endpoint layers, the SOC elevated the event from "background noise" to a high-confidence incident in minutes. Conditional-access policies stepped up authentication for at-risk users, EDR isolated the two workstations, and network controls blocked traffic to the suspect domains. Forensics confirmed the presence of tools typically deployed ahead of file-encrypting payloads. The incident never escalated to encryption. Post-incident, the team tuned detections to treat the triad—failed logins clustered by time, DGA-like DNS, and atypical invocation of archiving utilities—as a composite signal, and rotated weak credentials identified during the hunt. The key lesson was not the novelty of any single indicator but the value of fusing ordinary signals across domains.

Case study B: Cloud Credential Misuse and Control-Plane Forensics

A research university adopted multiple cloud providers for different departments. One department created an access key for a service account intended for nightly data ingestion, but the key leaked when a developer pushed configuration files to a public repository. Within hours, an external party used the key to enumerate storage buckets and modify a network policy that created an outbound egress path. Cloud audit trails recorded the API calls, including the origin IPs, user agent strings, and the specific resources touched. Flow logs captured a new pattern of egress to an unfamiliar autonomous system, and object storage access logs recorded requests for datasets outside the ingestion job's scope.

The security team's platform ingested these trails in near-real time. A detection for "sensitive action by credential with no recent history" fired because the service account had never performed network policy changes. A second detection for "novel egress to low-reputation ASN following control-plane change" confirmed the suspicion. Response actions rotated the keys, blocked the egress, and suspended the affected workloads. Because the audit logs were immutable and time-synchronized, the university could reconstruct exactly what was accessed and modified and communicate with affected stakeholders transparently. The post-mortem yielded durable changes: mandatory key vaulting, pre-commit secret scanning, and a policy that service accounts may not modify network or identity configurations.

Case study C: Third-party API Abuse in a Payments Workflow

An e-commerce platform integrated a third-party address-verification API to reduce shipping errors. Attackers discovered that the integration failed open: when the third-party was unavailable, the platform accepted the address without validation and logged only a generic warning. Over several days of intermittent outages at the vendor, fraud volume spiked. Application traces showed unusually high latencies on the address-verification call, while API gateway logs recorded repeated 5xx responses from the vendor. At the same time, the fraud-detection model's input features degraded because the address-verification result field was often null, which caused the model's confidence to drop and increased the manual review workload.

A retrospective analysis correlated the vendor's availability issues with fraud outcomes. The platform added two controls: a circuit breaker that failed and was closed for high-risk orders, and a local fallback validator for basic checks. It also altered logging to capture explicit fields about third-party call success and reason for failure, and shifted model training to include a feature for "vendor_unavailable." The lesson: third-party APIs are both a dependency and a data source; their health and semantics belong in security telemetry because business-logic attacks often ride on the seams between systems.

Common Pitfalls and How to Avoid Them

Several recurring mistakes undermine data-driven security. Programs sometimes centralize everything but fail to enrich with context, leaving analysts to chase IPs and hashes with no tie to owners or criticality. Others rely on a single source—say, endpoint telemetry—and miss control-plane or identity misuse that leaves little host-level residue. Teams may deploy detections without measuring precision and recall, flooding analysts with low-value alerts that erode trust. Pipelines may drop events silently during load or schema changes, creating false negatives that nobody notices until an incident demands reconstruction. Privacy can be an afterthought, resulting in excessive retention or overbroad access to raw identifiers. Each pitfall is avoidable with product-minded design: clear data contracts; pipeline health and schema validation; context enrichment as a first-class requirement; multi-layer visibility; detection engineering discipline; and explicit privacy, minimization, and retention policies.

Reference Mental Model

A useful mental model is to imagine three planes. The visibility plane captures reality through telemetry across identity, endpoint, network, application, and control-plane sources, as well as posture and intelligence. The understanding plane turns telemetry into knowledge through normalization, enrichment, correlation, and analytics, measured by quality and governed by policy. The action plane enforces decisions through controls and orchestrations in identity, network, endpoint, application, and cloud. Data flows up from visibility to understanding, decisions flow down from understanding to action, and outcomes are fed back as data to close the loop. A healthy program invests in each plane and, crucially, in the interfaces between them.

Conclusion

Security is ultimately a decisional discipline, and data serves as its essential substrate. Decisions about threat detection, incident response, risk prioritization, and policy enforcement all rely on the quality, availability, and contextualization of data. In mature organizations, data is not treated as an incidental by-product of operations but as a strategic asset—a product in its own right. High-value security programs assign ownership to data, define usage contracts, establish quality metrics, and develop forward-looking roadmaps for managing and leveraging that data across diverse security functions.

The scope of data that fuels modern cybersecurity is broad and heterogeneous. Security logs, network and DNS telemetry, endpoint and workload signals, identity and control-plane audit trails, application and database records, vulnerability assessments, and even external threat intelligence collectively form the observability layer upon which effective defense depends. These signals do not merely reflect operational activity; they provide evidence that enables organizations to reason under conditions of uncertainty, to reconstruct the narrative of attacks, and to make informed decisions about mitigation and recovery.

The advent of APIs, cloud-native architectures, and elastic computing resources has elevated both the richness and immediacy of this observability. Cloud service providers generate detailed telemetry that, when properly leveraged, can offer near real-time insights into system state and user activity. Yet this abundance of data introduces practical challenges. Organizations must manage not only sheer volume but also cost efficiency, privacy constraints, and governance obligations. The tension between exhaustive data collection and responsible stewardship is one of the defining challenges of modern cybersecurity.

To navigate these complexities, a lifecycle approach to data security is indispensable. This lifecycle encompasses stages of generation, collection, transport, storage, normalization, enrichment, analysis, action, and retirement. Each stage introduces opportunities and risks: for instance, collection methods determine completeness, normalization influences comparability, enrichment affects interpretability, and retention policies shape both evidentiary reliability and compliance exposure. By approaching data management as a disciplined lifecycle, organizations ensure that data remains trustworthy as evidence in forensic investigations and effective as fuel for advanced analytics and automated response.

Case studies throughout the field illustrate a recurring theme: single signals are rarely decisive. A lone log entry, packet trace, or vulnerability alert may not reveal the full scope of an attack. However, when multiple data sources are fused, correlated, and contextualized, organizations can transform noise into actionable insight. Timeliness amplifies this value, allowing defenders not only to understand what has happened but also to anticipate what may happen next. In this way, the discipline of data-centric cybersecurity is less about individual signals and more about their orchestration—turning fragmented observations into coherent, predictive, and ultimately actionable knowledge.

Practical Lab Ideas

1. **Building Observability with Logs and Telemetry**

In this lab, students instrument a small containerized microservice and enable structured application logs that include request IDs. They then generate synthetic identity events and DNS queries to simulate typical network activity. Using a simple pipeline, students normalize and enrich these logs with contextual metadata such as asset information and user identity. The exercise demonstrates how raw data can be transformed into actionable signals.

2. **Detection and Anomaly Analysis**

Building on the first exercise, students implement two detection methods: one rule-based (e.g., flagging repeated failed logins) and one statistical anomaly detector (e.g., detecting unusual query volumes). They then evaluate the performance of both methods against labeled datasets, comparing strengths and weaknesses. This highlights the challenge of balancing precision and recall in real-world security monitoring.

3. **Cloud Control-Plane Auditing**

In a second lab, students use free-tier cloud services to collect a small stream of control-plane audit events. They then configure a policy that generates an alert when a previously unused identity principal modifies a sensitive resource, such as a network security group. As a response exercise, students practice credential rotation and document a clear chain of custody, reinforcing the operational aspects of security data use.

Key Terms

1. Security data*:* Any information that, when collected and analyzed, improves confidentiality, integrity, availability, safety, or trust.
2. Telemetry: Instrumentation outputs—events, metrics, traces—that describe system behavior.
3. Audit trail*:* A chronological record of actions affecting systems or data.
4. Normalization: Mapping heterogeneous records into a common schema while preserving raw originals.
5. Enrichment*:* Attaching context—asset, identity, business, or threat—to raw events.
6. Lineage: Documented origin and transformations of data.
7. Immutability: A storage property that prevents alteration of stored records.
8. Endpoint telemetry: Process, file, registry/config, and memory activity from hosts or workloads.
9. Flow data*:* Summaries of network connections including endpoints, ports, and byte counts.
10. Identity telemetry: Authentication, authorization, and privilege-use events.
11. Control-plane*:* The administrative interface of cloud or SaaS used to configure resources and policies.
12. Tokenization / Pseudonymization*:* Substituting sensitive fields with surrogates to reduce exposure.
13. Detection engineering*:* The disciplined development, testing, and measurement of detection logic.
14. Base-rate fallacy: Misjudging probabilities when rare events are evaluated in noisy environments.
15. Schema-on-write/read*:* Modeling data at ingest time versus at query time.
16. Hot/warm/cold storage*:* Tiers of storage optimized for latency and cost.

Review Questions

1. Define cybersecurity and explain its relationship with the protection of digital data.
2. Why is data often referred to as "the new oil" in the digital economy?
3. Identify and describe the main categories of data (personal, financial, health, and intellectual property) relevant to cybersecurity.
4. Explain the concept of the **data lifecycle** and how it affects cybersecurity planning.
5. What is the difference between data at rest, data in transit, and data in use in terms of security needs?
6. What are the most common forms of cyber threats to sensitive data in the modern era?
7. Provide an example of a recent large-scale data breach and summarize its impact.
8. How do insider threats differ from external cyberattacks in terms of data risk?
9. Discuss the role of ransomware in compromising data integrity and availability.
10. How does the growth of cloud computing create new challenges for data security?
11. Why do governments consider data protection a matter of national security?
12. What are the legal implications of mishandling personally identifiable information (PII)?
13. Compare how the EU and the US approach data protection from a regulatory perspective.
14. What role do international treaties and cross-border agreements play in data governance?
15. Why is compliance with data protection regulations central to cybersecurity strategies?
16. How does data security influence organizational trust with customers and partners?
17. Explain the financial risks companies face following a major data breach.
18. In what ways do reputational consequences often outweigh direct financial penalties in breach scenarios?

19. What role does employee training play in protecting organizational data assets?
20. How do organizations balance between usability of data and security controls?
21. Describe the role of encryption in protecting sensitive data.
22. What is the function of multi-factor authentication in preventing unauthorized access to data?
23. How can data loss prevention (DLP) tools safeguard against leaks of sensitive information?
24. Why is continuous monitoring important in cybersecurity frameworks?
25. How do artificial intelligence and machine learning enhance data protection strategies?
26. Why is cybersecurity often described as a "cat-and-mouse game" between attackers and defenders?
27. Analyze the long-term implications of a large-scale data breach on consumer behavior.
28. Should companies be held legally responsible for breaches caused by third-party vendors? Why or why not?
29. Discuss the ethical considerations of governments using surveillance technologies to collect citizen data in the name of national security.
30. Imagine you are a Chief Information Security Officer (CISO): what three priorities would you set for protecting data in your organization, and why?

CHAPTER 2

Data Governance and Compliance

Learning Objectives

By the end of this chapter, readers will be able to:

1. Explain the role of data governance in modern organizations, including how governance frameworks ensure that data is managed as a valuable enterprise asset.
2. Differentiate between categories of data sensitivity, and evaluate appropriate classification and handling policies for personal, financial, healthcare, and proprietary information.
3. Analyze key legal and regulatory frameworks such as GDPR, HIPAA, and CCPA, and assess their implications for global data compliance strategies.
4. Evaluate the importance of audit requirements in ensuring transparency, accountability, and compliance with data protection standards.
5. Apply best practices for designing and implementing audits, including the use of checklists, continuous monitoring, and emerging technologies such as AI and blockchain.
6. Critically assess case studies of compliance failures and successes, drawing lessons for risk management and operational resilience.
7. Integrate governance, compliance, and auditing into a unified strategy that balances regulatory obligations with organizational agility and innovation.

Overview

In the modern digital economy, data has become both a strategic asset and a liability. Organizations across every sector—from healthcare to banking, from manufacturing to government—depend on data to deliver services, build customer trust, and drive innovation. Yet this same data is also a target for cybercriminals, corporate espionage, and even state-sponsored actors. As digital infrastructures expand in complexity, the governance and compliance structures surrounding data have become indispensable. Data governance refers to the overarching system of principles, policies, and practices that ensure data is properly managed across its entire lifecycle. Compliance, in turn, reflects adherence to regulatory frameworks and industry standards that define how sensitive data should be handled. Together, governance and compliance provide the guardrails that protect organizations from reputational harm, legal sanctions, and operational disruption.

The growing emphasis on data governance and compliance is not merely a response to external regulation, but also an internal necessity. A company that mismanages sensitive information risks eroding customer trust, losing competitive advantage, and exposing itself to costly breaches. High-profile incidents, such as the Equifax breach of 2017, which compromised the personal data of over 147 million individuals, underscore the dangers of inadequate governance and poor compliance. Conversely, organizations that excel in governance frameworks and compliance auditing often discover secondary benefits such as improved data quality, streamlined operations, and enhanced decision-making capacity.

This chapter examines the foundations of data governance and compliance, focusing on three pillars: classification and handling policies, legal frameworks around data security, and the audit requirements for sensitive data. Through real-world case studies, historical developments, and comparative analysis, it demonstrates how organizations can move beyond reactive measures toward proactive stewardship of digital information.

Data Classification and Handling Policies

The first step in any governance strategy is understanding the nature of the data an organization possesses and how it should be systematically categorized. Without classification, information becomes an amorphous pool—difficult to secure, hard to audit, and nearly impossible to manage in compliance with modern regulatory frameworks. Data classification provides the taxonomy that distinguishes between public, internal, confidential, and highly restricted information. It is not a purely academic exercise, but a practical one that shapes every aspect of the information lifecycle: how data is collected, where it is stored, how it is transmitted, who has access to it, and how it is ultimately destroyed.

For example, public data may be shared freely without consequence, such as a press release announcing quarterly earnings. Internal data may include organizational memos or employee directories, which, while not damaging if exposed, still require some protection. Confidential data can include customer purchase histories, contracts, or employee performance records—information that must be safeguarded to maintain trust and comply with privacy regulations. At the highest level, highly restricted data encompasses medical records, financial account details, defense research, or trade secrets, all of which demand advanced encryption, layered access controls, and meticulous handling.

The importance of such distinctions becomes evident in crisis scenarios. When Equifax suffered its infamous 2017 breach, millions of records containing personally identifiable information (PII) were compromised. One of the key criticisms was that the company had not treated certain consumer data with the level of classification and protective rigor it deserved. Conversely, in organizations where classification is tightly coupled with handling policies, a breach of low-level public or internal data might be inconvenient, but it rarely escalates into reputational or financial catastrophe.

Historical Evolution of Classification Systems

The roots of classification trace back to **military and government intelligence systems**. As early as the 20th century, national defense organizations were categorizing sensitive materials into levels such as "Confidential," "Secret," and "Top Secret." These categories were not arbitrary but corresponded to the degree of potential harm to national security should the information be exposed. The **US**

Department of Defense, for example, formalized classification protocols during World War II, establishing strict clearance systems to prevent espionage.

Over time, these frameworks migrated from government to the corporate world. With the digital transformation of the late 20th century, businesses recognized that information—not just physical assets—had become their most valuable resource. Intellectual property, financial strategies, and customer data needed to be protected with the same care once reserved for military intelligence. Thus, corporations adopted similar layered classification schemes.

By the 2000s, classification systems had become **industry-specific** and tied closely to regulatory landscapes. A **global pharmaceutical company** might classify clinical trial data as highly restricted, since it carries not only intellectual property concerns but also obligations under regulatory regimes like the **US Food and Drug Administration (FDA)** and the **European Medicines Agency (EMA).** Meanwhile, marketing brochures remain public, designed for unrestricted dissemination. In the financial sector, **payment card information** is considered highly sensitive, requiring compliance with the **Payment Card Industry Data Security Standard (PCI DSS)**. In healthcare, electronic health records (EHRs) are governed by the **Health Insurance Portability and Accountability Act (HIPAA)**, mandating specific handling protocols. Thus, what began as a military necessity evolved into a universal organizational discipline, with modern classification schemes shaped by **business needs, regulatory demands, and technological complexity.**

Categories of Data

An essential aspect of governance and compliance is the recognition that not all information is equal in its sensitivity, value, or potential risk exposure. Organizations, therefore, rely on structured classification schemes that assign different categories of protection to different data assets. These categories provide the foundation upon which handling policies, access controls, and security investments are built. Without such distinctions, businesses would either under-protect critical assets—leading to devastating breaches—or over-protect trivial data, wasting resources and impeding efficiency.

Most classification models employ a tiered taxonomy, typically ranging from *public* to *highly restricted* data. The terminology may vary across industries and jurisdictions, but the underlying principle remains the same: the more sensitive the data, the stronger the protections required.

Public Data represents the lowest tier of sensitivity. This category includes information deliberately intended for dissemination, such as press releases, corporate brochures, product catalogs, or published research reports. The mishandling of public data generally carries no material consequence, though even here, reputational risks can arise if inaccurate or outdated information circulates. For example, a multinational company that fails to update obsolete financial figures in its investor presentations can inadvertently mislead stakeholders and face regulatory scrutiny for poor disclosure practices.

Internal Data occupies a middle ground. It refers to operational material not meant for public consumption, but which, if exposed, would not result in severe damage. Staff directories, training manuals, and internal meeting notes typically fall into this category. While internal data breaches rarely trigger regulatory penalties, they may erode employee trust or provide adversaries with reconnaissance material that can be exploited in social engineering campaigns. A striking case involved a European bank whose leaked staff contact list enabled cybercriminals to craft highly targeted phishing emails that later compromised customer accounts.

Confidential Data is even more sensitive, encompassing business information whose unauthorized disclosure can cause financial, legal, or reputational harm. Examples include customer transaction histories, vendor contracts, strategic plans, or merger and acquisition documents. Confidential data requires strict handling policies, such as role-based access control, encryption at rest and in transit, and secure disposal procedures. The Sony Pictures breach of 2014 exemplifies the risks associated with poor protection of confidential assets: unreleased films, executive emails, and salary records were leaked, resulting in reputational damage and significant financial losses.

At the apex of the classification hierarchy lies **Highly Restricted Data**, representing the organization's crown jewels. This includes personally identifiable information (PII), protected health information (PHI), payment card details, proprietary algorithms, and trade secrets. Mishandling of highly restricted data not only jeopardizes customer trust but also triggers severe regulatory and financial penalties. For instance, under the General Data Protection Regulation (GDPR), breaches involving PII can result in fines of up to 4% of global annual revenue. Similarly, healthcare organizations under HIPAA face both civil and criminal liabilities for exposing PHI. A prominent example is the 2015 Anthem breach, where attackers gained access to nearly 80 million patient records, costing the company hundreds of millions in settlements and remediation.

It is critical to note that these categories are **neither static nor universally rigid**. Instead, they are shaped by the unique context of each industry and organization. In the healthcare sector, a patient's diagnosis or treatment plan is unequivocally classified as highly restricted due to its personal and legal sensitivity. However, aggregated or anonymized research datasets may be categorized as confidential, since their exposure carries less risk to individual privacy. Similarly, in the financial services industry, real-time trading algorithms are highly restricted, while historical stock performance reports may be classified as public. To illustrate the distinctions, table 2.1 presents a simplified corporate classification framework that many organizations adopt as a baseline before tailoring it to their specific environment.

Classification Tier	Examples of Data	Typical Protections Required	Consequences of Exposure
Public	Press releases, marketing brochures, product catalogs	None beyond accuracy and integrity	Minimal; reputational if inaccurate
Internal	Staff directories, training materials, project schedules	Basic access controls, monitoring of sharing	Low to moderate; may aid social engineering
Confidential	Customer transaction histories, contracts, executive communications	Encryption, role-based access, secure disposal	Moderate to high; financial loss, reputational damage
Highly Restricted	PII, PHI, credit card details, trade secrets, proprietary algorithms	Advanced encryption, strict access controls, auditing, legal compliance	Severe; regulatory fines, lawsuits, loss of trust

Table 2.1: Sample Data Classification Framework

This layered taxonomy allows organizations to allocate resources proportionally. Not every email requires military-grade encryption, nor should every marketing brochure be guarded behind multi-factor authentication. Instead, data classification ensures that protections are **risk-based**—scaled to the potential impact of misuse.

In practice, organizations often struggle with gray areas. For instance, is employee salary information confidential or highly restricted? Should anonymized but re-identifiable datasets be treated as restricted under privacy laws? These ambiguities highlight the need for governance frameworks that are **dynamic**, regularly reviewed, and aligned with evolving business practices and regulatory landscapes.

Data Handling Policies

While classification provides the foundation for data governance, it is the handling policies that give classification real meaning in practice. Without defined operational procedures, categories such as "confidential" or "highly restricted" remain abstract labels, easily ignored or inconsistently applied. Data handling policies translate these categories into actionable controls, ensuring that information is managed appropriately throughout its entire lifecycle.

At the core of handling policies lies the principle that **data has a lifecycle**—it is created, stored, transmitted, used, archived, and eventually destroyed. Each of these stages presents unique risks, and governance frameworks must provide rules for mitigating them. For example, a confidential vendor contract must be securely stored with access logs enabled, must not be transmitted over unsecured channels, and once its retention period expires, must be destroyed using methods such as digital wiping or physical shredding of print copies. The policies ensure that organizations avoid the common pitfall of accumulating "data debris" — obsolete but sensitive information left unprotected — which often becomes a target during cyberattacks.

Creation and Storage

When new information is generated—whether it is customer registration data, financial reports, or clinical trial results—policies should dictate how it is categorized from the outset. For highly restricted data, immediate encryption is typically mandated, ensuring that even if storage media are lost or stolen, the information remains unreadable. Storage requirements may vary across categories: public data can reside in open repositories, while confidential and highly restricted data require hardened servers, intrusion detection systems, and backup protocols with secure redundancy.

Transmission and Usage

The way data moves across organizational boundaries or within departments is often the most vulnerable point of exposure. Policies should mandate the use of secure transmission methods such as

Transport Layer Security (TLS) for emails or Virtual Private Networks (VPNs) for remote access. For highly restricted categories, end-to-end encryption combined with multi-factor authentication (MFA) ensures that both the channel and the access are protected. Furthermore, the principle of **least privilege** is often embedded in usage policies: employees should only have access to the exact data required for their roles. For example, a customer service representative may need access to billing history but not to full credit card numbers, which should be masked or tokenized.

Archival and Retention

A frequently overlooked aspect of data handling is the retention policy. Not all data should be stored indefinitely; in fact, excessive retention creates unnecessary liabilities. Regulatory frameworks such as the General Data Protection Regulation (GDPR) explicitly require organizations to minimize data retention to only what is necessary for the purpose originally collected. Handling policies, therefore, must specify retention timelines for each classification category. For instance, highly restricted medical data may need to be retained for seven years under healthcare law, whereas marketing campaign data may only be stored for 12–18 months. Automated archival systems, coupled with scheduled reviews, help enforce these rules while reducing human error.

Destruction and Disposal

The lifecycle concludes with secure destruction, a stage that is often underestimated in importance. Policies must articulate the appropriate disposal methods depending on classification. For public data, simple deletion may suffice. For confidential and highly restricted data, however, secure wiping tools, cryptographic erasure, or even physical destruction of storage media (such as degaussing hard drives) may be necessary. Several high-profile breaches have occurred because organizations discarded storage devices without properly sanitizing them, allowing attackers to later recover sensitive data from these remnants.

Automation and Enforcement

Modern handling policies increasingly rely on **automation technologies** to maintain compliance and reduce reliance on human vigilance. Data loss prevention (DLP) tools, for example, can automatically scan outgoing emails and attachments, blocking or quarantining transmissions that contain unencrypted confidential information. Similarly, identity and access management (IAM) systems can dynamically adjust user privileges based on role changes or behavioral anomalies. Logging and monitoring systems further enforce accountability, generating audit trails that demonstrate compliance with both internal and external requirements.

Data Category	Storage Policies	Transmission Policies	Retention & Disposal Practices
Public	Open access; minimal security required	Standard email or web transmission	Simple deletion when outdated
Internal	Stored on internal servers with access controls	Encrypted internal networks (VPN optional)	Retain as long as operationally relevant; deletion by IT policy
Confidential	Encrypted at rest, access logging enabled	TLS/SSL, VPN, masked identifiers	Defined retention periods; secure deletion/wiping
Highly Restricted	Strong encryption, MFA for access, redundant backups	End-to-end encryption, MFA, restricted channels	Strict retention limits; cryptographic wiping or physical destruction

Table 2.2: Examples of Handling Policies across Data Categories

Real-world experiences demonstrate the value of robust handling policies. In 2018, a major US government agency experienced a breach after employees routinely transmitted highly restricted personal records over unencrypted channels, violating handling policies. The lack of enforcement mechanisms allowed noncompliance to persist, ultimately resulting in identity theft for thousands of citizens. Conversely, companies with strong automation—such as financial firms that use tokenization to mask credit card data—have demonstrated how handling policies not only reduce breach risks but also simplify compliance audits.

By embedding handling policies into daily operations, organizations move from theoretical governance to **practical, enforceable safeguards**. These policies ensure that classification frameworks do not remain static charts but become living processes that protect information integrity, confidentiality, and availability across their full lifecycle.

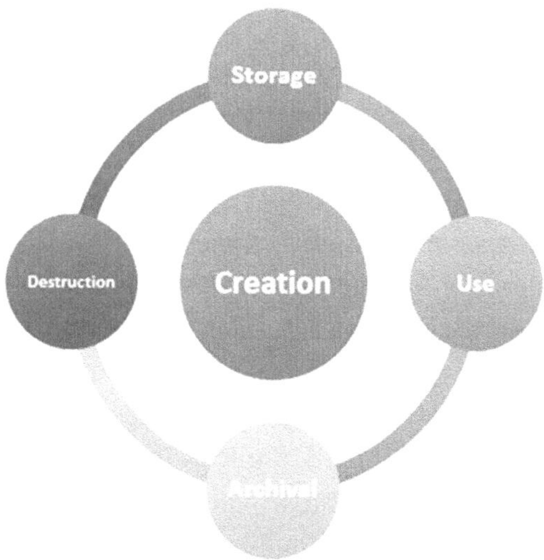

Figure 2.1: Lifecycle of Data Handlinsg

Narrative Example: Data Handling in the Healthcare Industry

Few industries highlight the stakes of data governance more starkly than healthcare. Unlike many sectors where the primary concern is financial loss or reputational harm, healthcare organizations manage information that is directly tied to human life, well-being, and dignity. The classification and handling of electronic health records (EHRs), imaging files, prescription histories, and insurance details can determine not only whether an organization avoids regulatory fines but also whether patients receive safe and timely treatment.

Consider the case of a midsized hospital network in the United States that was the subject of a federal investigation in 2019. The hospital had classified its EHRs as "confidential" rather than "highly restricted." On the surface, this may have seemed like a minor oversight in a taxonomy exercise, but the practical effects were devastating. Under the "confidential" label, access policies required only username and password authentication, with limited monitoring. This meant that administrative staff, contractors, and even non-medical personnel could access sensitive patient data without multi-factor authentication (MFA) or strict logging. Over time, several staff members—some malicious, others merely careless—downloaded large datasets onto unsecured devices. One laptop, later stolen from an employee's car, contained thousands of unencrypted patient records, leading to widespread identity theft and insurance fraud.

Improper handling was not confined to digital records. In another instance, printed discharge forms were discarded in unsecured recycling bins rather than shredded or pulped, violating the hospital's own written retention policies. Local journalists later recovered some of these documents, sparking a public scandal and drawing attention from regulators under the Health Insurance Portability and Accountability Act (HIPAA). Patients whose data were exposed reported fraudulent credit card applications, tax return fraud, and, in some cases, reputational damage when sensitive diagnoses became public.

In response to these failures, the hospital implemented a series of reforms that illustrate best practices in data handling. First, all patient-identifiable data were reclassified as "highly restricted," triggering a cascade of handling requirements: encryption at rest and in transit, access limited by MFA, and extensive logging of every interaction with EHR systems. The hospital also introduced a **"break-the-glass" protocol**, a concept now widely adopted across healthcare. Under this system, clinicians who need urgent access to restricted data—for example, during a trauma emergency in the intensive care unit—can override access barriers, but such actions generate detailed audit trails. These logs are reviewed post-incident to ensure that the access was justified and not a case of opportunistic browsing.

The hospital also improved its data destruction practices, investing in cross-cut shredders for paper records and cryptographic erasure for hard drives. Staff underwent mandatory training sessions emphasizing that improper disposal of even a single patient file can constitute a HIPAA violation, with potential civil and criminal penalties. Automation technologies such as Data Loss Prevention (DLP) software were deployed to monitor outgoing email traffic, blocking attempts to send unencrypted attachments containing protected health information (PHI).

The results were transformative. Within two years, the hospital reported zero major data-handling violations, regained public trust, and avoided millions of dollars in potential regulatory fines. More importantly, the changes underscored a cultural shift: data governance was no longer seen as an administrative burden but as a direct extension of patient care. As one hospital compliance officer explained, "When we mishandle patient records, we're not just breaking rules—we're breaking trust with the very people whose lives we're meant to protect."

Legal Frameworks around Data Security

Legal frameworks form the backbone of modern data governance and compliance. While internal policies may reflect an organization's culture or risk appetite, it is legislation and regulation that establish the binding obligations companies must observe. These frameworks do more than define categories of sensitive information; they prescribe, often in exacting detail, the conditions under which data may be collected, processed, transmitted, retained, and destroyed. Unlike voluntary codes of conduct, regulatory mandates are enforceable by courts and oversight bodies. Failure to comply is no longer a matter of reputational harm alone but carries direct and often severe consequences, including multimillion-dollar fines, civil lawsuits, class actions, or even the suspension of an organization's right to operate within a jurisdiction.

The emergence of legal frameworks governing data security can be traced to the rise of computerized records in the second half of the 20th century. Early laws were reactive, drafted in response to growing public unease over government surveillance and corporate misuse of personal data. One of the earliest and most influential examples was Germany's ***Hessen Data Protection Act of 1970,*** widely considered the world's first statute to regulate the storage and use of personal information by a government body. This innovation quickly spread across Europe, culminating in the ***OECD Guidelines on the Protection of Privacy and Transborder Flows of Personal Data (1980)***, which introduced principles such as purpose limitation, data minimization, and accountability. These guidelines influenced national legislation for decades to come, embedding the idea that individuals, not just institutions, have rights over their personal data.

By the late 1990s and early 2000s, the expansion of global e-commerce, cloud computing, and social media necessitated a stronger regulatory approach. Europe again led the way with the **European Union Data Protection Directive (1995/46/EC),** which harmonized privacy laws across Member States and introduced the requirement for organizations to notify supervisory authorities about their data processing activities. This directive was eventually superseded by the landmark **General Data Protection Regulation (GDPR)** in 2018. GDPR represented a paradigm shift: it moved from a compliance model based on notification to one of proactive accountability, requiring organizations to demonstrate privacy by design, conduct Data Protection Impact Assessments (DPIAs), and appoint Data Protection Officers (DPOs) for certain activities. Importantly, GDPR also asserted **extraterritorial reach**, meaning that non-EU organizations processing the data of EU citizens are subject to its rules.

Other regions developed parallel, though not identical, frameworks. In the United States, data protection evolved in a **sector-specific manner** rather than through a single overarching law. For instance, **HIPAA (1996)** governs healthcare data, **the Gramm-Leach-Bliley Act (1999)** regulates financial institutions, and **the Children's Online Privacy Protection Act (COPPA, 2000)** protects the digital privacy of minors. More recently, the **California Consumer Privacy Act (CCPA, 2018)** and its amendment, the **CPRA (2023)**, introduced broader consumer rights resembling GDPR, including the right to access, delete, and opt out of the sale of personal data. These laws reflect the growing demand for stronger privacy protections at the state level, even in the absence of a comprehensive federal statute.

In Asia, legal frameworks have expanded rapidly in the last two decades, reflecting the region's emergence as a hub of digital innovation. **Japan's Act on the Protection of Personal Information (APPI, 2003; amended in 2017)** is one of the oldest comprehensive privacy laws outside Europe, notable for its provisions on cross-border data transfers. **Singapore's Personal Data Protection Act (PDPA, 2012)** emphasizes consent-based processing, while **China's Personal Information Protection Law (PIPL, 2021)** establishes one of the world's most stringent regimes, modeled in part on GDPR but infused with national security considerations. PIPL's requirements on cross-border data localization and security assessments have major implications for multinational companies operating in China.

Beyond privacy-focused regulations, specific industries are governed by Sectoral security frameworks that impose technical and organizational controls. The **Payment Card Industry Data Security Standard (PCI DSS)** is a prime example. Though not a law, PCI DSS functions as a de facto regulatory framework, mandating encryption, access control, and regular penetration testing for all organizations that handle credit card data. Non-compliance can lead to hefty penalties from card networks and loss of the ability to process payments. Similarly, in the energy sector, the **North American Electric Reliability Corporation Critical Infrastructure Protection (NERC CIP) standards** mandate strict cybersecurity measures to safeguard the electric grid from attacks.

A defining feature of the modern regulatory landscape is the trend toward **extraterritorial enforcement.** GDPR has already issued billion-euro fines against non-European firms such as Amazon, Meta, and Google. China's PIPL has similar provisions requiring foreign firms that process Chinese citizens' data to establish local representatives and comply with domestic security reviews. This evolution means that compliance can no longer be managed purely at the national or regional level. Instead, global enterprises must adopt a harmonized strategy that accounts for the strictest applicable standard while remaining adaptable to local variations.

For organizations, the challenge lies not only in understanding the **substance of each law** but also in reconciling differences among them. For instance, GDPR emphasizes user consent and data subject rights, whereas US frameworks like HIPAA focus more on safeguarding the confidentiality and integrity of health records. China's PIPL imposes localization requirements, while the CCPA permits opt-out mechanisms but does not mandate data residency. Reconciling these conflicting obligations requires sophisticated governance structures, cross-border legal expertise, and in many cases, technological innovation such as privacy-enhancing technologies (PETs).

Ultimately, legal frameworks around data security are not static. They evolve in response to technological change, geopolitical concerns, and high-profile breaches that galvanize public opinion. The growing use of artificial intelligence, biometric data, and cross-border cloud infrastructure suggests that the next generation of laws will move beyond traditional privacy and into questions of **algorithmic accountability, fairness, and explainability**. Organizations that fail to anticipate these shifts may find themselves perennially reactive, caught between regulators and public outcry. By contrast, those that embrace compliance as a strategic imperative can transform legal obligations into competitive advantages, signaling trustworthiness and resilience in a digital economy where reputation is inseparable from governance.

Historical Development of Data Security Law

The legal protection of information predates the digital era, rooted in broader concerns about privacy, surveillance, and human rights. As early as the 1960s, the rise of computerized government registries and corporate databases provoked public debate about the dangers of centralized information systems. These anxieties crystalized in the 1970s, when nations such as Germany and Sweden pioneered the first data protection statutes, recognizing that automated record-keeping posed risks fundamentally different from traditional paper-based archives. The **Hessen Data Protection Act (1970)** in Germany is widely acknowledged as the world's first modern privacy law, setting a precedent for regulating personal information in an electronic environment.

In 1980, the **Organisation for Economic Co-operation and Development (OECD)** issued its **Guidelines on the Protection of Privacy and Transborder Flows of Personal Data,** a landmark in international privacy regulation. The OECD principles—such as data quality, purpose specification, use limitation, security safeguards, and accountability—introduced a blueprint for managing information responsibly. While nonbinding, these guidelines shaped the trajectory of national laws and influenced the design of later binding frameworks, embedding the concept of **fair information practices (FIPs)** into global discourse.

Europe emerged as the global pioneer in transforming privacy principles into comprehensive legislation. The **Data Protection Directive (95/46/EC),** adopted in 1995, harmonized protections across EU Member States, ensuring that personal data could flow freely within the Union while safeguarding individuals against misuse. This Directive established foundational rights such as access, rectification, and objection, while obligating organizations to implement adequate protections. In 2018, it was replaced by the **General Data Protection Regulation (GDPR),** which elevated privacy to a fundamental right and imposed unprecedented obligations on organizations worldwide. GDPR's innovations—such as the right to be forgotten, data portability, privacy by design, and extraterritorial reach—cemented its status as the most influential data law globally.

By contrast, the United States adopted a sector-specific approach, reflecting its emphasis on market-driven solutions and distrust of centralized regulation. Instead of one comprehensive statute, various laws targeted specific contexts: the Health Insurance Portability and

Accountability Act (HIPAA, 1996) for healthcare data, the Gramm-Leach-Bliley Act (GLBA, 1999) for financial information, and the Children's Online Privacy Protection Act (COPPA, 2000) for minors' online data. This fragmented system reflected different political priorities but left notable gaps, particularly in areas such as consumer profiling and online advertising. In response, states like California advanced their own rules, most prominently the California Consumer Privacy Act (CCPA, 2018) and its amendment, the CPRA (2023), which introduced consumer rights resembling GDPR.

Other regions quickly followed, tailoring frameworks to local socio-political contexts. Nigeria's Data Protection Regulation (NDPR, 2019) marked a significant step in Africa's engagement with digital rights, requiring consent-based processing and breach notification obligations. Similarly, Brazil's Lei Geral de Proteção de Dados (LGPD, 2020) consolidated over 40 fragmented statutes into a comprehensive law inspired by GDPR, balancing consumer protection with innovation. In Asia, Japan's Act on the Protection of Personal Information (APPI, 2003, amended 2017) and China's Personal Information Protection Law (PIPL, 2021) illustrate how different governments adapt core principles while embedding local priorities such as national security, data localization, or cross-border restrictions.

Taken together, these developments illustrate a global trajectory: as data becomes the "new oil," governments increasingly view privacy regulation not only as a tool of individual protection but also as an instrument of digital sovereignty. The historical evolution of data security law demonstrates a steady progression from voluntary guidelines to binding obligations, from national rules to extraterritorial regimes, and from narrow contexts to the recognition of data protection as a universal right essential for trust in the digital economy.

Year	Jurisdiction / Body	Regulation / Event	Significance
1970	Germany (Hessen State)	Hessen Data Protection Act	First modern privacy law, regulating computerized personal data.
1980	OECD	OECD Guidelines on Privacy and Transborder Flows of Personal Data	Established global principles of fair information practices (nonbinding).
1995	European Union	Data Protection Directive (95/46/EC)	Created baseline protections across EU; established rights of access, rectification, and objection.
1996	United States	HIPAA (Health Insurance Portability and Accountability Act)	Protected healthcare information; one of the first U.S. sector-specific laws.
1999	United States	GLBA (Gramm-Leach-Bliley Act)	Imposed safeguards for financial data.
2000	United States	COPPA (Children's Online Privacy Protection Act)	Restricted data collection from children under 13.
2003	Japan	Act on the Protection of Personal Information (APPI)	One of Asia's earliest comprehensive privacy laws.
2018	European Union	General Data Protection Regulation (GDPR)	Most influential global law; extraterritorial, introduced rights like portability and erasure.
2018	United States (California)	California Consumer Privacy Act (CCPA)	First U.S. state-level law resembling GDPR rights.
2019	Nigeria	Nigeria Data Protection Regulation (NDPR)	First African data protection framework of global significance.
2020	Brazil	Lei Geral de Proteção de Dados (LGPD)	Unified fragmented laws; modeled partly on GDPR.

Year	Jurisdiction / Body	Regulation / Event	Significance
2021	China	Personal Information Protection Law (PIPL)	Introduced strict consent rules, localization requirements, and national security provisions.
2023	United States (California)	California Privacy Rights Act (CPRA)	Expanded CCPA with stronger enforcement and consumer rights.

Table 2.1: Timeline of Major Data Security Laws and Regulations

Major Regional Frameworks in Data Security

The European Union: GDPR as a Global Standard

The General Data Protection Regulation (GDPR), which came into force in 2018, is widely recognized as the most consequential development in global data protection law. Its novelty lay in its breadth and enforcement power. By requiring informed, explicit consent and establishing rights such as the "right to be forgotten" and data portability, GDPR reshaped corporate practices worldwide. Importantly, its extraterritorial scope forced non-EU companies—from Silicon Valley tech giants to Asian e-commerce firms—to comply if they processed data belonging to EU residents. For example, in 2021, Amazon was fined €746 million by Luxembourg's data protection authority for GDPR violations, demonstrating the regulation's financial impact. Beyond fines, GDPR altered organizational culture: data protection became a board-level issue, with Data Protection Officers (DPOs) now a mandatory role in many corporations. Yet, scholars have also noted that GDPR's complexity disproportionately burdens small and medium enterprises, creating debates over fairness versus effectiveness.

The United States: A Patchwork Approach with CCPA/CPRA

Unlike the EU's comprehensive framework, the United States has historically adopted a sectoral approach to data protection, producing fragmented protections. However, California's Consumer Privacy Act (CCPA) of 2018—and its expansion via the California Privacy Rights Act (CPRA) in 2020—marked a turning point. These laws grant individuals rights to access, delete, and opt out of the sale of their personal information, echoing GDPR principles but tailored to US federalism. California's economic dominance, particularly in the tech sector, means that many national and even global companies align their practices with CCPA/CPRA, creating a "California effect." An example is Apple's introduction of global privacy nutrition labels for apps, influenced by Californian standards. Still, critics argue that CCPA lacks strong enforcement compared to GDPR, with fines capped at $7,500 per violation, making it less intimidating to corporate giants. Nevertheless, the law illustrates how subnational entities can influence global norms in the absence of federal legislation.

HIPAA and U.S. Sector-Specific Laws

Another cornerstone of American data security is the Health Insurance Portability and Accountability Act (HIPAA) of 1996, which focuses exclusively on healthcare information. HIPAA introduced the concepts of administrative safeguards (such as workforce training and access policies) and technical safeguards (like encryption, intrusion detection, and access logging). Enforcement is overseen by the US Department of Health and Human Services (HHS), which has levied significant fines, such as the $16 million penalty against Anthem Inc. in 2018 following a major healthcare breach. HIPAA demonstrates how sector-specific regulation can drive industry-wide compliance while leaving other sectors relatively under-regulated. Its success in establishing data security norms inspired later industry-focused legislation, but its siloed nature also highlights the unevenness of the US framework compared to comprehensive systems like GDPR.

Nigeria's NDPR: Africa's Emerging Data Protection Landscape

In 2019, Nigeria introduced the Nigeria Data Protection Regulation (NDPR), signaling Africa's rising commitment to digital rights. The NDPR requires organizations to obtain consent before processing data, appoint Data Protection Officers, and conduct regular audits. It represents a crucial step in harmonizing African privacy law with international standards, particularly given Nigeria's role as the continent's largest economy and its burgeoning fintech sector. Yet challenges remain, especially regarding enforcement capacity. Many organizations in Nigeria lack the resources or awareness needed to fully implement NDPR obligations, and the supervising authority—the National Information Technology Development Agency (NITDA)—has limited enforcement power compared to Europe's regulators. Nevertheless, the NDPR has sparked broader regional conversations and inspired similar initiatives in Kenya, South Africa, and Ghana, making it a landmark in Africa's regulatory trajectory.

Brazil's LGPD: A Latin American GDPR

Brazil's Lei Geral de Proteção de Dados (LGPD), enacted in 2020, reflects Latin America's growing focus on digital sovereignty. Like GDPR, LGPD grants individuals rights of access, correction, portability, and deletion, while obliging companies to adopt technical and organizational safeguards. The law created Brazil's National Data Protection Authority (ANPD), which can impose fines of up to 2% of company revenue. For multinational corporations operating in Brazil's massive consumer market, LGPD compliance has become non-negotiable. For example, WhatsApp was forced to adjust its privacy practices after ANPD raised concerns about inadequate disclosures in its terms of service. However, Brazil's enforcement environment is still evolving, with legal scholars debating how consistently the ANPD can impose sanctions. Despite these uncertainties, LGPD's introduction positioned Brazil as a regional leader, influencing neighboring countries to consider similar laws.

Comparative Reflection

Together, these frameworks illustrate both convergence and divergence in global data governance. Convergence is evident in the adoption of principles like consent, accountability, and breach notification, while divergence emerges in enforcement capacity, scope, and cultural priorities. For instance, GDPR embodies a rights-based European philosophy, whereas the US favors a market-driven, sector-specific approach. Nigeria's NDPR reflects the challenges of implementation in emerging economies, while Brazil's LGPD underscores the global diffusion of GDPR-style rules.

Case Study: Facebook and Cambridge Analytica

The Facebook–Cambridge Analytica scandal of 2018 is often regarded as a watershed moment in modern data governance. The controversy began when Cambridge Analytica, a political consulting firm, acquired personal data from millions of Facebook users through a seemingly innocuous personality quiz application. Although only about 270,000 users consented to the quiz, the app exploited Facebook's then-lax API rules to access the personal data of over 87 million individuals—most of whom had given no direct consent. This information was subsequently used to build psychographic profiles for targeted political advertising, including during the 2016 US presidential election and the UK's Brexit referendum, raising profound concerns about privacy, democracy, and corporate accountability.

Legal and Regulatory Failures

At the time, Facebook's data-sharing practices revealed serious gaps in compliance with emerging global privacy norms. Although the company argued that users had technically "agreed" to the terms of service, regulators and privacy scholars highlighted that consent was neither informed nor explicit, thereby breaching principles outlined in frameworks such as the OECD Guidelines (1980) and later codified in laws like the EU GDPR (2018). The incident exposed the inadequacy of relying solely on self-regulation by tech companies, emphasizing the necessity of robust, enforceable data protection laws.

Regulatory and Financial Consequences

The fallout was swift and severe. Public outrage led to multiple investigations across jurisdictions, including the United States, the United Kingdom, and the European Union. In 2019, the US Federal Trade Commission (FTC) imposed a record-breaking $5 billion fine on Facebook for privacy violations, one of the largest penalties ever levied against a technology company. Additionally, the UK's

Information Commissioner's Office (ICO) fined Facebook £500,000—the maximum allowed under the pre-GDPR regime, though critics argued that GDPR's newer, higher thresholds would have produced far larger sanctions. Beyond monetary penalties, Facebook was compelled to implement comprehensive privacy oversight mechanisms, including the creation of an independent privacy committee and mandatory third-party audits.

Reputational and Societal Impact

The reputational damage was equally significant. The hashtag #DeleteFacebook trended globally, trust in the platform plummeted, and CEO Mark Zuckerberg was summoned to testify before both the US Congress and the European Parliament. For many observers, the scandal underscored how data misuse could undermine democratic processes, shifting the debate about data security from a technical or compliance issue to a fundamental societal concern. Scholars argue that this case accelerated the political will behind GDPR enforcement in Europe and inspired analogous laws in other regions, such as Brazil's LGPD and Nigeria's NDPR.

In essence, the case demonstrates that data protection laws are not abstract legal frameworks—they directly influence corporate behavior, public trust, and even the integrity of democratic institutions. To understand the landscape, it is useful to compare how different regions regulate key aspects of data security.

Framework	Scope	Key Rights/ Obligations	Enforcement	Maximum Penalties
GDPR (EU)	Any entity processing EU residents' data	Consent, portability, erasure, breach notification	Supervisory authorities across EU	€20m or 4% of global revenue
CCPA/CPRA (California)	Businesses handling Californians' data	Right to know, opt-out of sale, deletion	California Privacy Protection Agency	$7,500 per violation

Framework	Scope	Key Rights/ Obligations	Enforcement	Maximum Penalties
HIPAA (U.S.)	Healthcare providers, insurers, business associates	Safeguards for medical data, breach reporting	U.S. Department of Health and Human Services	$1.5m per year per violation category
NDPR (Nigeria)	Controllers processing Nigerian data	Consent, audits, DPO appointment	National Information Technology Development Agency (NITDA)	2% of annual gross revenue
LGPD (Brazil)	Organizations processing Brazilian data	Similar to GDPR rights	ANPD (Brazilian authority)	2% of revenue, max 50m BRL

Table 2.2: Comparative Overview of Major Data Security Frameworks

Challenges of Compliance across Borders

For multinational corporations, ensuring compliance with data security regulations is far from straightforward. While the digital economy is global, data protection laws remain fundamentally territorial, reflecting the legal, cultural, and political priorities of individual jurisdictions. This mismatch creates a compliance minefield where a company must navigate overlapping, divergent, and sometimes directly conflicting rules.

Conflicting Legal Obligations

One major challenge is the divergence in definitions and the scope of consent. Under the European Union's GDPR, consent must be explicit, informed, and freely given, with individuals having the right to withdraw it at any time. In contrast, the United States' CCPA/CPRA permits broader implied consent in certain contexts, especially concerning data that is not deemed "sensitive." Nigeria's NDPR adds another layer, requiring organizations to secure lawful bases for processing but leaving certain operational ambiguities. These inconsistencies force corporations to implement complex, region-specific consent management systems, increasing both cost and compliance risk.

Another area of tension lies in data retention and deletion mandates. GDPR promotes the principle of data minimization, requiring that personal data be retained only for as long as necessary for its original purpose. However, US litigation culture often necessitates extensive data retention to comply with discovery obligations in legal disputes. Companies operating across both jurisdictions may therefore find themselves torn between minimizing data storage (to satisfy GDPR) and retaining large volumes (to satisfy US legal practice).

Breach Notification Timelines

Discrepancies in incident reporting deadlines further complicate compliance. GDPR requires organizations to notify supervisory authorities within 72 hours of becoming aware of a personal data breach. In contrast, the US operates a patchwork of state-level laws, some requiring notification within 30 days or "without unreasonable delay," while HIPAA specifies 60 days for healthcare breaches. Nigeria's NDPR requires data controllers to notify authorities within 72 hours, aligning with GDPR, but often lacks the enforcement rigor. For a multinational firm, this means managing breach response playbooks tailored to multiple timeframes—often under conditions of extreme pressure.

Data Localization and Sovereignty

Several countries, including China, Russia, and India, have enacted data localization requirements, mandating that certain categories of data be stored within national borders. While not directly covered by GDPR, NDPR, or HIPAA, such rules further complicate compliance by requiring firms to restructure IT infrastructure—sometimes duplicating systems region by region. This creates operational inefficiencies and cybersecurity vulnerabilities, while also raising costs.

Corporate Strategies for Harmonization

To address these challenges, many organizations adopt a strategy of compliance harmonization, applying the strictest standard globally as a baseline. For instance, a US company operating in Europe may adopt GDPR-level protections across all regions, even where local laws are more lenient. This not only reduces regulatory risk but also simplifies internal processes and enhances brand reputation. Some corporations further strengthen their approach by establishing centralized Data Protection Offices (DPOs), conducting privacy impact assessments (PIAs) for all major projects, and embedding privacy by design into software development lifecycles.

However, harmonization is not a silver bullet. It can be prohibitively expensive for smaller enterprises, and it may result in over-compliance that slows innovation or creates friction with customers used to more permissive practices. Moreover, governments increasingly assert data sovereignty, challenging the notion that a "one-size-fits-all" model can be sustained indefinitely.

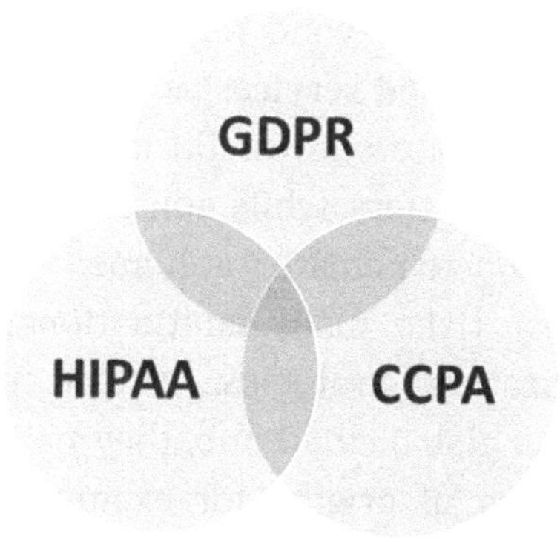

Figure 2.2: Overlap of Major Data Frameworks
A Venn diagram showing overlapping domains of GDPR, CCPA, HIPAA , and —with shared requirements (e.g., breach notification, consent) in the intersection, and unique obligations in separate circles

Narrative Example: Cross-Border Cloud Services

Consider a global e-commerce company that relies on US-based cloud infrastructure to manage its international operations. European customer data—including names, payment information, and purchase histories—is routinely stored on servers physically located in the United States. From the perspective of the General Data Protection Regulation (GDPR), such transfers are only lawful if appropriate safeguards are in place. These include Standard Contractual Clauses (SCCs), Binding Corporate Rules (BCRs), or adequacy decisions that recognize a non-EU jurisdiction as providing "essentially equivalent" protections.

The situation becomes more complicated when US law enters the picture. Under the Clarifying Lawful Overseas Use of Data (CLOUD) Act of 2018, American service providers can be compelled by US law enforcement to hand over data in their possession, custody, or control, regardless of where the data is physically stored. In practice, this means a US cloud provider hosting EU customer data can be legally obligated to disclose that information to US authorities—even if doing so directly conflicts with GDPR's restrictions on cross-border disclosures.

This tension produces a legal paradox: compliance with US law may trigger a violation of European law, and vice versa. For the company, the risks extend beyond regulatory fines. Customers may perceive the use of US-based services as a threat to privacy, eroding trust in the brand. Regulators in the EU may investigate or sanction the firm for unlawful transfers, while non-compliance with US orders can expose the company to penalties at home.

To mitigate these risks, many multinational firms have shifted toward data localization strategies. Instead of consolidating all customer data in one global cloud hub, they now host sensitive data within the jurisdiction of origin—for example, deploying regional data centers in the EU to handle European traffic. Some even pursue multi-cloud architectures, where different providers are used for different regions, or negotiate bespoke contractual arrangements with providers that include commitments to challenge overbroad government requests.

The broader lesson is clear: in the digital economy, jurisdictional conflicts are not hypothetical—they are operational realities. As regulatory fragmentation increases, compliance is no longer just about internal policy design but also about strategic infrastructure choices that balance efficiency with legal defensibility.

Real-World Parallel: Schrems II and the Collapse of Privacy Shield

The hypothetical e-commerce dilemma is not merely theoretical. In July 2020, the Court of Justice of the European Union (CJEU) delivered a landmark judgment in Data Protection Commissioner v. Facebook Ireland and Maximillian Schrems—popularly known as Schrems II. The case challenged the validity of the EU–US Privacy Shield, a transatlantic agreement that had governed personal data transfers since 2016.

The issue was whether US surveillance laws, particularly those enabling government access to foreign data (such as Section 702 of FISA and Executive Order 12333), provided "essentially equivalent" protection to that required under EU law. The CJEU ruled that they did not. Because US intelligence agencies could access European data without adequate safeguards or redress for EU citizens, the court invalidated Privacy Shield altogether.

This ruling sent shockwaves through global commerce. Overnight, more than 5,000 companies relying on Privacy Shield had to scramble for alternative mechanisms such as Standard Contractual Clauses (SCCs). Yet even SCCs were thrown into doubt, as the court warned that organizations must assess—on a case-by-case basis—whether the recipient country's legal system truly ensures adequate protection. For transfers to the US, this meant that SCCs alone might not suffice if government surveillance risks could not be mitigated.

The Schrems II decision illustrates the fragility of cross-border compliance mechanisms. It also highlights the growing willingness of courts and regulators to prioritize fundamental rights over economic convenience. Companies that had treated Privacy Shield certification as a routine checkbox suddenly faced existential legal and operational challenges. In the years since, many firms have adopted the very strategies described in the hypothetical example: data localization, encryption-at-rest with EU-held keys, and increased use of regional cloud providers. These shifts underline how legal conflicts between jurisdictions are not simply compliance headaches but drivers of technological architecture and business strategy.

The Tension between Innovation and Compliance

Technological innovation frequently outpaces the regulatory frameworks designed to govern it, creating a persistent tension between progress and compliance. Emerging fields such as artificial intelligence (AI), blockchain, and big data analytics challenge the very assumptions upon which existing data security laws were constructed. Traditional data protection regimes, built around clear distinctions between personal and non-personal data, lawful bases for processing, and user consent, often falter when confronted with systems that are opaque, distributed, and data-hungry.

AI illustrates this dilemma most vividly. Machine learning models, especially those built using deep neural networks, depend on access to large and often unstructured datasets. In practice, these datasets may contain sensitive personal information, sometimes without the explicit knowledge or consent of the individuals involved. Moreover, the "black-box" nature of many AI systems raises questions of explainability: if an algorithm denies a loan, selects a candidate for hiring, or influences medical treatment, how can organizations demonstrate compliance with principles such as fairness, transparency, and accountability as demanded by frameworks like the GDPR? Regulators have struggled to respond, and their efforts increasingly extend beyond data governance into the realm of algorithmic accountability. The European Union's proposed AI Act (2021) is perhaps the clearest example, introducing risk-based categories for AI applications and mandating rigorous testing, documentation, and oversight for "high-risk" systems.

Blockchain presents a different but equally disruptive challenge. The very qualities that make blockchain attractive—immutability, decentralization, and transparency—clash with legal requirements such as the "right to be forgotten" under the GDPR. Once data is written to a distributed ledger, deleting or altering it to comply with a user's erasure request becomes technically impractical, if not impossible. Similarly, identifying a "data controller" in a decentralized network often proves elusive, undermining accountability structures upon which existing regulations depend.

Big data analytics further complicates the compliance landscape. The value of big data lies in **secondary uses**—discovering patterns and insights not envisioned when the data was first collected. Yet, data protection laws typically limit processing to the purposes explicitly disclosed to the user at the time of collection. This creates a structural friction: the very innovation promised by big data is, by design, at odds with consent-driven models of regulation.

The tension between innovation and compliance is not new. Historical parallels can be drawn to earlier eras of technological disruption. For instance, the introduction of electronic health records (EHRs) in the 1990s prompted the creation of HIPAA to address security and privacy concerns in healthcare data. Likewise, the exponential growth of internet commerce in the early 2000s fueled the push for more robust consumer protection and anti-fraud legislation. Today, however, the scale and velocity of innovation—driven by global digital infrastructure and transnational data flows—make the regulatory lag far more consequential.

This evolving dialogue between law and technology underscores a critical lesson: compliance is not static. Regulatory frameworks are living systems, adapting to new risks and realities, while innovators must increasingly build legal and ethical considerations into design from the outset—a principle known as **"compliance by design."** Ultimately, the challenge lies not only in enforcing existing laws but also in shaping governance models flexible enough to accommodate future technologies without stifling their transformative potential.

Audit Requirements for Sensitive Data

If data classification provides the blueprint for what must be protected, and legal frameworks establish the binding rules for how that protection should occur, then auditing represents the practical enforcement mechanism that ensures governance is not a matter of aspiration but of demonstrable practice. Within the architecture of data governance, audits serve as the structured evaluation of whether an organization's policies, controls, and operations actually align with both internal standards and external regulatory mandates. Without audits, governance remains a theoretical exercise, confined to documents and declarations. With audits, governance becomes accountable, measurable, and ultimately defensible in the eyes of regulators, customers, and courts of law.

The purpose of auditing extends beyond mere compliance checks. At its most fundamental level, auditing serves as a guarantee of regulatory compliance, ensuring that the obligations established by laws such as the General Data Protection Regulation in Europe or the Health Insurance Portability and Accountability Act in the United States are not only acknowledged but also actively implemented. For example, GDPR requires timely breach notification and demonstrable consent management, while HIPAA mandates encryption, access controls, and regular training in healthcare contexts. An audit provides the mechanism to verify that such safeguards are in place, that breaches are reported within prescribed timelines, and that documentation exists to prove that policies are not just written but enacted.

Auditing also performs a vital role in providing operational assurance. Modern organizations are sprawling entities, often spanning multiple jurisdictions, subsidiaries, and cloud environments, each with its own unique data handling practices. Without periodic, structured assessment, there is little guarantee that a policy designed at the corporate level will be consistently applied on the ground. Audits create that connective tissue, enabling leadership to confirm that procedures are uniformly followed across departments and locations. This is particularly critical in an era of distributed cloud services, where sensitive data may traverse continents in milliseconds and oversight must account for infrastructures that are neither centralized nor static.

Beyond compliance and operational assurance, auditing reinforces a culture of accountability and transparency. Customers, partners, and regulators increasingly demand not only that organizations promise to safeguard data but also that they prove such claims through independent verification. Just as financial audits have long been central to deterring fraud and maintaining investor confidence, data audits in the digital era serve as a bulwark against both negligence and malfeasance. They deter the quiet erosion of standards that can occur over time, combat the phenomenon of "shadow IT" in which employees use unauthorized technologies to handle sensitive information, and provide a record of diligence that can mitigate liability in the event of an incident.

The analogy with financial oversight is particularly instructive. Investors and regulators do not accept a company's word that its balance sheets are accurate; they require external verification by independent auditors. Similarly, in the domain of data governance, stakeholders are no longer satisfied with assurances. They expect organizations to furnish evidence—through audits—that sensitive information is treated with rigor, consistency, and legal compliance. In this sense, auditing transforms data governance from a rhetorical commitment into a verifiable discipline—one that not only protects the organization from regulatory sanctions but also builds trust in the wider digital ecosystem.

Case Study: The Equifax Breach and the Absence of Effective Auditing

One of the most instructive examples of how inadequate auditing undermines data governance is the 2017 Equifax data breach, which exposed the personal information of over 147 million people. At its core, the breach stemmed not simply from a single technical vulnerability but from systemic failures in oversight and accountability. A critical software patch for the Apache Struts framework had been available for months before the breach, yet Equifax's systems remained unprotected. The lack of rigorous auditing meant no one verified whether vulnerability management policies were consistently enforced across the organization.

Regulators investigating the incident later emphasized that Equifax had policies in place requiring prompt patching of known vulnerabilities. However, what was missing was a mechanism to test whether those policies were actually followed—a textbook case of governance existing only on paper. An effective audit could have revealed the discrepancy between the written policy and operational practice, providing leadership with an opportunity to intervene before disaster struck. Instead, the gap persisted unnoticed until it culminated in one of the largest and most damaging breaches in history.

The fallout illustrates why auditing is indispensable. Equifax incurred a financial settlement of over $700 million, including compensation for affected consumers and penalties imposed by regulators. Perhaps even more damaging was the long-term erosion of trust. Consumers and lawmakers alike questioned whether an organization entrusted with such sensitive financial data could be relied upon in the future. The Equifax case demonstrates that in the absence of robust auditing, organizations may operate under the illusion of compliance while leaving themselves exposed to catastrophic risk.

What this narrative underscores is that auditing is not a bureaucratic burden but a safeguard against the very human tendency toward neglect, inconsistency, and complacency. Policies alone cannot prevent breaches; only the systematic verification of their implementation can. In this light, the Equifax scandal is less an anomaly and more a cautionary tale: without audits that connect governance to practice, even the most sophisticated organizations remain vulnerable.

Types of Audits

Auditing sensitive data is not a uniform exercise but rather a spectrum of practices that vary in purpose, scope, and authority. At one end of this spectrum are internal audits, which are conducted by an organization's own compliance or risk management teams. These audits are preventive in nature, designed to expose vulnerabilities before regulators intervene or attackers exploit them. They often focus on operational realities—whether staff are following established access protocols, whether encryption is consistently applied, or whether new software deployments introduce unmonitored risks. Because they are carried out by insiders, internal audits offer organizations the advantage of speed and familiarity with their own systems, but they also run the risk of bias or blind spots if not executed with rigor.

Complementing this internal perspective are external audits, which are carried out by independent firms. These reviews hold particular value because they provide an impartial assessment that can withstand external scrutiny. Regulators, investors, and customers tend to view external audits as more credible since they are less susceptible to internal politics or conflicts of interest. For many organizations, especially those operating in heavily regulated industries such as finance or healthcare, an external audit serves both diagnostic and reputational insurance purposes. Passing such an audit does not merely demonstrate compliance; it signals to stakeholders that the company is willing to subject itself to transparent accountability.

At the most formal end are regulatory audits, which are mandated by government bodies or industry regulators. Unlike internal or external audits that may be scheduled strategically, regulatory audits are compulsory and often unannounced. They are conducted with the explicit aim of measuring adherence to legal frameworks such as the Health Insurance Portability and Accountability Act (HIPAA) in the United States, the Payment Card Industry Data Security Standard (PCI DSS), or the European Union's General Data Protection Regulation (GDPR). Regulatory audits are often the most demanding, requiring extensive documentation, evidence of historical compliance, and the ability to demonstrate not only that protective measures are in place but also that they have been consistently applied over time.

While these categories differ in origin and emphasis, they are unified by a common goal: to establish whether sensitive data is adequately safeguarded. Each contributes in its own way to a layered system of assurance, where internal audits provide early detection, external audits deliver independent validation, and regulatory audits enforce compliance under the weight of law. Together, they transform the abstract principles of data governance into measurable, enforceable practices that can withstand both legal scrutiny and public expectation.

Consider the example of a large metropolitan hospital that handles millions of patient records each year. To ensure that it is protecting sensitive health information in line with HIPAA requirements, the hospital undertakes multiple layers of audits. Internally, its compliance team runs quarterly reviews of access logs to confirm that doctors and nurses only view the records of patients they are treating. These audits are proactive; if anomalies appear—for instance, an employee repeatedly accessing files outside of their department—the issue can be flagged and corrected before it escalates into a breach.

In addition to this, the hospital contracts an external cybersecurity firm to conduct penetration tests and evaluate the resilience of its encryption protocols. The external auditors bring a fresh perspective, challenging the hospital's internal assumptions and providing impartial assurance to the board of directors that the systems in place are not merely compliant on paper but robust against real-world threats.

Finally, the hospital is subject to regulatory audits by the US Department of Health and Human Services (HHS). These audits are legally binding and extend beyond operational practices to demand proof of historical compliance. For example, auditors may request evidence of staff training records, documentation of past breach notifications, or logs showing that backup systems are tested on schedule. Failure to provide such documentation can result not only in heavy fines but also in reputational harm that undermines patient trust.

Through this layered approach, the hospital demonstrates how internal, external, and regulatory audits intersect. Internal audits catch problems early, external audits provide credibility and independent validation, and regulatory audits enforce compliance under the law. Together, they exemplify how organizations transform abstract governance principles into operational safeguards that directly protect sensitive human data.

Tools and Methods

Modern audits rely on a mix of technical and procedural methods:

- Log Management: Collecting and reviewing logs from servers, applications, and databases to detect unauthorized access.

- Security Information and Event Management (SIEM): Systems like Splunk or IBM QRadar aggregate logs, correlate events, and generate alerts for anomalies.
- Forensic Analysis: Post-incident audits often include forensic reconstruction to determine how breaches occurred and whether governance failures were involved.
- Policy Auditing: Ensuring employees follow data handling rules, such as encryption of email attachments or proper disposal of printed documents.

Automation has become central to auditing. Continuous monitoring tools now provide real-time compliance checks, flagging violations instantly rather than months later. This shift reflects a broader evolution from periodic, checklist-based audits to dynamic, risk-based auditing.

Case Study: Capital One Data Breach (2019)

In July 2019, Capital One, one of the largest banks in the United States, disclosed a massive data breach that exposed the personal information of more than 100 million customers. The breach was traced to a misconfigured firewall on the company's cloud infrastructure, which allowed an external hacker to gain unauthorized access. While Capital One had invested heavily in cybersecurity controls and had even transitioned much of its infrastructure to the cloud in search of greater resilience, the incident revealed a glaring weakness: the absence of effective, continuous audit mechanisms to detect and remediate cloud misconfigurations.

Placed in the context of audit types, this case highlights the interplay and limitations of different approaches. Internal audits, while conducted regularly, were not designed to identify misconfigurations at the scale and speed required by cloud-native environments. External audits, typically scheduled annually, did not capture the ongoing technical risks that emerged in between reporting cycles. Even regulatory oversight, which later imposed an $80 million penalty through the Office of the Comptroller of the Currency (OCC), acted only after the breach had already occurred. In other words, Capital One was compliant in principle but operationally vulnerable in practice.

What was missing was a framework for automated, real-time configuration audits capable of flagging anomalous permissions or misalignments with security policies the moment they occurred. This incident underscores the evolution of auditing from static, compliance-driven exercises into dynamic, embedded safeguards. For cloud environments in particular, where systems change rapidly, the audit process must mirror that dynamism—moving beyond retrospective assurance to continuous monitoring.

The consequences were significant: reputational damage, regulatory fines, lawsuits, and diminished trust among customers who had entrusted the bank with highly sensitive financial data. More importantly, the breach became a cautionary tale for global enterprises navigating the balance between cloud innovation and audit rigor. As the case demonstrates, treating audits merely as a regulatory checkbox is insufficient; true governance requires aligning internal, external, and regulatory oversight with proactive, technology-driven resilience.

Healthcare Example: Implementing Audit Controls

A mid-sized hospital network in the United States provides a useful illustration of how audit requirements become operational safeguards under HIPAA. To comply with the law, the hospital deploys an advanced audit system that meticulously records every instance of access to patient records. Each transaction is logged with precise details: who accessed the data, when the access occurred, and under what justification. For instance, when a physician opens a patient's electronic health record (EHR) as part of a treatment plan, the log documents the action as legitimate and clinically justified. By contrast, if a system administrator attempts to view a patient file without a treatment-related reason, the audit system automatically flags the event for further review.

Over time, the accumulation of these audit trails begins to reveal broader behavioral patterns. Perhaps a nurse is found to be accessing an unusually high number of patient records compared to peers, or a staff member consistently attempts to access patient records outside normal working hours. These signals provide an early-warning system against insider threats and inappropriate disclosures, both of which represent significant risks in healthcare settings. The hospital is thus not only meeting HIPAA's legal obligations but also strengthening the protective shield around patient confidentiality and trust—two assets as critical as the medical treatments themselves.

The value of such a system extends beyond detection. By instituting clear policies that define how audit findings are reviewed, escalated, and acted upon, the hospital builds a culture of accountability where staff are aware that their interactions with sensitive data are both necessary and transparent. This reinforces professional responsibility while deterring negligence or malicious behavior. In effect, the audit log evolves from a passive repository of technical records into an active governance tool, simultaneously ensuring compliance, maintaining operational integrity, and safeguarding the well-being of patients.

The healthcare example also illustrates the importance of moving from ad hoc practices toward structured approaches. Organizations that rely on sporadic or informal audits risk overlooking subtle yet critical gaps in their security posture. By contrast, a formalized checklist of audit requirements provides a disciplined framework that ensures consistency across departments and timeframes. Such a checklist serves as a practical translation of abstract regulatory principles into daily operational procedures. It functions as a roadmap, guiding auditors to examine not only access controls and encryption standards but also training effectiveness, incident response preparedness, and third-party compliance. In this way, the checklist serves as a safeguard against omission, ensuring that no essential component of data protection is overlooked in the rush of clinical or administrative operations.

Requirement	Description	Example Practice	Frequency
Access Logging	Record all access to sensitive data	System logs capturing user ID, timestamp, and action	Continuous
Configuration Review	Validate security settings for servers, databases, and cloud	Automated scripts checking encryption settings	Monthly
Incident Response Audit	Assess how breaches are detected, contained, and reported	Tabletop exercises simulating a breach	Quarterly
Data Retention Compliance	Ensure obsolete sensitive data is deleted per policy	Scripts verifying deletion of aged records	Annual
Third-Party Vendor Review	Audit data protection measures of contractors and partners	Supplier questionnaires and site visits	Annual
Policy Training Verification	Confirm employees understand and apply data policies	Training completion logs	Annual

Table 2.3: Audit Checklist for Sensitive Data

The Audit Process Cycle

Auditing is not a one-off activity but rather a recurring cycle that reflects the dynamic nature of data governance. Unlike a static compliance measure, which can be implemented once and then left unattended, the audit process requires continuous iteration. This cycle begins with careful planning, during which auditors define the scope, objectives, and methodologies of their evaluation. Planning is not merely administrative; it determines whether the audit will successfully capture the risks most relevant to the organization's context. For instance, a hospital concerned with HIPAA compliance may prioritize monitoring access to patient records, while a financial institution operating under PCI DSS would place greater emphasis on payment card data security.

Once the scope has been established, the cycle moves into the execution or fieldwork stage. Here, auditors collect evidence through multiple methods: reviewing documentation, interviewing staff, inspecting systems, and testing controls. Evidence-gathering must be meticulous because the strength of an audit ultimately depends on the reliability of its findings. The process also benefits from triangulation, in which multiple data sources confirm or challenge the same conclusion, thereby reducing the risk of oversight.

Following evidence collection, auditors enter the evaluation stage, where the raw findings are analyzed against both internal policies and external regulatory requirements. This stage demands more than mechanical comparison; it requires judgment and interpretation. A configuration that is technically compliant might still be operationally insecure, while a minor deviation from procedure can, under certain conditions, signal systemic risk. Evaluating these nuances transforms the audit from a box-checking exercise into a meaningful governance practice.

The next stage involves reporting, where the results of the audit are documented in a structured, transparent manner. Audit reports must strike a careful balance: they should not only provide sufficient technical detail for IT and compliance officers to act on, but also include executive-level insights that translate findings into business risks and strategic priorities. The quality of the report directly affects whether corrective action will be taken or ignored, making communication as critical as discovery.

Finally, the audit cycle culminates in remediation and follow-up. Corrective measures are recommended, implemented, and then reassessed in subsequent audits to verify effectiveness. This stage closes the loop but also begins the next iteration of the cycle, reinforcing the idea that auditing is perpetual rather than terminal. In industries characterized by rapid technological change, such as healthcare or finance, this cyclical nature is particularly vital, ensuring that governance structures evolve alongside emerging threats and regulatory shifts.

When understood as a continuous loop of planning, execution, evaluation, reporting, and remediation, the audit process cycle becomes not just a compliance obligation but a strategic mechanism for resilience. Organizations that embrace this cycle embed accountability into their culture, transforming audits from occasional disruptions into steady rhythms of organizational learning and adaptation.

Figure 2.3: Audit Process Cycle

This cycle emphasizes that audits do not end with a report—they must feed into corrective actions and continuous improvement.

Future Directions: AI and Blockchain in Auditing

Auditing, much like the broader field of data governance, is entering a period of technological disruption. Traditional audit methods, often reliant on manual sampling, periodic review, and retrospective analysis, are proving inadequate in the face of increasingly complex data ecosystems. Emerging technologies such as artificial intelligence (AI) and blockchain are not merely supplementary tools but potential game-changers, capable of redefining how audits are conducted, how evidence is verified, and how accountability is preserved.

Artificial intelligence introduces a paradigm shift by moving auditing from periodic checks to continuous, real-time oversight. Machine learning algorithms, trained on historical audit data, can identify subtle anomalies that may elude human auditors—for instance, irregular login times, unusual volumes of data access, or behavioral deviations from an employee's typical patterns. By detecting these deviations in near real-time, AI systems transform auditing from a backward-looking exercise into a proactive mechanism of risk prevention. Moreover, natural language processing tools are being explored to automate the review of compliance documentation, accelerating a traditionally time-intensive process. Yet, the adoption of AI in auditing also raises profound challenges. Regulators increasingly demand explainability in algorithmic decision-making. An AI model that flags suspicious activities may be technically accurate, but if its reasoning cannot be clearly articulated, its evidentiary value in legal or regulatory proceedings can be questioned.

Blockchain technology, in contrast, offers radical transparency and immutability. At its core, blockchain functions as a distributed ledger where each transaction or event is cryptographically linked to the previous one, forming a chain resistant to tampering. Applied to auditing, this means that once an event—such as access to a patient record, financial transaction, or configuration change—is logged on the blockchain, it becomes virtually impossible to alter without detection. For healthcare systems governed by HIPAA or financial institutions under SOX (Sarbanes–Oxley Act), blockchain-based audit trails promise an unprecedented level of forensic accountability. However, blockchain also introduces regulatory paradoxes. Its immutability conflicts with legal principles such as the European Union's GDPR "right to be forgotten," which mandates that personal data be erasable upon request. Reconciling these opposing imperatives remains an open challenge for technologists, lawyers, and policymakers.

Imagine the audit environment of 2030. A multinational bank with operations across Europe, the United States, and Africa deploys an AI-driven audit system layered on a blockchain backbone. Every financial transaction, system update, and access attempt is instantly logged to the distributed ledger, creating a permanent, transparent record. The AI layer continuously scans these records, detecting deviations such as unusually high-value transfers occurring outside business hours or repeated access requests from unexpected geographies. When anomalies are found, the system automatically generates compliance alerts and proposes corrective actions, all of which are preserved in the blockchain trail for regulators to review. Instead of waiting for annual audits, regulators gain controlled access to the ledger in real time, allowing oversight to shift from episodic inspection to continuous assurance. For the bank, this dual system does more than protect against fraud or breaches—it builds trust with customers who know their financial data is monitored and safeguarded with a rigor that exceeds legal mandates.

Taken together, AI and blockchain suggest a future in which audits are no longer episodic compliance events but continuous, distributed, and deeply integrated into the operational fabric of organizations. The convergence of these technologies points to a world where auditors may evolve from inspectors into interpreters—professionals tasked less with uncovering data and more with contextualizing, explaining, and governing the insights produced by autonomous audit systems.

Ultimately, the promise of AI and blockchain in auditing is tempered by a recognition that technology alone cannot guarantee compliance. The ethical, legal, and cultural dimensions of governance remain central. Just as earlier innovations reshaped accounting and financial oversight, these new tools will only fulfill their potential if embedded within a governance culture that values transparency, accountability, and adaptability. In this sense, the future of auditing is not simply technological—it is socio-technical, evolving at the intersection of innovation, regulation, and organizational practice.

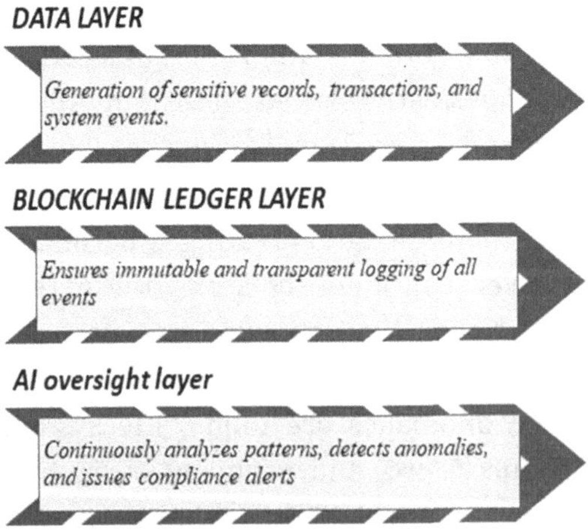

Figure 2.4: Conceptual Model of AI–Blockchain Audit Integration

Conclusion

Data governance and compliance are not abstract ideals confined to policy manuals or regulatory handbooks; they are dynamic, evolving practices that shape how organizations manage their most valuable — and, at times, most vulnerable — resource: information. In the digital economy, information has become both an asset and a liability. Organizations increasingly rely on data as the foundation of strategic decision-making, predictive analytics, customer engagement, and technological innovation. Yet, at the same time, the misuse, mismanagement, or unauthorized disclosure of data has consequences that extend far beyond financial loss. They touch on human dignity, privacy, societal trust, and, in certain sectors such as healthcare or critical infrastructure, even public safety.

At its most fundamental level, classification and handling policies provide the grammar of governance. By defining categories of sensitivity, establishing retention rules, and governing access privileges, classification systems create order from potential chaos. Without such taxonomies, organizations would struggle to distinguish trivial marketing data from life-critical medical records, or routine operational information from trade secrets. These frameworks represent the first step in the translation of ethical and strategic priorities into operational discipline.

Legal frameworks then step in to shape the boundaries of organizational conduct, anchoring internal practices in broader social expectations. The history of data protection law illustrates how societies have grappled with the power asymmetries inherent in data-driven economies. From the early OECD guidelines of the 1980s to landmark legislation such as the European Union's GDPR and California's CCPA, the legal trajectory has consistently moved toward empowering individuals, strengthening accountability, and expanding notions of consent, transparency, and proportionality. The emergence of laws governing artificial intelligence, such as the EU's proposed AI Act, signals the expansion of compliance beyond data itself toward the broader systems that process, infer, and decide upon it. Compliance, therefore, is not a fixed state but a moving target, constantly adjusting to the rhythm of technological progress and societal concern.

Auditing closes this circle by ensuring that governance and compliance are not aspirational but demonstrable. The audit process transforms lofty principles into verifiable action, providing regulators, customers, and boards with tangible evidence of accountability. Historically, auditing has long been a tool for establishing trust—financial audits dating back to mercantile economies helped stabilize trade by deterring fraud. In the digital context, data audits play a similar role by ensuring that internal negligence, shadow IT practices, or systemic vulnerabilities are detected and corrected before they cascade into crises. More than a regulatory necessity, audits are now a tool of operational resilience, enabling organizations to learn from their own patterns and mitigate threats proactively.

However, the true challenge lies not in adopting governance structures, legal frameworks, or audit protocols individually, but in orchestrating them together without stifling agility. Overly rigid governance regimes can slow the pace of innovation, discouraging experimentation in fields such as big data analytics, genomics, or financial technology. Conversely, weak compliance regimes expose firms to catastrophic risks, as high-profile breaches and scandals—from Facebook–Cambridge Analytica to the Capital One breach—have shown. Striking this balance requires more than technical solutions; it requires cultivating organizational cultures where compliance is not seen as a burden imposed by regulators, but as an integral element of corporate responsibility and strategic advantage.

Looking forward, the evolution of governance and compliance will be shaped by three interrelated dynamics. First, globalization ensures that compliance will continue to operate in a fragmented regulatory landscape, where multinational firms must harmonize rules across jurisdictions that may define consent, privacy, or retention in conflicting ways. The tension between the GDPR's strictures and the US CLOUD Act exemplifies this dilemma, pushing organizations toward solutions such as data localization or global baseline standards. Second, technological transformation will force the reinvention of compliance tools. Artificial intelligence, blockchain, and automation will not only generate new governance challenges but will also provide powerful new instruments for continuous monitoring, anomaly detection, and immutable audit trails. Finally, societal expectations will continue to rise. Consumers, investors, and civil society increasingly demand that organizations go beyond compliance and embrace ethical stewardship of data, addressing not only legal but also moral considerations in how information is collected, processed, and applied.

The organizations that succeed in this environment will be those that reframe compliance not as a static checklist but as a dynamic, strategic asset. They will embed governance into their DNA, integrate compliance seamlessly with innovation, and treat auditing as a continuous learning process rather than an external imposition. In so doing, they will not only avoid the costs of fines, breaches, and reputational crises but will also cultivate the trust that underpins durable relationships with customers, regulators, and society at large.

Practical Lab Ideas

1. Data Classification Exercise

- Provide students with a sample dataset that includes names, addresses, health information, and financial details.
- Ask them to classify the data into categories such as *Public, Internal, Confidential, and Restricted.*
- Discussion should highlight why classification matters and how it informs downstream security controls like encryption or retention policies.

2. Simulated Compliance Audit

- Divide students into "auditor" and "organization" groups.
- The "organization" is given a fictional company profile (e.g., a healthcare provider handling PHI).
- The "auditors" use a checklist derived from HIPAA or GDPR requirements to identify compliance gaps.

- Debrief on how organizations prepare for audits and the real-world tension between business operations and regulatory expectations.

3. Policy Development Lab

- Students draft a short data handling policy for a company expanding into Europe.
- They must address GDPR obligations: lawful basis for processing, consent mechanisms, and data subject rights.
- Class presentations compare approaches, reinforcing how legal frameworks shape governance.

4. Audit Log Review Exercise

- Provide anonymized log files (e.g., user access logs).
- Ask students to identify suspicious patterns, such as excessive access to sensitive records.
- This highlights how audit requirements translate into operational monitoring.

Looking Ahead

Data governance and compliance are not static disciplines; they evolve in response to shifting technologies, regulatory landscapes, and organizational priorities. As we move deeper into the study of cybersecurity, later chapters will explore data protection mechanisms (e.g., encryption, tokenization, and anonymization) that directly build upon the governance principles introduced here.

Emerging global regulations—such as evolving US state-level privacy laws, the EU's Digital Services Act, and cross-border data transfer frameworks—are reshaping how organizations must think about compliance. Furthermore, technologies such as artificial intelligence for compliance monitoring, continuous auditing platforms, and blockchain-based immutable logs are driving the field toward greater automation and transparency.

Students should understand that governance is not merely a legal checkbox; it is foundational to trust, resilience, and long-term strategic advantage. The next frontier of compliance will increasingly require balancing competing priorities: transparency versus privacy, automation versus explainability, and compliance enforcement versus business agility.

Key Terms

1. Data Governance – The framework of policies, processes, and standards that ensure effective and responsible data management across an organization.
2. Data Classification – The process of categorizing data according to sensitivity and criticality, guiding protection requirements.
3. Handling Policies – Organizational rules that dictate how different data classes must be stored, transmitted, accessed, and disposed of.
4. Compliance – Adherence to external legal or regulatory requirements governing data handling.
5. HIPAA (Health Insurance Portability and Accountability Act) – A US regulation governing the protection of health information.
6. PCI DSS (Payment Card Industry Data Security Standard) – A set of security standards for organizations handling credit card data.
7. GDPR (General Data Protection Regulation) – The European Union regulation that governs the collection, processing, and transfer of personal data.
8. Audit Trail – A chronological record that provides documentary evidence of data access, modification, or movement.
9. Regulatory Audit – A formal review mandated by government or industry regulators to ensure compliance with applicable laws and standards.
10. Operational Resilience – The ability of an organization to continue critical functions and maintain trust in the face of disruptions or security incidents.

Review Questions

1. Define data governance and explain its role in cybersecurity.

2. What is data compliance, and how does it differ from governance?
3. Why is data classification considered the foundation of governance policies?
4. Describe the main categories in a typical data classification framework.
5. How does proper data handling contribute to reducing cybersecurity risk?
6. What are the typical steps involved in developing a data classification policy?
7. Explain how labeling data as *public, internal, confidential,* or *restricted* impacts security controls.
8. Why is it important for organizations to train employees on data handling policies?
9. What are the risks of "shadow IT" in the context of data classification?
10. Provide an example of how misclassification of data can lead to a regulatory breach.
11. Summarize the key requirements of the General Data Protection Regulation (GDPR).
12. How does the US Health Insurance Portability and Accountability Act (HIPAA) shape healthcare data security?
13. Compare GDPR with the California Consumer Privacy Act (CCPA) in terms of user rights.
14. Why are international companies particularly challenged by conflicting data protection laws?
15. What role do sector-specific regulations like PCI DSS play in enforcing compliance?
16. Define the purpose of data audits in governance frameworks.
17. Distinguish between internal, external, and regulatory audits.
18. Why is continuous auditing more effective than periodic assessments?
19. How do audit logs help organizations detect insider threats?
20. What lessons did the Capital One (2019) breach provide about weaknesses in audit practices?

21. Why must compliance programs be tailored to an organization's industry and risk profile?
22. How does leadership commitment influence the success of governance frameworks?
23. Explain the role of third-party auditors in validating compliance.
24. How can checklists support audit readiness and reduce oversight failures?
25. What challenges do small and mid-sized organizations face in meeting audit requirements compared to large enterprises?
26. Should compliance with data protection laws be seen as a minimum requirement or as part of a broader ethical responsibility?
27. How can organizations balance the need for business agility with strict compliance obligations?
28. Evaluate the potential of blockchain-based audit trails for ensuring accountability.
29. Discuss whether artificial intelligence in auditing raises more opportunities or risks for governance.
30. Imagine you are a compliance officer: how would you prepare your organization for a surprise regulatory audit?

Part II

Data-Centric Security Controls

INTRODUCTION

Traditional approaches to cybersecurity have historically emphasized protecting the *perimeter* of organizational networks—erecting firewalls, intrusion detection systems, and endpoint defenses to prevent external actors from gaining unauthorized access. However, as digital ecosystems have grown more complex, perimeter-based defenses alone have proven insufficient. The rapid adoption of cloud computing, mobile devices, remote work, and third-party data sharing has blurred organizational boundaries, rendering the notion of a fixed "inside" and "outside" obsolete. In this context, data-centric security has emerged as a paradigm shift: rather than focusing exclusively on defending systems or networks, it prioritizes the protection of *data itself*, wherever it resides, however it moves, and whomever it is shared with.

At its core, data-centric security is anchored in the principle that information assets carry intrinsic value independent of the systems that host them. Protecting these assets requires embedding safeguards directly into the data lifecycle—from creation and classification to storage, transmission, usage, and eventual disposal. This contrasts with traditional models in which data was often left unprotected once attackers bypassed outer defenses. A data-centric approach assumes that breaches are inevitable; thus, the goal is to render stolen or mishandled data useless without proper authorization.

Several key concepts define this security philosophy. Data classification establishes the foundation by determining which information is sensitive (e.g., personally identifiable information, financial records, intellectual property) and thus requires heightened protection. Encryption serves as the most recognized mechanism for enforcing confidentiality, ensuring that data remains unreadable without the correct keys. Beyond encryption, access control mechanisms—including role-based access control (RBAC), attribute-based access control (ABAC), and emerging zero-trust models—govern who can interact with data and under what circumstances. Tokenization and data masking provide additional layers by substituting or obfuscating sensitive fields, thereby reducing the risk of exposure during analytics, testing, or third-party sharing.

Equally important is the role of data activity monitoring and auditing, which ensures visibility into how data is being accessed and used. In many regulatory environments, organizations are required not only to secure data but also to demonstrate that they have done so through transparent audit trails. Continuous monitoring detects anomalous usage patterns—such as excessive data downloads or unauthorized transfers—that may indicate insider threats or compromised accounts.

The importance of data-centric security controls has been magnified by regulatory frameworks such as the General Data Protection Regulation (GDPR), the Health Insurance Portability and Accountability Act (HIPAA), and the Payment Card Industry Data Security Standard (PCI DSS). These laws and standards impose obligations that go beyond network protection, requiring organizations to secure personal and financial data itself. Failure to implement robust data-centric controls has led to some of the most damaging breaches of recent years, where attackers exploited weak encryption, excessive privileges, or insufficient monitoring rather than bypassing traditional firewalls.

Looking forward, the data-centric model aligns closely with emerging paradigms such as zero trust architecture and confidential computing, both of which assume untrusted environments and seek to protect data even in use. This approach also dovetails with organizational efforts to build resilience and trust in a global digital economy, where data must flow securely across jurisdictions, platforms, and ecosystems.

In sum, data-centric security controls represent a strategic reorientation from defending boundaries to safeguarding the core asset: data itself. They are not merely technical measures but holistic practices that combine classification, encryption, access governance, monitoring, and auditing into a cohesive framework. As organizations continue to operate in increasingly distributed and interconnected environments, the adoption of data-centric controls will be essential to ensuring confidentiality, integrity, compliance, and ultimately, digital trust.

CHAPTER 3

Data Protection Mechanisms

Learning Objectives

By the end of this chapter, readers will be able to:

1. **Understand the foundations of data-centric protection** and explain why mechanisms such as encryption, key management, tokenization, and anonymization are essential for safeguarding sensitive information in modern digital ecosystems.
2. **Differentiate between encryption techniques**—symmetric, asymmetric, and hybrid—by analyzing their underlying principles, strengths, weaknesses, and real-world applications in securing data at rest, in transit, and in use.
3. **Explain the role of key management and PKI systems** in ensuring the effectiveness of encryption, including the processes of key generation, distribution, rotation, and revocation, as well as the trust model enabled by digital certificates and Certificate Authorities.
4. **Evaluate the use of tokenization, masking, and anonymization** as privacy-preserving techniques, identifying their regulatory relevance (e.g., PCI DSS, GDPR, HIPAA) and their role in reducing risk exposure while enabling business operations.
5. **Compare and contrast data protection mechanisms** to determine situational suitability, and demonstrate how they can be combined within a layered security architecture to achieve both compliance and resilience.

Overview

In the contemporary digital landscape, safeguarding information has become one of the most pressing concerns for organizations, governments, and individuals alike. Data is no longer confined to isolated mainframes or controlled organizational environments; instead, it flows constantly through cloud infrastructures, mobile devices, distributed supply chains, and global networks. In this highly interconnected setting, the question is not whether a system will be targeted but when and how such attempts will occur. Against this backdrop, protecting data directly—rather than relying solely on external defenses—has emerged as a fundamental requirement for ensuring confidentiality, integrity, and availability.

For decades, cybersecurity strategies were largely perimeter-based, built on the assumption that constructing strong firewalls, intrusion prevention systems, and access controls around networks would keep unauthorized users out. This model reflected an era when organizational boundaries were clearer, and data remained within physical or virtual walls. However, the rise of cloud computing, remote work, mobile applications, and cross-border collaboration has dissolved traditional perimeters. Data now exists in a perpetual state of motion—stored on third-party servers, transmitted across continents, or processed by external vendors. In such a fluid environment, perimeter defenses alone are insufficient, as breaches, insider threats, or even misconfigurations can expose sensitive information once it has left the "castle walls."

Data-centric protection represents a paradigm shift. Instead of focusing solely on defending the boundaries of networks or systems, it emphasizes the direct safeguarding of the data itself, regardless of where it resides or how it is transmitted. This approach recognizes that data may travel beyond organizational oversight and, therefore, must carry its security with it. In practical terms, this means embedding protection into the data through mechanisms that render it unreadable or unusable to unauthorized actors, while still allowing legitimate users and processes to access it as needed. Such mechanisms are not only technical safeguards but also compliance enablers, ensuring adherence to regulatory frameworks like the General Data Protection Regulation (GDPR), the Health Insurance Portability and Accountability Act (HIPAA), and the Payment Card Industry Data Security Standard (PCI DSS).

Within this framework, data protection mechanisms form the technical backbone of modern security practices. They translate abstract principles such as confidentiality, integrity, and accountability into enforceable measures. Encryption, for instance, transforms data into unreadable ciphertext, ensuring that even if information is intercepted, it remains meaningless without the appropriate cryptographic keys. Key management and Public Key Infrastructure (PKI) systems underpin this process by establishing trust, enabling secure distribution of keys, and governing their lifecycle. Meanwhile, tokenization, masking, and anonymization address another dimension of protection: reducing the exposure of sensitive data while preserving its utility for business operations, analytics, or research.

This chapter focuses on three focal areas—encryption, key management and PKI, and tokenization/anonymization—as the cornerstone techniques that enable organizations to operationalize data-centric protection. Each represents a unique, yet interdependent, layer of defense, collectively forming a robust strategy for mitigating risks in the digital era. By exploring their principles, applications, and limitations, this chapter underscores how effective data protection mechanisms serve not only as a bulwark against evolving threats but also as a foundation for trust, compliance, and sustainable digital innovation.

Encryption Techniques

Encryption is one of the oldest and most enduring techniques in the field of information security, serving as the primary method by which sensitive information is shielded from unauthorized access. At its core, encryption is the process of transforming readable data, known as plaintext, into an unreadable form, called ciphertext, through the use of mathematical algorithms and cryptographic keys. Only those in possession of the correct key are able to reverse this process—known as decryption—and restore the data to its original form. In modern contexts, encryption ensures the confidentiality of data by preventing adversaries from interpreting it, even if they manage to intercept or steal it. In addition, encryption contributes to integrity, since any unauthorized modification of ciphertext will generally result in unreadable or corrupted plaintext upon decryption.

The role of encryption in ensuring confidentiality and integrity has been consistent throughout history, though its mechanisms have evolved significantly with advances in mathematics and computing power. Early civilizations developed rudimentary forms of encryption to protect military and political communications. One of the most famous examples is the Caesar cipher, employed by Julius Caesar to secure messages by shifting letters in the Roman alphabet by a fixed number of positions. While ingenious for its time, such substitution techniques were vulnerable to frequency analysis, a method developed during the Middle Ages that exploited patterns in letter usage to crack ciphers.

The scientific foundation of cryptography expanded dramatically in the early modern period, particularly with the invention of polyalphabetic ciphers such as the Vigenère cipher, which used a series of shifting alphabets to complicate frequency analysis. During the twentieth century, mechanical and electromechanical devices, most notably the German Enigma machine in World War II, demonstrated the growing complexity of encryption. The breaking of Enigma by Allied cryptanalysts underscored a critical lesson that remains relevant: the security of an encryption system depends not only on its algorithm but also on the secrecy and management of its keys.

The advent of digital computing in the latter half of the twentieth century transformed encryption from a manual or mechanical process into a highly sophisticated field of applied mathematics. Modern cryptographic systems, such as the Data Encryption Standard (DES) in the 1970s and its successor, the Advanced Encryption Standard (AES), rely on complex mathematical operations that make brute-force attacks computationally infeasible within practical timeframes. These algorithms underpin much of today's secure communication, from online banking and e-commerce transactions to military and diplomatic correspondence.

Fundamentally, all encryption processes rely on a set of shared concepts that form the building blocks of cryptographic practice. Plaintext refers to the original, readable information that requires protection, whether it be an email message, a credit card number, or a medical record. Ciphertext is the unintelligible output produced when plaintext is processed by an encryption algorithm using a specific cryptographic key. The algorithm defines the mathematical procedure that governs how plaintext is transformed into ciphertext and back again. Finally, the key is a unique piece of information—analogous to a password—that determines the exact transformation performed by the algorithm. Importantly, it is not the secrecy of the algorithm but the secrecy of the key that ensures security, a principle often expressed in cryptography as Kerckhoffs's Principle, first articulated in the nineteenth century.

Symmetric Encryption

Symmetric encryption, also referred to as secret-key cryptography, is the most fundamental paradigm of data protection and remains a cornerstone of modern cybersecurity. In symmetric systems, the same key is used for both encryption and decryption, requiring that communicating parties securely share the key in advance.

Mathematically, the process can be expressed as:

$$C=E_k(P)$$

$$P=D_k(C)$$

Where:

- P = plaintext (original message)
- C = ciphertext (encrypted message)
- E_k = encryption function with key k
- D_k = decryption function with the same key k

This principle offers speed and efficiency, making symmetric encryption the method of choice for protecting large volumes of data, whether stored or transmitted. However, it introduces a major challenge: secure key distribution. If an adversary gains access to the key, the confidentiality of all communications is compromised.

Data Encryption Standard (DES)

The Data Encryption Standard (DES), adopted in 1977 by the US National Bureau of Standards (now NIST), was one of the most influential milestones in the history of modern cryptography. Developed in collaboration with IBM and refined with input from the National Security Agency (NSA), DES was designed to provide a standardized method for encrypting sensitive but unclassified government and commercial data. The algorithm uses a 56-bit key and processes information in 64-bit blocks through a series of 16 Feistel rounds. Each round applies a combination of substitution and permutation operations designed to obscure patterns and ensure diffusion of the input data.

For over two decades, DES was extensively deployed across sectors such as financial services, defense communications, and enterprise systems. Banks, for instance, relied on DES to secure Automated Teller Machine (ATM) transactions, while government agencies used it to protect diplomatic communications and classified documents. Its formal adoption as a federal standard not only spurred widespread industrial adoption but also contributed to the globalization of digital security practices, making DES one of the most widely recognized cryptographic algorithms of its time.

Despite its prominence, DES began to show significant weaknesses as computational power advanced. The most pressing vulnerability was its short 56-bit key length, which, although sufficient in the 1970s, became increasingly inadequate in the 1990s. With the growth of distributed computing and parallel processing, brute-force attacks became feasible. In 1998, the Electronic Frontier Foundation (EFF) built a specialized machine, known as the "Deep Crack," which was able to exhaustively search all possible DES keys in less than three days at a cost of approximately $250,000. This high-profile demonstration confirmed the impracticality of DES as a secure algorithm in the modern era.

In addition to brute-force vulnerabilities, DES also proved susceptible to differential cryptanalysis and linear cryptanalysis, two powerful methods of cryptanalysis that exploit statistical weaknesses in the algorithm's substitution-permutation structure. Although such attacks required large amounts of chosen or known plaintext, they further eroded confidence in the longevity of DES. By the late 1990s, DES was no longer considered a sufficient safeguard for sensitive information, prompting the search for more robust alternatives.

Triple Data Encryption Standard (3DES)

To extend the life of DES while a more permanent solution was being developed, cryptographers introduced the Triple Data Encryption Standard (3DES) in the late 1990s. As its name suggests, 3DES applies the DES algorithm three times to each data block, either with two independent keys (112-bit effective key length) or three independent keys (168-bit effective key length). This design significantly increased the computational cost of brute-force attacks, making 3DES a more secure interim solution than single DES.

The triple-encryption approach of 3DES provided a practical compromise: organizations could continue using existing DES hardware and software systems with relatively minimal modification, while still benefiting from a heightened level of security. For this reason, 3DES quickly became the default standard in banking and financial institutions, where it was widely used for encrypting payment card transactions, securing interbank communications, and protecting sensitive customer records. It also appeared in protocols such as IPSec and TLS during the transitional period before AES became the global standard.

However, the improvements of 3DES came at a cost. Applying DES three times inevitably increased its computational overhead, making the algorithm significantly slower than both DES and the emerging alternatives. The inefficiency of 3DES rendered it unsuitable for high-speed applications such as real-time video streaming or large-scale data encryption. Moreover, while 3DES increased key length and resilience, it still inherited structural weaknesses from DES, including susceptibility to certain cryptanalytic techniques such as meet-in-the-middle attacks, which reduced the effective security margin of the cipher.

By the early 2000s, the Advanced Encryption Standard (AES) was formally adopted, offering superior security and performance, effectively rendering 3DES an outdated solution. In recognition of its limitations, the National Institute of Standards and Technology (NIST) began deprecating 3DES in 2017, recommending its gradual retirement from use in government and commercial systems. Today, while 3DES may still appear in legacy environments for backward compatibility, it is widely regarded as unsuitable for protecting sensitive or long-term data in the modern cryptographic landscape.

Modern Standard: Advanced Encryption Standard (AES)

The Advanced Encryption Standard (AES) represents a major leap in symmetric encryption, both in terms of security and efficiency. Following the gradual obsolescence of DES and the interim use of 3DES, NIST initiated a global competition in the late 1990s to identify a new algorithm capable of meeting the evolving demands of the digital era. The winner, announced in 2001, was the Rijndael cipher, designed by Belgian cryptographers Vincent Rijmen and Joan Daemen. AES was subsequently adopted as the official US federal standard for symmetric encryption and rapidly became the global benchmark for securing digital data. Its adoption marked a transition from legacy systems to a modern, mathematically robust framework capable of supporting a wide range of applications, from enterprise data protection to internet communications.

AES operates on a block size of 128 bits, processing data in fixed-size chunks that are repeatedly transformed through a series of mathematical operations. The algorithm supports three key lengths — 128, 192, and 256 bits — which determine the number of transformation rounds: 10 for AES-128, 12 for AES-192, and 14 for AES-256. Each round incorporates four primary operations: byte substitution, which introduces non-linearity; row shifting, which rearranges bytes to increase diffusion; column mixing, which combines bytes within columns to further increase complexity; and round key addition, which integrates the cryptographic key at each stage to ensure security. This layered structure ensures that even minor changes to the input or the key produce vastly different ciphertext — a property known as the avalanche effect, which is fundamental to secure encryption.

One of AES's greatest strengths is its security against brute-force attacks. With a 256-bit key, the number of possible key combinations exceeds 22562^ {256}2256, a number so vast that even the most powerful supercomputers would require longer than the age of the universe to exhaustively search all keys. AES's design also incorporates resilience against known cryptanalytic techniques, including linear and differential attacks, making it robust against a wide array of sophisticated threats.

AES is also highly efficient and optimized for both hardware and software implementations. Modern CPUs include instruction sets specifically designed to accelerate AES operations, such as Intel's AES-NI, enabling encrypted communications and storage with minimal performance overhead. This efficiency makes AES suitable for high-volume applications such as cloud storage, streaming media, and enterprise database encryption, where speed is as critical as security.

Moreover, AES offers **flexibility** through its scalable key lengths. Organizations can select an appropriate key size based on the sensitivity of the data and anticipated security horizon. For instance, 128-bit AES may suffice for everyday communication, whereas 256-bit AES is recommended for highly sensitive information, including financial transactions, medical records, and government data.

Despite its strengths, AES is not without limitations. One primary concern lies in implementation vulnerabilities. Side-channel attacks, such as timing analysis or power consumption monitoring, can potentially expose secret keys if AES is implemented improperly in hardware or software. Additionally, poorly designed cryptographic protocols may introduce susceptibility to related-key attacks, though these are largely theoretical in well-engineered systems.

Today, AES forms the foundation of numerous critical security protocols and technologies. It is widely used in TLS (HTTPS) to secure web traffic, in VPN encryption to protect remote communications, and in disk encryption software such as Microsoft BitLocker and VeraCrypt, which safeguard data at rest. AES's combination of mathematical rigor, operational efficiency, and adaptability ensures its continued relevance as the global standard for symmetric encryption in the digital age. Table 3.1 shows the advantages of symmetric encryption.

Advantage	Description
High Speed and Efficiency	Symmetric algorithms are computationally faster than asymmetric algorithms, making them ideal for encrypting large volumes of data, such as database records, disk storage, or streaming media.
Low Computational Overhead	They require fewer mathematical operations, resulting in lower CPU and memory usage, which is particularly beneficial in performance-sensitive applications.
Mature and Well-Studied Algorithms	Algorithms like AES and DES have undergone decades of rigorous analysis, providing well-understood security guarantees and minimizing the risk of unknown vulnerabilities.
Strong Security for Bulk Data	When implemented with sufficiently long keys (e.g., AES-256), symmetric encryption is highly resistant to brute-force attacks and standard cryptanalytic methods.
Flexibility in Key Length	Algorithms such as AES allow multiple key lengths (128, 192, 256 bits), enabling organizations to balance security and performance based on their requirements.
Ease of Hardware and Software Implementation	Symmetric encryption can be efficiently implemented in both hardware and software; modern CPUs include specialized instructions (e.g., AES-NI) to accelerate operations.
Predictable Performance	Performance is largely deterministic, allowing predictable throughput in high-volume systems such as data centers or financial transaction networks.
Compatibility with Existing Systems	Symmetric encryption is widely supported across protocols and platforms (SSL/TLS, IPsec, database encryption, secure storage), ensuring interoperability in diverse environments.
Foundation for Hybrid Cryptosystems	It is often combined with asymmetric cryptography in hybrid systems, enabling secure key exchange via public-key methods while efficiently encrypting bulk data with symmetric keys.

Advantage	Description
Lower Energy Consumption	With reduced computational requirements compared to asymmetric algorithms, symmetric encryption is suitable for resource-constrained devices (IoT sensors, mobile devices) where energy efficiency is critical.

Table 3.1: Advantages of Symmetric Encryption

Limitations of Symmetric Encryption

While symmetric encryption is efficient and secure, it faces critical challenges, particularly in key management. Sharing and distributing the secret key safely among users can be difficult, and as the number of participants grows, scalability becomes a significant concern. Additionally, if the key is compromised, all encrypted data becomes vulnerable, creating a single point of failure.

Disadvantage	Description
Key Distribution Problem	The central challenge lies in securely distributing secret keys among all authorized parties. If keys are transmitted over insecure channels, they may be intercepted by attackers, compromising confidentiality. In large enterprises with distributed offices, securely sharing the same key across networks is both logistically complex and risky.
Scalability Challenges	Symmetric encryption does not scale efficiently in multi-user environments. A network with n participants requires maintaining $n(n-1)/2$ unique keys for secure pairwise communication, which becomes impractical for systems with hundreds or thousands of users.
Single Point of Failure	Since the same key is used for both encryption and decryption, compromise of the key immediately exposes all protected data. Insider threats, malware, or theft can render the encryption ineffective, as there is no separation between encryption and decryption keys.
No Built-In Authentication or Digital Signatures	Symmetric encryption provides confidentiality but does not inherently guarantee authenticity or integrity. Without additional mechanisms such as Message Authentication Codes (MACs) or HMAC, recipients cannot verify the sender's identity or detect tampering.
Vulnerability in Open or Untrusted Networks	Secure pre-exchange of keys is assumed in symmetric systems, but this is infeasible in open environments like the Internet. Symmetric encryption alone is inadequate for secure communications without the

	support of asymmetric protocols for key exchange.
Limited Flexibility for Multi-Party Communication	While efficient for two-party communication, symmetric encryption becomes cumbersome in group settings. Managing, rotating, or revoking keys for individuals requires re-encryption across the system, creating operational overhead.
Exposure to Cryptanalytic Attacks	Although modern ciphers such as AES remain robust, older algorithms like DES are vulnerable to brute-force, linear, or differential cryptanalysis. Security depends heavily on sufficient key length and correct implementation.
Disadvantage	**Description**
Key Rotation and Lifecycle Management Complexity	Maintaining long-term security requires regular key rotation, secure archival, and retirement. Poor key lifecycle management can lead to accidental reuse of compromised keys, undermining system integrity.
Incompatibility with Modern Security Requirements	Symmetric encryption cannot provide features such as digital signatures, non-repudiation, or scalable multi-party authentication. These functions require hybrid cryptosystems integrating asymmetric cryptography.
Resource Constraints in Key Storage	Large-scale systems must securely store numerous keys. Ensuring confidentiality, accessibility, and protection against leakage is challenging, especially in distributed, cloud, or IoT environments with limited secure storage capacity.

Table 3.2: Disadvantages of Symmetric Encryption

Real-World Applications of Symmetric Encryption

Symmetric encryption underpins a vast array of practical applications, safeguarding sensitive information across industries, communication channels, and digital infrastructures. Its efficiency and reliability make it particularly suitable for protecting data at rest, in transit, and even within distributed cloud environments.

- **Database Encryption**: One of the most critical applications of symmetric encryption is database protection, where large volumes of sensitive records must remain confidential. Financial institutions, for example, use AES to encrypt customer account information, transaction histories, and payment card data. Healthcare organizations similarly rely on symmetric algorithms to secure electronic health records (EHRs), clinical trial data, and personally identifiable information (PII), ensuring compliance with regulations such as HIPAA in the United States or the GDPR in Europe. By encrypting data at rest within databases, organizations mitigate the risk of unauthorized access, insider threats, and accidental leaks while maintaining operational efficiency, as symmetric algorithms can handle large datasets with minimal performance impact.

- **Internal Enterprise Communications***:* Within corporate networks, symmetric encryption is widely employed to secure **internal communications**. Virtual private networks (VPNs) use AES to encrypt traffic between remote employees and enterprise networks, protecting confidential emails, file transfers, and API communications from eavesdropping. File-sharing systems and collaborative platforms also integrate symmetric encryption to ensure that sensitive project documentation, intellectual property, and proprietary code remain confidential among authorized personnel. By providing fast, scalable protection for high-frequency internal communications, symmetric encryption allows organizations to maintain productivity without compromising security.
- **Cloud Storage**: The rise of cloud computing has dramatically increased reliance on symmetric encryption. Major cloud providers, including Amazon Web Services (AWS) and Microsoft Azure, implement AES-based encryption for data stored in services such as AWS S3, Azure Blob Storage, and other cloud-based file repositories. By encrypting data both at rest and in transit, these providers ensure that customer information is protected from external threats, malicious insiders, and potential misconfigurations. Symmetric encryption's speed and low computational overhead are crucial in cloud environments, where massive datasets must be encrypted and decrypted quickly to support scalable, on-demand services.
- **Mobile Messaging Applications***:* Symmetric encryption also plays a pivotal role in **mobile messaging platforms.** Applications such as WhatsApp, Signal, and Telegram employ

AES within broader cryptographic protocols to secure end-to-end communication. In these systems, symmetric keys are often dynamically generated for each session, providing high-speed encryption for text, voice, and multimedia messages while preserving confidentiality. Combined with asymmetric encryption for key exchange, symmetric encryption ensures that only intended recipients can decrypt messages, safeguarding user privacy and preventing interception by third parties.

Across these examples, the recurring theme is that symmetric encryption enables high-speed, scalable, and robust protection of sensitive data. Whether securing millions of financial transactions, protecting patient health records, encrypting corporate communications, or safeguarding personal messages on mobile devices, symmetric encryption remains a foundational mechanism in contemporary cybersecurity. Its efficiency enables organizations to maintain seamless operations while ensuring strong confidentiality and integrity.

Illustrative Model: Symmetric Encryption Workflow

Understanding symmetric encryption is greatly aided by visualizing the flow of data through its core processes. At its heart, symmetric encryption relies on a single shared key that is used for both encrypting and decrypting information. This key serves as the linchpin of confidentiality, as any compromise immediately jeopardizes all communications or data encrypted with it.

The conceptual workflow of symmetric encryption can be broken down into three primary stages: encryption, transmission, and decryption. In the encryption phase, plaintext — the original, readable information — is transformed using a symmetric encryption algorithm and the shared key. The algorithm applies mathematical operations, such as substitution, permutation, and mixing, to produce ciphertext — a scrambled version of the data that is unintelligible without the key. This transformation ensures that even if the ciphertext is intercepted during transmission, it cannot be understood by unauthorized parties.

Once encrypted, the data enters the transmission phase. The ciphertext may traverse networks, be stored on devices, or move between systems. Importantly, the ciphertext itself does not reveal any meaningful information without the key, preserving confidentiality during transport or storage.

Finally, the decryption phase reverses the process. Using the same shared key and a corresponding decryption algorithm, the ciphertext is converted back into plaintext, restoring the original information for authorized users. This round-trip transformation demonstrates the essential property of symmetric encryption: both encryption and decryption depend entirely on possession of the shared secret key. The flow can be summarized as illustrated in the table below.

Step	**Input**	**Process (with Shared Key k)**	**Output**
Encryption	Plaintext *(P)*	Encryption Algorithm *(E_k)*	Ciphertext *(C)*
Transmission	Ciphertext *(C)*	—	Ciphertext *(C)*
Decryption	Ciphertext *(C)*	Decryption Algorithm *(D_k)*	Plaintext *(P)*

Table 3.3: Cyclical and Interdependent Nature of Symmetric Encryption

This model illustrates the cyclical and interdependent nature of symmetric encryption. The same key is indispensable throughout, emphasizing the importance of secure key management. Furthermore, this workflow applies to a wide range of applications, including database encryption, cloud storage, secure communications, and mobile messaging systems. By conceptualizing the flow from plaintext to ciphertext and back, learners can grasp both the operational mechanics and the security rationale that underpins symmetric cryptography.

Asymmetric Encryption

As digital systems evolved, the limitations of symmetric encryption —particularly in key distribution and scalability — necessitated the development of a new paradigm: asymmetric encryption. Unlike symmetric systems, which rely on a single shared secret key, asymmetric encryption employs a pair of mathematically linked keys: a public key and a private key. The public key is openly distributed and can be used by anyone to encrypt data, while the private key is kept secret by its owner and is used to decrypt the corresponding ciphertext. This separation eliminates the need for secure channels to share encryption keys, addressing one of the core challenges of symmetric cryptography.

Principle of Operation

The fundamental principle of asymmetric encryption is based on mathematical functions that are easy to compute in one direction but difficult to reverse without specific knowledge (the private key). For instance, in RSA (Rivest–Shamir–Adleman), encryption relies on the computational difficulty of factoring large composite numbers. The public key is composed of a modulus (the product of two large primes) and an exponent, while the private key is derived from the same primes in a way that allows decryption. Attempting to reverse the process without the private key is computationally infeasible with current technology for sufficiently large key sizes, providing strong security guarantees.

Another prominent example is Elliptic Curve Cryptography (ECC), which relies on the mathematics of elliptic curves over finite fields. ECC achieves comparable security to RSA with significantly smaller key sizes, reducing computational overhead and bandwidth requirements. This efficiency makes ECC particularly attractive for resource-constrained environments, such as mobile devices, IoT sensors, and embedded systems, where performance and power consumption are critical considerations.

Asymmetric encryption offers several distinct benefits over symmetric methods. First, it provides scalability: each participant maintains a single private key and a publicly shared key, avoiding the exponential key growth problem faced by symmetric systems in multi-user networks. Second, it enables secure key exchange over untrusted channels. For example, in TLS (Transport Layer Security), asymmetric algorithms are used to exchange session keys, which are then used for faster symmetric encryption of bulk data. Third, asymmetric encryption supports digital signatures, ensuring data integrity, authenticity, and non-repudiation. A sender can sign a message with their private key, and any recipient can verify the signature using the sender's public key, guaranteeing that the message was not tampered with and confirming the sender's identity.

Despite its strengths, asymmetric encryption is computationally slower than symmetric encryption. The complex mathematical operations required for key generation, encryption, and decryption make it unsuitable for directly encrypting large volumes of data. Consequently, modern systems often adopt hybrid cryptosystems, where asymmetric encryption is used for key exchange and digital signatures, while symmetric encryption handles bulk data encryption efficiently. Additionally, asymmetric algorithms rely on the assumed hardness of specific mathematical problems (e.g., factoring in RSA and discrete logarithms in ECC), and advances in quantum computing pose a potential long-term threat to these foundations.

Asymmetric encryption is deeply embedded in modern digital infrastructure. SSL/TLS protocols, which secure HTTPS web traffic, rely on asymmetric encryption to exchange session keys and authenticate servers. Secure email protocols, such as S/MIME and PGP, use public/private key pairs to encrypt messages and provide digital signatures. In the blockchain domain, asymmetric cryptography ensures that transactions are signed by the legitimate owner of a wallet without revealing private keys, maintaining security and trust in decentralized systems. Additionally, asymmetric encryption enables secure software updates, digital certificates, and authentication systems, making it a cornerstone of contemporary cybersecurity practices.

Hybrid Approaches

While both symmetric and asymmetric encryptions offer distinct advantages, modern information systems increasingly rely on hybrid cryptosystems that combine the strengths of both methods. This approach leverages the speed and efficiency of symmetric encryption for bulk data protection while using asymmetric encryption to solve the critical challenge of secure key distribution. By integrating these techniques, hybrid systems achieve a balance between performance, scalability, and security, making them indispensable for contemporary digital communications and data protection.

The central principle of hybrid encryption is straightforward: asymmetric encryption is used to exchange or encrypt session keys, while symmetric encryption handles the actual transfer of large datasets. In practice, a sender generates a random, temporary symmetric key, commonly referred to as a session key, to encrypt the bulk data. This session key is then encrypted with the recipient's public key and transmitted alongside the encrypted data. Only the recipient, possessing the corresponding private key, can decrypt the session key and subsequently use it to decrypt the bulk data. This method ensures that large volumes of information are protected efficiently, without the computational overhead associated with encrypting all data asymmetrically.

A ubiquitous real-world example of this approach is HTTPS (Hypertext Transfer Protocol Secure), the standard protocol for secure web communications. When a user connects to a website, the server's public key is used to securely exchange a session key with the client. Once the session key is established, AES or another symmetric algorithm encrypts the remainder of the session, including web pages, form submissions, and multimedia content. This hybrid method combines the authentication and key distribution advantages of asymmetric encryption with the speed and performance of symmetric encryption, ensuring secure and responsive web experiences.

Hybrid systems are also widely employed in email encryption protocols, such as PGP (Pretty Good Privacy) and S/MIME

(Secure/Multipurpose Internet Mail Extensions). In these systems, the content of the email is encrypted with a symmetric session key, while the session key itself is encrypted using the recipient's public key. This guarantees that only the intended recipient can access the message, while minimizing computational load during encryption and decryption.

Similarly, cloud storage services and secure messaging applications utilize hybrid encryption extensively. Cloud platforms often encrypt user data with symmetric algorithms for efficiency, while key management and access control use asymmetric encryption to securely distribute keys to authorized users. Messaging apps such as Signal and WhatsApp implement hybrid schemes in their end-to-end encryption protocols, combining ephemeral symmetric session keys with asymmetric key exchanges to provide both high security and minimal latency.

The hybrid approach exemplifies the pragmatic integration of cryptographic methods, demonstrating that security is rarely a single-solution problem. By combining the complementary strengths of symmetric and asymmetric encryption, hybrid systems provide a scalable, efficient, and robust framework for protecting data across networks, devices, and global infrastructure. As digital environments continue to expand, hybrid cryptosystems remain a foundational element of secure communication and data protection strategies, balancing operational performance with uncompromising confidentiality and integrity.

Key Management and Public Key Infrastructure (PKI) Systems

Importance of Key Management

In the discourse on information security, cryptography is often framed as the cornerstone of digital protection. Textbooks, research papers, and industry whitepapers alike devote considerable attention to the design of encryption algorithms, comparing the strengths of block ciphers such as the Advanced Encryption Standard (AES) or public-key schemes like RSA and Elliptic Curve Cryptography (ECC). Yet, despite the sophistication of these mathematical constructs, it is not the algorithm itself that typically exposes organizations to compromise but rather the manner in which cryptographic keys—the lifeblood of encryption—are generated, stored, distributed, rotated, and revoked. Put simply, encryption is only as strong as the management of its keys.

The centrality of key management arises from the fact that keys are the ultimate gatekeepers of digital confidentiality, integrity, and authenticity. If an adversary gains control of a cryptographic key, the algorithm collapses into irrelevance, regardless of its mathematical robustness. A powerful illustration of this principle can be seen in the 2011 Sony PlayStation Network breach, where attackers were able to access internal systems partly due to inadequate protection of cryptographic credentials. Although Sony relied on established encryption mechanisms, the mishandling of keys undermined its security posture, leading to the exposure of over 77 million customer accounts. Such incidents underscore that encryption, in isolation, provides only theoretical protection; operational practices surrounding key management turn that theory into an effective or ineffective defence.

One of the foremost challenges in key management is secure distribution. In symmetric encryption systems, the same key must be shared between the sender and the recipient. If the distribution process is insecure, the confidentiality of the entire communication collapses. Historically, this problem was particularly acute before the advent of digital networks. During the Cold War, for example, intelligence agencies had to physically transport encryption keys via diplomatic pouches or couriers. The logistics of securely moving these keys across continents were costly, risky, and often vulnerable to interception. Even in the modern era, where asymmetric encryption can assist in secure key exchange, distribution challenges remain. Poorly configured key exchange protocols or reliance on outdated cryptographic standards can expose organizations to man-in-the-middle attacks, allowing adversaries to intercept or substitute keys in transit.

Beyond distribution, the secure storage of keys presents another persistent difficulty. A symmetric AES-256 key, for instance, provides near-impenetrable security against brute-force attacks. Yet if that key is stored in plaintext on a server's configuration file or embedded directly into application code, the encryption becomes meaningless. Adversaries who gain access to that environment can retrieve the key with minimal effort. To mitigate such risks, organizations increasingly rely on Hardware Security Modules (HSMs)—dedicated devices designed to generate, store, and manage cryptographic keys in secure, tamper-resistant environments. HSMs are frequently used in banking systems, certificate authorities, and cloud services where the compromise of keys can have catastrophic implications. However, even HSMs are not impervious to operational mismanagement, and their deployment requires rigorous governance frameworks.

Key rotation represents yet another essential, though often overlooked, dimension of management. Cryptographic keys, like physical locks, should not be used indefinitely. Over time, the probability of compromise increases due to advancing computational capabilities, insider threats, or simple operational mistakes. Consider the case of Wi-Fi Protected Access (WPA) encryption in wireless networks: when network administrators fail to update or rotate pre-shared keys, former employees or unauthorized individuals who once had legitimate access can exploit outdated keys to infiltrate the network. Rotation policies ensure that, even if a key is compromised, its window of utility is limited. Yet rotation is not without its own challenges. Poorly coordinated key changes can disrupt ongoing operations, lock out legitimate users, or result in data loss if archival systems remain tied to retired keys. This tension illustrates the delicate balance between operational continuity and security rigor.

Closely related to rotation is the need for effective key revocation. Circumstances often arise where a key must be invalidated before its scheduled expiration. This may occur when a system is decommissioned, when an employee with privileged access leaves an organization, or when a suspected breach raises the possibility that keys have been exposed. Failure to revoke compromised keys can lead to unauthorized access persisting undetected for months or even years. The consequences of neglecting revocation were vividly demonstrated in the 2013 compromise of Adobe Systems, where attackers stole encrypted user data alongside poorly protected keys. Even after the breach, the absence of timely revocation extended the risks for affected customers.

Taken together, these challenges highlight why key management is not merely a technical detail but the operational lifeline of data protection. Encryption without robust key management is akin to locking a vault but leaving the keys under the doormat. This principle is not limited to corporate environments. Governments, healthcare providers, financial institutions, and even individual users all depend on sound key practices. For instance, the Health Insurance Portability and Accountability Act (HIPAA) in the United States mandates strong safeguards for patient data, but compliance is impossible without adequate encryption key management. Similarly, the Payment Card Industry Data Security Standard (PCI DSS) explicitly requires organizations handling credit card transactions to implement rigorous key management protocols, recognizing that encryption alone does not ensure protection against fraud.

The importance of key management also extends to the geopolitical stage. National security agencies recognize that the control of cryptographic keys is a matter of sovereignty. The infamous "Clipper Chip" debate of the 1990s in the United States epitomized this struggle. The proposal sought to mandate government access to encryption keys through a built-in "escrow" system, sparking a heated controversy over privacy, civil liberties, and state surveillance. Although the initiative ultimately failed due to public opposition and technical flaws, it underscored the political weight carried by key management practices and the balance between state security and individual privacy.

Key Lifecycle Management

If key management sets the principles of cryptographic governance, then the key lifecycle embodies those principles in practice. Much like human life, cryptographic keys have a beginning, a period of maturity, and an end. Their journey encompasses secure generation, distribution, storage, usage, rotation, archival, and eventual destruction. Each stage presents vulnerabilities, and failure in any one area can compromise the confidentiality, integrity, and authenticity of vast digital ecosystems. Thus, lifecycle management is not an auxiliary task but the operational core of data protection.

The first stage, key generation, requires ensuring unpredictability and compliance with cryptographic standards. Weak random number generators have historically led to catastrophic breaches. The 2008 Debian OpenSSL flaw, in which a coding error reduced entropy to only 15 bits, produced millions of predictable keys, leaving SSL certificates and SSH logins trivially guessable. The lesson remains vital: strong algorithms are powerless if their keys are predictable. Today, cryptographically secure pseudo-random number generators (CSPRNGs) and hardware-based entropy sources, such as Trusted Platform Modules (TPMs), are standard to protect against such failures.

Once generated, keys must be distributed securely to authorized parties. Symmetric systems historically relied on physical transfer, as during World War II, when paper keying material was carried under armed guard—secure against interception but vulnerable to theft or espionage. The development of public key cryptography in the 1970s revolutionized this process, enabling secure exchange of session keys over insecure channels via RSA or Diffie–Hellman. Modern protocols like TLS rely on this principle, using asymmetric cryptography for the initial exchange before switching to faster symmetric keys for bulk encryption. Yet even here, poor configurations or expired certificates have repeatedly undermined security, showing that distribution is only as strong as its implementation.

Secure storage is the next concern. Keys left in plaintext in code repositories or configuration files pose a glaring risk, as seen in the 2017 Equifax breach, where weak credential management exposed data from 147 million people. To counter such threats, organizations rely on software vaults, Hardware Security Modules (HSMs), or cloud-based key management services like AWS KMS. These systems reduce risk but require careful configuration; mismanaged permissions can expose sensitive keys to malicious insiders or automated malware.

During the usage phase, keys actively encrypt, decrypt, or sign data, making them susceptible to side-channel attacks. These techniques, pioneered in the 1990s by Paul Kocher, exploit indirect signals such as power consumption or timing differences to extract secrets during computation. Even mathematically robust ciphers can be compromised if implemented carelessly. Constant-time algorithms, masking, and hardware shielding now form standard defences, underscoring the need for lifecycle management to consider both theoretical and practical attack surfaces.

Over time, all keys degrade in security, necessitating rotation. Regular replacement limits exposure if a compromise occurs and is often mandated by regulation, as in the PCI DSS for payment data. Yet rotation can be disruptive. A multinational bank, for example, that encrypts millions of records with a single symmetric key must regenerate, distribute, and re-encrypt at an enormous scale. Cloud-native solutions such as envelope encryption mitigate this by encrypting data with short-lived data encryption keys (DEKs), which are themselves secured by more easily rotated master keys. This layering reflects how lifecycle management evolves alongside technological complexity.

Closely related to rotation is archival. Retired keys may need preservation to ensure access to historical records, especially in finance or healthcare, where data must remain accessible for decades. Without archival, overly aggressive rotation can render old records unreadable. Yet archived keys must be guarded as carefully as active ones, since they provide a path into sensitive legacy data if mishandled.

The final stage is destruction. Simply deleting files is insufficient, as forensic tools can recover residual material. Standards such as NIST SP 800-88 prescribe rigorous techniques, including overwriting, cryptographic erasure, and even physical destruction of drives. Numerous breaches have occurred when decommissioned hardware containing residual cryptographic material was resold without proper sanitization, illustrating how failure at the lifecycle's end can undo decades of security discipline.

The consequences of weak lifecycle management are far from hypothetical. In 2019, a mismanaged key within Microsoft's Azure environment exposed user records due to a poorly rotated credential. Academic researchers continue to show that flawed key generation or revocation can undermine protocols once considered secure. Beyond technical risks, failures carry regulatory and reputational costs. Under the European Union's GDPR, negligence in cryptographic governance can lead to multimillion-euro fines. Reputational harm, often more damaging than fines, erodes public trust in organizations whose legitimacy rests on protecting sensitive information.

Ultimately, key lifecycle management transforms encryption from an abstract mathematical safeguard into a living process that mirrors organizational governance. Each stage—generation, distribution, storage, usage, rotation, archival, and destruction—forms a link in a chain of trust. When any link is broken, the entire chain is at risk; when each is fortified, organizations demonstrate not only technical competence but also a deep cultural commitment to security. The next discussion turns to Public Key Infrastructure (PKI), which builds on these lifecycle principles to coordinate trust across vast global networks.

Public Key Infrastructure (PKI)

If key lifecycle management governs the operational security of cryptographic systems, then Public Key Infrastructure (PKI) provides the overarching framework upon which digital trust is constructed. While symmetric encryption struggles with the challenge of securely distributing shared keys—a task that grows increasingly difficult in large-scale or global contexts—PKI addresses the fundamental question of how individuals and organizations, often complete strangers, can establish verifiable trust across insecure networks. PKI operationalizes asymmetric cryptography by embedding it within a broader system of policies, technical standards, and institutional actors. In this way, it is not only a technical mechanism but also a socio-technical infrastructure that fuses mathematical rigor with institutional trust.

The origins of PKI can be traced to the 1970s, when Whitfield Diffie and Martin Hellman introduced the revolutionary concept of public key cryptography, and when Ronald Rivest, Adi Shamir, and Leonard Adleman developed the RSA algorithm. These breakthroughs solved the problem of sharing public information securely by separating encryption and decryption into mathematically linked but distinct keys. Yet they also created a new challenge: how could one be certain that a given public key actually belonged to the person or organization it claimed to represent? Without a mechanism for verification, attackers could insert fraudulent public keys in so-called "man-in-the-middle" attacks. PKI emerged as the institutional solution to this verification problem, providing the assurance that digital identities could be reliably linked to cryptographic keys.

At the heart of PKI are Certificate Authorities (CAs), trusted organizations that issue digital certificates binding a public key to an identity. These certificates, formatted according to the X.509 standard, contain details such as the subject's name, the public key, the issuing CA, and the validity period. A CA guarantees the authenticity of a certificate through its own digital signature, which can be verified by others using the CA's public key. In this structure, trust is transitive: if users trust the CA, they also trust the certificates it issues. This creates what is known as a "chain of trust," anchored in a small number of root certificates that operating systems and browsers recognize by default. Registration Authorities (RAs) complement this structure by validating the identities of certificate requesters before certificates are issued, ensuring that the link between public keys and entities is legitimate.

PKI has become an invisible yet essential foundation of digital life. It underpins HTTPS, the secure version of the web's communication protocol, ensuring that connections between browsers and websites are authentic and encrypted. It supports email security protocols such as S/MIME, digital signatures for legal and governmental documents, and software code signing, which assure users that software has not been maliciously altered since publication. Government initiatives such as Estonia's e-Residency program rely on PKI to issue digital identities, enabling secure cross-border transactions and legally binding signatures. Even blockchain ecosystems, which often emphasize decentralization, employ PKI for securing wallets and interfacing with traditional systems.

Despite its success, PKI is not without weaknesses. The security of the entire system depends on the trustworthiness of root CAs, making them high-value targets for adversaries. Breaches such as the 2011 DigiNotar compromise or the misuse of certificates by CNNIC in 2015 exposed the fragility of the system and the dangers of centralization. These incidents demonstrated that if a CA is compromised, adversaries can issue fraudulent certificates that appear entirely legitimate, undermining user trust across the globe. To address these risks, the community has introduced mechanisms such as Certificate Transparency (CT) logs, which require all issued certificates to be publicly recorded in append-only ledgers that can be independently audited. Initiatives such as Let's Encrypt have further democratized PKI by automating certificate issuance, expanding secure communication to millions of websites and accelerating the universal adoption of HTTPS.

In reflecting on PKI, one must recognize its hybrid nature. While cryptographic algorithms such as RSA and elliptic curve cryptography provide the mathematical certainty necessary for secure key binding, PKI transforms these algorithms into a global trust system through the involvement of legal frameworks, technical standards, and international governance. It is, in effect, both a cryptographic system and a governance model. As digital ecosystems expand into domains such as the Internet of Things, autonomous systems, and cross-border digital identities, PKI's role will become even more critical. However, the emergence of quantum computing threatens to disrupt current algorithms, raising urgent questions about the resilience of PKI in a post-quantum era. Its future, therefore, rests not only on continued cryptographic innovation but also on vigilant governance, accountability, and global cooperation.

Challenges in Key Management and PKI

Although key management and Public Key Infrastructure (PKI) together provide the backbone of digital trust and secure communication, their implementation is riddled with practical challenges that stretch beyond the elegance of cryptographic mathematics. What appears sound in theory often proves fragile when confronted with the realities of organizational complexity, adversarial ingenuity, and global regulatory environments. Both key management and PKI sit at the intersection of technology, governance, and human oversight, and it is precisely this hybrid character that introduces vulnerabilities and obstacles. To understand the nature of these challenges is to appreciate why breaches, outages, and failures continue to plague even the most sophisticated organizations despite decades of advances in cryptographic science.

One of the most persistent issues in the field is the phenomenon of certificate sprawl. In modern enterprises, digital certificates are no longer limited to a few web servers or secure email gateways; they now underpin thousands of services, ranging from internal applications to multi-cloud environments and the proliferating universe of IoT devices. Each certificate carries an expiration date and requires monitoring to ensure timely renewal. Yet in sprawling infrastructures, maintaining centralized visibility often proves elusive. Certificates lapse unnoticed, and the consequences can be disruptive even without an active attacker. In 2020, Microsoft Teams suffered a global outage when an internal certificate expired, cutting off millions of users from communication tools at a critical moment during the COVID-19 pandemic. Such incidents expose the fragility of trust systems, demonstrating that neglect or administrative oversight alone can cause breakdowns comparable to deliberate attacks. The challenge is magnified in environments that rely heavily on automation, containers, and ephemeral services. In such contexts, certificates may be created and revoked dynamically, existing for minutes or hours rather than years, rendering traditional manual tracking obsolete. Organizations increasingly rely on automated certificate management platforms, but deploying these systems effectively requires integration across heterogeneous infrastructures, which is itself a formidable technical task.

The integrity of PKI also depends critically on the trustworthiness of Certificate Authorities. CAs occupy privileged positions as the ultimate arbiters of digital identity, but history shows that they are far from invulnerable—the DigiNotar compromise in 2011 stands as one of the most sobering reminders of this fragility. Attackers penetrated the CA's systems and issued fraudulent certificates for high-profile domains such as Google and Yahoo, which were subsequently used to intercept communications, particularly of dissidents and journalists in politically sensitive contexts. The fallout destroyed DigiNotar's credibility and forced its removal from trusted root stores, but the damage extended far beyond a single company: the entire PKI ecosystem was shaken by the realization that a single point of failure could jeopardize global trust. Similar concerns were raised by the Trustwave incident in 2012, in which the CA was found to have issued subordinate certificates to a corporate customer, enabling that customer to intercept TLS traffic. Although not a malicious breach, the case revealed how authority within PKI can be abused for surveillance. These events underscore a paradox: the very centralization of trust that makes PKI scalable also renders it brittle, because any lapse in integrity by one authority can ripple outward across the global internet.

Beyond present-day operational risks, the cryptographic foundations of PKI face an existential challenge from quantum computing. Most PKI implementations rely on RSA or Elliptic Curve Cryptography (ECC), both of which are susceptible to Shor's algorithm, a quantum method capable of efficiently solving the mathematical problems that underpin their security. While large-scale quantum computers capable of breaking these systems are not yet a reality, the principle of "harvest now, decrypt later" has already entered the lexicon of cybersecurity. Adversaries may be intercepting and storing encrypted communications today with the expectation that quantum breakthroughs will eventually allow them to decrypt the data retroactively. For sectors such as healthcare, finance, or government, where sensitive data may retain value for decades, this possibility is alarming. The transition to post-quantum cryptography is underway, with organizations such as NIST leading efforts to standardize algorithms that are resistant to quantum attacks. Yet migrating PKI on a global scale will not be trivial. Every digital certificate, protocol, and application that relies on RSA or ECC would need to be adapted, tested, and redeployed. This is not merely a technical transition but a societal one, requiring coordination among states, corporations, and regulatory bodies on an unprecedented scale.

Operational difficulties also manifest in the revocation and validation of certificates. While revocation mechanisms such as Certificate Revocation Lists and the Online Certificate Status Protocol were designed to ensure that compromised or expired certificates could be invalidated, both approaches suffer from structural weaknesses. CRLs can grow extremely large, burdening systems with the task of downloading and parsing them. OCSP, while more lightweight, introduces its own problems. It requires a real-time check with the issuing CA, which not only creates latency but also introduces privacy concerns, as it reveals to the CA the browsing habits of users. Failures of connectivity can also undermine the system: if a revocation check cannot be performed, many browsers adopt "soft fail" behaviors, continuing to trust certificates rather than risk denying legitimate users. This creates a dangerous asymmetry in which attackers can deliberately block OCSP traffic to ensure fraudulent certificates remain accepted. Partial remedies such as OCSP stapling and Certificate Transparency have improved matters, but the underlying tension between scalability, privacy, and reliability remains unresolved.

Regulatory and compliance pressures add yet another layer of difficulty. For industries like finance, government, or healthcare, the management of keys and certificates is not only a matter of security but also of legal obligation. Frameworks such as PCI DSS require rigorous control over cryptographic materials protecting payment card data, including mandates for rotation and auditing. Similarly,

HIPAA imposes strict standards on the protection of patient records. Achieving compliance requires institutions to implement not just technical controls but also procedural oversight, including staff training, access governance, and regular audits. For large organizations with dedicated security teams, these requirements can be met, albeit at high cost. For smaller entities, however, the burden is often prohibitive. Many lack the expertise or resources to implement enterprise-grade key management, leading to partial compliance or superficial adoption of standards. This creates a gap between regulatory expectations and practical capacity, leaving many organizations vulnerable despite nominal adherence to legal frameworks.

Finally, the global nature of PKI creates challenges of interoperability and political trust. The modern internet relies on hundreds of root CAs embedded in browsers and operating systems, yet not all roots are equally trusted across platforms. Users may find that a certificate accepted by one browser is rejected by another, undermining the seamlessness of digital trust. Geopolitical tensions exacerbate the problem. State-backed CAs, particularly those in authoritarian regimes, raise concerns that certificates may be weaponized for surveillance or censorship. The controversy surrounding CNNIC, China's government-affiliated CA, illustrates this tension. In 2015, when unauthorized certificates were discovered to have been issued by CNNIC, major browsers such as Google Chrome and Mozilla Firefox began distrusting its root certificates, sparking debates about sovereignty, surveillance, and the universality of digital trust. Such disputes highlight the fact that PKI is not purely technical but also geopolitical, reflecting broader struggles over control of the digital commons.

Taken together, these challenges reveal that key management and PKI are not static or settled disciplines but dynamic systems under constant pressure from technical, operational, and political forces. From certificate sprawl to CA compromise, from the looming threat of quantum computing to the limitations of revocation systems, from regulatory burdens to geopolitical fractures, the integrity of global trust depends on continuous adaptation. The mathematics of cryptography may remain robust, but the institutional scaffolding that allows societies to use those algorithms at scale is fragile, contingent, and perpetually contested. If encryption is the lock, then key management and PKI are the institutions that determine who holds the keys, how they are distributed, and under what conditions they can be trusted. The endurance of secure digital communication will therefore hinge not merely on mathematical breakthroughs but also on the collective ability of organizations, regulators, and societies to navigate the messy realities of trust in a connected world.

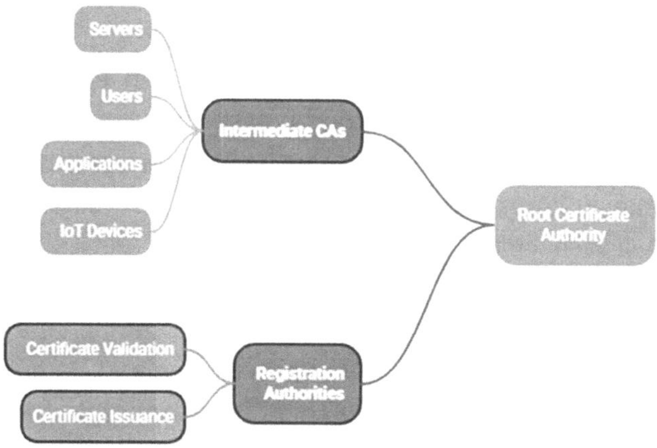

Figure 3.1: Integration with Other Data Protection Mechanisms

Tokenization and anonymization, while powerful in their own right, rarely exist in isolation within modern security architectures. Instead, they function most effectively as part of a layered, data-centric protection strategy that also encompasses encryption, key management, and Public Key Infrastructure (PKI). Integration of these techniques creates synergies, ensuring that weaknesses in one approach are compensated for by the strengths of another. This principle of defense-in-depth has been central to information security since the earliest military analogies were applied to digital systems: just as a fortress relies not only on its outer walls but also on inner gates, towers, and guards, so too must data security combine multiple layers to withstand evolving threats.

Consider a financial services environment where sensitive customer data—such as credit card numbers and personally identifiable information—is processed daily. Tokenization can be applied to replace account numbers with tokens, thereby minimizing exposure within transactional databases. However, the tokens themselves must be stored securely in a token vault, which is often protected using AES encryption. This layering ensures that even if attackers breach the database, they only gain access to non-sensitive tokens, and even if they reach the token vault, they encounter another layer of protection in the form of strong encryption. Such architectures demonstrate how tokenization and encryption, when combined, achieve resilience beyond what either can provide alone.

Anonymization, too, gains strength when integrated with other mechanisms. For instance, anonymized healthcare datasets used for clinical research may be transmitted across networks that are secured using PKI-based authentication and encryption protocols. Here, PKI ensures the authenticity of the sending and receiving parties, encryption protects the dataset during transmission, and anonymization ensures that even if the encrypted channel is compromised, no sensitive patient identifiers will be exposed. The combination thus provides confidentiality, integrity, and privacy simultaneously.

A particularly compelling example of integration arises in cloud environments. Organizations often use tokenization to minimize the storage of sensitive identifiers in multi-tenant systems, encrypt the token vaults under robust key management policies, and apply anonymization to datasets shared with third-party analytics providers. PKI then enables secure transmission across the distributed cloud infrastructure, creating a holistic model of trust and protection. This approach aligns with the "zero trust" security paradigm, which assumes that no component of a system can be inherently trusted, and therefore mandates rigorous, multi-layered controls at every stage of data handling.

Integration also has compliance implications. Many regulatory frameworks, such as the GDPR and HIPAA, encourage, or even mandate, pseudonymization and anonymization as part of privacy-by-design principles. When combined with encryption and PKI, these mechanisms help organizations demonstrate due diligence, accountability, and adherence to evolving standards. For example, an anonymized dataset transmitted over an encrypted TLS connection, authenticated by a trusted certificate authority, illustrates not only technical robustness but also regulatory alignment. By embedding tokenization and anonymization into broader architectures, organizations strengthen both their operational resilience and their legal defensibility.

Ultimately, integration underscores a fundamental truth: no single data protection mechanism can address the complexity of modern threats. Encryption ensures confidentiality, tokenization reduces data sensitivity, anonymization preserves privacy for analytics, and PKI establishes trust. Together, they form a composite system that is greater than the sum of its parts, enabling organizations to protect data across its lifecycle while still deriving value from it in ways that are compliant, secure, and operationally viable.

Challenges and Considerations

While tokenization and anonymization provide valuable tools for data protection, their practical deployment introduces challenges that organizations must navigate carefully. These challenges are not merely technical but extend to operational, regulatory, and even ethical dimensions. Understanding these limitations is essential for organizations that aspire to deploy these mechanisms effectively while balancing security, usability, and compliance.

Operational complexity is one of the most immediate concerns. Tokenization systems, particularly those deployed across large enterprises, require meticulous design and ongoing management. Each sensitive field in a database must be mapped to a corresponding token, and applications interacting with that database must be adapted to process tokens seamlessly without degrading functionality. The token vault itself must be maintained with strict security controls, redundancy, and monitoring. As organizations expand across multiple cloud platforms and geographies, managing tokenization consistently becomes even more challenging. For multinational banks, for example, integrating tokenization across global payment systems requires harmonization of token formats, synchronization of vaults, and compliance with multiple regulatory regimes. Such complexities can strain resources and create operational bottlenecks if not carefully planned.

Data utility trade-offs represent another critical limitation, particularly with anonymization. By design, anonymization removes granularity to protect individuals, but this very reduction can limit the value of the data for advanced analytics. In healthcare, for instance, transforming exact birthdates into age ranges can not only protect privacy but can also obscure meaningful patterns in rare disease research. Similarly, in retail analytics, over-generalizing geographic information may hinder the ability to detect regional consumer behavior trends. This trade-off between privacy and utility is a central tension in anonymization and demands careful calibration of methods such as generalization and noise addition. Striking the right balance requires collaboration between privacy experts, data scientists, and business stakeholders.

Regulatory scrutiny further complicates the adoption of tokenization and anonymization. Legal definitions of these terms vary across jurisdictions, and what qualifies as anonymized data under one regulatory framework may still be considered personal data under another. The GDPR, for example, sets a high bar for anonymization, requiring that data be irreversibly de-identified such that re-identification is impossible using "all means reasonably likely to be used." In contrast, the US HIPAA Privacy Rule provides more prescriptive standards for de-identification through either expert determination or a safe-harbor method of removing specified identifiers. Organizations operating globally must therefore navigate these definitional ambiguities and ensure their practices satisfy the most stringent applicable standard. Failure to do so not only exposes organizations to fines but also risks reputational damage if anonymization practices are challenged publicly.

Emerging threats also pose significant challenges. Advances in machine learning and big data analytics have increased the risk of re-identification, even from datasets that were once considered safely anonymized. Sophisticated algorithms can identify patterns, correlations, and outliers that effectively reverse anonymization by linking anonymized records with external data sources. This was starkly demonstrated in the Netflix Prize incident, where anonymized movie ratings were cross-referenced with publicly available IMDb data to re-identify users. Such cases highlight that anonymization is not static; what may be secure today can be vulnerable tomorrow as computational capabilities and external data availability grow. Organizations must therefore adopt a dynamic approach, continuously evaluating and updating anonymization techniques in response to emerging threats.

Another consideration is the ethical dimension of anonymization and tokenization. Even if data is legally anonymized, ethical questions may remain about its use. For example, anonymized mobility data collected during the COVID-19 pandemic raised concerns about surveillance and consent, despite being stripped of identifiers. Similarly, tokenized customer data used in financial profiling may raise ethical questions if used for discriminatory purposes. Organizations must therefore look beyond compliance to consider broader societal expectations and the potential for unintended consequences of their data practices.

Conclusion

This chapter has examined the critical mechanisms by which organizations can safeguard digital data in an increasingly interconnected and threat-prone environment. At the heart of modern cybersecurity lies the triad of encryption, key management/PKI, and tokenization/anonymization, which collectively ensure confidentiality, integrity, and regulatory compliance. Unlike perimeter-based approaches that aim to secure networks or systems, data-centric protection focuses directly on the asset itself, recognizing that breaches can bypass conventional defences if data is left unprotected. This paradigm shift underscores the growing importance of robust and integrated data protection mechanisms in the digital era.

Encryption remains the foundational technology for data confidentiality and integrity. The chapter traced its evolution from rudimentary ciphers, such as the Caesar cipher, to complex modern algorithms capable of securing massive digital infrastructures. Symmetric encryption, exemplified by AES, DES, and 3DES, offers efficiency and speed for bulk data processing but faces challenges in secure key distribution. Asymmetric encryption, using public/private key pairs (RSA, ECC), enables secure communication and digital signatures, providing scalability and trust at the cost of performance. Modern systems increasingly adopt hybrid approaches that combine the strengths of symmetric and asymmetric encryption, as seen in HTTPS protocols, to achieve both secure key exchange and efficient data transfer.

However, encryption alone is insufficient without proper key management. Effective key lifecycle management—from generation and distribution to rotation and revocation—is crucial to maintain the strength of encrypted data. Weak key practices can undermine even the most sophisticated algorithms. Public Key Infrastructure (PKI) provides the framework for secure asymmetric encryption, incorporating certificate authorities, registration authorities, and digital certificates. PKI enables trusted digital transactions, supporting applications from e-signatures to identity verification. Nonetheless, challenges remain, including certificate sprawl, potential CA compromise, and emerging threats such as quantum computing, all of which necessitate vigilant operational and regulatory oversight.

Complementing encryption and PKI are techniques that protect data by obscuring or transforming sensitive information. Tokenization replaces sensitive data with surrogate values, minimizing exposure while maintaining operational functionality, especially in payment processing. Data masking enables the safe use of production-like data for testing or analytics. Anonymization and pseudonymization reduce personal data exposure, aligning with regulations such as GDPR and HIPAA, though true anonymization remains difficult due to re-identification risks. Emerging techniques, including homomorphic encryption and differential privacy, further expand capabilities by enabling computation and statistical analysis on protected data without compromising privacy.

Key Terms

1. Data-centric protection focuses on securing the data itself rather than only the perimeter.
2. Encryption ensures confidentiality and integrity, with symmetric methods offering efficiency and asymmetric methods enabling secure key exchange and scalability.
3. Hybrid encryption combines symmetric and asymmetric strengths for practical implementations like HTTPS.
4. Effective key management is critical; weak practices can compromise encrypted data.
5. Public Key Infrastructure (PKI) supports trust in digital transactions via certificates and authorities.
6. Tokenization reduces sensitive data exposure in operational environments.
7. Data masking facilitates safe testing and analytics without revealing sensitive information.
8. Anonymization and pseudonymization enhance privacy and regulatory compliance but carry re-identification risks.
9. Emerging methods such as homomorphic encryption and differential privacy enable secure computation over sensitive data.
10. Integrating these mechanisms ensures resilience, trust, and regulatory adherence.

Review Questions

1. Define data protection mechanisms and explain why they are critical in the digital era.

2. Contrast perimeter-based security with data-centric protection.
3. Describe the historical evolution of encryption techniques.
4. Define plaintext, ciphertext, and encryption keys.
5. Explain the principle of symmetric encryption and provide examples.
6. Discuss the advantages and limitations of symmetric encryption.
7. Explain the principle of asymmetric encryption and provide examples.
8. Discuss the advantages and limitations of asymmetric encryption.
9. Describe how hybrid encryption approaches combine symmetric and asymmetric methods.
10. Explain how HTTPS uses hybrid encryption.
11. Discuss why encryption alone is insufficient without proper key management.
12. List and describe the stages of the key lifecycle.
13. Define Public Key Infrastructure (PKI) and explain its components.
14. Discuss the role of PKI in enabling trust in digital communications.
15. Identify common challenges in key management and PKI systems.
16. Define tokenization and explain its advantages and limitations.
17. Describe data masking and differentiate between static and dynamic masking.
18. Explain anonymization and pseudonymization and their differences.
19. Discuss the regulatory relevance of anonymization (e.g., GDPR, HIPAA).
20. Identify re-identification risks in anonymized datasets.
21. Explain the concept of homomorphic encryption and its applications.

22. Define differential privacy and describe its use in statistical analysis.
23. Provide examples of real-world applications of tokenization, masking, or anonymization.
24. Explain why integration of multiple data protection mechanisms is essential.
25. Predict future trends in data protection, including emerging encryption and privacy-preserving techniques.

CHAPTER 4

Data Access and Identity Management

Learning Objectives

By the end of this chapter, readers should be able to:

1. Differentiate between authentication and authorization by explaining their conceptual distinctions, historical evolution, and current models used in securing modern information systems.
2. Analyze common authentication mechanisms (passwords, multi-factor authentication, biometrics) and evaluate their strengths, weaknesses, and susceptibility to evolving attack vectors.
3. Examine the principles of authorization and understand how early discretionary access models evolved into structured frameworks such as access control lists, mandatory access control, and policy-driven systems.
4. Critically compare role-based access control (RBAC) and attribute-based access control (ABAC), identifying their use cases, advantages, and limitations in large-scale enterprise environments.
5. Assess the role of identity federation and Single Sign-On (SSO) in creating seamless yet secure user experiences across organizational and cloud ecosystems.
6. Apply zero-trust principles to data access and identity management, recognizing the shift from static, perimeter-based controls to adaptive, continuous verification models.

Overview

In the modern digital era, the protection of information has evolved beyond the traditional task of securing networks and databases. Encryption and perimeter defenses, while indispensable, can be rendered ineffective if the mechanisms that govern access are flawed. This reality has propelled data access and identity management (IAM) to the center of cybersecurity strategy. IAM ensures that only the right individuals, systems, or devices gain access to sensitive resources under the right conditions. As organizations embrace cloud computing, remote work, and global collaboration, identity has become the new perimeter, shaping trust, compliance, and resilience in digital ecosystems.

Historically, access control mechanisms began with simple user IDs and passwords in mainframe environments of the 1960s and 1970s. These rudimentary systems, though effective for small-scale computing, were ill-suited to large, distributed organizations. The emergence of formalized models, such as Bell and LaPadula's mandatory access control, highlighted the importance of structured policies for preventing unauthorized disclosure of classified information. Over time, IAM matured to encompass authentication—the process of verifying identity—and authorization, which determines the scope of actions permitted. Together, these form the backbone of secure digital interactions, aligning technical systems with organizational governance.

Today's IAM landscape is defined by increasing complexity. Cloud services decentralize data and applications, making static perimeter defenses obsolete. Remote and hybrid work have expanded attack surfaces, while the proliferation of Internet of Things (IoT) devices has multiplied the number of entities requiring trust and verification. In such contexts, IAM is more than a technical safeguard; it is a strategic enabler. It supports compliance with regulatory frameworks such as the General Data Protection Regulation (GDPR) and the Health Insurance Portability and Accountability Act (HIPAA), while also preserving operational efficiency and user productivity.

Modern IAM solutions go beyond passwords, embracing multi-factor authentication (MFA), biometrics, and passwordless authentication based on public-key cryptography. Authorization models have also advanced: role-based access control (RBAC) simplifies management by grouping users into roles, while attribute-based access control (ABAC) provides granular, context-aware decisions based on user, resource, and environmental attributes. These mechanisms underpin the zero trust model, which rejects the assumption that any user or device should be inherently trusted. Instead, access is continuously verified, reducing the risks posed by insider threats, stolen credentials, and lateral movement within networks.

At the same time, IAM addresses usability. Single Sign-On (SSO) and identity federation reduce credential fatigue by enabling users to access multiple services with a single identity, while standards such as SAML, OAuth, and OpenID Connect support secure collaboration across organizational boundaries. Yet challenges remain: misconfigured cloud access policies, over-privileged accounts, and phishing-driven credential theft have contributed to some of the most damaging breaches of the past decade.

Looking ahead, IAM is poised to be transformed by artificial intelligence, which enables adaptive, risk-based authentication, and by decentralized identity systems that empower individuals to manage their credentials without reliance on central authorities. Together, these innovations suggest that IAM will remain a critical frontier in cybersecurity, balancing the dual imperatives of protecting sensitive data and enabling digital trust.

Authentication and Authorization Models

At the core of identity and access management are two interdependent processes that together form the foundation of digital trust: authentication and authorization. These mechanisms, although often conflated, perform distinct yet complementary roles that govern how individuals, devices, and systems engage with sensitive digital resources. Authentication is the process of verifying identity—establishing with reasonable certainty that a user or system is who they claim to be—while authorization is the subsequent determination of what that authenticated entity is permitted to do once their identity is confirmed. Without the seamless integration of these two functions, even the most robust digital infrastructures remain vulnerable to misuse, exploitation, or catastrophic breaches. Their historical evolution — from rudimentary password systems to sophisticated zero-trust architectures — reflects the growing complexity of digital ecosystems and the pressing need for mechanisms that balance assurance, usability, and operational resilience.

Authentication has historically been the first line of defense in the struggle to safeguard access to information systems. In the earliest computing environments, this process was little more than the entry of a secret string, usually a password, to confirm a user's identity. Although this innovation was sufficient in the nascent age of isolated mainframes and limited user populations, it quickly revealed its limitations as networks expanded and systems became interconnected. Password reuse, susceptibility to brute-force attempts, and exposure to social engineering tactics made it increasingly clear that static, knowledge-based systems could not withstand the ingenuity and persistence of attackers. This realization gave rise to multi-factor authentication, which significantly strengthened identity verification by requiring a combination of different types of credentials. By incorporating something known, such as a password, with something possessed, such as a token or smart card, and something inherent, such as biometric traits, multi-factor approaches introduced layered defenses that were far more resistant to compromise. In recent years, adaptive authentication has added further sophistication by leveraging contextual cues like geographic location, device fingerprinting, and behavioral patterns to determine in real time whether additional checks are necessary. This risk-based approach ensures that security measures are stringent when anomalies are detected but remain minimally intrusive during normal activity, striking a critical balance between user convenience and security rigor.

Despite the technological evolution of authentication methods, it is important to recognize that identity verification is not purely a matter of mathematics or cryptography but equally a matter of human behavior and usability. Systems that impose excessive friction in everyday use risk alienating users, who may circumvent them in pursuit of convenience. Practices such as writing down complex passwords, sharing credentials, or attempting to disable multi-factor prompts often emerge when usability is sacrificed at the altar of security. Thus, effective authentication must always walk the delicate line between providing robust assurance and maintaining an experience that neither compromises productivity nor encourages insecure workarounds. This challenge becomes particularly acute in large, heterogeneous environments where user populations include employees, contractors, partners, and customers spread across different geographies and cultural contexts. For such organizations, authentication is as much a governance and design challenge as it is a technical one.

Once identity has been established, the task of authorization begins. Authorization is not concerned with verifying who a user is but with determining what that user can access and what actions they may perform. The principle of least privilege lies at the heart of this process, mandating that individuals or systems be granted only the minimal permissions required to accomplish their functions. This principle, though deceptively simple, is vital in limiting the damage that can result from accidental misuse, malicious insiders, or compromised accounts. Yet enforcing least privilege consistently proves difficult in practice. Over time, employees accumulate access rights as they move across roles or projects—a phenomenon known as privilege creep—that leaves them with far more extensive powers than they need. This surplus of privilege creates opportunities for exploitation, both deliberate and accidental, and undermines the protective intention of access control.

The historical development of authorization mechanisms mirrors the organizational structures of the institutions that adopted them. Early computing systems relied on rigid hierarchies, granting access according to static job functions in tightly controlled environments.

The formalization of this approach into Role-Based Access Control, or RBAC, in the 1990s provided administrators with an efficient method of assigning rights by linking them to predefined roles rather than to individual users. Although effective for organizations with stable, predictable structures, RBAC proved insufficient for modern enterprises characterized by fluid teams, contractors, and partners who often require temporary or conditional access. In response to these challenges, Attribute-Based Access Control, or ABAC, was developed. This model offers far greater flexibility by making access decisions based on a wide range of attributes, including the user's department, security clearance, the sensitivity of the resource, and contextual factors such as time of day or location. ABAC enables fine-grained, dynamic control that reflects the realities of modern organizations, where access decisions must often be sensitive not only to organizational hierarchy but also to compliance requirements, contractual obligations, and risk-based considerations. Moreover, authorization today is rarely a static determination; instead, it is embedded in systems that monitor, audit, and adapt access rights in real time, ensuring both compliance and responsiveness to emerging threats.

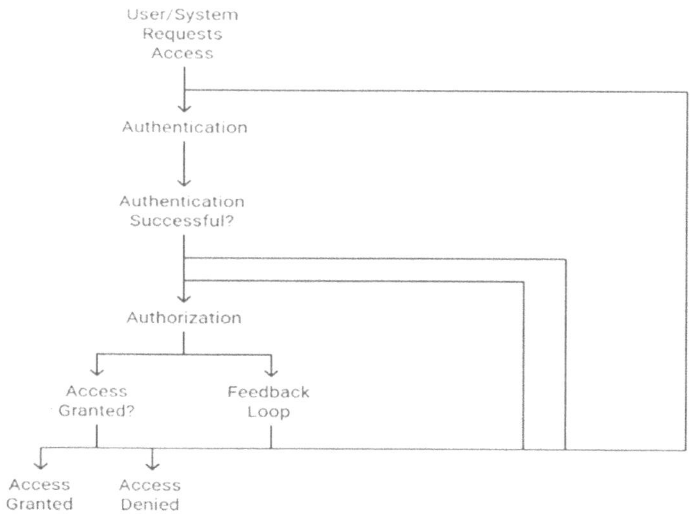

Figure 4.1: Conceptual Diagram of Authentication and Authorization Flow

Although authentication and authorization are distinct in function, their interrelationship is fundamental. Authentication answers the question of identity, while authorization specifies the boundaries of permissible action for that identity. A failure in either can undermine the integrity of the entire security framework. For instance, robust authentication without strong authorization can allow a verified employee to access highly sensitive resources far outside their role, creating unnecessary exposure. Conversely, sophisticated authorization rules are of little use if attackers can bypass authentication mechanisms to impersonate legitimate users. It is the seamless integration of these processes that defines the strength of an identity and access management system. The consequences of such failures are well illustrated by high-profile breaches. The 2013 Target breach, for example, occurred when attackers exploited credentials stolen from a third-party vendor responsible for HVAC systems. Authentication failed because the vendor's credentials were insufficiently protected, lacking multi-factor safeguards, while authorization failed because the vendor's account retained far more access than was necessary. The combination of these weaknesses allowed attackers to infiltrate Target's payment systems, ultimately exposing more than 40 million customer records and resulting in losses that exceeded $160 million. This breach underscored the dangerous ripple effects that occur when authentication and authorization are misaligned or insufficient.

By contrast, examples of successful integration demonstrate the transformative potential of well-designed IAM strategies. Google's BeyondCorp initiative is often cited as a model for rethinking the relationship between authentication and authorization. Abandoning traditional perimeter-based security approaches, BeyondCorp enforces continuous verification for every request, regardless of whether it originates within or outside the organizational network. Authentication is dynamic, continuously validated, and combined with context-sensitive authorization that considers factors such as device health, geolocation, and real-time risk assessments. This model, which came to define the broader "zero trust" paradigm, illustrates how tightly coupled identity verification and access decision-making can provide resilience in a world where traditional perimeters have collapsed under the weight of cloud computing, remote work, and ubiquitous connectivity.

The theoretical distinction between authentication and authorization can be further illuminated by considering their relationship as sequential and interdependent. Authentication always precedes authorization, as the system must first establish identity before determining permissions. Yet in practice, the relationship is recursive, as modern systems implement continuous monitoring and adaptive policies that reassess both identity assurance and access rights throughout a session. In this way, authentication and authorization are no longer discrete checkpoints but components of a living security ecosystem. The adoption of cloud-native IAM platforms such as Amazon Web Services' IAM, Microsoft's Azure Active Directory, and Okta exemplifies this integration in practice. These systems bring together multi-factor authentication, single sign-on, and fine-grained authorization rules within governance frameworks that also provide auditing, compliance reporting, and alignment with legal obligations such as GDPR or HIPAA. The result is an IAM ecosystem that is as much about governance and trust as it is about technical enforcement.

In sum, authentication and authorization are the twin pillars upon which digital trust is built. Their historical evolution reveals a trajectory of increasing sophistication, from static passwords to adaptive authentication, from rigid roles to dynamic, attribute-based policies. Failure in either can expose organizations to catastrophic breaches, while successful integration can enable secure, flexible, and scalable operations in complex digital ecosystems. More than technical mechanisms, they are socio-technical constructs that depend on human behavior, organizational policies, and regulatory environments as much as on cryptographic algorithms or access control engines. In an era increasingly defined by cloud computing, zero-trust architectures, and continuous digital transformation, authentication and authorization must be understood not as discrete technical functions but as interwoven, adaptive processes that safeguard the very fabric of trust in a digital society.

Role-Based and Attribute-Based Access Control

Modern identity and access management systems cannot function effectively without a robust framework to enforce authorization, and it is within this domain that structured access control models such as Role-Based Access Control (RBAC) and Attribute-Based Access Control (ABAC) play defining roles. These models represent distinct approaches to the perennial question of how organizations should govern "who gets access to what and under which conditions." They are not merely technical frameworks but conceptual paradigms that embody assumptions about organizational structure, governance, accountability, and adaptability in the face of dynamic digital ecosystems. Over time, these models have become embedded in regulatory guidance, compliance standards, and the very architectures of cloud and enterprise platforms, making their study not only a technical matter but also a socio-technical inquiry into how organizations manage risk, responsibility, and trust.

Role-Based Access Control (RBAC)

The origins of RBAC can be traced to the late twentieth century, when enterprises were grappling with increasingly complex IT environments and the inefficiencies of managing individual user permissions. The principle behind RBAC is deceptively simple: instead of assigning access rights to individual users directly, administrators define roles that correspond to organizational functions, and then map users to those roles. In this way, permissions are bundled according to responsibilities rather than identities. For example, in a hospital setting, the role of "Physician" may include access to electronic health records, diagnostic tools, and lab ordering systems, while a "Billing Clerk" is limited to patient accounts and insurance claim data. By abstracting permissions into roles, RBAC dramatically reduces administrative overhead, making access control scalable in organizations with thousands or even millions of users.

The elegance of RBAC lies not only in its administrative efficiency but also in its alignment with regulatory and governance principles. Frameworks such as HIPAA in healthcare, SOX in finance, and ISO/IEC 27001 emphasize the importance of accountability and auditability in data access. RBAC inherently supports these objectives because it produces clear, auditable mappings between responsibilities and access rights. When an auditor reviews a system, it is far easier to verify whether a nurse's role legitimately confers access to sensitive medical information than to analyze permissions scattered across thousands of individuals. In this sense, RBAC formalizes long-standing managerial practices into computational logic, reinforcing the idea that technology should mirror the organizational structure it serves.

The adoption of RBAC has also been strongly influenced by the need for regulatory compliance in critical industries. Financial services firms, for instance, are required by the Gramm-Leach-Bliley Act and related frameworks to implement controls that prevent excessive exposure to customer data. By assigning access based on job function—such as trader, compliance officer, or back-office clerk—institutions can ensure that employees receive only the access required for their duties. Similarly, government agencies often employ RBAC in classified environments to distinguish between security clearances, preventing individuals with "Confidential" access from inadvertently gaining entry to "Secret" or "Top Secret" systems.

Yet despite these advantages, RBAC has limitations in highly dynamic, decentralized, or cross-organizational environments. The rigidity of predefined roles can be a liability in industries where responsibilities evolve rapidly, such as in start-ups, agile software development teams, or multinational corporations engaged in project-based collaboration. In these contexts, creating new roles to capture every unique access permutation can lead to what administrators call "role explosion" — a proliferation of narrowly defined roles that becomes difficult to manage and undermines the very efficiency RBAC was intended to provide. Moreover, RBAC is often inadequate for managing temporary, context-dependent access.

For instance, if a contractor requires access to a system only for a week-long project, granting them a permanent role may create unnecessary risk unless manual intervention ensures timely revocation. These challenges highlight the static nature of RBAC in contrast to the fluid realities of contemporary digital environments.

Case studies illustrate both the strengths and weaknesses of RBAC in practice. Large healthcare providers such as the US Veterans Health Administration have historically relied heavily on RBAC to enforce compliance with HIPAA by ensuring that clinicians, nurses, and administrators operate within well-defined access boundaries. This approach reduces the likelihood of accidental disclosures and supports the extensive auditing required in regulated healthcare systems. However, when the COVID-19 pandemic forced many healthcare providers to rapidly reconfigure access rights to accommodate remote work, telehealth, and emergency response teams, RBAC systems often proved inflexible. Hospitals reported difficulties in quickly provisioning access to new temporary roles, such as remote triage nurses, without creating security gaps or administrative confusion. These disruptions underscored the limits of role-centric approaches in highly dynamic, crisis-driven contexts, paving the way for greater interest in more adaptive models such as ABAC.

Attribute-Based Access Control (ABAC)

While RBAC relies on the abstraction of organizational roles, ABAC offers a more granular, context-aware approach. Rather than relying exclusively on predefined roles, ABAC evaluates access decisions by considering a wide range of attributes relating to users, resources, actions, and environmental conditions. Attributes can include almost any definable characteristic: a user's department, job title, security clearance, or certification status; the sensitivity of the resource being accessed; the nature of the requested action, such as "read," "edit," or "delete"; and contextual factors like time of day, geographic location, or device security posture. Access control policies are then expressed in terms of logical rules that evaluate these attributes dynamically.

The flexibility of ABAC allows organizations to enforce security principles with far greater precision than RBAC alone. For example, in a hospital setting, ABAC can be used to grant a physician access to a patient's electronic health records only if the physician is assigned to that patient's care team, the patient has consented, and the request originates from within the secure hospital network. This multi-dimensional logic enforces not only the principle of least privilege but also contextual safeguards that reflect ethical and regulatory requirements. In the financial sector, ABAC enables institutions to enforce policies that traders may only initiate transactions above a certain threshold when logged in from approved terminals, during trading hours, and after multi-factor authentication. By encoding such fine-grained conditions, ABAC mitigates risks that would be difficult or impossible to capture in RBAC's role-centric structure.

The regulatory landscape has been a powerful driver for ABAC adoption. Regulations such as the European Union's General Data Protection Regulation (GDPR) emphasize purpose limitation, requiring that personal data be used only for specific, explicit, and legitimate purposes. ABAC supports this principle by allowing policies that condition access on declared purposes, thereby preventing data misuse even by legitimate users. Similarly, HIPAA's "minimum necessary" rule can be implemented through ABAC by ensuring that clinicians are granted only the information required for a specific treatment task, rather than blanket access to all patient data. In this way, ABAC not only increases security but also enhances compliance by translating regulatory obligations into enforceable technical policies.

Despite these strengths, ABAC is not without challenges. Its greatest advantage—flexibility—also contributes to its complexity. Defining, maintaining, and auditing policies that account for dozens or even hundreds of attributes can become an overwhelming task, particularly in large organizations with constantly evolving requirements. Unlike RBAC, where permissions are bundled into relatively stable roles, ABAC demands continuous oversight to ensure that attribute definitions remain accurate, up to date, and consistent across systems. The potential for misconfiguration is significant, and errors in policy definition can result in either excessive restriction, hindering productivity, or unintended access, creating security vulnerabilities. Furthermore, implementing ABAC requires sophisticated infrastructure capable of evaluating attribute-based rules at scale, which may not be feasible for organizations with legacy systems or limited technical capacity.

A case study illustrating ABAC in action is the US Department of Defence's migration toward attribute-based policies to manage access to classified information. Traditional RBAC models, though effective for standard role hierarchies, proved insufficient in highly complex environments where access must reflect not only security clearance but also mission-specific assignments, operational need-to-know, and situational context. By adopting ABAC, the Department was able to enforce policies such as permitting access to classified intelligence only if the individual possesses the requisite clearance, is currently assigned to the operation in question, and is connected via a secure, monitored device. This transition demonstrates how ABAC can provide the nuanced, adaptable control needed in environments where both security and agility are paramount.

Dimension	Role-Based Access Control (RBAC)	Attribute-Based Access Control (ABAC)
Core Principle	Access is granted based on predefined roles assigned to users.	Access is granted based on evaluation of attributes (user, resource, environment, action).
Granularity	Coarse-grained; permissions tied to roles, often hierarchical.	Fine-grained; supports complex, context-aware decisions.
Flexibility	Limited flexibility; adapting to dynamic conditions requires manual adjustments or role expansion.	Highly flexible; policies dynamically adjust based on real-time attributes.

Dimension	Role-Based Access Control (RBAC)	Attribute-Based Access Control (ABAC)
Scalability	Scales well in stable environments with fixed organizational structures.	Scales better in dynamic, cloud-based or multi-tenant environments where attributes evolve continuously.
Complexity of Management	Easier to administer with well-defined roles but can lead to "role explosion" in large organizations.	Complex to design and maintain due to attribute combinations and policy management.
Context Awareness	Minimal; context (time, location, device) rarely considered.	High; policies can evaluate contextual factors such as geolocation, device type, or time of access.
Compliance Support	Strong for static regulatory environments (e.g., SOX, HIPAA role mandates).	Strong for dynamic compliance needs (e.g., GDPR purpose limitation, conditional HIPAA access).
Implementation Cost	Lower upfront cost; supported by many enterprise IAM tools.	Higher upfront investment; requires advanced IAM platforms and policy engines.
Use Case Suitability	Best for structured organizations (finance, healthcare, government).	Best for dynamic, adaptive environments (cloud computing, research collaborations, global enterprises).
Example	A hospital assigns a "Physician" role granting access to all patient records.	A clinician can access a patient record only if on duty, patient consent is recorded, and device is secure.

Table 4.1: Comparative Analysis of RBAC and ABAC

Policy-Based Access Control (PBAC)

The evolution of RBAC and ABAC has given rise to a broader concept often referred to as policy-based access control, or PBAC. While RBAC and ABAC can be seen as distinct models, PBAC serves as an overarching paradigm that unifies them under the framework of policies. In PBAC, access rights are governed by explicitly defined rules, which may be based on roles, attributes, or hybrid combinations of both. These policies articulate the conditions under which access is granted or denied and may also specify obligations, such as requiring additional logging, enforcing multi-factor verification, or triggering alerts when sensitive data is accessed.

PBAC is particularly significant in cloud-native and multi-tenant environments where traditional organizational boundaries are porous and where access requirements evolve rapidly. For example, in software-as-a-service (SaaS) platforms that host multiple organizations on shared infrastructure, policies can be defined to ensure that data remains isolated by tenant while allowing administrators to manage exceptions in a scalable, auditable manner. Likewise, in industries governed by evolving compliance mandates, PBAC enables rapid adaptation: when regulations change, administrators can centrally update policies without re-engineering underlying systems.

The rise of PBAC reflects the recognition that real-world access control often requires a hybrid approach. Organizations rarely operate exclusively under RBAC or ABAC but instead blend elements of both. A financial institution may define broad roles for traders, analysts, and auditors while also using attribute-based rules to enforce transaction limits or geographic restrictions. A healthcare provider may rely on RBAC to define general categories of users, but deploy ABAC policies to ensure that clinicians can access records only for patients currently under their care. PBAC thus provides the governance layer that integrates different access models into a coherent strategy.

The theoretical significance of PBAC lies in its emphasis on policies as first-class citizens of access management. Instead of treating roles or attributes as the ultimate determinants of access, PBAC situates them within a policy framework that articulates both conditions and obligations. This approach not only increases flexibility but also enhances accountability, as policies can be versioned, audited, and aligned directly with organizational governance documents or regulatory requirements. In effect, PBAC bridges the gap between the technical implementation of access control and the institutional frameworks of accountability, ethics, and law.

A real-world example of PBAC in action can be found in large-scale cloud ecosystems such as Amazon Web Services (AWS) Identity and Access Management. AWS allows administrators to define policies that specify permissions in terms of both roles and attributes, encoded in JSON-based policy documents. These policies are explicit, machine-readable, and auditable, enabling fine-grained control that adapts as organizational needs evolve. Similar approaches are employed by Microsoft Azure and Google Cloud, all of which treat policy definition as the central mechanism for managing access in highly dynamic, multi-tenant environments.

Integrating RBAC, ABAC, and PBAC

The comparative analysis of RBAC, ABAC, and PBAC reveals not competition but complementarity. RBAC provides efficiency and auditability, ABAC delivers granularity and adaptability, and PBAC unifies these approaches under a governance-oriented framework. Organizations increasingly adopt hybrid strategies that combine the stability of roles with the flexibility of attributes, governed by explicit policies that align with compliance and operational objectives.

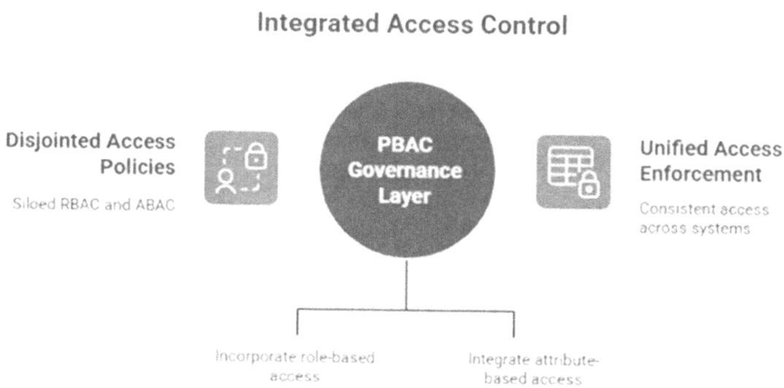

Figure 4.2: Conceptual Diagram of RBAC, ABAC, and PBAC Integration

Together, these models illustrate the maturation of access control from rigid hierarchies to dynamic, policy-driven ecosystems. As organizations navigate the complexities of cloud computing, global collaboration, and ever-shifting regulatory landscapes, access control models will continue to evolve. What remains constant, however, is the centrality of authorization frameworks in shaping not only the security posture of organizations but also their capacity to balance trust, efficiency, and accountability in the digital age.

Identity Federation and Single Sign-On

Identity Federation

The increasing reliance on distributed computing, cloud services, and global partnerships has redefined the way organizations conceptualize trust and identity. Historically, identity management was confined within organizational boundaries: employees were provisioned accounts in local directories, authenticated using internal systems, and authorized according to internal policies. This model worked effectively when enterprises were self-contained, with resources primarily on-premises and users mostly internal. However, as globalization, outsourcing, and cloud computing began to dominate the digital landscape, the limitations of such a siloed approach became evident. Organizations found themselves managing multiple overlapping credentials for contractors, suppliers, customers, and partners, creating inefficiencies, inconsistencies, and elevated risks. Identity federation emerged as the solution to these challenges, offering a framework through which identity could be portably asserted across trust boundaries without duplicating authentication systems.

At its core, identity federation is about establishing a trusted relationship between distinct identity domains, enabling a user authenticated in one domain to gain access to resources in another without the need to reauthenticate or manage separate credentials. This is achieved through the exchange of standardized assertions that verify identity, entitlements, and conditions of access. Unlike traditional account provisioning, federation avoids the proliferation of redundant accounts and passwords, thereby reducing both administrative burden and the attack surface associated with credential management. From a theoretical standpoint, federation extends the concept of digital identity from being a purely local construct to one that is transferable and recognized across organizational and even national borders.

The historical development of federation protocols reflects a progressive effort to formalize this transfer of trust. The Security Assertion Markup Language (SAML), introduced in the early 2000s, became one of the first widely adopted standards, particularly in higher education and government sectors. It enabled identity providers (IdPs) to assert authentication events to service providers (SPs) via XML-based messages, allowing a single authentication event to provide access to multiple applications. Building upon SAML's foundations, OAuth 2.0 introduced a more flexible, token-based approach that gained traction in consumer-facing environments, most notably powering the "Log in with Google/Facebook" model. OpenID Connect (OIDC), built on top of OAuth 2.0, further enhanced this model by providing a lightweight, JSON-based authentication mechanism that is now central to modern cloud identity platforms. These protocols collectively established a shared grammar for asserting and consuming identity, ensuring that federation could operate reliably and securely across heterogeneous systems.

In practice, the success of identity federation is tied to its ability to balance convenience with assurance. A global enterprise, for instance, may wish to allow contractors from a partner company to access its project management tools. Without federation, the enterprise would need to create and manage local accounts for each contractor, monitor their lifecycle, and bear the risk of forgotten or orphaned accounts after the contract ends. With federation, the enterprise can instead trust the contractor's home organization to authenticate its users, while enforcing its own authorization policies at the resource level. The contractor logs in once through their organization's identity provider, and through standardized federation protocols, gains access to the enterprise's applications. This arrangement not only streamlines the user experience but also distributes responsibility for authentication to the entity most capable of validating identity.

The academic community provides one of the most illustrative examples of federation in action. Initiatives such as InCommon in the United States and eduGAIN in Europe enable researchers, faculty, and students to use their home institution credentials to access resources across thousands of participating universities and research centers. A visiting scholar from one university can log into a research portal hosted by another institution without creating a new account, as the two domains trust each other's assertions through a federated network. This model has proven invaluable in large-scale scientific collaborations, such as those involving particle physics or genomic research, where seamless data sharing and collaboration are critical. Federation thus not only enhances security and efficiency but also acts as an enabler of knowledge exchange and innovation.

Despite these successes, identity federation is not without challenges. One persistent concern is the management of trust. Trust is not inherent; it must be negotiated and governed, often through legal agreements, operational policies, and technical safeguards. If one identity provider in a federation has weak security practices, the integrity of the entire federation can be compromised. This phenomenon, sometimes called "the weakest link problem," necessitates strong governance frameworks that define acceptable levels of assurance, incident response procedures, and compliance obligations. Moreover, federated systems must balance privacy concerns with usability. While federation reduces credential sprawl, it also creates opportunities to track user activity across domains, raising questions about consent, data minimization, and regulatory compliance under regimes such as the GDPR.

Looking ahead, federation is poised to evolve alongside other paradigms such as Zero Trust and decentralized identity. In Zero Trust architectures, federation plays a central role by ensuring that trust is established not only at the perimeter but continuously, across all interactions. Meanwhile, decentralized identity initiatives, often leveraging blockchain, aim to shift control of identity away from central providers, enabling individuals to store their identity assertions in cryptographic wallets. Whether centralized or decentralized, the trajectory of identity federation reflects an ongoing negotiation among efficiency, security, and sovereignty in the digital age.

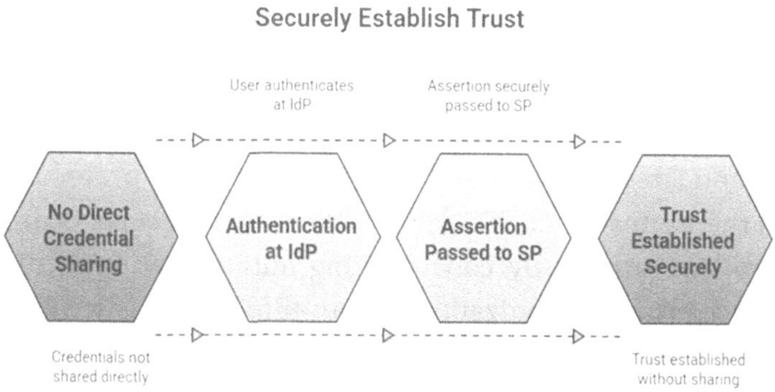

Figure 4.3: Identity Federation Trust Model

The above diagram shows the relationship between an Identity Provider (IdP), a Service Provider (SP), and the user. This figure illustrates how authentication is performed at the IdP, and how the assertion is securely passed to the SP, establishing trust without direct credential sharing.

Single Sign-On (SSO)

If identity federation enables trust across domains, Single Sign-On (SSO) enhances usability and security within and across them by reducing the number of separate authentication events a user must perform. At its simplest, SSO allows a user to authenticate once with a central identity provider and then access multiple applications or systems without re-entering credentials. Though deceptively straightforward in concept, SSO embodies a profound rethinking of how authentication should function in complex digital environments, balancing convenience with security in ways that reflect both technological and organizational imperatives.

The origins of SSO can be traced to early enterprise computing environments, where users were burdened with maintaining separate credentials for different applications, each with its own authentication mechanism. This proliferation of passwords, often referred to as "password fatigue," not only created usability problems but also heightened security risks. Users tended to reuse passwords across systems or select weak, easily memorable credentials, making them vulnerable to brute-force attacks or phishing. Helpdesks, overwhelmed with password reset requests, faced significant operational costs. SSO emerged as a practical response to these inefficiencies, initially implemented in proprietary enterprise systems and later generalized through standardized protocols.

At a theoretical level, SSO reflects the principle of centralization in identity management. By consolidating authentication into a single point of control, organizations can enforce consistent policies, strengthen monitoring, and streamline auditing. Instead of dozens of disparate systems each managing its own login procedures, SSO delegates authentication to a trusted identity provider. Once authenticated, the user receives a token or ticket—depending on the underlying protocol—that can be presented to other systems as proof of identity. The Kerberos protocol, developed at MIT in the 1980s, exemplified this approach by issuing time-limited tickets that enabled users to access multiple services without re-entering passwords. Later implementations extended this idea to web-based systems, where standards such as SAML, OAuth 2.0, and OpenID Connect now underpin modern SSO frameworks.

The practical benefits of SSO are evident across industries. Usability is perhaps the most immediate advantage: a clinician in a hospital, for instance, may need to access electronic health records, lab systems, imaging repositories, and billing platforms in quick succession. Without SSO, this clinician would be required to remember and repeatedly enter different passwords, a process that wastes time and interrupts workflow. With SSO, one authentication event provides seamless access across all relevant systems, improving efficiency and reducing the likelihood of errors. From a security perspective, SSO reduces the attack surface by minimizing the number of passwords that must be created, remembered, and stored. It also facilitates the integration of multi-factor authentication

(MFA), since the burden of MFA can be concentrated on the initial login, rather than imposed repeatedly.

However, the adoption of SSO introduces new challenges. Chief among them is the risk of a single point of failure. If the central authentication service becomes unavailable, users may be locked out of all dependent applications, disrupting business operations. More critically, if a user's credentials are compromised, an attacker can gain access to all systems linked to the SSO framework, amplifying the consequences of a breach. To mitigate these risks, organizations often pair SSO with layered security measures, such as adaptive authentication, anomaly detection, and robust session management. For example, even if a user is authenticated via SSO, access to sensitive applications may still trigger step-up authentication, requiring additional verification.

A well-documented case study illustrating the power and risks of SSO can be found in Google's implementation of its internal SSO system, known as BeyondCorp. Initially designed to eliminate reliance on a traditional corporate perimeter, BeyondCorp leverages SSO to centralize identity verification while applying continuous contextual checks. Employees authenticate once through a secure gateway, after which they gain access to a wide array of internal and cloud-based applications. This has significantly improved usability while supporting remote and mobile work. Yet, Google has also highlighted the importance of coupling SSO with ongoing risk analysis: if an account exhibits unusual behavior, additional challenges are issued, or access is revoked, thereby limiting the damage from compromised credentials. The BeyondCorp case demonstrates that while SSO enhances efficiency, it must be embedded in a broader zero-trust model to achieve resilience.

From a governance perspective, SSO simplifies compliance and auditing. Centralizing authentication logs allows organizations to trace user activity across multiple systems with greater accuracy, an essential capability under regulations such as HIPAA, PCI DSS, and GDPR. Instead of reconciling disparate audit trails, compliance teams can rely on the SSO system as a central source of truth for identity verification events. At the same time, SSO reinforces privacy principles by reducing the proliferation of stored credentials, thereby lowering the risk of breaches involving password databases.

As organizations continue their migration to cloud and hybrid environments, SSO has become an indispensable enabler of digital transformation. Cloud-based platforms such as Microsoft Azure Active Directory, Okta, and Ping Identity now offer enterprise-grade SSO solutions that integrate on-premises and cloud applications into a unified authentication framework. The demand for seamless access across SaaS platforms—Salesforce, Office 365, Zoom, and countless others—has made SSO not merely a convenience but a necessity.

Looking forward, the evolution of SSO is intertwined with emerging paradigms such as passwordless authentication and decentralized identity. Passwordless methods, leveraging biometrics or cryptographic keys, can further reduce reliance on vulnerable credentials, while decentralized identity frameworks promise to shift control of identity assertions toward the user, potentially transforming the traditional SSO model. In either case, the trajectory of SSO reflects an enduring pursuit: to reconcile usability, security, and governance in a way that supports the fluid, borderless nature of modern work.

Aspect	Benefits	Risks/Challenges
User Experience	Reduces password fatigue; improves workflow efficiency	Over-reliance may mask underlying security issues
Security	Fewer credentials stored and transmitted; easier to enforce MFA	Compromised credentials grant access to multiple systems
Operational Efficiency	Lowers helpdesk costs from password resets	Single point of failure can cause widespread disruption
Compliance & Auditing	Centralized logging supports regulatory reporting	Requires strong governance to manage trust relationships
Integration	Seamless access to cloud and on-premises applications	Complexity in hybrid environments may increase deployment risks

Table 4.2: Benefits and Risks of SSO

Integration with IAM Systems

The effectiveness of identity federation and Single Sign-On (SSO) does not lie in their isolated deployment, but in how seamlessly they integrate into the broader landscape of Identity and Access Management (IAM). IAM serves as the backbone of organizational security by defining policies, technologies, and processes that govern "who can access what, under which conditions." Federation and SSO extend IAM beyond traditional boundaries, connecting users, devices, and services across hybrid cloud, on-premises environments, and partner ecosystems. Integration, therefore, transforms these technologies from convenient add-ons into strategic enablers of trust, compliance, and resilience.

Historically, IAM systems evolved around closed enterprise environments. In the 1990s and early 2000s, organizations primarily relied on centralized directories such as Microsoft Active Directory (AD) and Lightweight Directory Access Protocol (LDAP)-based systems to manage user identities. These systems provided robust role-based access control (RBAC), allowing administrators to group users into roles that determined permissions across applications. However, the rapid rise of cloud computing, SaaS platforms, and external collaboration soon rendered these traditional models insufficient. Employees, contractors, and partners now require secure access to resources beyond the organizational perimeter, often from remote locations and unmanaged devices. This shift necessitated a new generation of IAM architectures that could integrate federation and SSO technologies while still leveraging the centralized governance of traditional directories.

At a theoretical level, integration between IAM, federation, and SSO can be seen as the convergence of three pillars: authentication, authorization, and accountability. Authentication, often centralized through SSO, verifies user identity. Authorization, managed through IAM systems, determines what resources a user can access once authenticated. Accountability, achieved through centralized logging and monitoring, ensures that all access attempts are auditable and compliant with regulatory requirements. When tightly integrated, these pillars form a closed security loop that enables dynamic, context-aware access control while preserving a seamless user experience.

Practical integration begins with aligning federation protocols—such as SAML, OAuth 2.0, and OpenID Connect—with IAM policy engines. For example, when a user authenticates via SSO using OAuth 2.0, the IAM system must interpret the identity claims contained in the access token and map them to appropriate roles or attributes within its internal model. This mapping is not always straightforward. An external partner may assert an attribute such as "contractor," but the internal IAM system may require finer-grained distinctions, such as project affiliation or security clearance. Without careful attribute harmonization, integration risks either over-provisioning (granting excessive privileges) or under-provisioning (blocking legitimate access).

The integration of federation and SSO with IAM also enables hybrid access control models that combine RBAC with Attribute-Based Access Control (ABAC). While RBAC provides simplicity and scalability, ABAC introduces granularity by evaluating contextual attributes such as time of access, device type, or location. For instance, an employee authenticated through SSO may be assigned a role that grants access to financial data, but ABAC rules can restrict this access to office-based devices during business hours. Such layered enforcement, made possible by IAM integration, reflects the growing influence of zero-trust security paradigms, where identity verification is continuous and context-aware rather than static.

A case study that illustrates the value of IAM integration comes from the financial services sector. A multinational bank faced the challenge of enabling thousands of employees and contractors to access a mix of legacy mainframe applications, cloud-based customer relationship management systems, and mobile platforms. By integrating federation and SSO with its IAM system, the bank established a unified identity architecture. Federation protocols allowed external contractors to authenticate using their home institutions' credentials, while SSO streamlined employee access to both on-premises and SaaS applications. The IAM system acted as the central policy engine, enforcing role-based and attribute-based rules across the environment. Importantly, the integration provided centralized audit logs, which proved critical during regulatory reviews under frameworks such as Basel III and GDPR. The result was not only improved user experience but also measurable reductions in unauthorized access incidents.

Despite these successes, integration introduces its own challenges. Complexity is one of the most significant hurdles. Hybrid environments often include legacy applications that were never designed to support modern federation protocols or token-based authentication. Retrofitting such systems to align with IAM policies can require costly middleware solutions or even application redesign. Moreover, governance complexity increases when integrating with external identity providers. Trust must be carefully established, and security teams must continuously validate that external assertions of identity and attributes meet internal standards.

Scalability is another consideration. As organizations expand their cloud footprints and enter into more federated relationships, IAM systems must handle growing volumes of authentication requests, attribute evaluations, and policy decisions in real time. Failure to scale effectively can lead to bottlenecks, downtime, or inconsistent policy enforcement. Modern solutions increasingly turn to cloud-native IAM platforms that offer elasticity and distributed architectures capable of supporting global enterprises.

The future of IAM integration with federation and SSO points toward even greater automation and intelligence. Machine learning models are being incorporated into IAM systems to detect anomalies in access patterns, automatically flagging or revoking suspicious sessions. Decentralized identity, supported by blockchain technologies, may eventually allow users to carry portable, verifiable credentials that federate seamlessly across domains without requiring centralized authorities. In this future landscape, IAM will continue to act as the policy and governance layer, integrating new technologies while preserving accountability.

Dimension	Benefits of Integration	Challenges of Integration
Security	Consistent enforcement of access policies across hybrid environments	Complexity of aligning attributes and roles across domains
Usability	Unified access experience for employees, partners, and contractors	Legacy applications may lack support for modern federation protocols
Compliance & Auditing	Centralized logs simplify regulatory reporting (e.g., GDPR, HIPAA, PCI DSS)	Governance complexity in establishing and maintaining trust with external IdPs
Scalability	Cloud-native IAM platforms enable global, elastic identity management	High transaction volumes require advanced infrastructure and continuous optimization
Strategic Value	Supports zero-trust architectures and digital transformation initiatives	Risk of vendor lock-in and high costs in integrating disparate systems

Table 4.3: IAM Integration Benefits and Challenges

Conclusion

This chapter has explored the critical role of data access and identity management (IAM) in modern cybersecurity, emphasizing how authentication, authorization, and access control frameworks underpin secure digital ecosystems. IAM is no longer merely a technical function; it is a strategic enabler that balances security, usability, compliance, and operational efficiency. Historically, identity and access control evolved from simple password-based authentication and static access assignments to sophisticated models that incorporate multi-factor verification, dynamic policy enforcement, and context-aware authorization. This evolution reflects the growing complexity of organizational structures, the decentralization of resources through cloud computing, and the expanding digital attack surface due to remote work, IoT devices, and global collaborations.

Authentication and authorization remain the twin pillars of IAM. Authentication establishes identity using mechanisms ranging from passwords to biometrics and adaptive risk-based verification, ensuring that the system accurately identifies users, devices, and processes. Authorization determines the scope of permissible actions for authenticated entities, implementing the principle of least privilege to reduce potential damage from accidental misuse, insider threats, or compromised credentials. The chapter highlighted how failures in either process can lead to catastrophic breaches, such as the 2013 Target incident, where inadequate authentication and excessive privileges enabled attackers to compromise millions of records.

Access control models, including Role-Based Access Control (RBAC) and Attribute-Based Access Control (ABAC), illustrate the trade-offs between administrative simplicity and contextual flexibility. RBAC streamlines access management by grouping users into roles aligned with organizational functions, supporting auditability and regulatory compliance, particularly in structured environments like healthcare and finance. ABAC, by contrast, evaluates attributes related to users, resources, actions, and environmental context, offering fine-grained, adaptive access control suited to dynamic, multi-tenant, or cloud-native systems. Policy-Based Access Control (PBAC) emerged as an integrative paradigm, unifying RBAC and ABAC under explicit policies to provide governance, accountability, and adaptability in complex ecosystems.

Identity federation and Single Sign-On (SSO) further extend IAM capabilities beyond organizational boundaries. Federation enables trusted identity assertions across domains, reducing credential sprawl and streamlining collaboration, while SSO consolidates authentication into a single, seamless user experience. When integrated with IAM systems, these technologies enhance security, enforce centralized policies, support regulatory compliance, and reduce operational inefficiencies. The chapter also emphasized the critical role of zero-trust principles, continuous verification, and adaptive access management in mitigating risks posed by perimeter-less networks.

Looking forward, IAM is poised for continued transformation. Artificial intelligence will drive adaptive, risk-aware authentication, while decentralized identity frameworks promise user-managed, portable credentials. Organizations that successfully integrate authentication, authorization, access control, federation, and SSO will achieve resilience, compliance, and operational efficiency, thereby establishing a foundation of trust in increasingly complex and interconnected digital landscapes.

Key Terms

1. IAM is central to cybersecurity, balancing identity verification, access control, usability, and compliance.
2. Authentication verifies identity; authorization defines permissible actions—both must be tightly integrated.
3. Multi-factor and adaptive authentication enhances security while preserving user convenience.
4. RBAC provides structured, role-based access; ABAC enables granular, context-aware access decisions.
5. PBAC unifies RBAC and ABAC under policy-driven governance.
6. Identity federation reduces credential sprawl and enables cross-domain access.
7. SSO enhances usability and supports centralized security and auditing.
8. Zero-trust principles require continuous verification and adaptive access management.
9. IAM integration with cloud, hybrid, and multi-tenant environments is crucial for scalability and compliance.
10. Emerging technologies such as AI and decentralized identity will further transform IAM practices.

Review Questions

1. Define Identity and Access Management (IAM) and explain its importance in modern cybersecurity.
2. Differentiate between authentication and authorization with historical examples.
3. Explain the principle of least privilege and its relevance to authorization.
4. Discuss the limitations of password-based authentication in large-scale systems.
5. Compare multi-factor and adaptive authentication in terms of security and usability.
6. Describe how human behavior affects authentication effectiveness.
7. Define Role-Based Access Control (RBAC) and its key benefits.
8. Identify scenarios where RBAC may be inadequate.
9. Explain the concept of "role explosion" in RBAC.
10. Define Attribute-Based Access Control (ABAC) and how it differs from RBAC.
11. Provide examples of ABAC in healthcare and finance.
12. Discuss regulatory drivers (GDPR, HIPAA) that influence ABAC adoption.
13. Identify challenges in implementing and maintaining ABAC.
14. Explain Policy-Based Access Control (PBAC) and its role in integrating RBAC and ABAC.
15. Provide a real-world example of PBAC in cloud ecosystems.
16. Define identity federation and explain how it supports cross-domain access.
17. Compare SAML, OAuth 2.0, and OpenID Connect in identity federation.
18. Explain the benefits and risks of Single Sign-On (SSO).
19. Analyze how SSO enhances usability and security in zero-trust environments.
20. Describe how IAM integration improves security, compliance, and operational efficiency.

21. Discuss the challenges of integrating legacy systems with modern IAM solutions.
22. Explain how zero-trust principles influence IAM design and continuous verification.
23. Describe the importance of auditability and centralized logging in IAM.
24. Provide a case study example illustrating the successful integration of RBAC, ABAC, federation, and SSO.
25. Predict future trends in IAM, including AI-driven adaptive access and decentralized identity.

CHAPTER 5

Cloud and API Data Security

Learning Objectives

By the end of this chapter, readers will be able to:

- Explain how cloud computing reshapes traditional data security practices.
- Analyze the shared responsibility model in cloud environments.
- Identify provider and customer obligations for data protection and compliance.
- Evaluate the role of APIs as both enablers of innovation and security risks.
- Describe the functions of API gateways, policies, and monitoring in securing data.
- Assess secure data pipeline design for data in transit, at rest, and in processing.
- Connect cloud and API security to regulatory requirements such as GDPR, HIPAA, and PCI DSS.
- Apply zero-trust and AI-driven approaches to strengthen cloud and API resilience.

Overview

Cloud computing has fundamentally reshaped the landscape of data management and digital operations. What began as an experimental technology offering elastic infrastructure has evolved into the backbone of global enterprise systems, powering everything from consumer applications to critical government services. Organizations increasingly adopt multi-cloud strategies, leveraging combinations of public, private, and hybrid environments to balance cost optimization, resilience, flexibility, and regulatory compliance. This evolution not only provides unprecedented scalability and efficiency, but also fragments the traditional security perimeter. Unlike earlier eras, when sensitive information was largely confined to corporate data centers, cloud adoption disperses data across geographic, technological, and organizational boundaries. Consequently, securing data in cloud environments is no longer about safeguarding a single, centralized repository; it is about protecting a constantly shifting ecosystem where data is in perpetual motion—stored, processed, and transmitted across diverse platforms and jurisdictions.

Central to this transformation are Application Programming Interfaces (APIs), which act as the connective tissue of modern cloud services. APIs enable interoperability between applications, systems, and services, allowing organizations to automate workflows, orchestrate infrastructure, and deliver real-time digital experiences. In a distributed, cloud-first world, APIs have become indispensable enablers of innovation. However, they also represent a critical security frontier. Poorly designed, unmonitored, or insecure APIs can expose sensitive information, create backdoors into systems, or allow attackers to escalate privileges. In fact, industry reports consistently identify API vulnerabilities as one of the fastest-growing categories of cyber threats, reflecting the dual role of APIs as both accelerators of digital transformation and potential vectors for compromise.

Equally important is the security of data pipelines, the complex flows that ingest, process, transform, and distribute data across multi-cloud and hybrid environments. Data pipelines underpin critical functions such as analytics, machine learning, and operational intelligence, often involving sensitive personal, financial, or intellectual property data. Without proper safeguards, these pipelines can inadvertently expose information at multiple points—whether in transit, during processing, or while temporarily stored in staging environments. The distributed and automated nature of pipelines makes them difficult to monitor comprehensively, increasing the risk of misconfiguration, unauthorized access, or unintentional data leakage. Ensuring end-to-end protection, therefore, requires a holistic strategy that integrates encryption, access control, logging, monitoring, and compliance frameworks into every stage of the data lifecycle.

The complexity of cloud and API security is further amplified by regulatory pressures and the globalized nature of data. Regulations such as the General Data Protection Regulation (GDPR), the Health Insurance Portability and Accountability Act (HIPAA), and the California Consumer Privacy Act (CCPA) impose stringent requirements on how organizations manage, share, and safeguard sensitive information. Cloud adoption often involves storing or transmitting data across national boundaries, raising questions of jurisdiction, sovereignty, and accountability. Missteps in handling such data not only undermine consumer trust but also expose organizations to severe financial and reputational penalties. As such, cloud and API security cannot be understood in isolation from the broader legal, ethical, and societal frameworks in which they operate.

This chapter sets out to examine the mechanisms, strategies, and best practices that define effective cloud and API data security in the twenty-first century. It explores how organizations can secure multi-cloud architectures, implement robust identity and access controls, and build resilient data pipelines that withstand both technical failures and malicious attacks. Equally, it considers how emerging paradigms such as zero-trust architecture, confidential computing, and AI-driven threat detection are reshaping approaches to security. By weaving together theoretical insights, technical solutions, and real-world case studies, the chapter seeks to equip readers with a comprehensive understanding of how to safeguard data in environments where change is constant and the stakes are higher than ever.

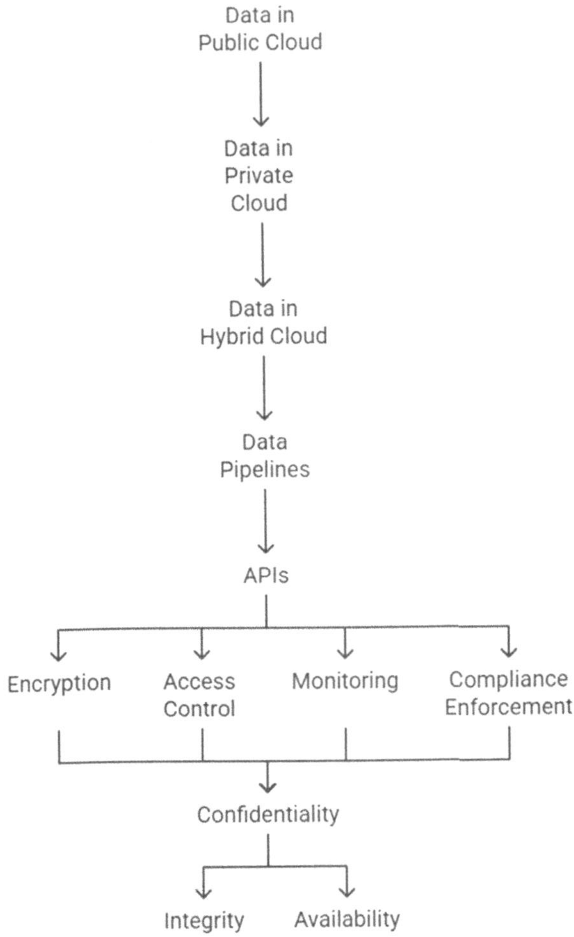

Figure 5.1: Cloud Data Ecosystem and Security Layers

This diagram illustrates the interconnected nature of modern cloud environments. Data resides across public, private, and hybrid clouds, flows through data pipelines for processing and transformation, and interacts with APIs that enable application and service integration. Security layers—encryption, access control, monitoring, and compliance enforcement—span all components, highlighting the end-to-end protection required to maintain confidentiality, integrity, and availability.

Protecting Data in Multi-Cloud Environments

Multi-cloud adoption offers organizations significant flexibility, scalability, and resilience. Besides, it also introduces a complex array of security challenges that require careful management. Unlike single-cloud deployments, where security policies, identity management, and compliance controls can be standardized and centrally monitored, multi-cloud environments span heterogeneous platforms, each with distinct configurations, operational practices, and native security models. Differences in encryption mechanisms, network segmentation strategies, and logging standards can create inconsistencies that attackers may exploit. For instance, an organization operating workloads on both Amazon Web Services (AWS) and Microsoft Azure must harmonize identity and access management across platforms while reconciling divergent security policies. Adding to this complexity, regional and international data protection regulations, such as Europe's GDPR, the US CCPA, or sector-specific requirements like HIPAA, must be enforced across all clouds. This creates a dual challenge: ensuring technical security while remaining compliant with potentially conflicting regulatory obligations.

A major risk in multi-cloud deployments arises from misconfiguration, which has consistently been among the leading causes of cloud data breaches. Cloud services offer immense configurability, but this flexibility also increases the likelihood of human or procedural errors. Misconfigured storage buckets, excessive permissions, improperly secured virtual networks, and open API endpoints can all inadvertently expose sensitive data. Historical incidents highlight the severe consequences of such oversights. For example, numerous breaches in recent years involved publicly accessible AWS S3 buckets containing millions of customer records, intellectual property, or internal analytics. The fallout from these breaches has included not only financial losses but also significant reputational damage, regulatory fines, and erosion of customer trust.

The operational complexity of multi-cloud security also complicates monitoring and incident response. Traditional security information and event management (SIEM) systems may struggle to provide a unified view across disparate platforms, making it difficult to detect anomalous activities or enforce consistent security policies. Furthermore, automated provisioning and deprovisioning of resources, common in dynamic cloud environments, can inadvertently leave security gaps if identity and access controls are not continuously synchronized across clouds. Organizations must therefore invest in centralized governance, cross-cloud visibility tools, and robust configuration management processes to maintain a secure posture.

Another consideration is the shared responsibility model inherent in cloud computing. While cloud providers secure the underlying infrastructure, organizations remain responsible for configuring services securely, managing encryption keys, and controlling access to their data. In multi-cloud contexts, this shared responsibility becomes more intricate, requiring teams to understand and implement the nuances of each provider's security framework. Misalignment between providers and internal policies can create vulnerabilities that attackers may exploit.

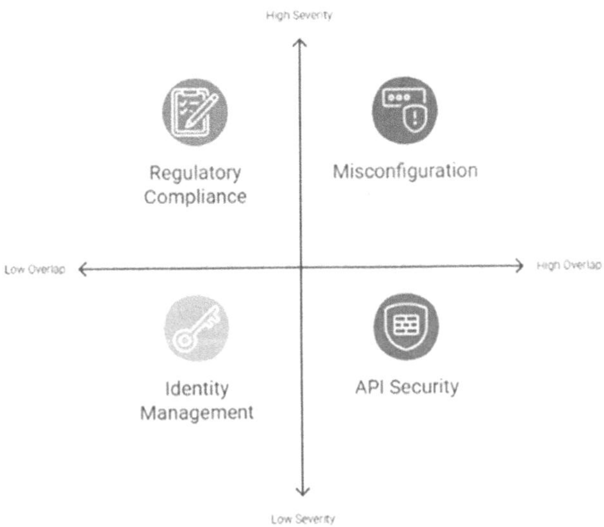

Figure 5.2: Multi-Cloud Security Platforms Overview

A visual showing multiple cloud platforms (AWS, Azure, GCP) with overlapping security concerns, highlighting areas like misconfiguration, regulatory compliance, identity management, and API security.

Data Protection Strategies

In the context of multi-cloud deployments, effective data protection requires shifting from perimeter-based approaches to data-centric security models that safeguard information regardless of its location or the platform on which it resides. This paradigm ensures that data remains secure as it moves between services, clouds, and geographic regions, addressing the inherent mobility and fluidity of modern enterprise workloads. End-to-end encryption is a cornerstone of this approach, ensuring that data remains unintelligible to unauthorized parties from the point of creation through transmission and storage. Encryption should encompass both data at rest and data in transit, with strong algorithms such as AES-256 and RSA/ECC-based key exchange, providing robust cryptographic guarantees.

Tokenization serves as an additional layer of protection, particularly for sensitive identifiers such as payment card information, personally identifiable information (PII), or health records. By replacing sensitive data with non-sensitive surrogates, tokenization reduces exposure in cloud applications while maintaining operational functionality. The original values are stored securely within token vaults, often reinforced with encryption and access controls, ensuring that even if application-level data is compromised, attackers cannot recover the underlying sensitive information. Role-based access policies further complement encryption and tokenization by enforcing the principle of least privilege, granting users and services access only to the resources necessary for their roles. Consistency in access control across multiple cloud platforms is critical, as discrepancies between providers can create exploitable gaps.

Key management is a particularly vital aspect of data protection. Organizations must retain control over the lifecycle of encryption keys, including generation, rotation, revocation, and storage.

Centralized key management solutions provide a unified interface for governing keys across multiple clouds, ensuring consistent policies and reducing operational errors. Cloud provider key management services can also be leveraged for cross-platform encryption, though organizations should evaluate provider-specific constraints and compliance implications. Secure handling of keys prevents unauthorized decryption and is often a regulatory requirement under frameworks such as GDPR, HIPAA, and PCI DSS.

Network-level protections supplement data-centric approaches by limiting exposure within cloud environments. Network segmentation, virtual private clouds (VPCs), and secure interconnects between clouds help contain potential breaches, preventing lateral movement of attackers once they gain access to a compromised system. By isolating workloads and enforcing strict network controls, organizations reduce the likelihood of widespread data compromise, even in the event of misconfigured services or compromised credentials.

Continuous monitoring and automated compliance audits are also essential. Multi-cloud environments are dynamic, with services and configurations changing rapidly. Automated tools can detect deviations from established security baselines, flag misconfigurations, and trigger remediation actions in real time. Monitoring should include log aggregation, anomaly detection, and behavioral analytics to proactively identify suspicious activity. Integrating these capabilities with centralized governance ensures that organizations maintain visibility, enforce security policies uniformly, and demonstrate compliance to auditors and regulators.

Case Study: Multi-Cloud Financial Platform

A leading global bank, operating across multiple continents, embarked on a hybrid multi-cloud strategy to leverage the scalability of public clouds while retaining sensitive workloads within private data centers. This approach allowed the bank to optimize costs, improve performance, and support disaster recovery, yet it introduced significant complexity in managing consistent security and compliance across heterogeneous platforms. Each cloud provider—AWS, Google Cloud, and the bank's private infrastructure—employed distinct identity management models, encryption services, network controls, and logging capabilities, creating the potential for gaps in protection if not carefully coordinated.

Initially, the bank faced challenges due to fragmented access policies and inconsistent encryption practices. For example, while AWS supported customer-managed keys (CMKs) with fine-grained IAM roles, Google Cloud's default configurations required adjustments to meet the bank's strict regulatory requirements, particularly under GDPR and local banking regulations. Misalignment of key rotation schedules and differing audit capabilities increased operational overhead and risk. To address these issues, the bank centralized its IAM governance, creating a unified role hierarchy and access matrix applicable across all environments. By standardizing roles and permissions, the bank enforced the principle of least privilege uniformly, reducing the likelihood of over-privileged accounts and limiting attack surfaces.

Encryption was standardized across clouds using AES-256 for data at rest and TLS 1.3 for data in transit. A centralized key management system allowed the bank to maintain control over key lifecycles, monitor usage, and implement automated rotation schedules. Tokens were also employed for sensitive payment and customer identifiers, reducing the exposure of personally identifiable information across operational systems and analytical platforms. The bank implemented additional security controls at the network layer, including virtual private clouds, segmentation, and secure interconnects between cloud providers and on-premises systems, limiting lateral movement and containing potential breaches.

Proactive monitoring and auditing played a critical role in maintaining the security posture. Automated tools aggregated logs from multiple clouds, performed anomaly detection, and triggered alerts when unusual access patterns were detected. Compliance dashboards enabled the bank to demonstrate regulatory compliance in real time, reducing the administrative burden of audits. Training and operational discipline were also emphasized, ensuring that security policies were understood and enforced by administrators, developers, and operational staff alike.

This case highlights several key lessons for multi-cloud security in financial services. First, centralized governance is essential to harmonize policies across disparate environments and prevent security gaps. Second, automation in monitoring, auditing, and key management enhances operational efficiency while reducing human error. Third, consistent encryption and tokenization practices mitigate the risk of data exposure, particularly in highly regulated industries. Finally, continuous vigilance, supported by structured operational processes, ensures that security evolves alongside the dynamic nature of multi-cloud infrastructures.

Component	Cloud / Environment	Security Measures Implemented	Purpose / Outcome
Identity & Access Management (IAM)	AWS, Google Cloud, Private Data Center	Centralized IAM policies, unified role hierarchy, least privilege enforcement	Reduced risk of over-privileged accounts and inconsistent access
Encryption	AWS, Google Cloud, Private Data Center	AES-256 at rest, TLS 1.3 in transit, centralized key management with automated rotation	Ensured data confidentiality, uniform encryption across platforms
Sensitive Data Protection	All Environments	Tokenization of payment and customer identifiers	Reduced exposure of personally identifiable information (PII)
Network Security	Multi-cloud connectivity	Virtual private clouds, network segmentation, secure interconnects	Minimized lateral movement and contained potential breaches

Component	Cloud / Environment	Security Measures Implemented	Purpose / Outcome
Monitoring & Auditing	AWS, Google Cloud, Private Data Center	Centralized log aggregation, anomaly detection, real-time compliance dashboards	Early detection of security incidents and streamlined regulatory reporting
Governance & Operations	Organization-wide	Training for administrators, developers, and operational staff; operational discipline	Ensured consistent policy enforcement and adherence to regulatory requirements

Table 5.1: Multi-Cloud Financial Platform Case Study Analysis

API Gateways and Security Policies

The Role of APIs in Modern Architectures

Application Programming Interfaces (APIs) have become the backbone of modern digital architectures, acting as the connective tissue that enables disparate applications, cloud services, and microservices to communicate and exchange data programmatically. Unlike traditional monolithic systems, where interactions were limited to tightly controlled internal interfaces, contemporary cloud-first and service-oriented architectures rely heavily on APIs to orchestrate workflows, provision resources, and integrate third-party services. APIs facilitate real-time data access, automated business processes, and the development of scalable, modular applications, making them indispensable for enterprises seeking agility, innovation, and operational efficiency.

Despite their operational advantages, APIs represent a significant attack surface within modern architectures. Each exposed endpoint potentially serves as a gateway for malicious actors seeking to exfiltrate sensitive data, manipulate system behavior, or escalate privileges. Unlike traditional web applications, which often benefit from well-established security controls such as network firewalls or perimeter defenses, APIs are programmatically accessible and frequently designed to be reachable across networks, increasing exposure. Vulnerabilities such as insufficient authentication, improper authorization, lack of input validation, and excessive data exposure have been repeatedly exploited in high-profile breaches, highlighting the criticality of API security. For instance, incidents in which unsecured API endpoints exposed customer records on cloud-based platforms underscore how a single misconfigured API can compromise the confidentiality, integrity, and availability of an entire system.

The security implications of APIs extend beyond technical considerations to operational and regulatory domains. Many APIs process sensitive data, including personally identifiable information (PII), financial transactions, or intellectual property, and their compromise can have legal and reputational consequences. Regulatory frameworks such as the General Data Protection Regulation (GDPR), the California Consumer Privacy Act (CCPA), and industry-specific standards such as PCI DSS mandate stringent controls over how data is accessed, transmitted, and logged, placing additional accountability on organizations to secure API interactions.

Securing APIs requires a layered approach that combines authentication, authorization, encryption, input validation, rate limiting, and continuous monitoring. Modern architectures increasingly adopt token-based authentication mechanisms, such as OAuth 2.0 and OpenID Connect, to ensure that only authorized clients and users can access endpoints. Role-based and attribute-based access control policies can further enforce fine-grained permissions, limiting exposure to sensitive resources based on identity, role, or contextual attributes. Transport Layer Security (TLS) ensures that data transmitted via APIs remains confidential and tamper-resistant, while structured logging and monitoring provide visibility into unusual patterns that may indicate attempted abuse or attacks.

The adoption of API gateways, management platforms, and threat detection tools has emerged as a best practice, allowing organizations to centralize security, enforce consistent policies, and integrate with identity and access management frameworks. In complex multi-cloud environments, API management platforms also facilitate governance, compliance reporting, and automated auditing, ensuring that enterprise-wide security objectives are consistently applied.

Securing APIs with Gateways

API gateways function as centralized enforcement points within modern application architectures, providing a unified layer of control for security, traffic management, and operational monitoring. Unlike individual microservices or server endpoints, which may implement security controls inconsistently, the gateway consolidates responsibilities such as authentication, authorization, input validation, rate limiting, and logging, effectively creating a defensive perimeter around all exposed APIs. This architectural pattern is especially critical in cloud-native and microservices-based environments, where the proliferation of endpoints across heterogeneous platforms can quickly become unmanageable without a central point of enforcement. By funneling all API traffic through a gateway, organizations can apply consistent security policies, reduce misconfiguration risks, and simplify operational oversight.

One of the primary security functions of API gateways is to enforce authentication protocols that validate the identity of clients or users before they can access services. Commonly adopted standards include OAuth 2.0, OpenID Connect, and JSON Web Tokens (JWT), which provide token-based, stateless authentication mechanisms. Implementing these protocols at the gateway level ensures that authentication checks are performed uniformly across all services, eliminating the need for each microservice to independently manage credential verification. This centralization reduces complexity, strengthens the security posture, and facilitates integration with identity and access management systems, including role-based and attribute-based access control frameworks. For example, a financial institution may require that any client requesting access to customer account data first present a valid OAuth token issued by the organization's identity provider, with the gateway verifying token validity, expiration, and associated permissions.

Beyond authentication, gateways handle authorization by enforcing fine-grained access control policies. Access rules can be based on user roles, attributes, contextual information such as geolocation or device type, and operational conditions, including time-of-day restrictions. By placing these checks at the gateway, organizations can ensure sensitive resources are consistently protected, preventing unauthorized actions such as data exfiltration or privilege escalation. Moreover, gateways often include input validation mechanisms that guard against injection attacks, malformed requests, or other malicious input, further reducing the attack surface for underlying services. Rate limiting and throttling features additionally protect APIs from denial-of-service attacks and abuse, maintaining system availability even under high traffic conditions.

Logging and monitoring represent another critical capability of API gateways. By capturing all requests and responses — including headers, parameters, and response codes — gateways create a comprehensive audit trail that supports compliance with regulatory frameworks such as GDPR, CCPA, HIPAA, and PCI DSS. Detailed logs enable security teams to conduct forensic investigations, identify suspicious patterns, and detect anomalous behavior that may indicate active attacks. Advanced API gateways can integrate with security information and event management (SIEM) systems and automated threat detection platforms, providing real-time alerts and analytics to support proactive defense. This combination of monitoring and logging transforms gateways into both a protective layer and a diagnostic tool, ensuring continuous visibility over API traffic.

Case studies illustrate the effectiveness of gateway-based security. For example, a global e-commerce platform that implemented an API gateway to mediate traffic between mobile applications, payment processors, and backend services successfully mitigated multiple attempts at credential stuffing and API scraping. By centrally enforcing OAuth authentication, role-based authorization, and rate limiting, the organization reduced operational overhead, maintained regulatory compliance, and significantly reduced its exposure to API-related breaches.

In summary, API gateways serve as a linchpin for secure, scalable, and auditable API management. By centralizing authentication, authorization input validation, rate limiting, and logging, gateways provide a coherent security framework that protects services from internal and external threats. They reconcile operational efficiency with compliance requirements, enabling organizations to confidently expose APIs across hybrid cloud and multi-tenant environments while maintaining robust defence-in-depth. The strategic deployment of API gateways is therefore essential for enterprises seeking to secure their digital ecosystems and maintain trust in an increasingly interconnected world.

Gateway Functions	Security Benefits	Practical Examples
Authentication	Ensures only verified users or clients can access APIs	OAuth 2.0 token validation for a banking mobile app
Authorization	Enforces fine-grained access control based on roles, attributes, or context	RBAC-based restriction of admin endpoints to authorized staff
Input Validation	Prevents injection attacks, malformed requests, and malicious payloads	Blocking SQL injection attempts on e-commerce product APIs
Rate Limiting & Throttling	Protects APIs from abuse, bot attacks, and denial-of-service (DoS)	Limiting requests per minute to prevent API scraping of pricing data
Logging & Monitoring	Provides audit trails for compliance, forensic analysis, and anomaly detection	Capturing all API calls to support GDPR compliance and integrate with SIEM
Traffic Management	Optimizes load distribution and protects backend services	Routing requests to multiple cloud regions while enforcing SSL/TLS encryption
Security Policy Enforcement	Centralizes rules for encryption, MFA, and session handling	Enforcing JWT token expiry, mandatory MFA for sensitive actions
Anomaly Detection & Alerts	Detects suspicious patterns and alerts security teams in real-time	Identifying repeated failed login attempts across multiple endpoints

Gateway Functions	Security Benefits	Practical Examples
Integration with IAM Systems	Ensures consistent identity and access governance across on-premises and cloud apps	Federated SSO integration with RBAC/ABAC for partner and employee access

Table 5.2: API Gateway Functions, Security Benefits, and Practical Examples

Real-World Example: SaaS Platform API Protection

In today's interconnected digital ecosystem, APIs serve as the backbone of Software-as-a-Service (SaaS) platforms, enabling seamless integration, real-time data exchange, and automated workflows. However, their ubiquity also makes them attractive targets for attackers seeking to exploit vulnerabilities in business logic, authentication mechanisms, or input handling. A notable example comes from a SaaS company providing cloud-based accounting services, which faced repeated attempts to compromise its API endpoints. These attempts included brute-force attacks aimed at exploiting weak authentication, injection attacks targeting input validation flaws, and high-volume request floods designed to disrupt service availability. Left unmitigated, such threats could have led to data exfiltration, regulatory violations, financial loss, and reputational damage, underscoring the critical importance of robust API security strategies.

To address these challenges, the company deployed an API gateway as a centralized security and management layer. The gateway performed multiple key functions. First, it enforced token-based authentication, ensuring that only authorized users and applications could interact with the platform's APIs. By leveraging standards such as OAuth 2.0 and JSON Web Tokens (JWTs), the gateway verified client identities, minimized password exposure, and prevented unauthorized access. Second, the gateway implemented strict rate-limiting policies to control the volume of requests from individual clients or IP addresses. This measure mitigated denial-of-service attacks, protected backend services from overload, and prevented automated credential-stuffing attempts. Third, anomaly detection capabilities allowed the gateway to monitor traffic patterns in real-time, flagging suspicious behaviors such as sudden spikes in failed authentication attempts, access from unusual geolocations, or irregular API call sequences.

The implementation of these measures had a profound impact on both security and operational efficiency. Security incidents declined significantly, while legitimate users experienced uninterrupted access, demonstrating that strong protections do not have to come at the cost of usability. Furthermore, the gateway's logging and monitoring features provided a rich audit trail, enabling the security team to analyze attack patterns, improve detection rules, and report compliance to regulatory bodies such as GDPR and PCI DSS. In essence, the case illustrates that API security is not solely a technical problem; it requires continuous operational oversight, proactive policy enforcement, and integration with broader identity and access management frameworks.

Beyond mitigating immediate threats, the experience also reinforced strategic lessons about API governance. Centralized enforcement via the gateway allowed the company to maintain consistent security policies across multiple services and cloud environments, reducing misconfiguration risk and supporting scalability. The deployment underscored the value of combining technical controls—such as authentication and rate limiting—with operational practices, including anomaly monitoring, logging, and regular security audits. By treating API security as a holistic discipline, the company was able to protect sensitive financial data, maintain user trust, and ensure regulatory compliance, demonstrating the best-practice model for SaaS providers operating in highly dynamic and exposed digital environments.

This case study highlights that in modern cloud architectures, security cannot be an afterthought. API gateways, when properly configured and continuously monitored, serve as both a protective barrier and an operational tool, bridging the gap between technical enforcement and real-world threat management. The integration of authentication, authorization, traffic management, and anomaly detection exemplifies a mature, multi-layered approach, illustrating that successful API security is as much about governance and visibility as it is about code-level defenses.

Secure Data Pipelines

Understanding Data Pipelines

Data pipelines are foundational components of modern information architectures, enabling the seamless movement of data from source systems through processing layers and into storage or analytical platforms. They underpin a wide array of business-critical functions, including real-time analytics, machine learning model training, operational dashboards, and automated decision-making processes. Since data pipelines often handle sensitive or regulated information—such as personally identifiable information (PII), financial transactions, or healthcare records—their security is paramount. A single vulnerability in the pipeline can expose data to unauthorized actors, resulting in breaches, regulatory violations, and reputational damage.

Securing data pipelines requires a multi-layered approach that encompasses both technical and operational controls. Encryption in transit and at rest ensures that data remains unreadable to unauthorized entities while moving between nodes or being stored in databases. Role-based or attribute-based access controls restrict which systems and users can interact with specific pipeline components, preventing privilege misuse. Additionally, authentication and authorization mechanisms must be enforced at each stage to verify the identity of entities requesting access. For example, ingestion points receiving data from third-party sources should authenticate the source system and validate data integrity before accepting it into the pipeline.

Operational monitoring is equally critical in protecting pipelines. Continuous logging of data flow, access events, and transformation activities allows organizations to detect anomalies indicative of malicious activity or configuration errors. Automated auditing and alerting mechanisms can notify security teams of irregular patterns, such as unusual data exfiltration attempts or unexpected access to sensitive datasets. This proactive oversight reduces the window of exposure and supports regulatory compliance with standards such as GDPR, HIPAA, and PCI DSS, which require demonstrable control over data-handling processes.

Furthermore, secure pipeline design often incorporates segmentation and isolation strategies. By partitioning data flows based on sensitivity or compliance requirements, organizations limit the potential impact of breaches or misconfigurations. For example, sensitive PII may be processed in an isolated environment with stricter access policies, while non-critical operational data flows through less restrictive pathways. Incorporating tokenization or anonymization within the pipeline can further reduce risk by ensuring that sensitive information is never exposed in clear text to downstream systems.

A case in point is a financial services firm managing high-frequency trading data. By implementing a secure pipeline architecture, the firm encrypted all data in transit, enforced multi-layer access controls, and monitored flows for abnormal patterns. This approach prevented unauthorized access to trading algorithms and client information, ensured compliance with financial regulations, and maintained the integrity of real-time analytics.

In essence, data pipelines are not merely channels for movement but critical points of control for maintaining the confidentiality, integrity, and availability of data across the organization. Their security demands a combination of technical safeguards, operational oversight, and policy-driven governance to ensure that information flows remain protected in increasingly complex, multi-cloud, and highly automated environments.

Securing the Pipeline

Securing data pipelines requires a comprehensive, multi-layered strategy that spans the entire data lifecycle, from ingestion to processing and storage. Encryption, both in transit and at rest, forms the first line of defense, ensuring that data cannot be read by unauthorized actors while moving between systems or residing in storage. Beyond encryption, tokenization and data masking are employed to protect sensitive fields during processing, allowing analytics and machine learning workloads to operate without exposing personally identifiable information (PII), financial data, or other confidential attributes. These techniques decouple sensitive information from operational datasets, reducing the impact of potential breaches and facilitating compliance with regulatory frameworks such as GDPR, HIPAA, and PCI DSS.

At each stage of the pipeline, strong authentication and authorization mechanisms are essential. Only verified and authorized processes, services, or users should be able to access, transform, or transfer data. Role-based or attribute-based access controls can enforce granular permissions, ensuring that each pipeline component interacts with data strictly in accordance with its function and clearance level. This minimizes the risk of privilege misuse, accidental leaks, or insider threats.

Data integrity controls complement these protections by safeguarding the accuracy and consistency of information throughout its journey. Techniques such as checksums, cryptographic signatures, and end-to-end verification provide assurance that data has not been altered or corrupted, whether accidentally or maliciously. These controls are particularly vital in real-time analytics and machine learning pipelines, where even minor deviations in data can compromise outcomes, predictions, or operational decisions.

Automation and continuous monitoring are equally critical in dynamic environments, especially cloud-native and multi-cloud architectures, where workloads can scale elastically. Real-time anomaly detection, logging, and alerting allow security teams to identify unusual patterns—such as unexpected access attempts, unusually high data throughput, or abnormal API calls—that may indicate an attack or misconfiguration. Automated responses, such as throttling, quarantine, or triggering additional authentication checks, enhance resilience and reduce the window of exposure.

The operational rigor of these measures is exemplified by organizations handling sensitive financial or healthcare data. For instance, a healthcare analytics firm processing patient records implemented tokenization and encryption throughout its ETL (Extract, Transform, Load) pipelines, while enforcing strict RBAC policies on each processing node. Continuous monitoring and integrity checks ensured that any deviations, such as unauthorized access attempts or processing errors, were immediately detected and remediated. This not only preserved patient confidentiality but also maintained trust and regulatory compliance.

Pipeline Stage	Security Measures	Purpose / Benefit	Example / Case Study
Data Ingestion	Authentication & Authorization, TLS/HTTPS Encryption	Ensures only authorized sources can input data; protects data in transit	A healthcare analytics firm validates API clients and encrypts incoming patient records
Data Processing	Tokenization, Data Masking, Role-Based/Attribute-Based Access Control (RBAC/ABAC)	Protects sensitive fields during transformation; enforces least-privilege access	Financial ETL pipelines tokenize credit card numbers to prevent exposure during processing
Data Storage	At-rest Encryption, Key Management, Access Controls	Protects data stored in databases or object storage; prevents unauthorized retrieval	Multi-cloud banks store encrypted customer records with centralized key management
Data Integrity	Checksums, Cryptographic Signatures, End-to-End Verification	Detects tampering or corruption during pipeline operations	Machine learning pipelines use hash checks to validate datasets before model training
Monitoring & Auditing	Logging, Anomaly Detection, Automated Alerts	Identifies unauthorized access, misconfigurations, or unusual activity; supports compliance audits	Cloud platforms monitor data flow in real-time and trigger alerts on suspicious patterns
API Interactions	API Gateway Security, Rate Limiting, OAuth/JWT Authentication	Prevents unauthorized API access, mitigates brute-force or DoS attacks	SaaS accounting platform enforces token-based authentication and request throttling

			via API gateways
Data Transmission	End-to-End Encryption, VPNs, Secure Interconnect	Protects data while moving between cloud environments, regions, or services	Multi-cloud organizations use encrypted channels to move analytics data across AWS, Azure, and GCP
Operational Governance	Automated Compliance Checks, Policy Enforcement, Access Reviews	Ensures security policies are consistently applied; reduces human error	Banks use automated scripts to detect S3 misconfigurations and enforce company-wide IAM policies

Table 5.4: Summarizing Key Security Measures for Data Pipelines

Case Study: Healthcare Data Analytics Pipeline

In recent years, healthcare organizations have increasingly turned to data-driven approaches to improve patient outcomes, optimize operational efficiency, and support medical research. However, the sensitive nature of patient information poses significant challenges in designing secure, compliant data infrastructures. One illustrative example is a consortium of hospitals that collaboratively implemented a comprehensive healthcare data analytics pipeline. The primary objective of this pipeline was to aggregate anonymized patient records from multiple institutions to support advanced research on disease prediction, treatment efficacy, and public health trends.

To protect the confidentiality and integrity of the data, the consortium adopted a multi-layered security strategy. At the network level, Transport Layer Security (TLS) encryption was implemented to secure data in transit, ensuring that patient records could not be intercepted or tampered with while being transmitted between hospitals, central servers, and analytics platforms. This measure is crucial in healthcare, where even minor data breaches can result in severe regulatory penalties under laws such as the Health Insurance Portability and Accountability Act (HIPAA) in the United States and the General Data Protection Regulation (GDPR) in the European Union.

In addition to encryption, the pipeline employed role-based access control (RBAC) mechanisms. RBAC ensured that only authorized personnel—such as researchers with approved credentials or data engineers responsible for pipeline maintenance—could access specific datasets. This granular access model significantly reduced the risk of insider threats and minimized accidental exposure of sensitive information. Furthermore, the consortium used tokenization for patient identifiers, replacing personally identifiable information with unique tokens that could be mapped back to the original data only in a secure environment. Tokenization not only enhanced privacy but also allowed researchers to analyze longitudinal data across institutions without compromising individual identities.

Beyond static security measures, the pipeline incorporated real-time monitoring and anomaly detection tools. These systems continuously tracked data access patterns and flagged unusual behaviors, such as excessive queries from a single user or attempts to access unauthorized datasets. By implementing automated alerts, the consortium was able to rapidly respond to potential breaches or policy violations, maintaining both data security and regulatory compliance.

The implementation of this secure pipeline demonstrates the feasibility of balancing privacy and innovation in healthcare analytics. By adhering to strict security protocols, the consortium enabled researchers to conduct complex analyses of large-scale, multi-institutional datasets while complying with HIPAA and GDPR requirements. The case highlights that robust pipeline security is not merely a regulatory obligation but a critical enabler of research-driven innovation.

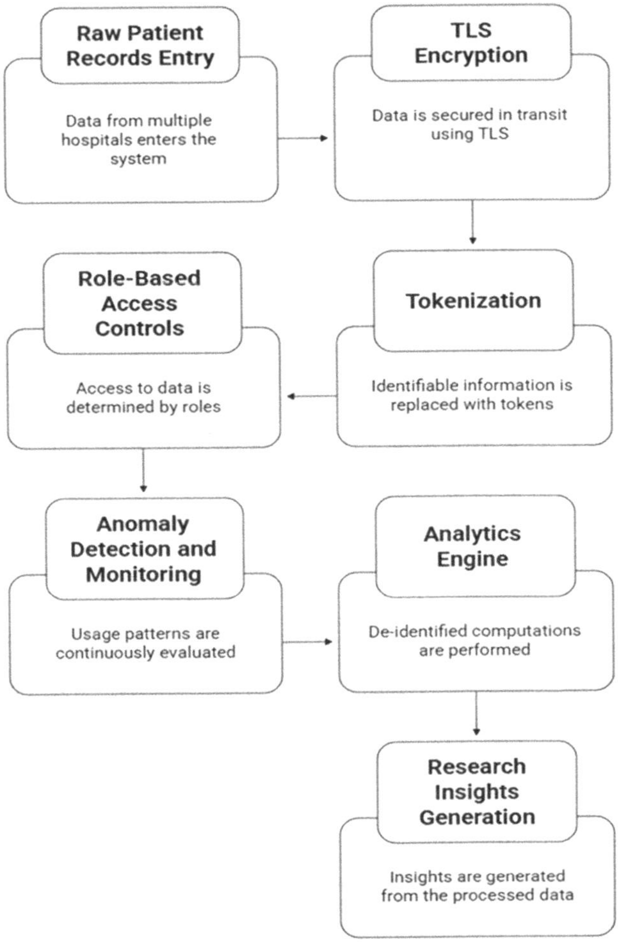

Figure 5.3: Schematic of the Healthcare Data Analytics Pipeline

The figure illustrates the architecture of the consortium's pipeline. Raw patient records from multiple hospitals are entered into the system, where TLS encryption secures data in transit. Tokenization replaces identifiable information with secure tokens. Role-based access controls determine who can access each dataset. Anomaly detection and monitoring modules continuously evaluate usage patterns, while the analytics engine performs de-identified computations and generates research insights. This layered approach ensures data privacy, regulatory compliance, and research efficiency simultaneously.

Overall, this case study underscores the importance of a holistic, proactive approach to data pipeline security. It illustrates that with careful planning and the right technical safeguards, it is possible to harness sensitive health data for meaningful insights, ultimately contributing to better patient care and more effective healthcare systems.

Conclusion

This chapter has examined the fundamental role of data governance, security, and compliance in contemporary organizational ecosystems, emphasizing that effective management of sensitive information is both a regulatory necessity and a strategic enabler. In today's data-driven landscape, organizations face unprecedented challenges as they strive to extract actionable insights from increasingly complex and voluminous datasets while simultaneously ensuring privacy, security, and ethical stewardship. The discussions in this chapter underscore that data governance extends beyond policy documentation, serving as a holistic framework that integrates technical safeguards, procedural rigor, and organizational accountability.

Central to effective data governance is the recognition of data as a strategic asset. Structured policies for classification, handling, and lifecycle management are essential to determine appropriate security measures, access controls, and retention schedules. By systematically categorizing data according to sensitivity and operational relevance, organizations can mitigate risks of unauthorized disclosure while maintaining operational efficiency. The healthcare data analytics pipeline case study exemplifies this approach: by aggregating anonymized patient records across multiple institutions, the consortium enabled advanced research while strictly enforcing privacy protections and regulatory compliance.

Legal and regulatory frameworks form another critical dimension of data governance. Laws such as HIPAA in the United States and GDPR in the European Union impose stringent requirements concerning consent, data minimization, transparency, and breach notification. Compliance with these frameworks is integral not only to avoid substantial penalties but also to maintain public trust and institutional credibility. Moreover, audit requirements highlight the importance of continuous monitoring, documentation, and accountability, reinforcing that governance and compliance are dynamic, ongoing responsibilities rather than one-time initiatives.

Technological safeguards complement policy frameworks, ensuring that data is protected both in transit and at rest. Encryption, tokenization, and role-based access controls provide essential layers of protection, while real-time monitoring and anomaly detection enable rapid identification of potential breaches or misuse. These measures demonstrate that security and innovation are not mutually exclusive; rather, well-implemented safeguards create a controlled environment in which organizations can safely perform analytics, conduct research, and generate operational insights.

A holistic approach to data governance integrates people, processes, and technology. Success requires collaboration among multiple stakeholders —including IT teams, compliance officers, legal advisors, and business leaders —to align technical capabilities with organizational goals and regulatory expectations. By embedding security, compliance, and ethical considerations into every stage of the data lifecycle, organizations can build resilient frameworks that not only protect information but also facilitate responsible innovation.

Key Terms

1. Data as a Strategic Asset: Proper governance treats data as a core organizational resource, requiring structured management and ethical utilization.
2. Multi-Layered Security: Encryption, tokenization, access controls, and monitoring provide comprehensive protection against internal and external threats.
3. Regulatory Compliance: Adherence to frameworks such as HIPAA and GDPR is essential for legal compliance, trust, and reputation.

4. Continuous Monitoring and Auditing: Ongoing evaluation and reporting are crucial to maintaining accountability and detecting potential breaches.
5. Enabler of Innovation: Robust governance supports analytics and research, allowing data-driven decision-making without compromising privacy.
6. Stakeholder Collaboration: Coordination among IT, compliance, legal, and business teams ensures alignment of objectives.
7. Holistic Approach: Integrating policies, technology, and processes creates resilient, scalable, and adaptable governance frameworks.
8. Ethical Responsibility: Organizations have a moral obligation to safeguard sensitive data, reinforcing societal trust.
9. Proactive Risk Management: Anticipating threats and implementing preventive measures minimizes exposure and strengthens credibility.
10. Scalability and Adaptability: Governance frameworks must be flexible to accommodate new technologies, expanding operations, and evolving regulations.

Review Questions

1. Define data governance and explain why it is critical in modern organizations.
2. Discuss the role of data as a strategic asset. How does this perspective influence governance policies?
3. What are the main components of a comprehensive data governance framework?
4. Explain the differences between data classification and data handling policies.
5. Describe the key legal and regulatory frameworks that influence data governance. Give examples.
6. How does HIPAA differ from GDPR in terms of data privacy and protection requirements?
7. Discuss the importance of audit requirements in data governance.

8. Explain the role of role-based access control (RBAC) in protecting sensitive data.
9. What is tokenization, and how does it enhance data privacy in analytics pipelines?
10. Describe the function of encryption in securing data both in transit and at rest.
11. Explain the concept of anomaly detection and its relevance in real-time data monitoring.
12. Using the healthcare data analytics case study, describe how multiple hospitals collaborated while maintaining compliance.
13. What are the risks associated with poor data governance practices?
14. Discuss how robust data security measures can enable innovation rather than restrict it.
15. Explain the relationship between people, processes, and technology in a holistic data governance approach.
16. How can organizations balance the need for data accessibility with privacy and security concerns?
17. Identify common challenges organizations face when implementing a multi-layered security strategy.
18. Describe proactive risk management strategies in data governance.
19. Explain the ethical responsibilities organizations have when handling sensitive data.
20. How can monitoring and auditing systems help organizations maintain compliance with evolving regulations?
21. Discuss the importance of stakeholder collaboration in successful data governance.
22. What are the key considerations when designing a scalable and adaptable data governance framework?
23. How does regulatory compliance influence organizational trust and reputation?
24. Explain the concept of continuous improvement in data governance and security processes.

25. Based on the chapter, outline a practical roadmap for implementing a secure and compliant data pipeline in a multi-institutional setting.

Part III

Security Analytics and Threat Intelligence

INTRODUCTION

The modern cybersecurity landscape is defined by complexity, speed, and unpredictability. Cyber adversaries are becoming increasingly sophisticated, exploiting technological vulnerabilities, human error, and gaps in traditional security defenses to launch attacks that can compromise sensitive data, disrupt operations, and damage organizational reputation. Against this backdrop, conventional security measures—such as perimeter-based firewalls, signature-based antivirus, and rule-driven intrusion detection systems—are no longer sufficient. The dynamic and evolving nature of cyber threats demands an intelligence-driven approach that leverages data, analytics, and predictive insights to anticipate, detect, and respond to security incidents effectively. Part III of this text, Security Analytics and Threat Intelligence, explores these advanced approaches and examines how organizations can harness data and intelligence to achieve proactive, resilient cybersecurity.

At the core of this part is security analytics, the discipline of transforming raw security data into actionable insights. Organizations generate vast volumes of information across multiple systems, including network traffic logs, endpoint telemetry, application activity records, cloud infrastructure events, and external threat feeds. Individually, these data points are of limited use; however, when analyzed collectively using advanced statistical, machine learning, and behavioral techniques, they reveal patterns, anomalies, and trends that indicate potential threats. Security analytics enables organizations to move beyond reactive defense, providing the capacity to detect unusual behaviors, identify ongoing attacks, and support automated or guided response mechanisms. Through analytics, security teams gain enhanced situational awareness, improved visibility across complex infrastructures, and the ability to prioritize interventions based on risk.

Threat intelligence complements security analytics by providing context-rich information about adversaries, vulnerabilities, attack vectors, and emerging tactics, techniques, and procedures (TTPs). Threat intelligence can be classified into strategic, operational, tactical, and technical levels, each serving distinct organizational purposes—from guiding executive decision-making to enabling real-time threat mitigation and automated detection. By integrating threat intelligence into security operations, organizations gain the ability to anticipate potential attacks, preemptively strengthen defenses, and respond with precision to minimize damage. Threat intelligence also facilitates collaborative cybersecurity efforts, enabling organizations to share insights and warnings to collectively defend against global threats.

Together, security analytics and threat intelligence form a synergistic framework for data-driven cybersecurity decision-making. Analytics identifies suspicious patterns and anomalies, while threat intelligence contextualizes these findings within a broader threat landscape. This combination supports predictive threat modeling, enabling organizations to forecast potential attacks, prioritize security investments, and allocate resources efficiently. It also enhances compliance reporting, supports forensic investigations, and reduces response times by enabling automated or semi-automated actions based on high-confidence indicators of compromise.

The integration of these approaches is not without challenges. Large and diverse datasets, high rates of false positives, and rapidly evolving attack techniques can complicate detection and analysis. The quality, timeliness, and relevance of threat intelligence significantly influence the effectiveness of security decisions. Moreover, organizations must balance automation with human oversight, ensuring that analytical models are continually refined and aligned with operational realities. Addressing these challenges requires robust data management practices, sophisticated analytical tools, and a culture of continuous learning within security teams.

In essence, Part III emphasizes the transition from reactive to intelligence-driven security operations. By leveraging analytics and threat intelligence, organizations can not only detect and respond to attacks more effectively but also anticipate threats before they materialize, creating a proactive security posture. The chapters in this section explore critical concepts, methodologies, and technologies in depth, including anomaly detection, predictive threat intelligence, and the role of machine learning in cybersecurity, providing readers with a comprehensive understanding of how to operationalize data-driven threat detection and response in modern enterprise environments.

CHAPTER 6

Security Monitoring with Data Analytics

Learning Objectives

By the end of this chapter, learners should be able to:

1. Understand the importance of data collection in security monitoring.
2. Explain the role of data normalization in cybersecurity.
3. Identify key functions and benefits of SIEM platforms.
4. Understand SOAR platforms and their integration with security operations.
5. Analyze the use of logs for intrusion detection.
6. Apply data-driven security monitoring practices in real-world scenarios.

Overview

In contemporary cybersecurity practices, organizations face an ever-increasing volume, variety, and velocity of digital threats. Traditional perimeter-based defenses, such as firewalls and antivirus systems, are no longer sufficient to ensure organizational security. Modern threats are often sophisticated, distributed, and persistent, making proactive monitoring and early detection critical. Security monitoring with data analytics has therefore emerged as a cornerstone of contemporary cyber defense strategies. By leveraging data-driven approaches, organizations can gain real-time visibility into their digital environment, identify anomalous behavior, and respond efficiently to security incidents.

Security monitoring begins with the systematic collection of data from all relevant sources, including servers, network devices, endpoints, cloud services, applications, and security appliances.

These sources generate extensive logs and telemetry, capturing events such as authentication attempts, network connections, file access, configuration changes, and application behavior. The heterogeneity of these data sources presents challenges in analysis, as inconsistent formats, timestamps, and metadata can impede correlation and interpretation. To address this, normalization is employed to transform raw, unstructured logs into standardized formats. Normalized data enables cross-system correlation, ensuring that security events are accurately contextualized, reducing false positives, and supporting advanced analytical techniques.

Once data is collected and normalized, Security Information and Event Management (SIEM) platforms serve as the central analytical hub. SIEM systems aggregate, analyze, and visualize data to provide actionable insights into potential threats. They enable real-time detection of anomalies, suspicious activity, and policy violations. Security Orchestration, Automation, and Response (SOAR) platforms complement SIEM capabilities by automating response workflows, integrating threat intelligence feeds, and coordinating remediation actions across multiple systems. The combined deployment of SIEM and SOAR ensures rapid detection, investigation, and response, reducing mean time to detection (MTTD) and mean time to response (MTTR), while improving operational efficiency for security teams.

A key aspect of security monitoring is the use of logs for intrusion detection. By correlating data across multiple sources, organizations can identify patterns that signify malicious activities, such as repeated login failures, unusual network connections, or anomalous access to sensitive resources. Advanced analytical techniques, including behavioral analytics and anomaly detection, further enhance the capability to detect sophisticated attacks that bypass traditional defenses. Case studies have shown that enterprises leveraging data-driven monitoring can detect complex intrusions, lateral movement within networks, and potential data exfiltration before significant damage occurs.

The adoption of data analytics in security monitoring also supports regulatory compliance. Many standards, including GDPR, HIPAA, and PCI DSS, require continuous monitoring, logging, and reporting of security events. Data-driven monitoring provides the necessary audit trails and documentation, ensuring transparency and accountability. Additionally, the insights gained through analytics allow organizations to continuously refine their security posture, identify systemic weaknesses, and proactively address emerging threats.

Collecting and Normalizing Security Data

Effective security monitoring begins with the systematic collection of security data from all relevant sources within an enterprise environment. Modern organizations operate increasingly complex IT ecosystems, encompassing physical servers, virtual machines, endpoints such as laptops and mobile devices, network infrastructure including switches, routers, and firewalls, cloud-based services, and diverse applications. Each component generates logs that capture operational events, user activities, configuration changes, and system alerts. These logs are indispensable for understanding system behavior, identifying security incidents, and reconstructing attack sequences during post-incident investigations. However, the diversity of data formats, timestamping conventions, and metadata structures presents a significant challenge. For example, a firewall may log traffic in a flat, delimited format, while an endpoint agent produces JSON-formatted telemetry, and a cloud application exports logs in XML. Attempting to analyze these sources in their native forms without standardization can lead to missed correlations, overlooked threats, and incomplete situational awareness.

Normalization is a critical process that addresses these challenges by converting heterogeneous logs into a consistent, structured format. The process begins with parsing raw log entries to extract relevant fields such as timestamps, source and destination IP addresses, user identifiers, event types, and status codes. Next, these extracted fields are aligned to a common time reference, often using coordinated universal time (UTC), to ensure accurate chronological correlation across multiple sources. Event types are then mapped to a standardized taxonomy or classification system, allowing analysts to recognize similar security events irrespective of their origin.

Additionally, data representations, such as numerical units or categorical labels, are unified to prevent misinterpretation during analysis. For instance, different systems may record login success as 'success' or 'true'; normalization standardizes these to a common representation, enabling automated systems to process them correctly.

Beyond enabling cross-system correlation, normalization directly impacts the accuracy and efficiency of anomaly detection and automated response mechanisms. By providing a structured dataset, normalization allows machine learning models, rule-based engines, and statistical tools to operate effectively. It reduces false positives caused by inconsistent data representation and increases the likelihood of detecting subtle patterns that indicate emerging threats. Furthermore, normalization supports scalability, allowing large volumes of data to be aggregated, analyzed, and stored efficiently without losing context or semantic meaning.

Finally, high-quality data collection and normalization also underpin compliance and audit requirements. Regulations such as GDPR, HIPAA, and PCI DSS mandate comprehensive monitoring and accurate reporting of security events. Without normalized, standardized data, organizations risk failing audits, misreporting incidents, or being unable to demonstrate effective monitoring practices. Therefore, organizations must implement robust logging standards, continuous validation mechanisms, and automated normalization pipelines to ensure that collected data is reliable, timely, and actionable. In sum, the collection and normalization of security data form the foundation for modern, proactive security monitoring, enabling accurate threat detection, rapid incident response, and informed decision-making across complex IT landscapes.

Benefits of Data-Driven Intrusion Detection

Data-driven intrusion detection has become a cornerstone of modern cybersecurity, enabling organizations to identify and respond to threats more effectively than traditional perimeter-based approaches. One of the primary benefits of this approach is early identification of threats. By continuously monitoring and analyzing data from diverse sources—including network traffic, system logs, application events, and endpoint telemetry—security teams can detect anomalies and suspicious patterns that may indicate malicious activity at an early stage. Unlike reactive measures that respond only after a breach, data-driven intrusion detection systems (IDSs) can proactively identify emerging threats, including zero-day attacks, lateral movement, and insider threats, thereby preventing escalation and reducing potential damage to organizational assets.

In addition to early detection, data-driven intrusion detection enhances situational awareness across systems. Traditional monitoring methods often rely on siloed logs or isolated alerts, limiting the ability of analysts to see the broader context of an attack. In contrast, data-driven approaches leverage normalization, correlation, and advanced analytics to provide a holistic view of the security landscape. This integrated perspective enables security teams to understand the scope, sequence, and potential impact of an attack, enabling more informed decision-making and prioritization of response efforts. By visualizing relationships among events across multiple systems and layers, organizations can identify coordinated attacks and anticipate potential escalation points before critical systems are compromised.

Another significant advantage is support for regulatory compliance and reporting. Many industries are governed by regulations such as GDPR, HIPAA, and PCI DSS, which mandate continuous monitoring of security events and accurate reporting of incidents. Data-driven intrusion detection systems generate comprehensive logs, detailed alerts, and structured reports that provide an auditable trail of security activities. This not only ensures compliance with legal and regulatory requirements but also demonstrates due diligence to stakeholders, including customers, partners, and regulators. Automated reporting features reduce the administrative burden on security teams, allowing them to focus on proactive threat mitigation rather than manual data compilation.

Finally, data-driven intrusion detection contributes to the reduction of mean time to detection (MTTD) and mean time to response (MTTR). By leveraging advanced analytics, pattern recognition, and automated alerting mechanisms, organizations can quickly identify and validate potential threats. Early detection allows security teams to respond rapidly, containing threats before they spread and minimizing operational and financial impact. In complex enterprise environments, where attacks can traverse multiple layers and systems within minutes, reducing MTTD and MTTR is critical for maintaining resilience and business continuity. Additionally, automated correlation and response capabilities, often integrated through SIEM and SOAR platforms, further enhance efficiency by executing predefined remediation steps, reducing manual intervention, and accelerating incident resolution.

Case Study: Using Logs for Intrusion Detection

In the era of data-driven cybersecurity, intrusion detection has evolved from basic signature-based systems to sophisticated analytics leveraging logs from multiple sources across an enterprise. Logs—chronological records of system events, network communications, and user activities—are invaluable for identifying potential threats, reconstructing attack sequences, and supporting regulatory compliance. This case study demonstrates how a mid-sized enterprise utilized comprehensive log analysis to detect a complex cyberattack, highlighting the benefits of normalization, correlation, and cross-system analytics in enhancing security monitoring.

Enterprise Context

The organization in question operates a hybrid IT environment encompassing on-premises servers, cloud-based applications, remote endpoints, and network devices such as firewalls and VPN gateways. Daily operations generate substantial log data from diverse sources, including web servers, endpoint protection systems, application servers, and intrusion detection systems. However, each source produces logs in distinct formats with varying field structures, timestamp conventions, and metadata standards. Before adopting a data-driven approach, the security team experienced frequent false positives, delayed detection of genuine threats, and limited insight into coordinated attack patterns that spanned multiple systems.

Recognizing these challenges, the enterprise implemented a Security Information and Event Management (SIEM) platform. The SIEM system aggregated logs from all sources and normalized them into a structured, unified format. Normalization involved parsing raw logs, extracting relevant fields, standardizing timestamps, mapping event codes to a consistent taxonomy, and aligning data units for compatibility. This process enabled cross-system correlation and ensured that anomalies were detected accurately and efficiently.

Detection of the Intrusion

During routine monitoring, the SIEM platform identified unusual authentication patterns. The logs revealed multiple failed VPN login attempts from geographically distant IP addresses targeting administrative accounts. Simultaneously, endpoint security logs indicated repeated account lockouts, while web server logs showed attempts to access sensitive administrative pages outside normal operational hours. Firewall logs corroborated these findings by highlighting suspicious inbound traffic originating from IP ranges previously associated with malicious activity.

By normalizing and correlating these diverse data streams, the security team quickly identified a coordinated brute-force attack targeting high-privilege accounts. Table 6.1 illustrates the critical normalized events that facilitated early detection:

Log Source	Event Description	Timestamp	User/Host	Anomaly Indicator
VPN Gateway	Failed login attempts	2025-07-15 02:15	UserA	Multiple failures from unusual IP
Endpoint Security	Account lockout triggered	2025-07-15 02:16	UserA	Repeated authentication failures
Web Server	Access to administrative pages	2025-07-15 02:17	UserA	Access outside business hours
Firewall	Suspicious inbound traffic	2025-07-15 02:18	192.168.15.32	Known malicious IP range

Table 6.1: The Critical Normalized Events That Facilitated Early Detection

Event Flow Analysis

Once the attack was flagged, the team analyzed the sequence of events to understand the attack vector and potential lateral movement within the network. Figure 6.1 provides a conceptual diagram of the event correlation workflow, demonstrating how different system logs interact to reveal attack patterns:

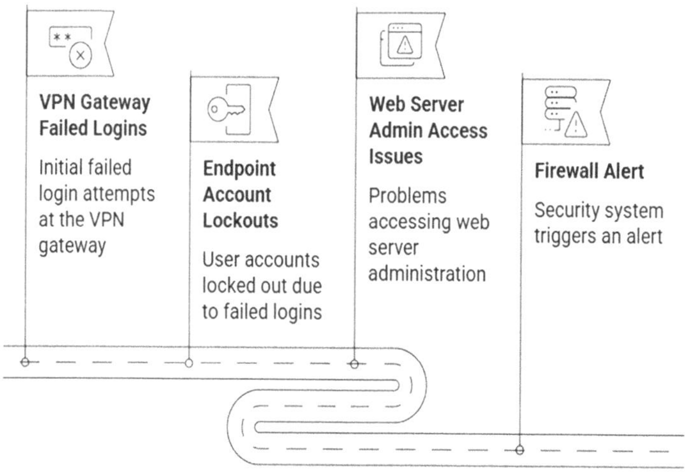

Figure 6.1: Event Correlation sequence

This cross-system analysis revealed that the attacker attempted to escalate privileges by targeting multiple endpoints and exploiting weak authentication processes. By combining log data from various sources, the security team gained a comprehensive view of the attack progression that would have been difficult to achieve through isolated log analysis.

Automated Response

The organization's Security Orchestration, Automation, and Response (SOAR) platform facilitated rapid mitigation once the attack was detected. Automated workflows temporarily disabled compromised accounts, blocked malicious IP addresses at the firewall, and triggered alerts for further investigation. Endpoint logs were used to identify compromised devices, while network flow data helped trace the attacker's lateral movement. The investigation revealed that the initial intrusion vector was a phishing email containing a credential-stealing payload.

The use of normalized logs and automated response significantly reduced both the mean time to detection (MTTD) and mean time to response (MTTR). The integration of SIEM and SOAR platforms ensured that critical security events were detected in near real-time and responded to promptly, minimizing potential damage.

Impact and Metrics

The adoption of data-driven intrusion detection demonstrated measurable improvements in security performance. The table below summarizes key metrics before and after implementation.

Metric	Before Implementation	After Implementation
Mean Time to Detection (MTTD)	6 hours	15 minutes
Mean Time to Response (MTTR)	4 hours	30 minutes
False Positives per Day	120	18
Incidents Escalated to SOC	35%	5%

Table 6.2: Key metrics before and after Implementation

These results indicate that comprehensive log normalization and correlation not only enhance threat detection but also improve operational efficiency and reduce alert fatigue among security personnel.

SIEM and Soar Platforms

Security Information and Event Management (SIEM) and Security Orchestration, Automation, and Response (SOAR) platforms represent foundational technologies in contemporary cybersecurity operations, serving as critical enablers of data-driven security monitoring. The increasing complexity of organizational IT environments, coupled with the exponential growth of data from endpoints, networks, cloud services, and applications, has rendered traditional, manual security monitoring approaches inadequate. SIEM and SOAR platforms bridge this gap by providing centralized, intelligent frameworks that collect, normalize, correlate, and act on security data in real time, significantly enhancing the effectiveness of threat detection and incident response.

A SIEM platform primarily functions as a centralized repository for security data, aggregating logs and events from diverse sources including servers, firewalls, intrusion detection systems, endpoints, and cloud applications. By unifying these heterogeneous data streams, SIEM systems enable analysts to perform real-time correlation of events, uncovering patterns indicative of potential attacks that might otherwise go unnoticed. For example, repeated failed login attempts across multiple systems, when correlated with unusual outbound network traffic, may reveal the early stages of a coordinated intrusion. Moreover, SIEM solutions provide dashboards, visualizations, and reporting capabilities that support both operational decision-making and regulatory compliance, offering a comprehensive view of the organization's security posture.

In contrast, SOAR platforms complement SIEM capabilities by emphasizing automation and orchestration of security operations. Whereas SIEM focuses on detection and alerting, SOAR platforms enable organizations to define automated response workflows that can remediate threats without human intervention. SOAR systems integrate with a broad range of security tools, including endpoint protection platforms, threat intelligence feeds, firewalls, and network monitoring systems, and orchestrate these disparate technologies into a cohesive operational framework. For instance, if a SIEM alert identifies a phishing email targeting multiple employees, a SOAR platform can automatically quarantine affected mailboxes, block the sender at the firewall, trigger endpoint scans, and document the response process for audit purposes. This orchestration not only accelerates response times but also reduces human error, enhancing overall security resilience.

The integration of SIEM and SOAR creates a synergistic ecosystem where detection and response capabilities are tightly aligned. SIEM systems generate alerts by analyzing incoming security data and identifying anomalous patterns, while SOAR platforms act on these alerts through preconfigured workflows, automating containment, investigation, and reporting processes. This combination significantly reduces the mean time to detect (MTTD) and mean time to respond (MTTR), ensuring that threats are mitigated before they can inflict substantial damage. Furthermore, SIEM-SOAR integration facilitates continuous learning; alerts and response outcomes can be fed back into the system to improve threat models and refine detection rules, fostering an adaptive and proactive security posture.

Despite their advantages, deploying SIEM and SOAR platforms is not without challenges. Effective utilization requires skilled personnel capable of configuring data feeds, tuning correlation rules, and designing automated workflows. Organizations must also address alert fatigue, ensuring that systems prioritize critical events to prevent analysts from being overwhelmed by false positives. Nevertheless, when implemented thoughtfully, these platforms serve as the backbone of modern cybersecurity operations, providing organizations with the tools needed to transform raw data into actionable intelligence and maintain robust, resilient defenses against evolving threats.

Security Information and Event Management (SIEM) platforms constitute a cornerstone of contemporary cybersecurity operations, providing organizations with a centralized mechanism to monitor, analyze, and respond to security events across heterogeneous IT environments. As organizations increasingly rely on complex infrastructures comprising on-premises servers, cloud services, endpoints, applications, and network devices, the volume and diversity of log data have grown exponentially. SIEM platforms are specifically designed to aggregate this disparate data, enabling security analysts to gain a unified view of the organization's security posture, while facilitating the rapid detection of potential threats.

At their core, SIEM platforms integrate three primary functional layers: collection, normalization, and correlation/analysis. The collection layer focuses on acquiring logs and telemetry data from all relevant sources. This includes system logs from servers and workstations, network traffic from switches and firewalls, application logs, cloud infrastructure logs, and even telemetry from security appliances such as intrusion detection and prevention systems. Effective collection ensures that no critical event is overlooked, forming the foundational data pool upon which all subsequent analyses depend.

Following collection, the normalization layer transforms heterogeneous log data into a consistent, standardized schema. Each system generates logs in different formats, with varying field names, timestamps, and metadata conventions. Without normalization, it becomes difficult to correlate events across systems or to apply automated analysis consistently. Normalization processes parse raw logs, extract relevant fields, standardize time stamps, and map event types to a common taxonomy, allowing SIEM platforms to analyze data holistically rather than as isolated events. This step is critical for ensuring the accuracy and reliability of threat detection algorithms.

The correlation and analysis layer constitutes the core intelligence of SIEM systems. Here, the platform identifies patterns, anomalies, and relationships between events that may indicate security incidents. Correlation rules can be predefined, such as detecting repeated failed login attempts, or adaptive, using behavioral analytics to identify deviations from baseline activity. For instance, a series of failed login attempts on a web server combined with simultaneous unusual outbound network traffic may signify a brute-force attack followed by potential exfiltration. By linking these events, SIEM platforms enable analysts to detect complex attack scenarios that individual logs alone would not reveal.

Beyond detection, SIEM platforms provide extensive alerting, reporting, and visualization capabilities. Dashboards aggregate information into intuitive displays, enabling security teams to monitor overall system health and threat activity in real time. Automated alerts notify analysts of potential incidents, while historical reporting supports compliance with regulatory frameworks such as GDPR, HIPAA, and PCI DSS.

SIEM adoption also enhances situational awareness and operational efficiency. By centralizing security data and automating correlation processes, organizations reduce mean time to detect (MTTD) and enable more effective prioritization of threats. Furthermore, modern SIEM solutions increasingly incorporate advanced analytics, machine learning, and threat intelligence feeds, allowing proactive detection of emerging threats rather than merely reactive identification.

In practice, SIEM platforms serve as both a defensive and investigative tool, enabling organizations to detect intrusions, monitor compliance, and support forensic investigations. Their value lies in consolidating disparate data streams into actionable intelligence, enabling security teams to respond rapidly to evolving threats while maintaining a comprehensive understanding of the enterprise security landscape.

Security Orchestration, Automation, and Response (SOAR) platforms have emerged as a critical evolution in enterprise cybersecurity, addressing the limitations of traditional Security Information and Event Management (SIEM) systems. While SIEM platforms focus on detecting, aggregating, and correlating security events, they typically require significant manual effort for incident investigation and remediation. SOAR platforms, in contrast, extend these capabilities by introducing automation, orchestration, and structured workflow management, enabling organizations to respond to security incidents faster, more accurately, and consistently.

At the core of SOAR platforms is orchestration, which integrates multiple security tools and data sources into a unified operational framework. Modern organizations often deploy a heterogeneous mix of technologies, including firewalls, intrusion detection/prevention systems (IDS/IPS), endpoint protection platforms (EPP), cloud security solutions, and threat intelligence feeds. SOAR platforms bridge these tools, creating coordinated workflows that enable automated or semi-automated response actions. For example, if a SIEM system detects a phishing attempt targeting an employee, the SOAR platform can orchestrate a sequence of responses: isolate the affected endpoint, block the malicious sender, quarantine suspicious files, and update threat intelligence databases. By centralizing these actions, SOAR reduces human dependency, minimizes error, and accelerates response times.

Automation is another defining feature of SOAR platforms. Predefined playbooks enable security teams to execute repetitive tasks automatically while ensuring consistency across incidents. These playbooks can include containment measures, system scans, user notifications, and ticketing processes. Automated workflows not only shorten the mean time to response (MTTR) but also allow security analysts to focus on high-value activities such as threat hunting and strategic risk mitigation. Importantly, many SOAR systems incorporate conditional logic and decision points, allowing analysts to approve or override automated actions when necessary, thus maintaining a balance between efficiency and human oversight.

A third key component of SOAR platforms is incident documentation and reporting. Every action taken during an automated or semi-automated workflow is logged, creating a comprehensive audit trail. This supports regulatory compliance, internal audits, and post-incident review processes. For example, during a ransomware attack simulation, the SOAR platform can document which endpoints were isolated, which files were quarantined, and which alerts triggered each automated response. This level of documentation provides transparency, accountability, and actionable insights for continuous improvement in security operations.

Feature	SIEM	SOAR
Primary Function	Detection & Alerting	Orchestration & Automated Response
Data Sources	Logs & Telemetry	SIEM, EDR, Threat Intelligence, Firewalls
Automation	Limited	Extensive
Workflow Management	Minimal	Centralized & Playbook-driven
Response Speed	Analyst-dependent	Real-time or near-real-time automation
Reporting & Audit	Basic	Comprehensive and regulatory-compliant

Table 6.3: The Comparative Benefits of SIEM and SOAR Systems

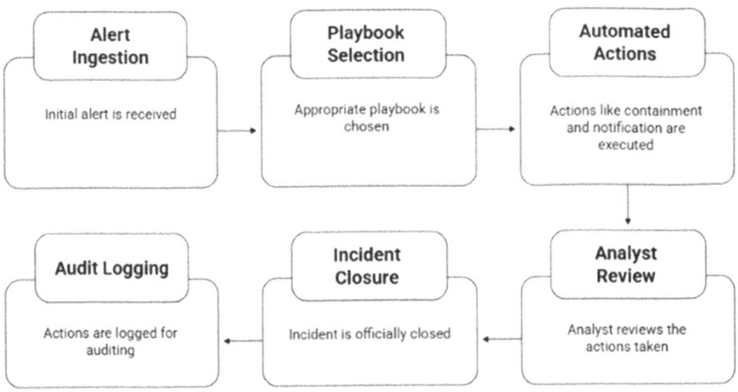

Figure 6.2: SOAR Workflow Sequence

SOAR platforms also integrate **threat intelligence** into incident response. By leveraging external threat feeds, historical incident data, and contextual risk scoring, SOAR platforms prioritize alerts and tailor automated actions based on severity and criticality. For instance, a malware alert on a high-value server may trigger immediate automated containment, whereas a similar alert on a non-critical endpoint might be routed for analyst review. This prioritization enhances resource allocation and ensures that security teams address the most pressing threats first.

Key Capabilities of SOAR

Security Orchestration, Automation, and Response (SOAR) platforms have become integral to modern cybersecurity operations, offering a range of capabilities that enhance efficiency, consistency, and effectiveness in incident detection and response. While SIEM platforms primarily focus on aggregating and analyzing security data, SOAR extends these capabilities by enabling actionable, automated, and collaborative security workflows. The key capabilities of SOAR can be broadly categorized into four areas: orchestration, automation, incident management, and collaboration.

Orchestration refers to the ability of SOAR platforms to integrate with multiple security systems, tools, and data sources within an enterprise environment. Organizations typically operate a diverse array of security technologies, including firewalls, endpoint protection platforms, intrusion detection systems, cloud security solutions, and threat intelligence feeds. Orchestration allows these tools to operate in a coordinated manner, creating unified workflows that streamline security operations. For example, when a phishing attack is detected, orchestration ensures that endpoint isolation, email blocking, and threat intelligence updates occur in a cohesive sequence, reducing the likelihood of oversight and enhancing operational efficiency.

Automation is a defining feature of SOAR systems, enabling predefined tasks and responses to be executed without human intervention. Automation significantly reduces both the mean time to detect (MTTD) and the mean time to respond (MTTR) to security incidents. Routine but critical tasks—such as scanning files, isolating compromised endpoints, or updating firewall rules—can be automatically triggered by specific alerts. By minimizing manual intervention, automation not only accelerates response times but also reduces the risk of human error, ensuring consistency across repeated actions. Importantly, modern SOAR platforms often incorporate conditional logic and exception handling, allowing security analysts to oversee automated processes and intervene only when complex judgment is required.

Incident management encompasses the systematic tracking, documentation, and analysis of security events throughout their lifecycle. SOAR platforms centralize incident management by maintaining comprehensive logs of alerts, investigations, and remediation actions. This capability supports compliance with regulatory frameworks, such as GDPR, HIPAA, and PCI DSS, which require detailed records of security incidents. Effective incident management also facilitates post-event reviews and continuous improvement by providing insights into recurring attack vectors and system vulnerabilities.

Collaboration represents another critical capability of SOAR platforms, enabling seamless coordination among internal security teams as well as external stakeholders, including managed security service providers (MSSPs) and law enforcement agencies when necessary. Collaborative features, such as shared dashboards, automated notifications, and integrated communication tools, help ensure that all relevant parties are informed and engaged during an incident. This reduces delays in decision-making and improves the overall effectiveness of the security operation.

The table below summarizes the key capabilities of SOAR platforms, highlighting their functionality and the associated benefits.

Capability	Description	Benefit
Orchestration	Connects multiple security tools	Streamlined security workflows
Automation	Executes predefined tasks automatically	Faster response, reduced errors
Incident Management	Tracks lifecycle of security events	Improved accountability and documentation
Collaboration	Supports communication across teams	Enhances coordination and situational awareness

Table 6.4: The Key Capabilities of SOAR Platforms

These core capabilities collectively transform how organizations approach security operations. By integrating orchestration, automation, incident management, and collaboration, SOAR platforms not only enhance operational efficiency but also strengthen the overall security posture. They enable security teams to act decisively on threats, maintain comprehensive documentation for audits and compliance, and coordinate effectively across organizational boundaries. As cyber threats grow increasingly sophisticated and pervasive, the adoption of SOAR platforms ensures that organizations remain proactive, resilient, and capable of mitigating risks with speed and precision.

Integration of SIEM and SOAR

Although Security Information and Event Management (SIEM) and Security Orchestration, Automation, and Response (SOAR) platforms serve distinct purposes within the cybersecurity ecosystem, their integration offers a holistic approach to monitoring, detecting, and responding to threats. SIEM platforms excel at collecting and normalizing data, correlating events, and generating alerts that indicate potential security incidents. However, their functionality often stops at detection and alerting, leaving security analysts to manually investigate and respond. SOAR platforms, in contrast, operationalize the insights provided by SIEM, automating response actions, orchestrating workflows across diverse security tools, and documenting the incident lifecycle. Together, SIEM and SOAR create a comprehensive security operations framework that combines real-time threat detection with rapid, consistent remediation.

The integration process begins with data ingestion and normalization. SIEM platforms aggregate logs and telemetry from servers, endpoints, firewalls, applications, and cloud environments, transforming them into standardized formats suitable for analysis. Once normalized, this data is subject to event correlation and analysis, enabling SIEM to detect patterns indicative of attacks—such as brute-force login attempts, lateral movement across networks, or anomalous traffic from suspicious IP addresses. These correlated events generate alerts that serve as the primary input for SOAR systems.

At this stage, SOAR platforms assume responsibility for orchestrating responses. Leveraging predefined playbooks, SOAR systems can automatically contain threats, block malicious actors, isolate compromised devices, and initiate forensic investigations. For example, if SIEM identifies multiple failed login attempts followed by unusual outbound traffic from a critical server, SOAR can execute a response workflow: disabling the affected user account, isolating the server from the network, notifying the security team, and updating the firewall rules to prevent further exploitation.

In addition to automation, SOAR platforms enhance workflow management and incident documentation. Every response action—whether automated or analyst-approved—is logged to create an audit trail. This ensures compliance with regulations such as GDPR, HIPAA, and PCI DSS, which mandate detailed reporting of security incidents. Moreover, integrating SIEM and SOAR improves situational awareness, enabling analysts to monitor real-time threats and responses from a centralized dashboard rather than working with siloed tools.

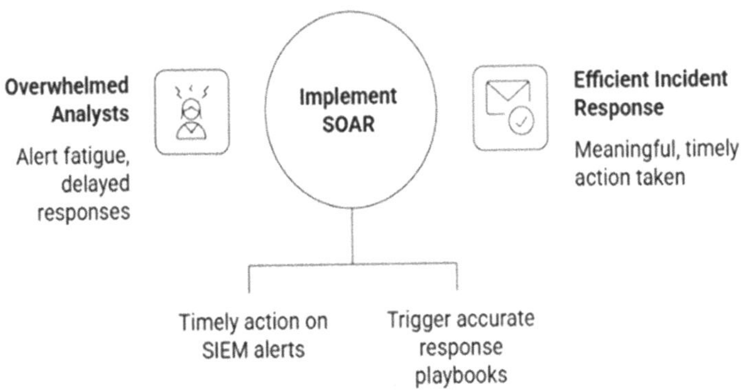

Figure 6.3: SIEM-SOAR Synergy

This workflow highlights the symbiotic relationship between detection and response. SIEM identifies anomalies and escalates them as alerts, while SOAR ensures those alerts translate into meaningful, timely action. Without SOAR, SIEM alerts risk overwhelming analysts with sheer volume, leading to alert fatigue and delayed responses.

Conversely, without SIEM, SOAR platforms would lack the comprehensive, normalized data necessary to trigger accurate response playbooks.

The benefits of integration are manifold. First, it reduces Mean Time to Detect (MTTD) and Mean Time to Respond (MTTR), two critical performance indicators in cybersecurity. Second, it alleviates the burden on human analysts by automating repetitive tasks such as IP blocking, endpoint isolation, or user account suspension. Third, it fosters consistency and accuracy in responses, ensuring incidents are handled according to standardized workflows rather than ad hoc decision-making. Finally, it strengthens organizational resilience by creating a feedback loop: SOAR platforms feed incident documentation and lessons learned back into SIEM systems, refining correlation rules and improving future detection.

Case Study: Using Logs for Intrusion Detection

Intrusion detection is a fundamental component of modern cybersecurity operations, and leveraging logs for this purpose exemplifies the power of data-driven monitoring. Organizations today operate in highly complex digital environments, where servers, endpoints, network devices, applications, and cloud infrastructures generate vast volumes of log data. These logs contain granular details of system activities, user behavior, network connections, and application transactions. When systematically collected, normalized, and analyzed, these datasets provide invaluable insight into anomalous activities that can signify cyber threats or ongoing attacks.

A practical example of this approach can be observed in an enterprise environment where security analysts monitored web server access logs in conjunction with firewall and network traffic logs. Individually, each log type offered a limited perspective. Web server logs, for instance, recorded authentication attempts, page requests, and session durations, while firewall logs documented network connection attempts, blocking traffic, and suspicious inbound or outbound flows. Network traffic logs captured packet-level data and provided insight into bandwidth usage, unusual ports, or unexpected data transfers. When correlated, however, these logs painted a comprehensive picture of system activity, enabling analysts to identify subtle indicators of compromise that might otherwise go unnoticed.

In this case study, a series of repeated failed login attempts on a critical web application was flagged. While such attempts alone could be attributed to user error, further correlation with network logs revealed that the source IP addresses were geographically dispersed and associated with known malicious networks. Simultaneously, endpoint telemetry revealed abnormal attempts to access sensitive files across multiple servers. By integrating these diverse logs, the analysts detected a pattern consistent with a brute-force attack designed to compromise privileged accounts. This multi-source correlation illustrates the necessity of normalization and structured data aggregation; without these processes, the disparate logs would have remained siloed, significantly delaying detection.

Beyond initial detection, the analysis uncovered evidence of lateral movement within the enterprise network. By examining network flow data alongside endpoint telemetry, the security team observed unusual internal connections between servers that rarely communicated. These connections coincided with anomalous activity on a subset of user accounts, indicating that an attacker had successfully gained access to an initial endpoint and was attempting to propagate across the network to access sensitive resources. Recognizing this early enabled the organization to implement containment measures, such as isolating affected systems, resetting compromised credentials, and deploying additional endpoint monitoring to prevent further propagation.

This case study also demonstrates the importance of integrating security analytics platforms, such as SIEM and SOAR, to enhance detection capabilities. SIEM platforms collected and normalized logs from multiple sources, allowing real-time correlation and alerting. When alerts were generated, SOAR systems enabled the automated execution of containment workflows, including network segmentation, endpoint isolation, and notification of the incident response team. The combination of these technologies ensured that the attack was detected and mitigated before critical data exfiltration occurred.

The insights derived from this log-based monitoring were not limited to immediate threat mitigation. Analysis of the attack patterns informed the organization's risk assessment and threat modeling. For instance, the geographic dispersion of IP addresses used in the attack highlighted the need for enhanced geolocation-based access controls. Similarly, the discovery of lateral movement prompted a reevaluation of internal segmentation and privilege management, reducing the attack surface for future incidents.

The case demonstrates that comprehensive log analysis, supported by normalization and analytics platforms, is critical for detecting sophisticated attacks. By correlating data across systems, organizations gain visibility into complex attack vectors, improve mean time to detection (MTTD), and enhance overall resilience. Furthermore, such practices ensure that cybersecurity efforts are proactive rather than reactive, enabling organizations to anticipate potential threats and implement controls that reduce risk exposure.

Log Source	Indicators Detected	Response Measures Implemented
Web server access logs	Repeated failed login attempts	Account lockouts, enhanced MFA enforcement
Firewall logs	Traffic from suspicious IPs	IP blocking, geolocation-based rules
Network flow logs	Unusual internal connections	Network segmentation, additional monitoring
Endpoint telemetry	Abnormal file access and process activity	Endpoint isolation, forensic imaging

Table 6.5: Types of Logs Analyzed, the Indicators Identified, and the Response Measures Implemented

Conclusion

Chapter 6 has explored the vital role of data analytics in modern security monitoring, emphasizing how organizations can leverage structured and normalized data to strengthen their cybersecurity posture. Effective monitoring begins with the systematic collection of logs from diverse sources, including servers, endpoints, network devices, applications, and cloud services. These raw data streams, in isolation, provide limited visibility; however, when transformed through normalization processes into consistent and structured formats, they enable comprehensive correlation, anomaly detection, and actionable insights. Normalization ensures that security analysts can effectively compare events across heterogeneous systems, reduce false positives, and detect subtle indicators of compromise that might otherwise remain hidden. The integrity, timeliness, and completeness of collected data directly influence the accuracy of threat detection and the effectiveness of incident response.

The chapter also highlighted the centrality of SIEM and SOAR platforms in contemporary security operations. SIEM systems serve as the foundation for log aggregation, event correlation, and real-time monitoring. By consolidating data from multiple sources, SIEM platforms enable the identification of patterns indicative of potential attacks, facilitating rapid detection and situational awareness. The discussion of SIEM capabilities underscored their role in alert generation, anomaly detection, and dashboard visualization, enabling security teams to prioritize and investigate incidents effectively.

SOAR platforms complement SIEM by automating response workflows, orchestrating cross-tool interactions, and streamlining incident management. Unlike SIEM, which primarily focuses on detection, SOAR platforms execute predefined actions, such as isolating compromised endpoints, blocking malicious IP addresses, or notifying relevant teams, thereby reducing the mean time to response (MTTR) and minimizing human error. The integration of SIEM and SOAR creates a holistic security ecosystem in which threat detection and remediation are closely linked, resulting in faster, more efficient, and more consistent incident management. Figure 6.1 in this chapter illustrates this integrated workflow, showing how normalized data flows from collection and correlation in SIEM systems to automated responses and orchestration within SOAR platforms.

The practical case study of using logs for intrusion detection reinforced these concepts by illustrating how multi-source log correlation can uncover sophisticated attacks, such as lateral movement within an enterprise network. By analyzing web server, firewall, network flow, and endpoint logs together, security analysts identified unusual behaviors, detected an ongoing malware campaign, and implemented rapid containment measures. This example emphasizes the importance of combining normalization, analytics platforms, and automated response mechanisms to improve detection accuracy and resilience against advanced threats.

Key Terms

1. Security Data Collection – The systematic gathering of logs and telemetry from servers, endpoints, network devices, applications, and cloud systems.
2. Data Normalization – The process of converting heterogeneous security data into a standardized, structured format for analysis.
3. Log Analysis – Examination of collected logs to detect patterns, anomalies, and potential security threats.
4. SIEM *(Security Information and Event Management)* – A platform that aggregates, normalizes, correlates, and analyzes security events in real-time to provide alerts and situational awareness.
5. SOAR *(Security Orchestration, Automation, and Response)* – A platform that automates incident response, orchestrates security tools, and manages incident workflows.
6. Event Correlation – Linking related events from multiple sources to identify potential security incidents.
7. Anomaly Detection – Identifying deviations from normal behavior that may indicate security threats.
8. Mean Time to Detection *(MTTD)* – The average time taken to detect a security incident after it occurs.
9. Mean Time to Response *(MTTR)* – The average time taken to respond and remediate a detected security incident.
10. Endpoint Telemetry – Data collected from user devices, including activity logs, system events, and behavioral patterns.

11. Threat Intelligence – Information about potential or current attacks that can be used to anticipate, prevent, or mitigate security incidents.
12. Incident Lifecycle – The stages of a security incident, including detection, investigation, containment, remediation, and documentation.
13. Orchestration – Coordination and integration of multiple security tools and processes to respond to threats effectively.
14. Automation – Execution of predefined security tasks without human intervention to increase efficiency and reduce errors.
15. False Positive – A security alert that incorrectly identifies benign activity as a threat.
16. Correlation Rules – Predefined logic or patterns used by SIEM systems to link events and detect threats.
17. Dashboard Visualization – Graphical representation of security events, trends, and metrics for situational awareness.
18. Real-Time Monitoring – Continuous observation of security events as they occur.
19. Forensic Analysis – Detailed investigation of collected logs and data to determine the root cause and impact of security incidents.
20. Normalized Schema – A standard structure used to unify data from various sources.

Review Questions

1. Define security data collection and explain its significance in modern cybersecurity practices.
2. What is data normalization, and why is it critical for effective security monitoring?
3. Describe the differences between heterogeneous and standardized log formats.
4. Explain how data quality impacts threat detection.
5. What are SIEM platforms, and what role do they play in security operations?
6. List the three primary functions of a SIEM system.
7. How does event correlation enhance anomaly detection in SIEM platforms?

8. Discuss the advantages of integrating multiple data sources in a SIEM system.
9. What is SOAR, and how does it complement SIEM capabilities?
10. Explain the key functions of SOAR: orchestration, automation, incident management, and collaboration.
11. Provide an example of an automated response that a SOAR platform can execute.
12. How do SIEM and SOAR integration workflows improve incident response efficiency?
13. What is the significance of mean time to detection (MTTD) in security monitoring?
14. How does mean time to response (MTTR) influence organizational resilience against threats?
15. Define endpoint telemetry and explain its role in intrusion detection.
16. What is threat intelligence, and how can it be leveraged in SIEM and SOAR platforms?
17. Explain the importance of anomaly detection in identifying sophisticated attacks.
18. Discuss the limitations of relying solely on logs without normalization and correlation.
19. How can dashboards and visualizations improve situational awareness for security analysts?
20. Provide an example of a real-world incident where log analysis helped detect a threat.
21. Explain the concept of the incident lifecycle and its stages.
22. What challenges can organizations face when collecting and normalizing security data?
23. Compare false positives and false negatives in the context of security alerts.
24. How does automated orchestration in SOAR platforms reduce human error?

CHAPTER 7

Machine Learning in Cybersecurity

Learning Objectives

By the end of this chapter, learners should be able to:

- Understand the role of machine learning in cybersecurity.
- Differentiate between anomaly detection techniques.
- Apply unsupervised learning methods for anomaly detection.
- Apply supervised learning methods for threat classification.
- Understand real-time anomaly detection.
- Explain predictive threat intelligence.
- Evaluate risk-prioritization strategies using predictive models.
- Identify limitations of machine learning models.
- Understand model validation and monitoring requirements.
- Integrate human expertise with ML systems.
- Critically assess AI-driven security solutions.

Overview

The rapid evolution of cyber threats, combined with the exponential growth of data in digital environments, has significantly increased the complexity of cybersecurity challenges. Traditional rule-based security mechanisms, such as signature-based intrusion detection systems and predefined firewall rules, are often effective at identifying known threats; however, they struggle to detect novel, sophisticated, or stealthy attacks. Modern cyber adversaries employ tactics that evolve quickly, exploit zero-day vulnerabilities, or operate under the radar of conventional defenses. In response to these challenges, machine learning (ML) has emerged as a transformative technology in cybersecurity, providing advanced capabilities that complement traditional security methods and improve overall organizational resilience.

Machine learning enables security systems to automatically analyze vast amounts of historical and real-time data, recognize complex patterns, and detect anomalies that deviate from established behavioral baselines. This analytical capability enables organizations to identify previously unseen threats, including zero-day exploits, insider threats, and subtle indicators of compromise. By employing both supervised and unsupervised learning algorithms, ML models can perform classification, clustering, and predictive analysis on network traffic, user behavior, system logs, and endpoint activity. Supervised learning relies on labeled datasets to detect known threat signatures and predict the likelihood of future attacks, while unsupervised learning detects unusual patterns without prior knowledge of specific attack types, making it particularly effective in discovering unknown threats. The combination of these approaches provides more comprehensive coverage, reducing blind spots that traditional methods may leave uncovered.

Beyond anomaly detection, machine learning enables predictive threat intelligence — the proactive identification of potential attacks before they occur. By analyzing historical attack data, threat feeds, and vulnerability reports, ML algorithms can identify patterns and trends that indicate likely attack vectors, high-risk assets, or targeted vulnerabilities. For example, analyzing phishing campaigns, malware propagation, or network reconnaissance activities can provide actionable intelligence, enabling security teams to prioritize defences, allocate resources efficiently, and implement preemptive mitigation strategies. This predictive capability shifts organizations from reactive to proactive cybersecurity postures, improving overall operational readiness and resilience against cyber threats.

Despite its numerous advantages, deploying machine learning in cybersecurity introduces new challenges and risks. The effectiveness of ML models depends heavily on the quality, quantity, and diversity of training data; biased, incomplete, or outdated datasets can lead to false positives, false negatives, or misclassification of threats.

Furthermore, sophisticated adversaries may employ adversarial attacks to manipulate model inputs and evade detection. Additionally, complex models, such as deep neural networks, often lack transparency and interpretability, making it difficult for security analysts to understand the rationale behind alerts. To mitigate these risks, continuous model validation, monitoring, and integration with human expertise are essential, ensuring that ML complements human decision-making rather than introducing additional vulnerabilities.

This chapter delves into the role of machine learning in cybersecurity, exploring its applications in anomaly detection and predictive threat intelligence, as well as the limitations and risks associated with AI-driven models. By understanding these concepts, security practitioners and researchers can leverage machine learning to enhance detection capabilities, streamline incident response, and strengthen organizational security resilience in an increasingly complex cyber threat landscape.

Anomaly Detection Techniques

Anomaly detection represents one of the most critical applications of machine learning in modern cybersecurity. At its core, anomaly detection involves identifying patterns of behavior or activity that deviate from a learned baseline of "normal" operations. These deviations, when correctly interpreted, often signal potential security threats, ranging from malware infections and unauthorized access attempts to insider threats and sophisticated advanced persistent threats (APTs). Unlike signature-based detection systems, which require prior knowledge of threats, anomaly detection can identify previously unknown attack patterns, making it particularly valuable for proactive defense in dynamic, complex IT environments.

The foundation of anomaly detection lies in understanding normal system behavior. In practice, this involves collecting comprehensive data from a wide variety of sources, including network traffic, endpoint activity, application logs, authentication records, and system process metrics. Machine learning algorithms then analyze this data to establish statistical or behavioral baselines. For example, in network traffic monitoring, the baseline may consist of typical packet volumes, access frequencies, or protocol usage patterns for each endpoint or subnet. Any significant deviation—such as a sudden spike in outbound connections to an unfamiliar IP address—can be flagged as anomalous for further investigation. Figure 7.1 illustrates the basic principle of anomaly detection: normal behavior is represented as a clustered region, and anomalies are points outside this cluster.

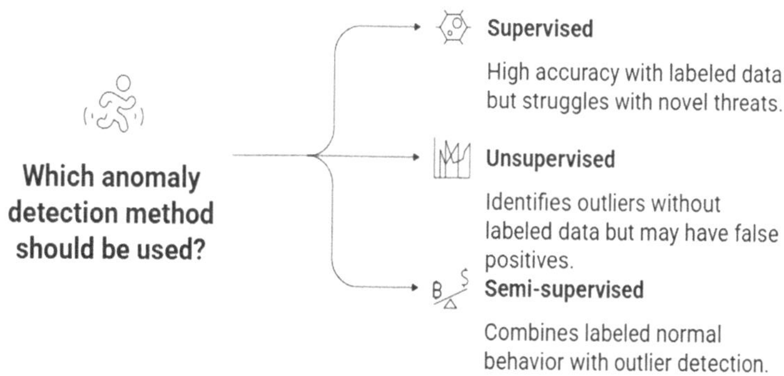

Figure 7.1: Conceptual Diagram of Anomaly Detection in Cybersecurity

Machine learning approaches to anomaly detection are typically categorized into supervised, unsupervised, and semi-supervised methods. In supervised anomaly detection, models are trained on labeled datasets that include examples of both normal and malicious activity. The model learns to classify incoming observations accordingly. While this approach can achieve high accuracy when ample labeled data is available, it struggles to identify novel threats that are not represented in the training set. Conversely, unsupervised anomaly detection does not require labeled data. Instead, it identifies outliers or deviations based on statistical properties or clustering methods. For instance, k-means clustering or density-based techniques such as DBSCAN can group normal behavior and flag data points that do not conform to any cluster. Semi-supervised approaches combine elements of both, often using labeled normal behavior while treating deviations as potential anomalies.

A practical example can be found in user behavior analytics (UBA), a subset of anomaly detection that monitors user activity patterns to identify insider threats. Consider an employee who typically accesses internal databases from the corporate network during business hours. If machine learning models detect that the same credentials are used to access sensitive systems at unusual times from an external IP address, this deviation triggers an alert. By correlating this behavior with other metrics, such as the volume of data accessed or the use of unusual system commands, analysts can prioritize investigations and potentially prevent data exfiltration before significant harm occurs.

Network anomaly detection is another critical application. Traditional intrusion detection systems (IDS) rely on signature-based patterns, which fail against zero-day exploits or sophisticated attacks that mimic legitimate traffic. Machine learning algorithms, however, can model normal network flows and flag deviations indicative of malicious activity. For example, a sudden surge in DNS queries to an external domain or a new pattern of communication between previously unrelated hosts may signal the presence of command-and-control traffic used by malware. Table 7.1 provides a comparison of common anomaly detection techniques and their applicability in cybersecurity contexts.

Technique	Description	Strengths	Limitations
Statistical Profiling	Uses statistical models to define normal ranges	Simple, interpretable	Sensitive to noise, assumes normal distribution
Clustering-Based Detection	Groups similar data points; outliers are anomalies	Handles unlabeled data, adaptable	Computationally expensive for large datasets
Neural Networks / Autoencoders	Learns compressed representations of normal behavior	Detects complex patterns	Requires substantial data and computational resources

Technique	Description	Strengths	Limitations
One-Class SVM	Classifies normal data in high-dimensional space	Effective for sparse anomalies	Sensitive to hyperparameters
Time-Series Analysis	Models sequential behavior over time	Captures temporal anomalies	Requires careful modeling of seasonality and trends

Table 7.1: Comparison of Anomaly Detection Techniques

One of the critical challenges in anomaly detection is balancing sensitivity and specificity. Highly sensitive models may detect every deviation but generate a large number of false positives, overwhelming security teams. Conversely, models tuned for specificity may miss subtle but critical indicators of compromise. Hybrid approaches often integrate multiple detection methods and incorporate feedback loops to continuously refine model accuracy. For instance, analysts may label detected anomalies as true positives or false positives, feeding this information back into supervised or semi-supervised models for ongoing improvement.

Another key consideration is the evolving threat landscape. Attackers may deliberately attempt to evade detection by blending malicious activity with normal traffic patterns or mimicking legitimate user behavior. Adversarial machine learning, in which attackers manipulate input data to deceive models, represents a growing concern. Robust anomaly detection systems, therefore, combine ML-driven insights with threat intelligence, contextual analysis, and human expertise to validate alerts and reduce the likelihood of evasion.

Real-world applications of anomaly detection extend across industries. Financial institutions use anomaly detection to monitor transactional patterns and detect fraudulent behavior, such as unusual transfers or unauthorized access to sensitive accounts. Healthcare organizations leverage it to identify unauthorized access to patient records. Industrial control systems (ICS) employ anomaly detection to monitor sensor readings and operational metrics, helping prevent cyber-physical attacks. Across all domains, integrating anomaly detection with automated incident response —

for example, through SOAR platforms — ensures timely mitigation and reduces potential damage.

Unsupervised Learning Methods

Unsupervised learning plays a pivotal role in modern cybersecurity, particularly in the detection of anomalies that may indicate malicious activity. Unlike supervised learning, which requires labeled datasets to train models to recognize known threats, unsupervised learning algorithms operate without prior knowledge of attack signatures. This makes them exceptionally valuable for identifying novel or zero-day threats that traditional signature-based systems cannot detect. By analyzing the intrinsic structure and distribution of data, unsupervised models can identify deviations from normal behavior, flagging potential security incidents that might otherwise go unnoticed.

Clustering techniques are among the most commonly used unsupervised approaches. Algorithms such as k-means and DBSCAN (Density-Based Spatial Clustering of Applications with Noise) group data points with similar characteristics into clusters representing normal behavior. Data points that fall outside these clusters are considered anomalies. For instance, in network traffic analysis, k-means can model normal packet flow patterns for different endpoints. If a host suddenly initiates connections that do not fit any established cluster—such as unusual high-volume transfers to an external IP—this behavior can be flagged for further investigation. DBSCAN, on the other hand, identifies dense regions of data and labels sparse points as outliers, which is particularly useful in detecting rare but potentially dangerous events, such as lateral movement within a network during an advanced persistent threat (APT).

Another powerful technique is Principal Component Analysis (PCA), which reduces the dimensionality of large datasets while preserving the most significant variance. PCA transforms correlated variables into a smaller set of uncorrelated components, simplifying the identification of patterns and deviations. In cybersecurity applications, PCA can reveal abnormal activity by highlighting deviations along key components of network or system metrics. For example, a sudden spike in CPU usage or unusual file access patterns across endpoints may appear as outliers in the transformed feature space, signaling potential malware execution or unauthorized access.

Autoencoders, a class of neural networks, represent another effective unsupervised approach. Autoencoders are trained to reconstruct input data from a compressed latent representation. Normal behavior is learned during training, and deviations during reconstruction result in high reconstruction error scores, which can be interpreted as anomalies. In practical terms, autoencoders can monitor system logs, application metrics, or user activity patterns, flagging events that significantly deviate from the learned normal behavior. This makes them particularly effective for detecting subtle attacks or insider threats that may not trigger conventional alerts.

One of the key advantages of unsupervised learning in cybersecurity is its adaptability. Because these models do not rely on labeled data, they can continuously learn from evolving system behavior and adapt to changing environments. However, there are challenges, including sensitivity to noise and the risk of false positives, which require careful tuning of model parameters and thresholds. Integrating unsupervised detection with other security measures, such as SIEM platforms or human analyst validation, ensures that alerts are actionable and reduces the likelihood of alert fatigue.

Supervised Learning Methods

Supervised learning represents a cornerstone of modern cybersecurity analytics, leveraging historical, labeled datasets to train models that can accurately distinguish between benign and malicious activity. Unlike unsupervised learning, which identifies anomalies based solely on deviations from normal patterns, supervised learning requires well-curated datasets containing examples of both normal and malicious behavior. These datasets enable algorithms to learn associations between observed features and the corresponding class labels, allowing the model to make predictions on new, unseen data with a degree of confidence.

Classification algorithms are among the most commonly used supervised learning techniques in cybersecurity. Decision trees, for instance, create hierarchical structures where each node represents a decision based on specific feature thresholds, leading to leaf nodes that classify behavior as normal or suspicious. These models are interpretable and can provide insights into the reasoning behind each classification, making them valuable for compliance and auditing purposes. Random forests, an ensemble of decision trees, improve predictive accuracy by combining multiple tree outputs to reduce overfitting and increase generalization across diverse datasets.

Support Vector Machines (SVMs) offer another effective approach, particularly for binary classification problems. SVMs identify optimal hyperplanes that separate malicious and normal data points in a high-dimensional feature space. This capability is particularly useful in network intrusion detection, where multidimensional features such as packet size, source IP, destination port, and protocol type can be analyzed simultaneously to detect abnormal traffic patterns.

Deep Neural Networks (DNNs) and other deep learning architectures have also become prevalent in supervised cybersecurity applications. By learning hierarchical feature representations, DNNs can detect complex patterns that may be missed by traditional algorithms. For example, in malware detection, raw executable file attributes can be fed into a neural network, which automatically learns distinguishing characteristics between benign software and malware. Similarly, user behavior analytics can leverage DNNs to identify subtle deviations from established usage patterns that indicate insider threats.

A significant advantage of supervised learning is its high accuracy for known attack types. By training models on comprehensive labeled datasets, security teams can achieve reliable detection and classification of familiar threats, reducing false positives and improving incident response efficiency. However, the reliance on historical data introduces limitations. Models may struggle to detect zero-day attacks or novel threats that were not represented in the training data. Additionally, the quality of predictions depends heavily on the accuracy, completeness, and representativeness of the labelled datasets. Poor-quality data, class imbalance, or outdated information can lead to biased models and misclassifications, undermining security effectiveness.

To address these limitations, many cybersecurity systems integrate supervised learning with unsupervised techniques in hybrid models. In such configurations, unsupervised models identify anomalous activities that may indicate novel threats, while supervised models validate and classify known attack types. This combination improves overall detection coverage, reduces false positives, and enables more adaptive and resilient security monitoring.

In practice, supervised learning models are widely applied in malware detection, spam and phishing identification, intrusion detection systems (IDS), and threat intelligence analysis. For instance, email security solutions often employ random forests or DNNs to classify incoming messages as spam, phishing, or legitimate based on features such as sender reputation, header analysis, and textual content patterns. By continuously retraining models with newly labeled incidents, organizations can maintain high detection accuracy in the face of evolving threats.

Hybrid Approaches

Hybrid approaches in machine learning combine the strengths of both supervised and unsupervised techniques to provide a more robust and comprehensive cybersecurity defense. While supervised learning excels at accurately classifying known threats based on labeled data, it often struggles to detect previously unseen attacks or subtle anomalies. Conversely, unsupervised methods are adept at identifying deviations from normal behavior but can generate higher false positives due to lack of explicit context. By integrating these two paradigms, hybrid models leverage the complementary advantages of each, enabling more accurate detection of both known and novel threats.

In a typical hybrid system, unsupervised algorithms such as clustering, principal component analysis (PCA), or autoencoders first analyze incoming data streams to detect unusual patterns or outliers. These anomalies are flagged as potentially suspicious and passed to supervised models for classification. For example, in a network intrusion detection scenario, an autoencoder might identify a sudden spike in outbound traffic from a particular host, signaling anomalous behavior. A supervised classifier, trained on historical attack signatures, then evaluates whether this anomaly corresponds to a known threat, such as data exfiltration malware, or represents a benign irregularity.

Hybrid approaches can also employ semi-supervised learning, which uses a small set of labeled data combined with a larger set of unlabeled data to improve model generalization. This is particularly valuable in cybersecurity environments where labeling every incident is impractical due to volume or complexity. Semi-supervised models can learn patterns from the abundant unlabeled data while using labeled examples to guide classification, thus enhancing both sensitivity and precision in threat detection.

A practical example of hybrid modeling can be seen in user and entity behavior analytics (UEBA). Here, unsupervised techniques detect deviations from baseline user activity—such as unusual login times, atypical file access, or abnormal data transfers—while supervised models classify these deviations based on known insider threat patterns. This layered approach reduces false positives while ensuring early identification of potential malicious activities.

Method	Strengths	Weaknesses	Example Use Case
Supervised Learning	High accuracy for known threats	Poor at detecting unknown threats	Malware classification, phishing detection
Unsupervised Learning	Detects novel or zero-day attacks	Higher false positive rate	Anomaly detection in network traffic
Hybrid Approach	Combines strengths of both; adaptive	More complex to implement and maintain	UEBA, advanced intrusion detection, threat intelligence

Table 7.2: Comparison of Hybrid, Supervised, and Unsupervised Methods

Hybrid approaches also support continuous learning and adaptation, which is essential in dynamic cybersecurity environments. As new threats emerge and attack techniques evolve, models must be retrained regularly. By combining unsupervised anomaly detection with supervised classification, hybrid systems can identify unknown attack patterns while refining classification accuracy for recurring threats. This adaptability enhances resilience against advanced persistent threats (APTs), polymorphic malware, and sophisticated social engineering attacks.

Predictive Threat Intelligence

Predictive threat intelligence represents a transformative application of machine learning in cybersecurity, enabling organizations to anticipate and mitigate potential threats before they manifest into active incidents. Unlike traditional reactive security measures, which respond only after attacks occur, predictive intelligence leverages historical data, threat feeds, vulnerability databases, and behavioral trends to forecast probable attack vectors and identify assets at heightened risk. This proactive approach enables organizations to allocate resources efficiently, implement preventive measures, and minimize the likelihood and impact of cyberattacks.

At its core, predictive threat intelligence relies on machine learning algorithms that analyze vast datasets to uncover correlations, trends, and emerging patterns. Historical attack data, for example, can reveal recurring tactics, techniques, and procedures (TTPs) employed by threat actors. By modeling these TTPs over time, predictive systems can anticipate how attackers might adapt or evolve their strategies. Threat feeds, which provide near-real-time information on newly discovered vulnerabilities, malware signatures, and phishing domains, further enhance predictive capability by incorporating external intelligence into internal security models. Behavioral analysis of user and network activity complements these sources, highlighting deviations from typical patterns that may indicate potential threats before they escalate.

One practical application of predictive threat intelligence is in phishing prevention. By analyzing past phishing campaigns, machine learning models can identify characteristics that increase the likelihood of success, such as email subject patterns, sender domains, target user roles, or the timing of attacks. Predictive models can then score incoming emails for risk and inform adaptive defense measures, including enhanced spam filtering, dynamic access restrictions, or targeted user training. For example, if a financial department historically receives a high volume of phishing attempts, predictive analytics can flag high-risk emails for additional scrutiny or temporarily restrict suspicious attachments, mitigating potential compromise.

Similarly, predictive intelligence can aid in vulnerability management. By combining historical exploit data with internal asset inventories and system configurations, machine learning models can prioritize vulnerabilities that are most likely to be targeted in the near future. This supports proactive patching strategies, where critical systems are updated or reinforced before they are exploited, reducing the window of exposure. Organizations can also simulate potential attack scenarios, using predictive outputs to stress-test defenses and identify gaps in their security posture.

Application Area	Data Sources	Predictive Outcome	Example Use Case
Phishing Detection	Historical campaigns, email metadata	Identify likely phishing targets and attack methods	Adaptive email filtering, user training
Vulnerability Management	Patch databases, exploit trends	Prioritize high-risk vulnerabilities	Proactive patching and risk mitigation
Malware Propagation	Threat feeds, endpoint telemetry	Forecast potential spread of malware	Network segmentation, containment strategies
Insider Threat Detection	User behavior logs, access patterns	Detect abnormal activity indicating insider risk	Targeted monitoring, access restrictions

Table 7.2: Predictive Threat Intelligence Applications

Predictive threat intelligence also supports strategic decision-making at the organizational level. Security teams can use predictive insights to plan defensive investments, allocate staff and budget to high-priority areas, and design policies that anticipate emerging threats. For example, if predictive models indicate a likelihood of ransomware targeting supply chain vendors, organizations can preemptively enforce stricter access controls, backup strategies, and incident response drills focused on that vector.

Despite its advantages, predictive intelligence is not without limitations. Its accuracy depends on the quality, completeness, and timeliness of the underlying data. Models trained on outdated or biased datasets may generate inaccurate forecasts, leading to misallocated resources or missed threats. Additionally, attackers may deliberately alter their behavior to evade predictive systems, requiring continuous retraining and monitoring of the models. Integrating human expertise remains essential, as analysts can contextualize model outputs, validate predictions, and make informed decisions when uncertainty arises.

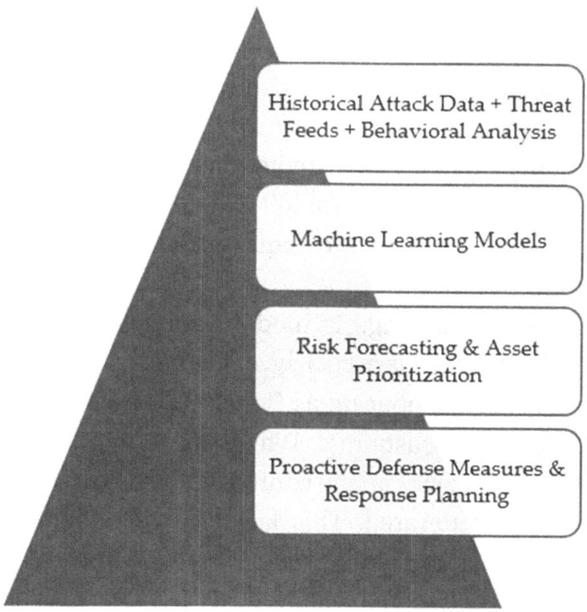

Figure 7.2: Predictive Threat Intelligence Workflow

Limitations and Risks of AI Models

While machine learning (ML) has revolutionized cybersecurity, enabling advanced threat detection, anomaly identification, and predictive intelligence, it is important to recognize its inherent limitations and risks. The efficacy of any ML-based security system is fundamentally dependent on the quality, completeness, and relevance of its training data. Models trained on biased, incomplete, or outdated datasets can produce inaccurate outputs, generating false positives or false negatives that undermine security operations. False positives, for example, may overwhelm security teams with unnecessary alerts, while false negatives can allow genuine threats to go undetected, exposing critical systems to compromise.

A particularly serious risk arises from adversarial attacks, where malicious actors deliberately manipulate inputs to deceive AI systems. In cybersecurity contexts, such attacks can take subtle forms. Attackers may modify malware features, network traffic characteristics, or system behavior patterns just enough to evade ML detection, without triggering conventional signature-based alerts. For instance, polymorphic malware can continuously change its code structure, bypassing models trained on previous malware samples. Similarly, attackers may inject noisy or deceptive data into anomaly detection models, skewing predictions and reducing system reliability. These adversarial strategies highlight that AI systems are not immune to manipulation and require robust countermeasures to maintain effectiveness.

Another critical challenge is model interpretability. Many high-performing ML models, particularly deep neural networks (DNNs) and ensemble methods, operate as "black boxes," producing outputs without transparent reasoning. While these models may detect complex patterns, security analysts often cannot easily discern why a specific alert was generated. This lack of explainability can erode trust, hinder decision-making, and impede effective human-AI collaboration. For example, when a DNN flags unusual network behavior, analysts need interpretative insights to decide whether to isolate a system, initiate forensic analysis, or ignore the alert. Without interpretability, organizations risk over-reliance on automated outputs or misapplication of incident response protocols.

Mitigating these risks requires a multi-layered approach. Continuous model validation is essential to ensure performance in real-world environments. Regularly testing models against fresh data and emerging threat patterns allows organizations to detect degradation in accuracy and recalibrate accordingly. Human oversight is equally critical, providing context, judgment, and decision-making capabilities that ML alone cannot replicate. By combining automated detection with expert evaluation, organizations can balance speed and accuracy while minimizing operational errors.

Emerging strategies such as adversarial training—where models are exposed to intentionally modify malicious inputs—can improve robustness against evasion techniques. Similarly, explainable AI (XAI) approaches aim to enhance transparency, allowing analysts to understand the reasoning behind predictions and integrate insights into security workflows effectively. Regular dataset updates, informed by threat intelligence feeds and incident reports, are necessary to maintain model relevance, especially in rapidly evolving cyber threat landscapes.

Risk Factor	Description	Mitigation Strategy
Data Quality	Biased, incomplete, or outdated datasets	Continuous dataset curation and validation
Adversarial Attacks	Manipulation of inputs to bypass detection	Adversarial training, model hardening
Model Interpretability	Black-box nature of complex models	Explainable AI techniques, human oversight
False Positives/Negatives	Incorrect classification of benign or malicious activity	Hybrid models, continuous performance monitoring
Evolving Threats	Rapid emergence of novel attack methods	Integration of real-time threat intelligence feeds

Table 7.3: Key Risks and Mitigation Strategies for ML in Cybersecurity

Conclusion

Chapter 7 has explored the transformative role of machine learning (ML) in modern cybersecurity, highlighting its applications, benefits, and inherent limitations. The increasing complexity and frequency of cyber threats have rendered traditional, rule-based security systems insufficient for detecting sophisticated attacks, zero-day exploits, and insider threats. Machine learning, with its ability to identify patterns, adapt to evolving threat landscapes, and predict future attacks, offers a powerful complement to conventional security measures.

Anomaly detection represents a foundational application of ML in cybersecurity. By analyzing deviations from normal behavior, organizations can detect threats that do not conform to known signatures or pre-defined rules. Both unsupervised and supervised learning methods contribute to anomaly detection, each with distinct advantages. Unsupervised models, such as clustering, principal component analysis (PCA), and autoencoders, are effective against emerging threats and previously unseen attack vectors because they do not require labeled datasets. Supervised learning models, including decision trees, random forests, support vector machines (SVMs), and deep neural networks (DNNs), rely on historical, labeled data to predict and classify known attacks. Hybrid approaches that combine supervised and unsupervised learning can improve detection coverage while reducing false positives, providing a more comprehensive defense strategy.

Predictive threat intelligence extends the capabilities of ML beyond reactive measures. By analyzing historical attack patterns, threat feeds, and vulnerability data, ML models can forecast likely attack vectors, identify high-risk assets, and prioritize mitigation strategies. For example, analyzing phishing campaigns over time can reveal likely targets and attack methodologies, allowing organizations to deploy preemptive countermeasures such as enhanced email filters, user awareness training, or adaptive access controls. Similarly, predictive models can anticipate vulnerable points in network infrastructure or software systems, enabling proactive patching and resource allocation. Through predictive intelligence, security operations shift from a reactive posture to a proactive, strategic approach, reducing response times and improving organizational resilience.

Despite these advantages, ML in cybersecurity is not without limitations. Model performance is highly dependent on data quality, completeness, and relevance. Biased, incomplete, or outdated datasets can lead to false positives, false negatives, and blind spots. Adversarial attacks—where attackers manipulate inputs to evade detection—pose an additional risk, particularly against unsupervised anomaly detection or black-box deep learning models. Interpretability remains a challenge; complex ML models often lack transparency, making it difficult for analysts to understand why certain events are flagged. Mitigating these limitations requires continuous model validation, adversarial training, explainable AI (XAI) techniques, and integration with human expertise.

Key Terms

1. Machine Learning (ML): An AI technique that learns patterns from data to make predictions or detect threats without explicit programming.
2. Anomaly Detection: Identifying deviations from normal behavior to spot suspicious activity or attacks.
3. Supervised Learning: ML approach using labeled datasets to classify known threats.
4. Unsupervised Learning: ML approach analyzing unlabeled data to detect new or unknown threats.
5. Hybrid Models: Combine supervised and unsupervised learning to improve detection accuracy.
6. Predictive Threat Intelligence: Forecasting potential attacks using historical and behavioral data.
7. Zero-Day Exploit: A vulnerability unknown to vendors, and exploitable before patches are available.
8. Insider Threat: Malicious or negligent actions by internal personnel.
9. Adversarial Attack: Manipulating inputs to deceive ML systems.
10. False Positive: Benign activity incorrectly flagged as malicious.
11. False Negative: Malicious activity incorrectly deemed safe.

12. Decision Tree: ML algorithm using tree-like structures to classify events.
13. Random Forest: Ensemble of decision trees improving classification accuracy.
14. Support Vector Machine (SVM): Algorithm separating data into classes using optimal boundaries.
15. Deep Neural Network (DNN): A multi-layered model learning complex patterns for threat detection.
16. Autoencoder: A neural network that detects anomalies by reconstructing input data.
17. Clustering: Grouping similar data points to identify unusual activity.
18. Principal Component Analysis (PCA): Reduces data dimensions to detect patterns and outliers.
19. Black-Box Model: ML system with opaque decision-making, difficult to interpret.
20. Explainable AI (XAI): Techniques making ML decisions understandable for analysts.
21. Model Validation: Ensuring that the ML model performs accurately on new data.
22. Data Bias: Skewed datasets causing inaccurate predictions.
23. Threat Feed: Source of threat intelligence data for model updates.
24. Network Traffic Analysis: Examining network data for suspicious patterns.
25. Predictive Analytics: Using ML to forecast future security incidents.

Review Questions

1. Define machine learning in the context of cybersecurity.
2. Explain why traditional rule-based systems may fail against advanced cyber threats.
3. What is anomaly detection, and how does it contribute to cybersecurity?
4. Describe the difference between supervised and unsupervised learning in anomaly detection.

5. Provide examples of unsupervised learning techniques used in cybersecurity.
6. How do autoencoders detect anomalies in network traffic?
7. Explain the role of clustering algorithms such as k-means in detecting unusual activity.
8. Discuss the limitations of supervised learning models when faced with zero-day attacks.
9. What are hybrid ML models, and why are they useful in cybersecurity?
10. Define predictive threat intelligence and its significance in proactive defense.
11. How can historical attack data inform predictive models?
12. Give an example of how predictive analytics can prevent phishing attacks.
13. What are the key risks associated with ML-based cybersecurity models?
14. Explain the concept of adversarial attacks in ML security systems.
15. Why is model interpretability critical for human analysts?
16. What are false positives and false negatives, and how do they affect security operations?
17. How does deep learning improve detection capabilities in cybersecurity?
18. Describe the role of data quality in ML model effectiveness.
19. Explain the concept of black-box models and their challenges.
20. How can explainable AI (XAI) enhance trust in ML systems?
21. What strategies can organizations use to mitigate the limitations of ML models?
22. Discuss the importance of continuous model validation in cybersecurity.
23. How does combining supervised and unsupervised methods reduce detection errors?
24. Describe the role of ML in identifying insider threats.
25. In what ways does predictive threat intelligence shift the cybersecurity posture from reactive to proactive?

CHAPTER 8

Data-Driven Incident Response

Learning Objectives

By the end of this chapter, learners should be able to:

- Understand the role of digital forensics in investigating security incidents.
- Identify methods for examining compromised systems, logs, network traffic, and memory dumps.
- Analyze how root-cause analysis uncovers exploited vulnerabilities and attack methods.
- Demonstrate how to integrate logs, telemetry, authentication records, and threat intelligence for attack reconstruction.
- Reconstruct the sequence and scope of an attack using correlated data.
- Utilize correlation insights to prioritize remediation, strengthen defenses, and generate verifiable evidence.
- Describe how automated workflows accelerate containment and mitigation of security threats.
- Implement automation for isolating endpoints, revoking credentials, and blocking malicious activity.
- Recognize the benefits of combining human expertise with data-driven automated response to enhance resilience and reduce mean time to response (MTTR).
- Assess the advantages of integrating forensic analysis, data correlation, and automation in incident response.
- Understand how data-driven incident response supports compliance, reporting, and proactive security posture.

- Explore methods to balance automated actions with strategic human decision-making in incident handling.

Overview

In today's complex cyber threat landscape, organizations face an increasing number of sophisticated attacks that can compromise sensitive data, disrupt operations, and damage reputations. Effective incident response is no longer a reactive process; it must be data-driven, proactive, and capable of rapidly mitigating threats while providing actionable insights for long-term resilience. Data-driven incident response leverages advanced analytics, comprehensive forensic investigation, and automated workflows to ensure that security incidents are detected, analyzed, contained, and remediated efficiently. By systematically integrating data from multiple sources—including system logs, network traffic, endpoint telemetry, authentication records, and threat intelligence feeds—security teams can reconstruct the sequence of events surrounding an attack, identify vulnerabilities, and implement corrective measures that prevent recurrence.

At the heart of data-driven incident response is digital forensics, a discipline that examines compromised systems, memory dumps, and other digital evidence to uncover how an attack occurred. Forensic analysis enables organizations to trace attackers' actions, determine the scope of damage, and gather evidence needed for legal or regulatory compliance. When combined with root-cause analysis, which identifies the underlying vulnerabilities and methods exploited, organizations gain a holistic understanding of security incidents. This dual approach ensures that defenses are strengthened not only to mitigate current threats but also to prevent future breaches, supporting a proactive cybersecurity posture.

Another critical aspect of effective incident response is data correlation for attack reconstruction. Modern attacks often span multiple systems and involve complex techniques such as lateral movement, privilege escalation, and data exfiltration. Isolated data points provide limited visibility, whereas correlating logs and telemetry from diverse sources creates a comprehensive timeline of malicious activity. This holistic reconstruction enables security teams to assess the full impact of an incident, prioritize remediation efforts based on risk, and derive insights that inform both operational and strategic decisions. Data correlation also plays a key role in internal reporting and external compliance requirements, ensuring that all actions taken during an incident are documented, verifiable, and auditable.

In addition to human-driven analysis, automation has become a cornerstone of modern incident response. Automated workflows, often integrated with Security Orchestration, Automation, and Response (SOAR) platforms, allow organizations to respond to threats rapidly and consistently. Tasks such as isolating infected endpoints, revoking compromised credentials, blocking malicious network traffic, and triggering alerts can be executed automatically, significantly reducing the time between detection and mitigation. Automation not only minimizes potential damage but also frees security analysts to focus on strategic activities such as threat hunting, vulnerability management, and continuous improvement of incident response processes.

By combining forensic investigation, data correlation, and automation, data-driven incident response enables organizations to maintain resilience against an evolving threat landscape. It provides a structured, evidence-based approach to managing security incidents, enhances the speed and accuracy of decision-making, and ensures that organizations can recover quickly while continuously strengthening their defenses. This chapter explores these components in detail, providing a comprehensive understanding of how data-driven methodologies transform incident response from a reactive necessity into a proactive strategic advantage.

Forensics and Root-Cause Analysis

Data-driven incident response relies heavily on the integration of forensics and root-cause analysis (RCA) to provide a holistic understanding of security incidents. Digital forensics serves as the systematic process of collecting, preserving, and analyzing digital evidence from affected systems, including servers, endpoints, network devices, and cloud environments. This involves examining log files, memory dumps, disk images, and network traffic to reconstruct the sequence of events, identify compromised assets, and determine the methods employed by attackers. Forensic investigations not only support immediate incident mitigation but also produce verifiable evidence for regulatory compliance, legal proceedings, and internal accountability.

Root-cause analysis complements forensic efforts by focusing on the underlying vulnerabilities, misconfigurations, or procedural gaps that allowed the incident to occur. By identifying these systemic weaknesses, RCA enables organizations to implement corrective measures, strengthen security controls, and reduce the likelihood of similar attacks in the future. Techniques such as fault tree analysis, event sequence mapping, and dependency analysis are commonly used to trace incidents back to their origin, providing actionable insights for continuous improvement.

Together, forensics and RCA create a structured framework for proactive cybersecurity. While forensics provides empirical evidence and a chronological reconstruction of events, RCA interprets these findings to uncover deeper systemic issues. Organizations that integrate both approaches benefit from enhanced threat visibility, faster remediation, and a stronger security posture. This combined methodology ensures that incident response is not merely reactive but forms part of a continuous cycle of detection, analysis, and prevention, ultimately improving resilience against evolving cyber threats.

Digital Forensics

Digital Forensics in Incident Response

Digital forensics is a critical component of data-driven incident response, encompassing the systematic identification, preservation, analysis, and presentation of digital evidence from compromised systems. The primary objective of digital forensics is to reconstruct the sequence of events during a cybersecurity incident, allowing organizations to understand how an attack unfolded, identify affected assets, and determine the methods used by adversaries. Sources of digital evidence are diverse and include system logs, application logs, network traffic captures, memory dumps, disk images, cloud service records, and endpoint telemetry. Each source provides unique insights, contributing to a comprehensive understanding of the incident.

Modern enterprises generate massive volumes of data on a daily basis. For instance, a large multinational corporation may produce millions of log entries across endpoints, firewalls, intrusion detection systems, and cloud services each day. Without effective digital forensics practices, critical indicators of compromise (IOCs) may go unnoticed, allowing attackers to remain active and carry out further malicious activities undetected. The ability to systematically collect and analyze these logs is therefore essential for timely threat detection, remediation, and compliance with regulatory requirements.

Evidence Source	Description	Purpose in Forensics
System Logs	OS-level logs, event logs, audit trails	Identify login attempts, privilege escalations
Application Logs	Logs from business or web applications	Detect unusual behavior, unauthorized access
Network Traffic Logs	Firewall, IDS/IPS, and network flow data	Trace lateral movement and data exfiltration
Memory Dumps	RAM snapshots captured during incidents	Analyze malware behavior, inspect running processes
Disk Images	Complete copies of storage media	Recover deleted files, identify forensic artifacts
Cloud Service Logs	Logs from AWS, Azure, GCP, and SaaS platforms	Track user activity, detect API misuse

Table 8.1: Digital Forensics Evidence Source Analysis

Automated forensic tools significantly enhance investigative efficiency and accuracy. Software such as EnCase, FTK (Forensic Toolkit), Autopsy, and X-Ways allow analysts to create forensic images, search for malicious binaries, and recover deleted or hidden data. For network-based forensics, tools like Wireshark and Zeek provide packet-level visibility, enabling the tracing of attack paths and lateral movement across the network. By integrating system, application, and network-level evidence, digital forensics offers a comprehensive picture of an incident, informing both immediate response and long-term security improvements.

Forensic Workflow

Forensic investigation is a cornerstone of data-driven incident response, providing a systematic method to uncover the root cause, scope, and impact of cybersecurity incidents. To ensure reliability, reproducibility, and legal defensibility, forensic investigations follow a structured workflow that integrates technical rigor with procedural compliance. This workflow not only facilitates accurate evidence collection and analysis but also supports regulatory adherence and legal scrutiny.

Step 1: Incident Detection

The process begins with incident detection, where security teams identify anomalous activity or breaches through multiple channels. Alerts may originate from Security Information and Event Management (SIEM) systems, intrusion detection/prevention systems (IDS/IPS), endpoint monitoring, or direct user reports. Effective detection requires real-time monitoring and correlation of diverse datasets to distinguish genuine threats from false positives. Early and accurate detection is critical to minimize dwell time—the duration an attacker remains undetected within a network.

Step 2: Evidence Collection

Once an incident is detected, the next step is evidence collection. This involves gathering relevant logs, system snapshots, network traffic captures, and other digital artifacts. Maintaining a strict chain of custody is essential during this phase to ensure that evidence is admissible in legal or regulatory proceedings. Collecting comprehensive evidence allows forensic analysts to capture the full scope of the attack, including compromised endpoints, malicious files, and anomalous user activity.

Step 3: Preservation & Imaging

Preservation and imaging aim to create exact, forensically sound copies of volatile and non-volatile data, preventing any modification or tampering of original evidence. Disk imaging tools generate bit-for-bit replicas of storage media, while memory snapshots capture the system state, including running processes, open connections, and in-memory malware. This phase ensures that investigators can analyze the data without compromising the integrity of the original sources.

Step 4: Data Analysis

During data analysis, forensic investigators leverage both automated tools and manual techniques to identify malicious activity, anomalous behavior, and the presence of malware. Tools such as EnCase, FTK, Autopsy, and X-Ways enable comprehensive searches for hidden, deleted, or encrypted files. Network-level analysis using Wireshark or Zeek allows analysts to trace lateral movement, exfiltration paths, and command-and-control traffic. The objective is to extract actionable intelligence from raw evidence, providing insights into attacker techniques and tactics.

Step 5: Timeline Reconstruction

Timeline reconstruction synthesizes findings into a chronological sequence, revealing the progression of the attack. By mapping events such as initial compromise, privilege escalation, lateral movement, and data exfiltration, security teams gain a clear understanding of the attack lifecycle. Visualizing the sequence of events facilitates decision-making, helps identify vulnerabilities exploited, and supports root-cause analysis.

Step 6: Reporting & Documentation

The final phase involves comprehensive reporting and documentation, which serves multiple purposes: informing stakeholders, supporting compliance audits, and providing legal evidence if required. Reports typically include descriptions of evidence sources, analysis methodologies, reconstructed timelines, identified vulnerabilities, and recommended mitigation strategies. Proper documentation ensures transparency, accountability, and knowledge retention for future incident response efforts.

By adhering to this structured workflow, organizations can conduct forensic investigations that are methodical, defensible, and actionable, laying the foundation for robust root-cause analysis and continuous improvement of cybersecurity defenses.

Root-Cause Analysis

While digital forensics primarily addresses the question, *"What happened?"*, root-cause analysis (RCA) seeks to answer *"Why did it happen?"* and *"How could it have been prevented?"* RCA delves deeper into the underlying factors that allowed an incident to occur, identifying vulnerabilities, misconfigurations, human errors, and process gaps that attackers exploit. Understanding root causes is essential for organizations not only to remediate the immediate incident but also to strengthen long-term security posture and reduce the likelihood of recurrence.

For instance, consider a ransomware attack initiated through a phishing email. Digital forensics can determine which endpoints were compromised, the malware variant used, and the extent of data encryption. RCA, however, investigates the deeper systemic reasons that allowed the attack to succeed. The phishing attempt may have succeeded due to multiple contributing factors: insufficient employee cybersecurity training, inadequate email filtering controls, outdated software lacking patches, the absence of multi-factor authentication, or weak access management policies. By systematically analyzing these factors, organizations can implement targeted preventive measures, such as user education programs, enhanced email scanning, endpoint segmentation, and stricter access policies.

RCA Techniques

Several structured methodologies are commonly employed to perform RCA in cybersecurity, ensuring a thorough and methodical approach:

- **Fault Tree Analysis (FTA):** FTA uses a top-down approach to visualize multiple contributing factors that lead to a security incident. The incident itself is placed at the top of the tree, with branches representing different failure points or vulnerabilities. By tracing each branch to its contributing events, security teams can identify critical weaknesses and prioritize remediation strategies.
- **Five Whys Analysis:** This iterative questioning technique involves repeatedly asking *"Why?"* to peel back layers of cause and effect. For example, why was the ransomware successful? Because the user clicked a malicious link. Why did they click it? Because training on phishing recognition was insufficient. Repeating this process helps uncover systemic issues beyond the immediate technical failure.
- **Fishbone (Ishikawa) Diagrams:** Fishbone diagrams categorize root causes into major domains such as human factors, processes, technology, policies, and training. Each branch explores potential contributing factors systematically, providing a clear visual representation of causality.

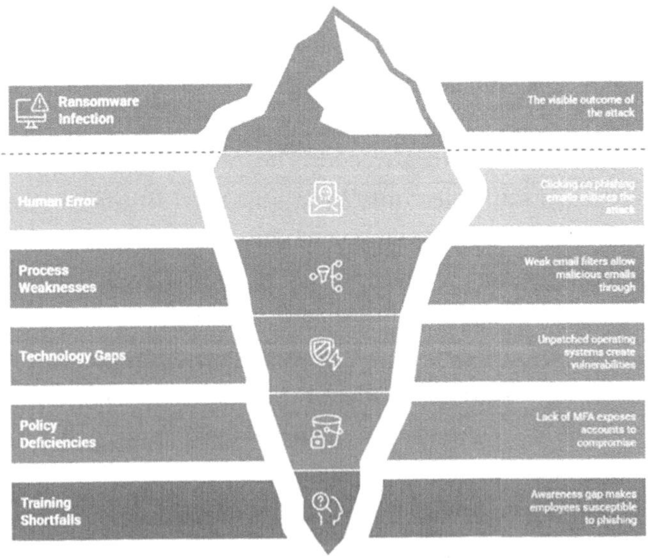

Figure 8.1: Phishing-Induced Ransomware Incident

In this example, each branch identifies a specific factor that contributed to the ransomware infection. Human error (clicking a phishing email), process weaknesses (weak email filtering), technological gaps (unpatched operating systems), policy deficiencies (absence of multi-factor authentication), and training shortfalls (lack of employee awareness) collectively enabled the attack.

By addressing each contributing factor, organizations can implement preventive controls. Human factors can be mitigated with continuous security awareness programs. Process weaknesses can be addressed through automated email sandboxing and stricter filtering rules. Technology gaps require timely patch management and endpoint segmentation, while policy and procedural shortcomings can be strengthened through access control policies and multi-factor authentication enforcement.

Integrating RCA with Digital Forensics

RCA is most effective when combined with digital forensics, forming a cohesive investigative framework. Forensics provides the factual basis of *what* occurred, while RCA uncovers the *why* and *how*. Together, they enable organizations to generate comprehensive incident reports, remediate vulnerabilities, and implement proactive controls. Furthermore, RCA supports compliance requirements and internal audit processes by documenting systemic risks and demonstrating continuous improvement efforts.

Case Study Example

In a real-world scenario, a medium-sized enterprise experienced a ransomware attack that encrypted several critical databases. Digital forensics revealed that the attack vector was a phishing email sent to a finance team member. RCA identified multiple root causes: insufficient phishing training, delayed software patching on database servers, lack of endpoint isolation, and weak password policies. The organization subsequently implemented a layered defense strategy, including endpoint segmentation, automated patch management, enhanced email security, and mandatory multi-factor authentication. Post-implementation, simulated phishing tests showed a 70%

reduction in successful phishing clicks, and no similar ransomware incidents occurred over the following year, demonstrating the efficacy of RCA-driven improvements.

Integration with Threat Intelligence

While digital forensics and root-cause analysis (RCA) establish the foundational understanding of *what happened* and *why it happened* during a cybersecurity incident, the integration of threat intelligence adds a critical external layer of insight. Threat intelligence provides information about malware signatures, attacker tactics, techniques, and procedures (TTPs), as well as indicators of compromise (IOCs) collected from global threat landscapes. By combining forensic data, RCA insights, and threat intelligence, organizations gain a holistic understanding of attacker behavior, enabling more precise incident classification, informed prioritization of remediation efforts, and anticipation of potential follow-on attacks.

Digital forensics produces an evidence-based account of affected systems, compromised endpoints, and the chronological sequence of malicious activity. RCA extends this analysis by investigating the underlying systemic vulnerabilities, misconfigurations, and procedural gaps that attackers exploited. However, internal analyses alone are often insufficient for understanding the broader context of cyber threats. Threat intelligence fills this gap by providing up-to-date knowledge of global attack campaigns, malware variants, and exploit techniques. For example, correlating a malware sample identified during forensic analysis with threat intelligence feeds can reveal the malware family, its associated TTPs, and its connections to known adversaries. This integrated perspective equips incident responders to understand not just the technical impact of the attack, but also the attacker's intent, methodologies, and potential future actions.

RCA Output	Threat Intelligence Role	Example Use Case
Malware observed	Signature & behavior analysis	Determine malware family & MITRE ATT&CK mapping
Attack vector identified	Known exploits & CVE data	Apply patches proactively
Lateral movement paths	Indicators of compromise (IOCs)	Block similar future movement
Potential targets & assets	Risk scoring & adversary tactics	Prioritize high-value assets for monitoring

Table 8.2: Integrating Threat Intelligence into RCA

This integrated approach significantly improves the accuracy of incident classification. For instance, if forensic analysis uncovers a ransomware payload across multiple endpoints and RCA identifies a phishing email as the initial entry point, threat intelligence can contextualize the attack by linking it to a known global campaign targeting finance departments via exploit kits. Armed with this information, security teams can prioritize patching vulnerable systems, reinforce access controls, and enhance monitoring for high-risk assets likely to be targeted in subsequent attacks.

Moreover, integrating threat intelligence facilitates proactive defense strategies. Mapping RCA findings to documented TTPs allows organizations to anticipate lateral movement, privilege escalation, or exfiltration attempts. For example, a ransomware strain known to exfiltrate sensitive data before encryption may prompt security teams to implement heightened data monitoring, enhanced logging, and stricter network segmentation. Awareness of CVEs exploited during the attack further enables immediate patching and preemptive scanning of other systems sharing the same vulnerabilities.

From a governance and compliance perspective, incorporating threat intelligence into RCA enriches reporting and regulatory documentation. Incident reports can communicate not only the technical and procedural details of a breach but also provide a broader understanding of attacker intent, threat context, and global trends. Such comprehensive reporting supports internal risk assessment, strategic decision-making, and adherence to regulatory requirements, ensuring that security operations move from reactive mitigation to informed, intelligence-driven action.

In essence, the integration of forensic data, RCA, and threat intelligence transforms incident response from a purely diagnostic process into a proactive, strategic capability. By leveraging these combined insights, organizations can better prevent recurrence, strengthen defenses, and anticipate emerging threats, creating a resilient and intelligence-informed cybersecurity posture.

Challenges in Forensics and RCA

Effective digital forensics and root-cause analysis (RCA) are essential components of a robust incident response strategy. However, organizations face several practical challenges when implementing these methodologies in modern, data-intensive environments. One of the foremost challenges is the volume and variety of data generated across enterprise systems. Contemporary organizations produce massive quantities of logs from cloud services, network infrastructure, endpoints, and applications. This data is often highly heterogeneous, with differing formats, timestamps, and contextual metadata. Correlating such diverse datasets manually can overwhelm analysts and significantly slow the investigative process. Without automation and structured workflows, critical indicators of compromise (IOCs) may be overlooked, allowing attackers to operate undetected for extended periods.

Another critical concern is maintaining evidence integrity and chain-of-custody. The forensic process must ensure that all collected data is preserved in its original form, with a documented trail of who accessed it and how it was handled. Any deviation from proper evidence-handling procedures can jeopardize the legal admissibility of digital evidence and compromise compliance with regulatory requirements such as GDPR, HIPAA, or industry-specific mandates. In high-stakes investigations, even minor lapses in chain-of-custody can invalidate findings in legal proceedings or audits.

Encrypted data further complicates forensic investigations. The widespread use of encryption, while vital for protecting sensitive information, introduces additional technical barriers. Encrypted files, memory, and network traffic require specialized decryption techniques or tools to extract meaningful forensic evidence. Analysts must balance the need for decryption with privacy and legal constraints, often necessitating collaboration with security teams, legal departments, or cloud service providers.

Time sensitivity is another major challenge. Certain forms of digital evidence are highly volatile, such as memory dumps, in-memory malware processes, or transient network traffic. Delays in detecting incidents or collecting evidence can result in the permanent loss of crucial information, limiting the accuracy of the investigation and the ability to reconstruct events accurately. Rapid response, structured data collection protocols, and proactive monitoring are essential to mitigate these risks.

To address these challenges, organizations should adopt a set of **best practices** aimed at maintaining forensic readiness and improving the efficiency and reliability of RCA. This includes implementing automated triage and log-correlation tools to process large datasets quickly and accurately. Regular tabletop exercises and incident simulations can prepare teams for real-world scenarios, testing workflows, decision-making, and communication protocols. Clear evidence-handling procedures, including standardized collection, preservation, and documentation processes, ensure compliance and maintain data integrity. Additionally, organizations should establish secure storage for forensic data, employ role-based access controls, and integrate forensic workflows with threat intelligence to enhance situational awareness and expedite analysis.

By recognizing these challenges and adhering to best practices, enterprises can strengthen their forensic and RCA capabilities. This ensures that investigations are not only thorough and timely but also defensible in regulatory or legal contexts. Ultimately, a structured, proactive approach to digital forensics and root-cause analysis enables organizations to respond effectively to security incidents, minimize operational impact, and implement preventive measures to reduce the likelihood of recurrence.

Case Study: Enterprise Malware Breach

In a real-world scenario, an enterprise network was compromised by sophisticated malware introduced via phishing emails. Forensic investigation included analyzing endpoint telemetry, firewall logs, and cloud service activity. Memory dumps revealed malware injecting into legitimate processes. RCA identified that the initial compromise resulted from:

1. Lack of multi-factor authentication on remote access.
2. Delayed patching of critical endpoint vulnerabilities.
3. Insufficient employee awareness training.
4. The combined forensic and RCA approach allowed the security team to:
5. Remove malware and restore affected systems.
6. Implement preventive controls, including MFA, email filtering, and automated patch management.
7. Produce detailed reports for regulatory compliance and executive review.

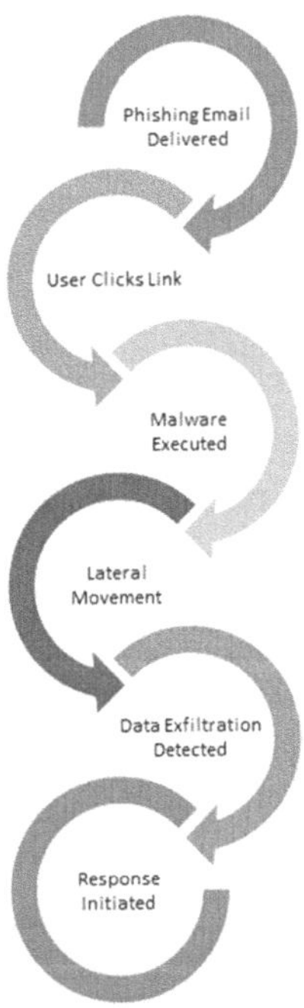

Figure 8.2: Timeline Reconstruction of the Attack

Best Practices

1. Maintain **forensic readiness** with pre-configured logging and evidence collection procedures.
2. Use **automated tools** for initial triage, while keeping manual investigation for nuanced cases.
3. Ensure **chain-of-custody** and integrity of evidence for compliance and legal purposes.
4. Integrate **threat intelligence** to contextualize findings and anticipate future threats.
5. Conduct **post-incident RCA** to improve security policies, patch management, and employee training.

Data Correlation for Attack Reconstruction

Modern cybersecurity incidents often involve multiple stages, systems, and attack vectors. A single source of data, such as a firewall log or endpoint alert, rarely provides the full picture of an attack. **Data correlation** is the process of integrating diverse sources of security-relevant information to reconstruct the sequence, scope, and impact of an incident. By correlating network logs, endpoint telemetry, authentication records, and threat intelligence feeds, security teams can map the flow of an attack, identify compromised assets, and formulate effective remediation strategies.

The Role of Data Correlation in Incident Response

The primary goal of data correlation is to transform **disparate security events** into a cohesive understanding of an incident. For example, repeated login failures observed in authentication logs may initially seem benign. However, when correlated with unusual network traffic patterns and endpoint process anomalies, these events may indicate a brute-force attack followed by lateral movement.

Data correlation improves incident response in several ways:

1. Enhanced Situational Awareness: Analysts can visualize the attack across multiple systems and understand the tactics, techniques, and procedures (TTPs) employed by adversaries.

2. Comprehensive Attack Reconstruction: Correlation helps identify the sequence of malicious actions, from initial compromise to final objectives, such as data exfiltration or ransomware deployment.
3. Prioritization and Resource Allocation: By understanding which systems or data assets were targeted, organizations can prioritize remediation and containment efforts effectively.
4. Legal and Regulatory Compliance: Correlated evidence supports forensic reporting and internal/external audits, ensuring verifiable documentation of incidents.

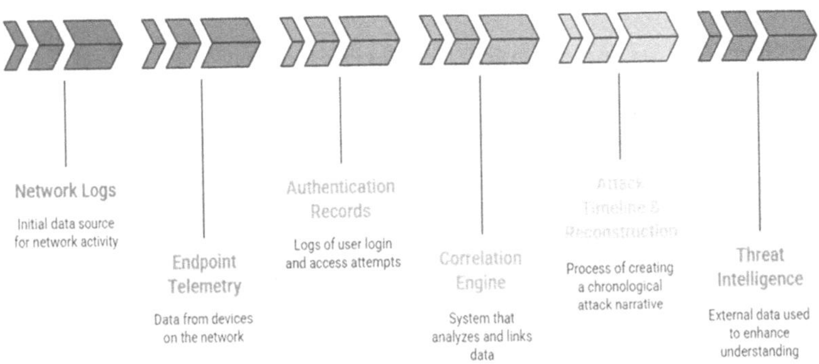

Figure 8.3: Conceptual Diagram of Data Correlation in Attack Reconstruction

In this workflow, the correlation engine ingests and normalizes data from multiple sources, identifies relationships between events, and outputs actionable insights, including attack timelines, affected assets, and probable attack vectors.

Data Sources for Correlation

Effective attack reconstruction requires integrating a wide variety of sources, each contributing unique insights:

Data Source	Contribution to Correlation	Example Use Case
Network Logs	Track traffic flows, identify unusual connections	Detect lateral movement between servers
Endpoint Telemetry	Monitor running processes, file access, malware behavior	Identify malware execution or persistence
Authentication Records	Log user login attempts, access anomalies	Detect credential misuse or insider threats
Firewall & IDS/IPS Logs	Record blocked or suspicious traffic	Map intrusion attempts and blocked vectors
Threat Intelligence Feeds	Provide context about known malware, exploits, TTPs	Correlate internal events with external threats
Cloud & SaaS Logs	Track API usage, file access, administrative actions	Identify misuse of cloud resources

Table 8.3: Common Data Sources and Correlation Contributions

Correlation Techniques

Data correlation relies on several techniques to connect events meaningfully:

1. Rule-Based Correlation: Predefined rules link events with known relationships. For example, repeated failed logins followed by a successful login from the same IP may trigger an alert.
2. Statistical Correlation: Identifies patterns that deviate from normal baselines. For instance, unusual spikes in network traffic combined with endpoint alerts may indicate data exfiltration.
3. Machine Learning-Based Correlation: Advanced models detect complex relationships and hidden patterns, flagging suspicious sequences that might evade rule-based approaches.

Visualization Tools

Visualization is essential for understanding complex attacks. Security teams use timeline charts, graph-based visualizations, and heat maps to represent correlated data.

Visualization Type	Description	Example Use Case
Timeline Chart	Chronological event sequence	Trace malware propagation
Graph-Based	Nodes represent entities; edges represent interactions	Map lateral movement across endpoints
Heat Map	Highlight activity intensity or frequency	Identify most targeted assets

Table 8.4: Visualization Approaches

Figure 8.4: Stages of a Multi-Stage Attack

Case Study: Multi-Stage Breach Reconstruction

In a real-world incident, an enterprise network was infiltrated by sophisticated malware delivered through a targeted phishing campaign. The malware was designed to evade traditional signature-based defenses, highlighting the necessity of a data-driven, forensic-led approach to incident response. Initial detection arose from anomalous endpoint behavior and unusual network traffic patterns, prompting the security operations team to initiate a structured forensic investigation.

The **digital forensic analysis** involved collecting and examining endpoint telemetry, firewall logs, and cloud service activity. Memory dumps revealed that the malware injected itself into legitimate processes, allowing it to operate stealthily while exfiltrating sensitive data. Analysis of system and application logs provided insight into the malware's lateral movement across the network, including attempts to escalate privileges and access high-value assets. Cloud service activity logs confirmed unauthorized access attempts to shared drives and sensitive applications, further illustrating the breadth of the compromise.

Concurrently, **root-cause analysis (RCA)** was performed to identify the systemic vulnerabilities and gaps that facilitated the attack. Three key factors were uncovered: the absence of multi-factor authentication (MFA) on remote access points, delayed patching of critical endpoint vulnerabilities, and insufficient employee awareness training regarding phishing threats. By understanding these root causes, the organization could implement controls to prevent recurrence.

The integration of forensic findings and RCA allowed the security team to take immediate, targeted actions. Malware was eradicated from compromised endpoints, and systems were restored from secure backups. Preventive measures, including deployment of MFA for all remote access, implementation of email filtering with phishing detection, and automated patch management, were introduced to strengthen the security posture. Additionally, the team generated comprehensive reports detailing the incident timeline, the nature of the compromise, and corrective actions taken, satisfying regulatory requirements and providing actionable intelligence for executive review.

This case study underscores the value of combining digital forensics, RCA, and threat intelligence in incident response. Forensics provided a clear picture of what happened and which systems were affected. RCA revealed why the compromise occurred and what systemic weaknesses were exploited. Together, these methodologies allowed the organization to remediate the incident efficiently, implement preventive controls, and enhance future resilience against similar attacks. It exemplifies how a data-driven, structured approach to cybersecurity enables organizations to respond decisively to complex, evolving threats.

Benefits of Data Correlation

Data correlation is a cornerstone of effective incident response, as it allows security teams to combine information from multiple sources to gain a holistic understanding of attacks. By integrating network logs, endpoint telemetry, authentication records, and threat intelligence feeds, analysts can reconstruct a comprehensive timeline of malicious activity. This consolidated perspective reduces blind spots that may occur when examining events in isolation, ensuring that subtle indicators of compromise are not overlooked. For instance, correlating failed login attempts from an endpoint with abnormal outbound network traffic can reveal potential data exfiltration attempts that might otherwise go undetected.

In addition to providing a complete view of incidents, data correlation supports the prioritization of remediation efforts. By assessing the severity and potential impact of correlated events, security teams can allocate resources to address the most critical threats first, thereby minimizing operational disruption and potential data loss. This prioritization is particularly valuable in large enterprise environments where hundreds of alerts may be generated daily.

Data correlation also enhances forensic reporting, allowing organizations to produce detailed documentation suitable for internal audits, regulatory compliance, and legal proceedings. By linking observed behaviors, exploited vulnerabilities, and impacted systems, correlated data provides verifiable evidence that demonstrates due diligence in investigating and mitigating security incidents. Furthermore, insights gained from correlated analysis can inform preventive measures. For example, patterns revealed during correlation may highlight weaknesses in network segmentation, gaps in patch management, or deficiencies in employee security training, guiding organizations toward proactive interventions that reduce the likelihood of similar incidents in the future.

Challenges and Best Practices

Despite its advantages, effective data correlation presents several challenges. One primary issue is the sheer volume and heterogeneity of security data generated by modern enterprises. Logs may come from multiple vendors, cloud services, endpoints, and network devices, each with distinct formats and standards. Integrating this diverse data while preserving accuracy and context is a non-trivial task. Additionally, maintaining data integrity and ensuring real-time correlation are essential, as delays or errors in processing can allow threats to propagate unchecked.

To address these challenges, organizations should implement centralized log aggregation and normalization platforms. Centralization ensures that all relevant data is collected and standardized into a consistent format, which is a prerequisite for accurate correlation. Automated correlation engines can then analyze these normalized logs to identify relationships and patterns that suggest malicious activity. While automation accelerates detection and response, human analyst oversight remains critical for interpreting complex or ambiguous events, validating alerts, and reducing false positives.

Integrating threat intelligence into correlation workflows further enhances context and situational awareness. For example, associating an observed IP address with known malicious infrastructure or linking a malware hash to a global threat database allows security teams to distinguish between benign anomalies and serious threats. Regular testing and validation of correlation rules and machine learning models ensure that the system remains effective as new attack techniques emerge and the IT environment evolves. These best practices collectively enable organizations to leverage data correlation to strengthen incident detection, response, and overall cybersecurity resilience.

Automating Incident Response with Data

In today's cybersecurity landscape, the velocity, volume, and sophistication of attacks often surpass the capacity of human analysts to respond effectively. Traditional manual incident response processes, while thorough and methodical, can be slow and inconsistent, particularly in organizations with large-scale infrastructures generating high-volume alert streams. Delays in responding to threats increase the risk of data exfiltration, operational disruption, and reputational damage. Consequently, automation has become a cornerstone of modern incident response, leveraging data analytics to accelerate detection, coordination, and remediation activities.

Automated incident response systems draw upon insights generated from security monitoring platforms such as Security Information and Event Management (SIEM), Security Orchestration, Automation, and Response (SOAR), and endpoint detection tools. These systems continuously collect and analyze vast amounts of security data, converting raw logs, telemetry, and alerts into actionable intelligence. Once a potential threat is identified, automated workflows can execute predefined mitigation steps, including isolating affected endpoints, revoking compromised credentials, blocking malicious IP addresses, or triggering alerts to incident response teams. By executing these responses rapidly and consistently, automation significantly reduces both the mean time to detect (MTTD) and mean time to respond (MTTR), critical metrics in operational security.

A practical example of automation in action can be seen in the handling of phishing attacks. When a phishing email is detected through email security gateways or anomaly detection in SIEM logs, an automated workflow may quarantine the email, notify the intended recipient, and initiate a scan of affected endpoints for potential compromise. Simultaneously, the SOAR platform can enrich the alert with threat intelligence, including indicators of compromise (IOCs) associated with the phishing campaign, and document all actions taken for audit purposes. This orchestration ensures that human analysts are not overwhelmed by repetitive tasks while maintaining a high standard of accuracy and response speed.

Automation also enhances consistency and compliance in incident response. Manual processes can vary across teams and shifts, creating gaps in coverage and potential errors. Automated playbooks standardize responses based on best practices and organizational policies, ensuring that each incident is handled in accordance with pre-approved procedures. Additionally, these playbooks generate comprehensive logs of all actions taken, facilitating internal reporting, regulatory compliance, and post-incident review. For example, automated containment of ransomware infections, coupled with documented forensic snapshots of affected systems, enables organizations to meet regulatory requirements while preserving evidence for further investigation.

The integration of machine learning and analytics into automated incident response further strengthens its effectiveness. Predictive models can anticipate the progression of attacks, identify high-risk assets, and dynamically adjust mitigation strategies. For instance, if a malware strain is known to propagate laterally across endpoints, the system can proactively isolate network segments and alert administrators to potential target machines. Such predictive automation transforms incident response from a reactive activity into a proactive defense mechanism, improving organizational resilience against sophisticated, multi-stage attacks.

However, automation is not a substitute for human expertise. Complex incidents often require nuanced judgment, contextual understanding, and strategic decision-making that cannot be fully encoded into workflows. Best practices emphasize a hybrid approach, where automation handles high-volume, repetitive, or time-sensitive tasks, while skilled analysts focus on investigation, threat hunting, and decision-making. This combination optimizes operational efficiency, ensures comprehensive threat mitigation, and allows security teams to adapt dynamically to evolving threat landscapes.

The Role of Automation in Incident Response

The primary goal of automation in incident response is to ensure that detected threats are addressed rapidly, consistently, and in a repeatable manner. In high-volume security environments, where SIEM and endpoint monitoring systems generate thousands of alerts daily, human analysts alone cannot maintain the necessary pace or accuracy to respond effectively. By integrating automated processes with human oversight, organizations can achieve accelerated response times, operational efficiency, improved accuracy, and proactive threat mitigation.

Automation enables the execution of predefined actions as soon as a threat is detected. For instance, if a malware alert is triggered by endpoint telemetry, automated playbooks can isolate affected machines, block malicious IP addresses, revoke compromised credentials, and initiate network-wide scans—all within seconds. This capability reduces the mean time to detect (MTTD) and the mean time to respond (MTTR), minimizing the window in which attackers can cause damage. In contrast, manual intervention may take hours, during which lateral movement, privilege escalation, or data exfiltration can occur.

Consistency is another critical advantage. Predefined workflows standardize responses according to organizational policies and best practices, reducing variability that may arise from different analysts, shifts, or locations. Automation ensures that containment, notification, and remediation actions are executed accurately across all affected systems. This repeatability not only strengthens security posture but also enhances compliance with regulatory requirements, as consistent processes provide verifiable audit trails for legal and governance purposes.

Operational efficiency is enhanced by relieving security analysts from repetitive or time-consuming tasks. Instead of manually isolating endpoints or scanning logs, analysts can focus on advanced tasks such as threat hunting, anomaly investigation, vulnerability management, and root-cause analysis. For example, once automated systems flag a potential insider threat through anomalous behavior in network traffic, analysts can concentrate on understanding the broader context, identifying systemic vulnerabilities, and implementing strategic controls to prevent recurrence.

Automation also supports proactive threat mitigation. Advanced systems can leverage predictive analytics, historical incident data, and threat intelligence to anticipate attack progression. For example, if a ransomware variant is known to attempt lateral movement and exfiltrate sensitive files before encryption, automated workflows can isolate critical servers, block file transfer protocols, and alert administrators in advance of widespread compromise. This proactive approach transforms incident response from a reactive activity into a forward-looking defense strategy, significantly reducing potential operational and financial impact.

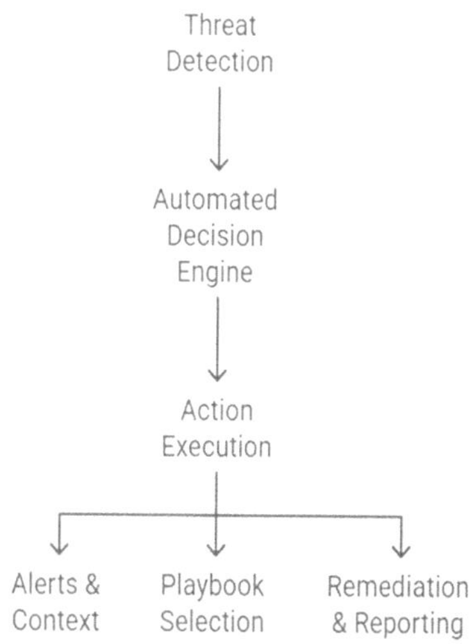

Figure 8.5: Conceptual Framework for Automated Incident Response

In this framework, incoming alerts are enriched with contextual information from multiple sources, including threat intelligence feeds, endpoint telemetry, and network activity logs. The automated decision engine evaluates the threat, selects an appropriate playbook, and executes remediation steps across the relevant systems. Simultaneously, detailed records of all actions, decisions, and outcomes are generated, supporting compliance audits, post-incident review, and continuous improvement of response strategies.

By integrating automated processes with human oversight, organizations can balance speed and accuracy with strategic analysis. While automation handles routine, repetitive, or high-volume tasks efficiently, security professionals focus on complex investigations, threat modeling, and proactive defense. This hybrid approach ensures that data-driven incident response remains resilient, adaptive, and capable of addressing the evolving cyber threat landscape.

Data Sources for Automation

Automated incident response relies on the integration of diverse data sources to accurately detect, analyze, and respond to cyber threats in real time. These inputs provide the raw information necessary for triggering workflows, making informed decisions, and executing predefined actions. Key sources include SIEM alerts, endpoint detection and response telemetry, threat intelligence feeds, and network monitoring data. By leveraging multiple data streams, organizations can ensure comprehensive visibility, reduce false positives, and improve the effectiveness of automated workflows.

SIEM Alerts form the primary layer of detection in automated response systems. Security Information and Event Management platforms continuously aggregate logs from endpoints, servers, applications, and network devices. When anomalies are detected, such as repeated failed login attempts or unusual data transfers, SIEM generates alerts that can automatically trigger corresponding response playbooks. For example, a spike in failed authentication attempts across multiple endpoints may prompt an automated workflow to temporarily lock affected accounts and notify administrators, reducing the risk of brute-force attacks.

Endpoint Detection and Response (EDR) systems provide detailed telemetry about processes, files, and user activities on endpoints. EDR data enables automation platforms to isolate infected machines, terminate malicious processes, and perform forensic snapshots without human intervention. In a ransomware scenario, EDR telemetry might reveal a process encrypting multiple files on a workstation. An automated response can immediately isolate that endpoint from the network, preventing lateral movement and limiting potential data loss.

Threat Intelligence Feeds enrich automated response actions with external context about known threats, malware signatures, malicious IP addresses, and TTPs of threat actors. By incorporating threat intelligence, automated systems can dynamically update firewall rules, IDS/IPS signatures, and endpoint policies to proactively block identified threats. For instance, if a known phishing campaign targeting finance departments is observed globally, threat feeds can inform the automation engine to flag and quarantine related emails across the organization before users engage with them.

Network Telemetry captures traffic flows, anomalies, and patterns indicative of lateral movement, privilege escalation, or data exfiltration. Automated response platforms use this telemetry to throttle anomalous traffic, block suspicious IP addresses, and dynamically implement network segmentation. For example, detecting an unusual outbound data stream to an unrecognized external server may trigger automated firewall adjustments and generate alerts for analyst review, effectively preventing sensitive data exfiltration.

Data Source	Automation Use Case	Benefit
SIEM Alerts	Trigger workflow playbooks for anomalies	Faster response to incidents
EDR Telemetry	Automatically isolate infected endpoints	Contain malware spread
Threat Intelligence Feeds	Update firewall/IDS rules dynamically	Prevent known threats from infiltrating
Network Telemetry	Block suspicious IPs, throttle anomalous traffic	Mitigate lateral movement and exfiltration

Table 8.5: Key Data Inputs and Automation Use Cases

Integrating these data sources enables a holistic, multi-layered approach to automated incident response. Workflows can prioritize alerts by severity, correlate endpoint and network anomalies, and execute preventive measures in real time. For example, a combined detection of unusual outbound traffic (network telemetry), a new malicious process (EDR), and a known malware signature (threat intelligence feed) can trigger an automated containment sequence while notifying the security operations center for further investigation.

Automation Workflows and Playbooks

Central to effective automated incident response are playbooks, which serve as predefined sequences of actions triggered when specific security conditions are detected. Playbooks translate detection signals—such as alerts from SIEM platforms, endpoint telemetry, or threat intelligence feeds—into a structured response workflow that can be executed consistently and efficiently. By formalizing response procedures, playbooks ensure that security operations teams act quickly and accurately, minimizing human error and improving incident containment.

Playbooks can vary from relatively simple rule-based sequences to sophisticated AI-driven orchestration processes. In simpler implementations, a specific alert may trigger a direct action, such as isolating a compromised endpoint. In more advanced systems, playbooks incorporate decision engines that analyze multiple data sources, evaluate contextual threat information, and select the optimal response workflow dynamically. This integration allows automated responses to adapt to evolving attack patterns and organizational priorities.

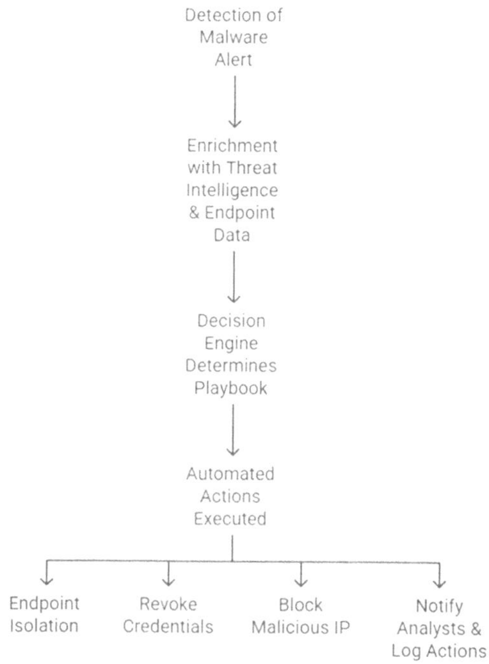

Figure 8.6: Sample Automated Incident Response Workflow for Malware Detection

In the example workflow above, the system first detects a malware-related alert, which is then enriched with contextual data from threat intelligence feeds and endpoint telemetry. This enrichment ensures that the automated response considers not only the immediate threat but also any relevant patterns, adversary indicators, or environmental factors. The decision engine evaluates the collected information and selects the appropriate playbook. Finally, the system executes a series of automated actions, such as isolating affected endpoints, revoking compromised credentials, blocking malicious IP addresses, and notifying analysts, while logging all activities for compliance and post-incident review.

Step No	Action	Data Required	Automation Tool Used
1	Detect suspicious email	Email gateway logs	SIEM/Email Security
2	Analyze attachment/link	Threat intelligence feed	SOAR/EDR
3	Quarantine email and affected endpoints	Endpoint telemetry	SOAR
4	Notify user and security team	Incident logging system	SOAR/Communication
5	Document incident	SIEM and playbook logs	Automated Reporting

Table 8.6: Example of Playbook Steps for Phishing Email Response

The table illustrates a typical playbook for handling phishing emails, showing the integration of multiple data sources and automation tools. Each step corresponds to a specific action informed by input data, with the entire process executed consistently across all affected systems. This ensures that similar incidents are handled uniformly, reducing the likelihood of missed threats or human error.

Playbooks also enhance operational efficiency by freeing security analysts from repetitive tasks, allowing them to focus on high-value activities such as threat hunting, forensic investigation, and strategic planning. Furthermore, the consistent documentation produced by automated playbooks supports regulatory compliance, audits, and internal reporting requirements.

By incorporating playbooks into an automated incident response framework, organizations achieve several critical objectives: rapid threat containment, standardized response procedures, continuous monitoring, and improved integration with broader security analytics and threat intelligence systems. The result is a resilient, proactive, and scalable approach to incident response capable of keeping pace with increasingly sophisticated cyber threats.

Integration with SIEM and SOAR Platforms

Automation in incident response does not operate in isolation; it is most effective when integrated with Security Information and Event

Management (SIEM) and Security Orchestration, Automation, and Response (SOAR) systems. SIEM platforms serve as the foundational detection layer, aggregating logs from diverse sources—such as endpoints, network devices, applications, and cloud services—and correlating them to generate alerts for potential security incidents. These alerts provide the raw input that drives automated response mechanisms, ensuring that timely action can be taken without waiting for manual intervention.

SOAR platforms act as the orchestration layer, receiving alerts from SIEM systems and determining appropriate response workflows through predefined playbooks. By leveraging automation engines, SOAR can execute tasks such as endpoint isolation, credential revocation, network blocking, and alert notifications while maintaining comprehensive logging and reporting. This orchestration ensures that security responses are not only consistent but also aligned with organizational policies and threat intelligence insights.

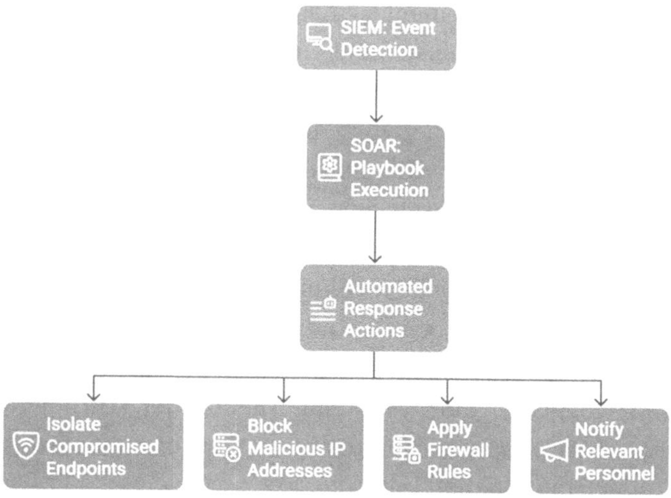

Figure 8.7: Integration of SIEM, SOAR, and Automation in Incident Response

The figure illustrates the dynamic interplay between detection, orchestration, and automation. Initially, the SIEM platform identifies anomalous or suspicious activity and generates an alert. This alert triggers a corresponding SOAR playbook, which specifies the sequence of automated response actions. The automated actions, in turn, can include isolating compromised endpoints, blocking malicious IP addresses, applying firewall rules, and notifying relevant personnel.

Importantly, this integrated approach establishes a continuous feedback loop. Automated actions are monitored and evaluated in real-time, allowing analysts to review and escalate incidents that require human judgment. The outcomes of these incidents—successful containment, partial remediation, or false positives—inform the refinement of playbooks and automation rules. Over time, this iterative process enhances the accuracy, efficiency, and reliability of automated incident response.

Integration with threat intelligence further strengthens this ecosystem. SIEM and SOAR platforms can enrich alerts with contextual data, such as known malware signatures, adversary tactics, and exploit indicators. Automation engines leverage this information to prioritize response actions, apply targeted mitigations, and prevent lateral movement or data exfiltration. For example, if a SIEM alert indicates suspicious outbound traffic and threat intelligence confirms a known exfiltration pattern, the SOAR platform can automatically trigger network throttling, endpoint isolation, and escalation notifications simultaneously.

This integrated model not only accelerates incident containment but also reduces operational burdens on security teams. Analysts are no longer overwhelmed by high volumes of alerts or routine response tasks; instead, they can focus on advanced threat hunting, forensic investigations, and strategic risk mitigation. Furthermore, the structured logging and reporting generated throughout the automation cycle support regulatory compliance, audit readiness, and executive decision-making.

In practice, organizations that adopt this integrated approach often achieve significant improvements in key metrics such as mean time to detection (MTTD) and mean time to response (MTTR). By combining SIEM's detection capabilities, SOAR's orchestration and automation, and continuous analyst oversight, enterprises can maintain resilience against rapidly evolving cyber threats while ensuring operational efficiency, accuracy, and compliance.

Case Study: Automated Incident Response in a Ransomware Outbreak

Ransomware attacks represent one of the most urgent and destructive threats facing modern enterprises, particularly in sectors like financial services, healthcare, and critical infrastructure. The speed at which ransomware propagates across endpoints often outpaces the capacity of manual response teams, making automation a critical component of effective incident containment. The following case study illustrates the application of a data-driven automated incident response system in mitigating a ransomware outbreak in a financial services organization.

The incident began when a SIEM platform detected unusual file encryption activity on multiple endpoints within the corporate network. These alerts were correlated with endpoint telemetry, which confirmed that ransomware processes were actively executing. This combination of detection and verification triggered the organization's SOAR platform, which automatically initiated predefined playbooks designed for ransomware containment. The playbooks included several coordinated actions executed without human intervention, ensuring rapid and consistent mitigation:

- Endpoint Isolation: Infected systems were immediately disconnected from the corporate network to prevent further lateral movement.
- Account Revocation: User accounts associated with the initial infection were automatically suspended to halt any unauthorized access attempts.
- Network Blocking: External IP addresses communicating with the ransomware command-and-control (C2) servers were dynamically blocked at the firewall and intrusion prevention systems.
- Analyst Notifications: Real-time alerts, including enriched forensic data, were sent to the security operations center for oversight and verification.

- Automated Reporting: Incident logs, telemetry, and threat intelligence enrichment were compiled automatically into reports to satisfy internal and regulatory compliance requirements.

The integration of SIEM, SOAR, and automation drastically reduced the mean time to response (MTTR) from several hours—typical for a manual response scenario—to under ten minutes. As a result, the ransomware propagation was effectively contained, preventing significant data loss and minimizing operational disruption. This rapid mitigation also allowed analysts to focus on strategic tasks, such as identifying the root cause of the infection, analyzing malware behavior, and refining defensive controls for future resilience.

Beyond operational efficiency, this case highlights additional benefits of a data-driven automated response system. By leveraging enriched data and threat intelligence within the playbooks, the organization was able to anticipate potential lateral movement and preemptively block attack vectors. Furthermore, the automated documentation provided a verifiable audit trail, facilitating compliance with regulatory frameworks such as GDPR, SOX, and PCI DSS, and supporting internal post-incident reviews and lessons-learned sessions.

This scenario underscores the strategic value of automation in cybersecurity operations. High-speed attacks like ransomware demand rapid, coordinated responses that combine detection, orchestration, and remediation. Organizations that integrate SIEM and SOAR with automated workflows can achieve faster containment, reduced operational burden, and improved overall resilience against increasingly sophisticated cyber threats.

Benefits of Data-Driven Automation

Data-driven automation has become a cornerstone of modern incident response, particularly in environments where high-volume alerts and sophisticated attacks exceed human operational capacity. One of the primary benefits is rapid threat mitigation. By executing predefined workflows immediately upon detection, automated systems contain malware, isolate compromised endpoints, revoke credentials, and block malicious network traffic in real time. This rapid intervention minimizes operational disruption, prevents lateral movement of attackers, and reduces the overall impact on critical assets. For example, in a ransomware outbreak scenario, automated playbooks can contain the infection across multiple endpoints within minutes, compared to hours required for manual intervention.

Another key advantage is operational efficiency. Automation reduces the repetitive workload on security analysts, who otherwise would spend significant time manually triaging alerts, isolating systems, and compiling incident reports. By offloading routine tasks to automated processes, analysts can focus on strategic functions such as threat hunting, root-cause analysis, and system hardening. This not only improves staff productivity but also enhances the organization's overall security posture.

Consistency and compliance represent additional benefits. Standardized automated playbooks ensure that every security event is handled according to established procedures, minimizing the risk of human error. Furthermore, automated logging and reporting create a verifiable audit trail that supports regulatory compliance with frameworks such as GDPR, SOX, PCI DSS, and HIPAA. Organizations can demonstrate that threats were addressed systematically and according to policy, reinforcing accountability and transparency.

Finally, automation provides scalability. As enterprises grow in size and complexity, the volume of security alerts can increase exponentially. Automated response systems can scale to handle thousands of alerts simultaneously without proportional increases in staffing or operational cost. This allows organizations to maintain robust incident response capabilities even in high-demand environments.

Benefit	Description	Example Use Case
Rapid Threat Mitigation	Immediate execution of predefined workflows	Containment of ransomware before lateral movement
Operational Efficiency	Analysts focus on strategic tasks	Threat hunting, vulnerability assessment
Consistency and Compliance	Standardized actions with automated documentation	Regulatory reporting, audit readiness
Scalability	Handles high alert volume without added staff	Enterprise-wide intrusion detection response

Table 8.7: Key Benefits of Data-Driven Automation

Challenges and Best Practices

Despite these advantages, data-driven automation is not without challenges. False positives remain a critical concern; automated systems may act on incorrect or low-confidence alerts, potentially disrupting legitimate business operations. Complexity is another challenge, as developing, testing, and maintaining comprehensive playbooks for diverse attack scenarios is resource-intensive and requires specialized expertise. Additionally, integration issues can arise if SIEM, SOAR, endpoint telemetry, and network tools do not communicate seamlessly, creating gaps in detection or response. Lastly, human oversight is essential; while automation handles routine tasks efficiently, critical decisions—such as releasing sensitive data or authorizing high-risk actions—must remain under analyst control.

To address these challenges, several best practices are recommended. Organizations should implement tiered automation, where high-confidence actions, such as endpoint isolation or blocking known malicious IPs, are executed automatically, while low-confidence alerts are escalated to human analysts for validation. Continuous playbook updates informed by threat intelligence and post-incident lessons ensure that automated workflows remain effective against evolving attack vectors. Monitoring and auditing automated actions help detect errors, inefficiencies, or unintended consequences. Finally, integrating automation with human expertise creates a hybrid response model, combining the speed and consistency of machines with the contextual judgment and strategic thinking of security analysts.

Figure 8.8: Hybrid Automated Incident Response Model

This integrated approach ensures organizations benefit from automation while maintaining accuracy, adaptability, and compliance. By implementing these best practices, enterprises can maximize the effectiveness of data-driven incident response, reduce risk exposure, and maintain resilience against sophisticated, high-speed cyber threats.

Conclusion

Chapter 8 has explored the critical role of data-driven approaches in modern incident response, emphasizing the synergy between forensic investigation, root-cause analysis, data correlation, and automation. Effective incident response is no longer a reactive process; it demands proactive, evidence-based strategies to detect, contain, and remediate cyber threats efficiently. The chapter demonstrated that forensic investigations form the foundation for incident understanding, enabling organizations to reconstruct events, identify exploited vulnerabilities, and implement corrective measures. Root-cause analysis ensures that breaches are not merely addressed superficially but are used to enhance systemic defenses, reduce recurrence, and support compliance with legal and regulatory frameworks.

Data correlation further extends the effectiveness of incident response by integrating disparate sources of information, including network logs, endpoint telemetry, authentication records, and threat intelligence feeds. By synthesizing this information into a coherent timeline, security teams gain a holistic view of attacks, uncovering complex patterns such as lateral movement, privilege escalation, and data exfiltration. This comprehensive understanding supports prioritized remediation, improves strategic planning, and provides verifiable evidence for legal, regulatory, or internal reporting purposes.

Automation emerges as a key enabler in modern security operations, reducing both human workload and response latency. Data-driven automated workflows enable rapid threat containment by isolating affected systems, revoking compromised credentials, blocking malicious traffic, and triggering alerts to response teams. Automation ensures consistency and precision while freeing analysts to focus on proactive threat hunting, vulnerability management, and decision-making. The integration of real-time analytics with automated response mechanisms transforms incident management from a reactive activity to a proactive, continuous defense strategy.

Throughout this chapter, several practical frameworks and workflows were presented, highlighting the interplay between manual forensic expertise, correlation of diverse data sources, and automated response actions. Case studies demonstrated how these processes enable early detection, precise containment, and informed mitigation, minimizing operational disruption and financial loss. Organizations that embrace a data-driven approach to incident response achieve higher resilience, faster recovery, and greater alignment with cybersecurity best practices.

This Data-driven incident response represents a paradigm shift from isolated, manual processes to integrated, analytics-based security operations. By combining forensics, correlation, and automation, organizations can detect threats more accurately, respond faster, and continuously improve their security posture. The insights gained from these processes not only mitigate immediate risks but also inform long-term strategies, building organizational resilience in an increasingly complex and adversarial cyber landscape.

Key Terms

1. Digital Forensics – The systematic investigation and analysis of digital evidence to reconstruct events and understand security incidents.
2. Root-Cause Analysis (RCA) – A methodology for identifying the underlying causes of security incidents to prevent recurrence.
3. Incident Response (IR) – Structured processes for detecting, investigating, mitigating, and recovering from security events.
4. Data Correlation – Integration of multiple data sources to reveal relationships and reconstruct attack sequences.
5. Endpoint Telemetry – Monitoring data from devices (computers, mobile devices) used to detect anomalies and attacks.
6. Lateral Movement – Techniques used by attackers to navigate within a network to access additional resources.
7. Privilege Escalation – Exploiting vulnerabilities to gain higher access rights than initially permitted.
8. Data Exfiltration – Unauthorized transfer of sensitive data outside an organization's network.
9. Automation in IR – Use of automated tools and workflows to execute repetitive or time-sensitive response actions.
10. Playbook – Predefined set of procedures guiding automated or manual incident response steps.

11. Threat Intelligence Feed – Stream of data providing information about known threats and indicators of compromise (IOCs).
12. Mean Time to Detect (MTTD) – Average time taken to identify a security incident.
13. Mean Time to Respond (MTTR) – Average time taken to contain and mitigate a security incident.
14. Chain of Custody – Documentation of evidence handling to ensure its integrity and admissibility.
15. Security Orchestration – Integration and coordination of multiple security tools and processes for efficient operations.

Review Questions

1. What is the primary goal of data-driven incident response?
2. How does digital forensics contribute to understanding cyber incidents?
3. Define root-cause analysis and explain its importance in incident response.
4. How can network logs be used to reconstruct an attack timeline?
5. What is endpoint telemetry, and why is it critical for incident response?
6. Explain the concept of lateral movement and its implications.
7. How does privilege escalation affect organizational security?
8. What is data exfiltration, and how can it be detected?
9. Discuss the benefits of integrating multiple data sources for attack reconstruction.
10. How does data correlation improve situational awareness for security teams?
11. What are the advantages of automating incident response workflows?
12. Describe a sample automated workflow for isolating affected endpoints.
13. How does automation reduce mean time to detect (MTTD) and mean time to respond (MTTR)?

14. What role do threat intelligence feeds play in incident response?
15. Explain the importance of maintaining a chain of custody during forensic investigations.
16. How can playbooks enhance consistency in response actions?
17. Compare manual versus automated incident response strategies.
18. Discuss common challenges in implementing automated incident response.
19. How can data-driven IR support regulatory compliance?
20. Give an example of correlating authentication logs and network traffic for attack reconstruction.
21. What is the relationship between forensic analysis and root-cause identification?
22. How do real-time analytics improve the effectiveness of incident response?
23. Discuss the role of human expertise in a largely automated IR environment.
24. What are the risks of relying solely on automation without human oversight?
25. How does integrating forensics, data correlation, and automation contribute to organizational resilience?

Part IV

Practical Implementations

INTRODUCTION

The increasing sophistication of cyber threats has moved data security and analytics from a conceptual framework into a strategic necessity that organizations must implement with precision. While theoretical models and high-level strategies provide the blueprint for securing digital infrastructure, their true value is realized only through practical implementation in real-world environments. Practical implementation refers to the operationalization of security policies, analytical frameworks, and technological tools in ways that directly protect systems, detect anomalies, and enable timely responses to evolving threats. In modern cyber defense, this step is particularly critical because adversaries exploit not the weaknesses of theory, but the gaps that emerge in applied practice.

Implementing robust data security begins with embedding protective mechanisms across the full data lifecycle—creation, storage, transmission, processing, and eventual disposal. Encryption technologies, for instance, must be consistently integrated into both in-transit and at-rest scenarios to prevent unauthorized interception. Equally, access controls and authentication protocols need to be tailored to organizational contexts, ensuring that only legitimate users interact with sensitive data. However, effective implementation extends beyond technical measures; it involves creating workflows, policies, and cultural awareness that reinforce security at every organizational layer. Practical implementation, therefore, combines technological rigor with human adaptability, embedding security into daily operations rather than treating it as an afterthought.

Analytics plays an equally significant role in operationalizing cyber defense strategies. In practice, analytics involves the deployment of systems capable of ingesting massive data streams—logs, traffic patterns, user behaviors—and translating them into actionable intelligence. Modern Security Information and Event

Management (SIEM) systems, combined with User and Entity Behavior Analytics (UEBA), exemplify how advanced analytics can move from theory to real-world defense by identifying patterns that indicate malicious activity. For instance, a practical implementation may involve correlating login attempts from unusual geolocations with abnormal data transfer volumes to flag potential insider threats or compromised accounts. The success of such systems depends not only on sophisticated algorithms but also on seamless integration with existing infrastructure and workflows.

One of the defining challenges of practical implementation is the gap between theoretical security designs and the constraints of operational environments. Budget limitations, legacy systems, and workforce expertise often dictate the feasibility of deployment. For example, while zero-trust architecture is widely recognized as a best-practice model, its practical rollout requires step-by-step adoption, continuous monitoring, and retraining of staff, which can be resource-intensive. Similarly, while advanced machine learning models may promise predictive threat detection, their effectiveness depends on clean, representative data and the ability to minimize false positives, which in practice requires iterative calibration and human oversight.

Importantly, practical implementation is never a one-time exercise but a continuous process of adaptation. Cyber adversaries constantly refine their tactics, techniques, and procedures, which means that security measures and analytical tools must be regularly updated, tested, and evaluated. Practical implementation, therefore, embodies a cycle: deploy, monitor, assess, and refine. Organizations that excel in cyber defense are those that can operationalize theoretical insights quickly, align them with regulatory and business requirements, and maintain the agility to respond to novel attack vectors as they emerge.

In summary, practical implementation represents the bridge between the conceptual foundations of data security and analytics and their tangible impact on organizational resilience. It demands a balance between technology, process, and human expertise, ensuring that strategies are not confined to policy documents but are actively defending systems in real time. By grounding cyber defense efforts in practical, adaptable, and iterative applications, organizations can transform abstract models into effective shields against the complex threat landscape of the digital age.

CHAPTER 9

Vulnerability and Risk Assessment Using Data

Learning Objectives

By the end of this chapter, readers should be able to:

1. Define key concepts of vulnerability, threat, and risk in the context of cybersecurity and data protection.
2. Explain the role of data in identifying, quantifying, and prioritizing vulnerabilities within organizational systems.
3. Understand frameworks and methodologies commonly used in vulnerability and risk assessment (e.g., NIST, ISO 27005, and FAIR).
4. Differentiate between qualitative and quantitative approaches to risk assessment and their practical applications.
5. Apply data-driven techniques to evaluate system vulnerabilities and predict potential exploitation scenarios.
6. Interpret vulnerability assessment outputs, including CVSS scores, penetration test reports, and automated scan results.
7. Assess the impact and likelihood of risks by leveraging historical incident data, threat intelligence, and analytics.
8. Integrate vulnerability data into organizational decision-making, including prioritization of remediation efforts.
9. Develop a risk treatment plan that aligns with business objectives, compliance requirements, and resource constraints.
10. Evaluate the effectiveness of risk mitigation strategies through continuous monitoring and feedback loops.

11. Recognize limitations and challenges in data-driven vulnerability and risk assessment, including data quality issues and false positives.
12. Explore emerging trends such as AI-driven risk prediction, automation in vulnerability management, and adaptive defense strategies.

Overview

In cybersecurity discourse, three interrelated terms—vulnerability, threat, and risk—form the backbone of any discussion on security management. *Vulnerability* refers to a weakness or flaw in a system, application, process, or network that can be exploited to compromise confidentiality, integrity, or availability. Examples include unpatched software, weak authentication mechanisms, or misconfigured servers. A *threat* is any circumstance or actor—malicious or accidental—that has the potential to exploit these vulnerabilities. This can range from external hackers and insider threats to natural disasters or human error. *Risk*, by extension, is the calculated likelihood that a threat will exploit vulnerability and the potential impact of such exploitation on organizational assets, business operations, and stakeholders. Thus, risk serves as the practical intersection between vulnerabilities and threats, guiding organizations in determining which security issues require urgent attention and resources.

In the modern cyber defense landscape, traditional approaches to vulnerability and risk assessment are no longer sufficient. The increasing complexity of IT ecosystems—spanning cloud environments, mobile devices, IoT systems, and hybrid infrastructures—has dramatically expanded the attack surface. At the same time, cyber adversaries have become more agile, leveraging automation, machine learning, and global threat intelligence to execute highly targeted attacks. In this environment, data-driven approaches are indispensable. Unlike static checklists or periodic audits, data-driven methods continuously ingest, process, and analyze diverse data sources—system logs, vulnerability feeds, penetration test results, and behavioral analytics—to provide dynamic, context-rich assessments. This integration of analytics into vulnerability management allows organizations to not only identify potential weaknesses but also to quantify their risks in real time, prioritize remediation based on business impact, and measure the effectiveness of their defense strategies.

The evolution of vulnerability assessment reflects the larger trajectory of cybersecurity itself. In the early stages of the field, assessments were largely manual, relying on human auditors who examined code, configurations, and policies. While valuable, these methods were time-consuming, prone to oversight, and difficult to scale. The second phase emerged with the rise of automated vulnerability scanners in the late 1990s and early 2000s, such as Nessus or Qualys, which enabled organizations to identify known vulnerabilities more efficiently across larger infrastructures. However, these tools often produced overwhelming volumes of findings without effective prioritization, leading to alert fatigue. The current era has shifted toward intelligence-driven and risk-centric models. These approaches integrate vulnerability scanning with contextual data, business asset valuation, and predictive analytics. They leverage frameworks such as the Common Vulnerability Scoring System (CVSS) alongside advanced machine learning techniques to rank vulnerabilities not only by technical severity but also by exploitability and organizational relevance. This historical progression underscores the field's movement from reactive detection toward proactive and predictive defense.

The objective of this chapter is to explore how vulnerabilities and risks can be systematically assessed using data-driven methodologies. It seeks to clarify the principles of risk scoring, illustrate the importance of prioritization based on business impact, and demonstrate how vulnerability assessment can be seamlessly integrated into modern development lifecycles such as Agile and DevOps. In doing so, the chapter emphasizes both the theoretical underpinnings and the practical realities of operationalizing these frameworks. By the end, readers will understand how data transforms vulnerability and risk assessment from a static compliance exercise into a dynamic, adaptive component of modern cyber defense—one that is essential for safeguarding organizational assets in an increasingly hostile digital environment.

Foundations of Vulnerability and Risk Assessment

Understanding the foundations of vulnerability and risk assessment is critical to developing a systematic approach to modern cyber defense. At its core, this process requires a clear conceptual distinction among vulnerabilities, threats, and risks, as these terms often overlap in both technical and managerial discussions but serve distinct purposes in shaping defense strategies. A vulnerability refers to a specific weakness in a system, such as outdated software, default configurations, or insufficient encryption practices, which creates an opportunity for exploitation. A threat, by contrast, is the potential cause of an unwanted incident, ranging from cybercriminals exploiting a flaw to environmental hazards such as a power outage disrupting a data center. Risk emerges at the intersection of these two concepts, representing the probability that a threat will exploit a vulnerability and the potential consequences if such an event occurs. This triangular relationship is often visualized in risk management frameworks as a formula: Risk = Threat × Vulnerability × Impact. In practice, this formula underscores that not every vulnerability equates to a high risk. For instance, a critical vulnerability in a system isolated from external access may present far less risk than a lower-severity flaw in a mission-critical, internet-facing application.

Traditionally, organizations approached vulnerability and risk assessment through static, checklist-driven methodologies. Early assessments often relied on manual audits in which security professionals examined system configurations, network layouts, and codebases against best-practice guidelines. This approach, while systematic, was heavily resource-intensive and prone to human error. The logic behind manual auditing was that security experts, applying their knowledge, could identify flaws before adversaries did. Yet as enterprise infrastructures expanded and digitization accelerated, the limitations of this approach became apparent. Manual audits could not keep pace with the constant influx of new vulnerabilities—now cataloged at a rate of more than 25,000 annually in the Common Vulnerabilities and Exposures (CVE) database. Moreover, periodic audits provided only a snapshot in time, leaving organizations exposed between assessments.

The emergence of automated vulnerability scanning represented a significant shift in practice. Tools such as Nessus, OpenVAS, and Qualys enabled enterprises to systematically scan networks, applications, and endpoints for known vulnerabilities at scale. Automated tools dramatically reduced the labor required to identify flaws, delivering reports within hours rather than weeks. However, these tools also introduced challenges, particularly the tendency to generate overwhelming volumes of results with limited prioritization. For example, a single network scan might return thousands of vulnerabilities, many of which are redundant, misclassified, or irrelevant to business operations. This gave rise to what practitioners call "alert fatigue," where security teams, overwhelmed by the volume of findings, struggle to distinguish between critical risks and inconsequential issues.

In response, the field evolved toward data-driven vulnerability and risk assessment, which incorporates analytics, contextualization, and automation into the process. Data-driven approaches go beyond identifying whether a vulnerability exists to evaluating its exploitability, relevance, and potential business impact. By combining internal telemetry, such as system logs or asset inventories, with external threat intelligence feeds, organizations can assess not just whether a flaw is present but whether it is actively being targeted in the wild. For instance, an SQL injection vulnerability in a low-priority application might appear severe based on technical scoring alone, but if no active exploits are observed in current threat intelligence, its risk rating may be adjusted downward. Conversely, a seemingly minor misconfiguration in a cloud service may be escalated to high risk if data analysis reveals it aligns with tactics observed in recent attack campaigns. The logic of data-driven assessment is thus rooted in contextual prioritization, enabling organizations to focus on remediation efforts that deliver the greatest reduction in real-world risk.

Regulatory and compliance frameworks have also played a central role in shaping the evolution of vulnerability and risk assessment. The National Institute of Standards and Technology (NIST) provides detailed guidelines for risk management and vulnerability assessment, notably in its Risk Management Framework (RMF) and the NIST Cybersecurity Framework. These frameworks emphasize a structured approach to identifying, assessing, and mitigating risks while embedding continuous monitoring as a core principle. Similarly, ISO/IEC 27005 offers international standards for information security risk management, providing organizations with a consistent methodology to identify, evaluate, and treat risks. On the legal front, regulations such as the General Data Protection Regulation (GDPR) in the European Union and the Health Insurance Portability and Accountability Act (HIPAA) in the United States mandate that organizations implement adequate security measures to protect sensitive data. These laws often carry significant financial and reputational penalties for non-compliance, further incentivizing enterprises to adopt rigorous, data-driven approaches to vulnerability management.

A comparative case example illustrates the difference between traditional manual audits and automated vulnerability scanning. Consider a mid-sized financial services company conducting a quarterly manual security audit of its internal systems. The audit team, over the course of several weeks, identifies misconfigurations in firewall rules, outdated patches in certain servers, and inconsistent password policies. While these findings are valid, the process consumes valuable staff time and leaves a significant gap between assessments. In contrast, when the same company deploys an automated vulnerability scanner, thousands of issues are flagged in a single sweep, including known CVEs affecting software libraries and services not previously examined in the audit. However, the scanner produces so many results that the security team struggles to prioritize, leaving critical vulnerabilities unaddressed amid less significant issues. A data-driven enhancement to this process would involve integrating vulnerability scanner outputs with a risk analytics engine, which applies contextual data such as asset criticality, exploit availability, and business impact. In this enhanced model, vulnerabilities affecting customer-facing banking applications are prioritized above flaws in low-importance internal systems, enabling the company to allocate remediation resources more effectively.

The analysis of these foundations demonstrates that vulnerability and risk assessment is no longer merely a technical exercise but a multi-dimensional process shaped by technological advancements, regulatory requirements, and organizational priorities. Data-driven assessment represents a natural evolution along this trajectory, enabling alignment of technical findings with business realities. In practice, this means that modern organizations must combine the strengths of automation, analytics, and compliance alignment to transform raw vulnerability data into actionable risk intelligence. By doing so, they not only achieve regulatory compliance but also build resilience against the increasingly sophisticated threat landscape.

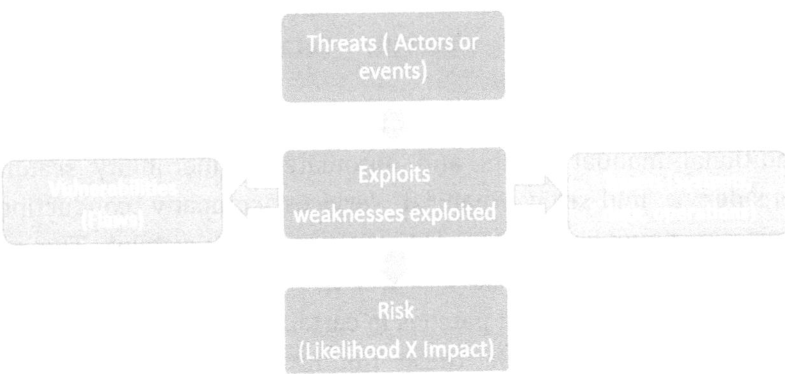

Figure 9.1: Relationship between Vulnerabilities, Threats, and Risk

Risk emerges only when vulnerabilities intersect with threats targeting valuable assets. Without an exploitable vulnerability, a threat may be harmless; without a meaningful asset, exploitation may be inconsequential.

Approach	Key Features	Advantages	Limitations
Manual Audits	Human-led inspection of systems, configs, and processes against policies/standards	Deep contextual understanding, tailored recommendations	Time-consuming, limited scalability, snapshot-only results, prone to human error
Automated Scanning	Tools (e.g., Nessus, OpenVAS, Qualys) scan for known vulnerabilities	Scalable, fast, detects large volumes of issues across environments	High false positives, overwhelming data, lacks business context
Data-Driven Assessment	Integration of analytics, threat intel, asset value, and automated scanning	Prioritized results, real-time insights, alignment with business impact	Requires quality data, advanced tools, and skilled analysts

Table 9.1: Comparative Overview of Vulnerability Assessment Approaches

Data Sources for Risk Assessment

Risk assessment in cybersecurity is only as strong as the data that underpins it. Just as a medical diagnosis depends on reliable test results, the accuracy of vulnerability and risk analysis depends on the quality, diversity, and relevance of the data feeding into the process. Modern enterprises generate vast amounts of security-relevant data every second, from system logs and endpoint telemetry to vulnerability databases and penetration test findings. The challenge lies not in the absence of data but in harnessing it effectively, ensuring that raw information is transformed into actionable intelligence that supports timely and prioritized decision-making.

At the foundation of this process are **system logs**, which provide detailed records of activities across servers, networks, and applications. Logs can capture user logins, system errors, configuration changes, and attempted intrusions. For example, an unusual series of failed login attempts in authentication logs may suggest a brute-force attack in progress. When analyzed in isolation, such logs may appear routine or ambiguous. However, when correlated with network traffic showing abnormal outbound connections, they can reveal a larger attack narrative. Logs are therefore indispensable for identifying vulnerabilities that are actively probed and exploited, bridging the gap between static system weaknesses and dynamic threat behavior.

Complementing logs is network traffic data, often collected through intrusion detection systems (IDS) and intrusion prevention systems (IPS). Traffic analysis helps identify anomalies such as sudden surges in outbound traffic, unusual port activity, or communication with known malicious IP addresses. For example, a data exfiltration attack may manifest as consistently large data transfers to an unrecognized external host. Network telemetry not only identifies the exploitation of vulnerabilities but also offers insight into attacker tactics and persistence mechanisms. In risk assessment, this data allows organizations to measure the real-world impact of vulnerabilities rather than relying solely on theoretical severity scores.

Another crucial category of data is endpoint telemetry, captured through endpoint detection and response (EDR) solutions. Endpoints—laptops, mobile devices, IoT systems—are often the weakest link in an organization's defense perimeter. Telemetry from these devices can reveal suspicious activities such as privilege escalation, unauthorized application execution, or attempts to disable security controls. For example, if an EDR solution detects repeated privilege escalation attempts on a workstation, it may indicate an attacker exploiting a known local vulnerability. Incorporating such data into the risk assessment process ensures that vulnerabilities in user devices are not overlooked, especially since endpoints often serve as entry points into wider enterprise systems.

In addition to internal telemetry, external vulnerability databases and threat intelligence feeds provide critical data. Public repositories, such as the Common Vulnerabilities and Exposures (CVE) database and the National Vulnerability Database (NVD), catalog known vulnerabilities along with identifiers, descriptions, and severity scores. The MITRE ATT&CK framework offers structured information on adversarial techniques, tactics, and procedures, allowing analysts to map vulnerabilities to potential attack paths. Commercial and open-source threat intelligence feeds further enrich this data, supplying real-time updates on actively exploited vulnerabilities, exploit kits circulating in underground markets, and threat actor campaigns. For example, if intelligence reports highlight that ransomware groups are exploiting a specific VPN vulnerability, organizations can immediately elevate its priority, regardless of its base CVSS score.

Penetration testing results and red-team exercises are another valuable data source. Unlike automated scanners, these assessments simulate real-world attack scenarios, identifying vulnerabilities that may not be captured by traditional tools. A penetration test, for example, might reveal that while a system has strong technical controls, weak social engineering defenses make it highly vulnerable to phishing campaigns. Similarly, red team engagements often expose systemic weaknesses in incident response and detection, offering a broader perspective on organizational risk. These findings complement automated data by highlighting gaps in human processes and organizational culture, which technical scanning alone cannot address.

Despite the abundance of data, challenges remain in ensuring data quality and accuracy. Large-scale vulnerability scans often produce false positives, flagging issues that may not exist or are irrelevant to the organization's context. Conversely, false negatives—overlooked vulnerabilities—pose an equally dangerous problem. Moreover, data silos, where different teams collect and store security data independently, hinder comprehensive analysis. To mitigate these issues, organizations are increasingly adopting centralized security data platforms, such as Security Information and Event Management (SIEM) and Extended Detection and Response (XDR) systems. These platforms integrate diverse data streams into a unified environment, enabling correlation, contextualization, and prioritization.

To illustrate the importance of diverse data sources, consider the case of the 2017 Equifax breach. Attackers exploited a known vulnerability in the Apache Struts framework. While the CVE had been published months earlier, Equifax's patch management system failed to update the affected servers in time. Internal logs recorded suspicious activity, but the signals were not correlated across teams, delaying detection. In this case, the vulnerability data was available, but inadequate integration and prioritization of internal telemetry left the organization exposed. Had Equifax combined external CVE intelligence with internal log analysis and automated patch prioritization, the breach—impacting over 140 million individuals—might have been mitigated.

A useful way to conceptualize data sources is through a comparative framework that highlights their role in risk assessment.

Data Source	Examples	Contribution to Risk Assessment
System Logs	Authentication logs, system events	Reveal anomalies, detect brute force, privilege misuse
Network Traffic	IDS/IPS alerts, flow data	Identify exfiltration, lateral movement, malicious comms
Endpoint Telemetry	EDR alerts, device activity	Highlight endpoint exploitation and malware persistence
Vulnerability Databases	CVE, NVD, vendor advisories	Provide known vulnerabilities and severity data
Threat Intelligence Feeds	MITRE ATT&CK, commercial intel	Indicate active exploits, attacker TTPs, emerging threats
Penetration Tests / Red Teams	Simulated attacks, social engineering	Uncover systemic weaknesses and validate controls

Table 9.2: Key Data Sources in Vulnerability and Risk Assessment

The strength of vulnerability and risk assessment lies not in any single data source but in the integration of multiple inputs. Logs, traffic data, telemetry, external intelligence, and simulated attacks each provide a partial view of organizational risk. When combined and contextualized through modern analytics platforms, they offer a comprehensive perspective that enables organizations to not only detect vulnerabilities but also prioritize remediation according to real-world threat landscapes. In an era of expanding attack surfaces and increasingly sophisticated adversaries, the ability to leverage diverse, high-quality data sources is not optional—it is the very foundation of effective cyber risk management.

Risk Scoring with CVSS and Data Models

The quantification of cybersecurity risk is central to modern defense strategies. With the growing number of vulnerabilities disclosed each year—over 25,000 in recent databases—security teams face the daunting challenge of deciding which issues require urgent attention and which can be deferred. Without standardized and context-aware scoring systems, organizations risk either underestimating threats that can lead to catastrophic breaches or overcommitting limited resources to issues of lesser impact. Risk scoring frameworks address this challenge by offering systematic approaches to vulnerability prioritization.

Two major paradigms dominate this domain: the Common Vulnerability Scoring System (CVSS), which provides a rule-based, universally recognized standard for assessing vulnerability severity, and data-driven risk scoring models, which utilize analytics, statistical inference, and machine learning to adapt dynamically to real-world conditions. These two approaches are complementary: CVSS offers simplicity and transparency, while data-driven methods incorporate context, prediction, and intelligence.

Model Type	Input Factors	Strengths	Limitations	Use Case Example
CVSS-only (v2/v3)	Static vulnerability characteristics (attack vector, complexity, privileges required, impact metrics)	Standardized across industries, simple to calculate, widely recognized in compliance frameworks	Ignores exploit likelihood, real-time context, and asset value; produces "risk inflation" when applied alone	Assigning a universal severity score for published CVEs
ML-based Predictive Models	Historical vulnerability data, exploit timelines, threat intel feeds, attacker behavior indicators	Predictive power (exploit likelihood), reduces false positives, dynamic adaptation to new threats	Requires quality data; model interpretability may be limited; risk of bias in training data	Predicting which 5–10% of vulnerabilities are likely to be exploited
Probabilistic (Bayesian) Models	Prior probabilities, updated evidence from threat intelligence and incident reports	Handles uncertainty well, updates risk dynamically, aggregates systemic risk across environments	Complex to implement; requires continual data updates; not easily understood by non-experts	Estimating likelihood of exploitation for emerging vulnerabilities
Hybrid Models (CVSS + Contextual Data)	CVSS base score, exploit availability, business impact, asset exposure, patching feasibility	Balanced approach: standardization plus context, improves prioritization accuracy, flexible	Requires data integration from multiple sources, implementation costs	Prioritizing vulnerabilities in mixed environments (e.g., production vs. test servers)

Table 9.3: Comparison of Risk Scoring Models

The Common Vulnerability Scoring System (CVSS)

The CVSS was first introduced in 2005 under the sponsorship of the National Infrastructure Advisory Council (NIAC) and has since been maintained by the Forum of Incident Response and Security Teams (FIRST). It has evolved through three major versions—CVSS v1, v2 (2007), and v3 (2015, with v3.1 in 2019)—each iteration addressing criticisms of its predecessor. Today, CVSS is widely adopted by vendors, government agencies, and enterprises as the baseline system for describing and comparing vulnerabilities.

At its core, CVSS is built on three groups of metrics:

1. Base Metrics – These describe the intrinsic characteristics of vulnerability that do not change over time. Examples include *Attack Vector* (network, adjacent, local, and physical), *Attack Complexity* (low or high), *Privileges Required, User Interaction*, and impacts on *Confidentiality, Integrity, and Availability.*

2. Temporal Metrics – These reflect factors that evolve, such as the availability of exploit code or official patches. For instance, vulnerability with a known, public exploit is scored more severely than one without.
3. Environmental Metrics – These allow organizations to adapt the base and temporal scores to their specific environment. For example, a vulnerability affecting a mission-critical payment system would be rated higher in a financial institution than in an academic research lab.
4. Together, these metrics produce a score between 0.0 and 10.0, which is then mapped into qualitative categories: Low (0.1–3.9), Medium (4.0–6.9), High (7.0–8.9), and Critical (9.0–10.0).

Example of CVSS in practice: The infamous EternalBlue exploit, which targeted Microsoft's SMB protocol and was weaponized in the WannaCry ransomware outbreak, received a CVSS v3 score of 8.1 (high). While this accurately reflected its technical severity, the subsequent widespread exploitation demonstrated that CVSS alone was insufficient to capture the true risk, which included mass worm-like propagation and devastating economic impact.

Strengths of CVSS:

- **Universality**: Provides a common language for vendors, security analysts, and policy makers.
- **Transparency**: Every metric is explicitly defined, ensuring reproducibility of scores.
- **Integration**: Widely adopted in vulnerability management systems and compliance frameworks.
- **Limitations of CVSS**:
- **Static nature**: Scores do not automatically update as threat conditions change.
- **Context blindness**: CVSS does not consider asset value, business processes, or adversary intent.
- **Over-simplification**: Two vulnerabilities with close scores (e.g., 8.8 and 9.0) may be worlds apart in practical impact.

In essence, CVSS provides an essential baseline but should not be mistaken for a complete risk assessment.

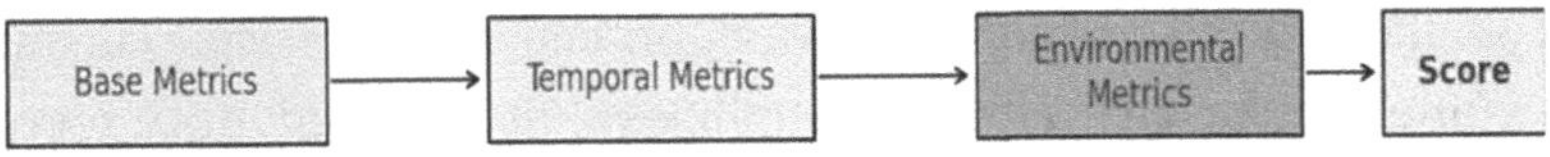

Figure 9.2: CVSS Scoring Workflow

Data-Driven Risk Scoring Models

The limitations of CVSS have spurred the development of data-driven approaches that integrate real-time threat intelligence, organizational context, and predictive analytics. Unlike CVSS, which is rule-based and largely static, these models evolve continuously as new data becomes available.

Sources of Data in Risk Scoring Models:

- **Threat intelligence feeds**: Indicators of compromise, exploit kit activity, malware campaigns.
- **Exploit databases**: Information on whether proof-of-concept or weaponized exploits exist.
- **Dark web and social media monitoring**: Signals of adversary interest in specific vulnerabilities.
- **System telemetry:** Logs, intrusion detection system alerts, and asset inventories.
  - **Historical exploitation patterns**: Statistical models of how similar vulnerabilities were exploited.

By fusing these data points, machine learning models can assign probabilities that a vulnerability will be exploited within a certain timeframe.

A prime example is the Exploit Prediction Scoring System (EPSS), developed by the FIRST community to complement CVSS. Unlike CVSS, EPSS produces a probability score (0 to 1) reflecting the likelihood that a vulnerability will be exploited in the next 30 days. For instance, while many vulnerabilities receive high CVSS scores, EPSS analysis shows that only a fraction of them are ever exploited. This distinction is crucial for overburdened security teams who must prioritize limited resources.

  - **Case illustration:** In 2021, researchers compared vulnerabilities with CVSS scores above 9.0 to EPSS predictions. They found that fewer than 5% of those vulnerabilities were actually exploited in the wild, underscoring that CVSS severity alone can mislead prioritization. EPSS, by contrast, highlighted vulnerabilities with moderate CVSS scores that had high exploitation probabilities, enabling more efficient patching strategies.

Advantages of Data-Driven Models:

- Dynamic adaptability: Scores update as threat landscapes evolve.
- Contextual intelligence: Models can integrate asset value and business criticality.
- Predictive capability: Forecasts potential future exploitation.

Challenges of Data-Driven Models:

- Opacity: Machine learning algorithms may function as "black boxes," reducing transparency.
- Data dependency: Accuracy hinges on the completeness and quality of threat intelligence.
- Standardization gap: Unlike CVSS, there is no universally mandated model, leading to fragmentation across vendors.

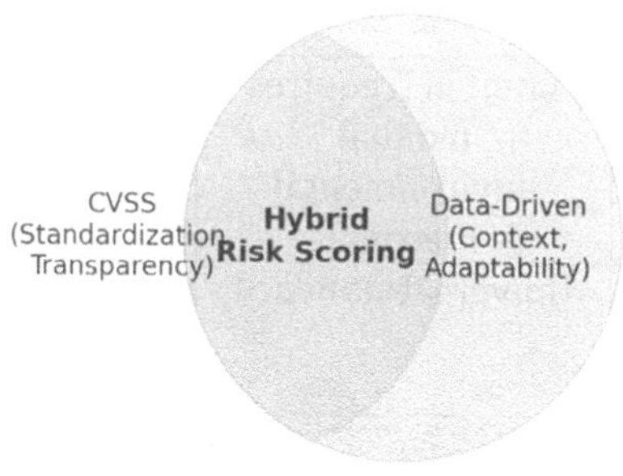

Figure 9.3: Hybrid Risk Scoring Models

Comparative Analysis and Hybrid Approaches

The coexistence of CVSS and data-driven models raises an important question: which system should organizations rely on? In practice, the most effective strategy is not to choose one over the other but to **combine their strengths.**

- CVSS offers baseline standardization. It is indispensable for vendors who must communicate severity across a broad audience, and for regulatory compliance, where consistent reporting is required.
- Data-driven models offer contextual refinement. They enable organizations to filter through thousands of CVSS-rated vulnerabilities and focus on those that present imminent, real-world danger.

A hybrid approach typically looks like this: an organization uses CVSS to generate an initial pool of vulnerabilities rated "High" or "Critical." Then, a data-driven model such as EPSS or a vendor-specific scoring engine re-ranks these vulnerabilities based on exploitability, asset importance, and threat activity. This layered process ensures that resources are directed not only toward theoretically severe vulnerabilities but also toward those that are actively dangerous.

Dimension	**CVSS**	**Data-Driven Models**
Basis	Rule-based metrics (static)	Threat intelligence, analytics, ML (dynamic)
Output	Severity score (0–10)	Probability / risk-adjusted score
Transparency	High (open rubric)	Often lower (black box algorithms)
Context sensitivity	Limited (requires manual environmental metrics)	High (can incorporate asset value and threat landscape)
Adoption	Universal standard	Fragmented, vendor-specific, emerging standards

Table 9.4: CVSS vs. Data-Driven Models

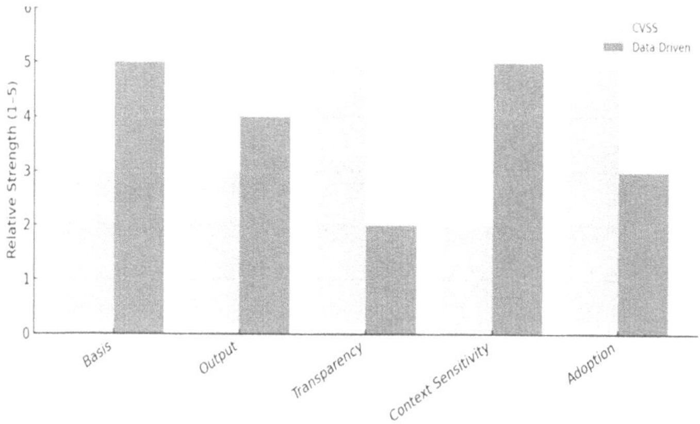

Figure 9.4: Comparison of CVSS and Data-Driven Models

Prioritization Based On Business Impact

The modern cyber defense landscape is characterized by an overwhelming number of vulnerabilities discovered on a daily basis. Large organizations routinely find tens of thousands of potential flaws across their systems, applications, and devices. Yet it is neither technically feasible nor economically rational to attempt to patch every single vulnerability at once. This practical constraint gives rise to the critical discipline of prioritization, in which vulnerabilities are ranked not only by their technical severity but, more importantly, by their business impact. While severity scoring frameworks such as the Common Vulnerability Scoring System (CVSS) remain central to technical evaluation, they provide only part of the picture. What ultimately matters to an organization is the extent to which a given vulnerability can disrupt its mission, compromise its assets, damage its reputation, or trigger regulatory and financial penalties.

Prioritization based on business impact acknowledges that vulnerabilities cannot be understood in isolation from the systems they affect. A flaw on a test server with no connection to production systems may be rated as severe in technical terms but practically insignificant to the business. Conversely, a medium-scoring flaw in a payment gateway, a hospital's electronic health record system, or a manufacturing plant's control network can lead to catastrophic consequences. The task of the modern cyber defender, therefore, is not simply to chase down the highest technical scores but to understand vulnerabilities within the broader context of organizational value and risk appetite.

Business Context in Cyber Risk

The classical definition of cyber risk is often expressed as a function of threats, vulnerabilities, and impact. Traditional vulnerability assessments emphasized the technical characteristics of flaws—the ease of exploitation, the privileges required, and the potential damage to confidentiality, integrity, and availability. However, these evaluations ignored the fact that not all systems are created equal. Business prioritization requires embedding technical assessment into the hierarchy of organizational assets and services.

Imagine, for instance, a retail company that operates multiple digital platforms. A critical vulnerability discovered on a test environment accessible only to a handful of developers is of limited concern compared to the same vulnerability on the firm's e-commerce payment servers. The latter system processes thousands of transactions daily and directly supports revenue generation. Here, the same technical weakness has radically different implications.

To conceptualize this, many risk management frameworks propose viewing cyber risk as a multiplicative function:

$$\text{Business Risk} = \text{Technical Severity} \times \text{Business Criticality}$$

This model reinforces the idea that business impact is a distinct axis of measurement, equal in importance to technical severity. The challenge lies in accurately mapping vulnerabilities to business assets and assigning appropriate weights to those assets. This often requires maintaining a dynamic asset inventory and a configuration management database that categorizes systems into different tiers of criticality. In practice, systems are often classified into mission-critical assets (such as payment processing servers or hospital life-support systems), supportive assets (such as HR portals or employee email), and peripheral assets (such as test environments).

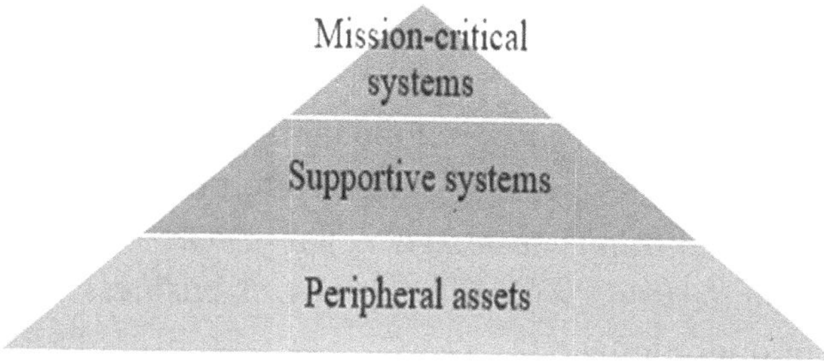

Figure 9.5: An Asset Criticality Pyramid Illustrating How Vulnerabilities on Different Tiers Carry Different Business Impacts

Quantitative and Qualitative Approaches to Prioritization

Organizations have developed two broad schools of thought for embedding business impact into vulnerability prioritization: **qualitative models and quantitative models.**

Qualitative models are grounded in categorical language. Vulnerabilities are labeled as "High," "Medium," or "Low" based on expert judgment, and results are often displayed using heatmaps or risk matrices. In such matrices, one axis represents the likelihood of exploitation and the other represents the potential business impact. A vulnerability that is highly exploitable and carries significant business impact is placed in the "red zone," requiring immediate remediation, while vulnerabilities with low likelihood and limited impact fall into "green" or "yellow" zones. These models are attractive because of their simplicity and visual clarity. They allow executives, board members, and non-technical stakeholders to grasp relative priorities without needing to interpret technical jargon.

However, qualitative models also have inherent weaknesses. Their reliance on subjective assessment can introduce inconsistency across organizations or even across different teams within the same enterprise. Furthermore, the broad categories of "high" or "medium" risk can oversimplify complex realities, making it difficult to conduct cost-benefit analyses or justify resource allocation decisions in precise terms.

In response to these limitations, quantitative models seek to translate cyber risk into financial language. The FAIR methodology (Factor Analysis of Information Risk) is the most prominent example. FAIR decomposes risk into two components: the probable frequency of a loss event and the probable magnitude of its financial impact. This allows organizations to assign dollar values to vulnerabilities, facilitating comparisons with other types of business risk, such as credit risk or operational risk.

For example, consider a payment server vulnerability that, if exploited, might allow attackers to steal customer card data. Using historical data and threat intelligence, analysts estimate that such an event can occur once per year, with an average loss magnitude of two million dollars due to fines, customer compensation, and reputational damage. The quantitative risk, under FAIR, would then be expressed as an expected annual loss of two million dollars. This transforms an abstract technical problem into a tangible financial one, allowing executives to weigh the cost of patching against the expected savings in avoided losses.

Dimension	Qualitative Models (e.g., Heatmaps, Risk Matrices)	Quantitative Models (e.g., FAIR)
Basis of Evaluation	Expert judgment, categorical scales (High/Med/Low)	Statistical modeling, probabilistic analysis, financial quantification
Ease of Use	Simple, intuitive, easy for executives to understand	Complex, requires data collection and modeling expertise
Output Format	Color-coded charts, ordinal risk levels	Expected financial loss values (e.g., $2M annual loss)
Accuracy & Precision	Subject to bias, inconsistent across evaluators	More precise, consistent, data-driven
Resource Requirements	Minimal data required, low cost	High data requirements, modeling tools, skilled analysts
Decision-Making Value	Useful for quick prioritization, board-level communication	Enables ROI analysis, insurance planning, cost-justified decisions

Dimension	**Qualitative Models (e.g., Heatmaps, Risk Matrices)**	**Quantitative Models (e.g., FAIR)**
Limitations	Oversimplification, lack of financial context	Complexity, difficulty in obtaining reliable data

Table 9.5: Comparison of Qualitative vs. Quantitative Approaches to Business Impact Prioritization

Strategic Models for Business Impact Prioritization

Beyond methodological frameworks, organizations must also grapple with the strategic challenge of embedding prioritization into daily operations. This involves aligning vulnerability management with enterprise mission, regulatory requirements, and operational realities.

One important dimension is the linkage between vulnerabilities and mission-critical systems. Consider an airline whose operations depend on reservation systems and aircraft scheduling software. A vulnerability in these systems can lead not only to financial losses but also to catastrophic reputational harm and passenger safety concerns. Thus, even a moderately severe vulnerability on such systems may be treated as the highest priority.

Another strategic consideration is the use of analytics to rank asset value. Advanced security platforms now integrate business metadata into vulnerability dashboards. These platforms combine asset inventories, revenue data, and interdependency mapping to calculate an "asset value score" for each system. Vulnerabilities in high-value assets are automatically escalated, while those in lower-value assets are deprioritized. This creates a dynamic prioritization process that adapts as business conditions evolve.

A further challenge lies in balancing compliance-driven priorities with operational ones. Regulatory frameworks such as the General Data Protection Regulation (GDPR), the Health Insurance Portability and Accountability Act (HIPAA), and the Payment Card Industry Data Security Standard (PCI DSS) impose strict remediation deadlines for vulnerabilities affecting sensitive data or financial systems. Compliance obligations may require organizations to patch certain vulnerabilities even if their immediate business impact appears modest. Conversely, operational realities, such as system uptime requirements, may delay patching critical assets, forcing organizations to deploy compensating controls. Strategic prioritization, therefore, requires constant negotiation between these competing pressures.

Case Examples across Industries

The value of business impact prioritization becomes most apparent when examined in real-world industries. In the financial sector, a large bank discovered vulnerabilities across employee email servers, teller systems, and online payment platforms. While CVSS scores rated many of these vulnerabilities equally, business impact analysis revealed that payment platforms were mission-critical, processing millions of dollars in daily revenue and subject to PCI DSS compliance. Prioritizing these systems allowed the bank to reduce financial exposure by over half in a single quarter while postponing remediation of lower-risk systems to scheduled maintenance windows.

In the healthcare industry, a hospital system faced vulnerabilities in both its electronic health record (EHR) platform and in IoT-enabled infusion pumps deployed in patient wards. Technically, the EHR vulnerabilities carried higher CVSS scores due to the potential for data theft. Yet a business impact analysis revealed that exploitation of IoT vulnerabilities could directly threaten patient safety — an impact dimension not captured by technical severity metrics. As a result, the hospital redirected resources to secure its IoT infrastructure, segmenting vulnerable devices and accelerating vendor patch timelines. This decision highlighted the necessity of considering patient safety as a core element of business impact.

Manufacturing provides yet another case study. A global manufacturer identified vulnerabilities in both its corporate IT systems and its industrial control systems (ICS) that managed production lines. CVSS assigned "critical" scores to email server flaws, while some ICS vulnerabilities received lower ratings. However, a business impact analysis revealed that an exploited ICS vulnerability could shut down entire production facilities, resulting in daily losses exceeding five million dollars and significant disruption to supply chains. By reprioritizing ICS vulnerabilities, the manufacturer avoided tens of millions of dollars in potential losses and increased resilience across its global operations.

Secure Software Development Lifecycle (SSDLC)

The Secure Software Development Lifecycle (SSDLC) provides a structured framework for incorporating security considerations into every phase of software creation. Unlike traditional software lifecycles, which often relegated security testing to the end of the release cycle, SSDLC integrates vulnerability assessment into the planning, design, coding, testing, deployment, and maintenance stages.

For example, during the requirements and design phase, security architects assess the threat landscape and model potential attack vectors against system components. Tools such as Microsoft's STRIDE threat modeling or the OWASP Top 10 provide structured ways of identifying likely vulnerabilities before any code is written. By capturing these risks early, developers can design safeguards into the architecture itself, such as enforcing input validation, encryption standards, and secure authentication mechanisms.

In the coding and implementation phase, static code analysis becomes critical. Static Application Security Testing (SAST) tools scan source code for known insecure coding patterns such as SQL injection risks or hardcoded credentials. Rather than waiting until testing or deployment, these vulnerabilities are flagged for developers at the moment of creation.

Finally, in the testing and maintenance phases, dynamic assessment techniques—such as penetration testing or Dynamic Application Security Testing (DAST)—validate how the application behaves at runtime. Integration of these results into a central vulnerability management platform ensures that remediation tasks are tracked and prioritized based on business impact.

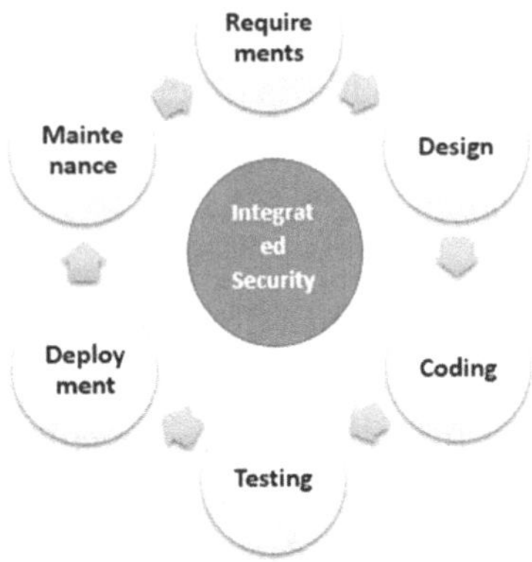

Figure 9.6: A Circular SSDLC Model Showing the Software Lifecycle Stages with Security

Continuous Vulnerability Management in CI/CD

In the era of DevOps and continuous delivery, software is no longer released in discrete versions but as a stream of incremental updates. This demands continuous vulnerability management within CI/CD pipelines. Each build, whether a minor patch or a feature release, must undergo automated security checks before deployment.

Modern pipelines integrate a combination of tools:

- SAST (Static Application Security Testing) analyzes source code during the build process.
- DAST (Dynamic Application Security Testing) runs simulated attacks on deployed test environments to discover runtime flaws.
- IAST (Interactive Application Security Testing) combines static and dynamic techniques, instrumenting the application during execution to provide real-time feedback on vulnerabilities.
- RASP (Runtime Application Self-Protection) tools embed protective agents within the application itself, detecting and blocking malicious activities during operation.

By orchestrating these tools into automated workflows, organizations transform vulnerability management into a gatekeeper function for deployment. For example, a build may be automatically halted if a high-severity vulnerability is detected, preventing insecure code from reaching production.

Beyond tool integration, pipelines now incorporate automated risk scoring. By correlating scan results with CVSS metrics, exploit likelihood data, and business impact models, security dashboards provide developers and product managers with clear visibility into which vulnerabilities must be addressed immediately. This prevents "alert fatigue" by filtering out low-risk issues while highlighting those most likely to result in exploitation.

Metrics also play a central role. Common measures of secure code quality include the mean time to remediate vulnerabilities (MTTR), the percentage of builds passing security gates, and the defect density normalized per thousand lines of code. Tracking these metrics across multiple sprints enables organizations to demonstrate security improvements over time.

Phase in Pipeline	Tool	Primary Function	Example Output
Build	SAST	Scan source code for insecure patterns	Hardcoded passwords detected
Test	DAST	Probe running app for runtime flaws	SQL injection vulnerability
Staging	IAST	Monitor execution with instrumentation	Validation bypass attempt logged
Production	RASP	Protect app at runtime	Malicious payload blocked

Table 9.6: CI/CD Security Tool Integration

Shift-Left Security

The concept of "shift-left security" captures the idea of embedding security earlier in the development lifecycle—literally shifting security testing to the "left" on the project timeline. The rationale is clear: vulnerabilities identified in production are exponentially more expensive to fix than those detected during design or coding. Industry studies consistently show that a vulnerability caught during requirements may cost less than $100 to remediate, while the same flaw discovered after deployment can cost upwards of $10,000 once patching, downtime, and customer remediation are included.

Shifting left means empowering developers with tools and training to recognize and fix vulnerabilities as they write code. Modern integrated development environments (IDEs) now include plugins that provide real-time vulnerability detection, suggesting secure coding patterns as developer's type. Machine learning models are also emerging that analyze historical defect patterns to predict which code segments are most likely to introduce vulnerabilities. For example, a model might learn that certain modules dealing with authentication or cryptographic functions historically generate more high-severity flaws. Developers can then apply heightened scrutiny or targeted peer review to those areas.

Beyond cost savings, shift-left security improves developer ownership of security outcomes. Rather than treating security as an external function enforced by auditors or testers, developers become active participants in risk management, reducing the "us versus them" mentality that historically divided engineering and security teams.

Case Studies

Case 1: Reducing Remediation Backlog in a Fintech DevOps Team

A mid-sized financial technology company faced a growing backlog of over 7,000 unresolved vulnerabilities flagged by periodic penetration tests. Despite dedicated remediation sprints, the backlog grew faster than developers could patch due to the rapid pace of feature releases. To address this, the company integrated SAST and DAST directly into its Jenkins CI/CD pipeline. Vulnerabilities were automatically scored based on both CVSS severity and business context, with critical payment-system flaws prioritized above peripheral features. Within three months, the backlog was reduced by 60%, and average MTTR fell from 45 days to 12 days. This not only improved compliance with PCI DSS requirements but also reassured major banking partners, strengthening the company's competitive position.

Case 2: Scaling Vulnerability Assessment in Open-Source Projects

An open-source cloud orchestration project struggled with maintaining security across a globally distributed contributor base.

Vulnerabilities often went unnoticed until after deployment, undermining user trust. The project leadership adopted a shift-left model, requiring contributors to run lightweight SAST checks before submitting pull requests. Additionally, GitHub Actions workflows were configured to run automated DAST scans on every merge into the main branch. Over the course of a year, the project observed a 70% reduction in high-severity vulnerabilities reaching production. More importantly, community contributors became more engaged in secure coding practices, demonstrating that even decentralized, volunteer-driven projects can scale vulnerability assessment when it is integrated directly into the development workflow.

Tools and Technologies for Vulnerability and Risk Assessment

The discipline of vulnerability and risk assessment is inseparable from the technologies that support it. As digital infrastructures grow in complexity and scale, manual methods of security evaluation have become inadequate. Modern organizations must rely on a wide ecosystem of specialized tools to detect, evaluate, prioritize, and remediate vulnerabilities before they are exploited. These tools vary from traditional vulnerability scanners to highly integrated enterprise platforms that provide continuous risk visibility and automated response mechanisms. Increasingly, cloud-native and artificial intelligence–driven solutions are also reshaping the landscape, enabling faster, more accurate, and more scalable assessments. Understanding the strengths and limitations of these tools is essential for building a comprehensive vulnerability management strategy.

At the foundation of vulnerability assessment lie scanners that systematically probe networks, systems, and applications for known weaknesses. These scanners may be either open-source or commercial, and the choice between the two often reflects an organization's resources, regulatory obligations, and tolerance for customization. Open-source scanners, such as OpenVAS and Nmap, are attractive for their accessibility and flexibility. They provide security teams with the ability to modify scanning rules, integrate findings into custom workflows, and build community-driven knowledge bases. Such tools are especially valuable for smaller organizations or academic environments where budget constraints make commercial solutions prohibitive. However, they often require greater expertise to configure, interpret, and maintain, and their support and update cycles may not match the rigor demanded by enterprise environments.

Commercial scanners, by contrast, such as Qualys, Tenable Nessus, or Rapid7 InsightVM, bring a different value proposition. They are backed by vendor support, regular updates aligned with emerging threats, and advanced reporting functionalities designed to meet compliance frameworks like PCI DSS, HIPAA, or ISO 27001. Many of these platforms provide continuous scanning capabilities that integrate with enterprise IT workflows, offering dashboards that link technical vulnerabilities to business risks. Commercial offerings typically include service-level agreements, dedicated technical support, and compliance-ready documentation, all of which are critical for highly regulated industries such as finance, energy, or healthcare. Yet, the reliance on vendor ecosystems can limit flexibility, and costs may escalate rapidly as infrastructure scales. The decision between open-source and commercial tools is therefore not binary but contextual, depending on organizational maturity, industry requirements, and the balance between budgetary constraints and operational security needs.

Beyond scanners, modern risk assessment increasingly relies on platforms that aggregate and analyze data from across the enterprise. Security Information and Event Management (SIEM) systems serve as centralized repositories that collect logs, alerts, and telemetry from disparate systems. They enable analysts to correlate events, detect anomalies, and contextualize vulnerabilities within broader attack patterns. SIEM solutions such as Splunk, IBM QRadar, or ArcSight have become indispensable in environments where raw vulnerability data alone is insufficient to understand the full scope of risk exposure. However, SIEM platforms often struggle with alert fatigue, generating a flood of events that overwhelm analysts.

To mitigate this challenge, Security Orchestration, Automation, and Response (SOAR) platforms have emerged as complementary technologies. SOAR tools automate repetitive tasks such as triaging vulnerability alerts, initiating patch workflows, or isolating affected assets. By embedding playbooks into operational pipelines, SOAR systems reduce response times and ensure consistency in remediation efforts. They also allow organizations to standardize their incident handling across teams and geographies, a critical feature for multinational corporations. Governance, Risk, and Compliance (GRC) platforms add another dimension, focusing on aligning vulnerability and risk assessment with broader business objectives. These tools help organizations translate technical vulnerabilities into governance terms, ensuring that executives and regulators can evaluate security posture in relation to strategic goals, compliance mandates, and industry benchmarks. Together, SIEM, SOAR, and GRC platforms form the backbone of enterprise risk management, providing a continuum from technical detection to governance-level reporting.

The rise of cloud computing has introduced both new challenges and new tools into the vulnerability management domain. Traditional on-premises scanners are often ill-suited for dynamic cloud environments where assets appear and disappear within seconds. Cloud providers have responded by developing native vulnerability and risk assessment tools tailored to their platforms. For instance, Amazon Web Services offers Amazon Inspector, a service that automatically assesses workloads for software vulnerabilities and unintended network exposure. Microsoft Azure provides the Azure Security Center, a unified infrastructure security management system that evaluates configurations, detects threats, and recommends hardening measures. Similarly, Google Cloud Platform delivers the Security Command Center (SCC), which offers comprehensive visibility into risks across resources, data, and workloads. These cloud-native tools integrate seamlessly with their respective ecosystems, leveraging metadata and platform telemetry to provide context-aware assessments. Their advantage lies in scalability and real-time adaptation to the fluid nature of cloud infrastructure. Yet their utility is often constrained by vendor lock-in, and organizations operating in multi-cloud environments must grapple with integrating disparate cloud-native tools into a unified vulnerability management strategy.

The most transformative development in recent years has been the integration of artificial intelligence and machine learning into vulnerability assessment platforms. Traditional scanners rely heavily on signature-based detection, which is inherently reactive, flagging only known vulnerabilities cataloged in databases such as the Common Vulnerabilities and Exposures (CVE) list. AI-driven platforms move beyond this by analyzing behavioral patterns, anomaly detection, and predictive modeling to identify emerging risks. For example, machine learning algorithms can prioritize vulnerabilities by evaluating not just their technical severity but also their likelihood of exploitation in the wild, based on threat intelligence feeds and adversarial behavior models. This allows organizations to focus remediation efforts on vulnerabilities that pose the greatest real-world risk rather than those that simply score high on theoretical severity scales.

Furthermore, AI-powered platforms enable continuous, adaptive learning. As new exploits are observed in global environments, algorithms refine their detection and scoring models without requiring manual updates. This dynamic capability is particularly crucial in addressing zero-day vulnerabilities, where traditional patch-driven approaches may lag behind attacker activity. AI also enhances scalability: instead of overwhelming analysts with thousands of alerts, intelligent systems cluster vulnerabilities, identify common root causes, and recommend prioritized remediation strategies. Some advanced systems even simulate attacker behavior to test exploitability within specific organizational contexts, bridging the gap between abstract vulnerability detection and concrete risk assessment.

Despite these advances, AI-driven platforms are not without limitations. Their effectiveness depends on the quality and diversity of training data, and adversaries can attempt to manipulate or evade detection through adversarial machine learning techniques. Moreover, the opacity of some AI models poses challenges for auditability and regulatory compliance, as organizations may struggle to explain how certain risk scores were generated. Nonetheless, the trajectory of development strongly suggests that AI and machine learning will become central to the future of vulnerability and risk assessment, augmenting human expertise with computational speed and pattern recognition at scales impossible for manual analysis.

Category	Examples	Primary Functions	Advantages	Challenges/ Limitations
Open-Source Vulnerability Scanners	OpenVAS, Nmap, Nikto	Network and system scanning, service enumeration, basic vulnerability detection	Cost-effective, customizable, strong community support, transparency of source code	Requires expertise to configure and interpret, limited vendor support, slower update cycles
Commercial Vulnerability Scanners	Tenable Nessus, Qualys, Rapid7 InsightVM	Continuous scanning, compliance reporting, integration with enterprise workflows	Regular updates, vendor support, compliance-ready reporting, enterprise scalability	High licensing costs, potential vendor lock-in, less customization than open-source
SIEM Platforms	Splunk, IBM QRadar, ArcSight	Log aggregation, correlation of security events, anomaly detection	Centralized visibility, regulatory compliance support, scalable event analysis	Alert fatigue, expensive infrastructure, requires skilled analysts
SOAR Platforms	Palo Alto Cortex XSOAR, IBM Resilient	Automated incident response, playbook execution, workflow orchestration	Faster response times, consistency in remediation, reduced analyst workload	Complex deployment, reliance on accurate playbooks, integration challenges
GRC Platforms	RSA Archer, MetricStream	Governance, compliance mapping, risk reporting to executives	Aligns technical vulnerabilities with business objectives, supports audits	May not capture technical granularity, costly in large enterprises
Cloud-Native Security Tools	AWS Inspector, Azure Security Center, GCP Security Command Center	Cloud workload assessment, misconfiguration detection, continuous monitoring	Seamless integration with cloud services, scalable, real-time adaptation to dynamic assets	Vendor lock-in, siloed capabilities in multi-cloud environments, reliance on provider's ecosystem
AI/ML-Driven Platforms	Darktrace, Qualys VMDR with ML, CrowdStrike Falcon Spotlight	Predictive risk scoring, anomaly detection, exploit simulation, automated prioritization	Adaptive learning, real-time detection of emerging threats, prioritization based on exploitability	Opaque algorithms ("black box"), risk of adversarial evasion, regulatory concerns around explainability

Table 9.7: Comparative Overview of Tools and Technologies for Vulnerability and Risk Assessment

Challenges and Limitations

While tools and technologies for vulnerability and risk assessment have grown remarkably sophisticated, they are not without inherent challenges and limitations. The effectiveness of any security program depends not only on the adoption of advanced platforms but also on the quality of the underlying data, the organizational capacity to interpret and act upon findings, and the delicate balance between automation and human judgment. Understanding these limitations is essential for designing realistic, resilient strategies that acknowledge the imperfections of current methodologies.

A fundamental challenge lies in the completeness and accuracy of the data that fuels vulnerability assessment processes. Scanners and monitoring platforms often rely on vulnerability databases such as the Common Vulnerabilities and Exposures (CVE) list or vendor advisories. While these repositories are extensive, they are never exhaustive, and significant delays can occur between the discovery of a vulnerability and its official publication. Moreover, the data itself can reflect biases: vulnerabilities that affect widely deployed commercial software tend to receive more attention than those targeting niche systems, even if the latter may pose substantial risks in certain environments. In cloud and IoT ecosystems, where new configurations and devices proliferate rapidly, data gaps can be even more pronounced. The result is an incomplete risk picture that can leave organizations blind to emerging or underreported threats. This incompleteness forces security leaders to make decisions with imperfect information, often erring on the side of caution but at the expense of efficiency and resource allocation.

Another enduring limitation is the problem of false positives and alert fatigue. Vulnerability scanners frequently flag potential issues that may not be practically exploitable, leading to inflated reports that overwhelm analysts. For example, a system may register a vulnerability because a library exists in its file system, even though the library is not loaded or accessible in runtime contexts. Similarly, configuration assessments may generate warnings that are technically correct but irrelevant in a particular operational environment. When such false positives accumulate, analysts face the danger of desensitization, treating all alerts as noise rather than as meaningful indicators of risk. This "cry wolf" effect not only erodes trust in vulnerability management tools but also diverts attention from genuine threats. Alert fatigue is especially acute in organizations with high-velocity digital operations, where thousands of events are generated daily. Without effective prioritization and filtering mechanisms, security teams risk missing the proverbial needle in the haystack.

Compounding these issues is the persistent skills and resource gap that many organizations face in implementing vulnerability and risk assessment programs. Advanced tools demand trained personnel capable of configuring them, interpreting results, and integrating findings into broader security and governance workflows. Yet the global cybersecurity workforce shortage means that many enterprises struggle to recruit and retain professionals with the requisite expertise. Smaller organizations, in particular, may deploy scanning tools without the human capital needed to act upon the findings, leaving vulnerabilities unpatched or misclassified. Even when skilled analysts are available, resource constraints — such as limited budgets, competing IT priorities, and fragmented organizational structures — often limit the scope of vulnerability assessments. In practice, this gap manifests as "shelfware": expensive tools purchased and deployed but underutilized because organizations cannot sustain the operational investment needed for effective use. The resource imbalance is further exacerbated by the speed of technological change, as analysts must continuously update their knowledge to keep pace with evolving attack techniques and tool updates.

The increasing reliance on automation introduces another set of challenges. Automated vulnerability management and risk assessment systems promise speed and consistency, but they cannot replace the nuanced judgment of human analysts. Algorithms may excel at identifying known vulnerabilities or correlating telemetry data, yet they struggle to interpret business context or weigh trade-offs that involve human, ethical, or strategic dimensions. For example, an automated tool may recommend immediate patching of a critical server vulnerability, but a human analyst might recognize that applying the patch during peak operational hours can disrupt mission-critical services. Similarly, automated prioritization models may misjudge the risk of a vulnerability if they fail to account for unique organizational factors, such as the presence of compensating controls or the criticality of a specific asset. Striking a balance between automation and human expertise is therefore critical. Organizations that rely too heavily on automation risk making brittle decisions that fail under complex, real-world conditions, while those that resist automation entirely risk inefficiency and delays in detection and response.

These limitations underscore a broader truth: vulnerability and risk assessment cannot be treated as a purely technical process. It is an interdisciplinary challenge that requires not only advanced tools but also organizational adaptability, skilled professionals, and governance structures that bridge the gap between raw data and strategic decision-making. Incomplete data, false positives, skills shortages, and overreliance on automation each represent distinct obstacles, but they are also interrelated. Poor data quality amplifies the problem of false positives, which in turn increases alert fatigue and strains already limited human resources. Meanwhile, the temptation to lean on automation grows stronger as resource gaps widen, yet such reliance may backfire without sufficient human oversight.

Recognizing these interdependencies allows organizations to adopt more realistic expectations and to design layered strategies that mitigate the limitations of each tool. For instance, pairing automated vulnerability scanning with expert review can reduce false positives, while investing in training and cross-functional collaboration can alleviate the skills gap. Similarly, diversifying threat intelligence sources can help reduce data incompleteness, while embedding contextual risk analysis ensures that vulnerabilities are assessed not only in technical terms but also in relation to business priorities. Ultimately, the challenges and limitations of vulnerability and risk assessment should not be viewed as insurmountable obstacles but as structural constraints within which organizations must operate intelligently. By acknowledging and addressing these limitations, security leaders can strengthen resilience and move closer to the elusive goal of proactive, comprehensive risk management.

Future Directions and Emerging Trends

The field of vulnerability and risk assessment is in a state of rapid evolution, shaped by advances in technology, the increasing sophistication of adversaries, and the shifting demands of regulatory and business environments. While current practices provide important foundations for organizational security, they are not sufficient to meet the challenges of tomorrow. The next phase of vulnerability management will move beyond reactive scanning and patching toward predictive, adaptive, and globally coordinated approaches. Four emerging trends—predictive risk assessment through artificial intelligence and big data analytics, the integration of threat-informed defense models, the rise of automated remediation and self-healing systems, and the global harmonization of regulatory frameworks—are poised to redefine the landscape of cybersecurity risk management.

A central trajectory in this evolution is the development of predictive risk assessment powered by artificial intelligence and big data analytics. Traditional vulnerability management often relies on backward-looking indicators, focusing on known weaknesses cataloged in vulnerability databases or revealed through scanning. This reactive orientation leaves organizations perpetually one step behind adversaries. By contrast, predictive models aim to anticipate vulnerabilities and exploit attempts before they materialize. Leveraging machine learning techniques, organizations can correlate vast datasets that include threat intelligence feeds, exploit kit activity, system telemetry, and even geopolitical indicators. For instance, if data analytics reveal a sudden increase in exploit activity targeting a specific software stack on underground forums, predictive models can raise the risk rating of similar vulnerabilities in enterprise systems, even if no attack has yet occurred locally. Such forward-looking capabilities allow security teams to shift from passive defense to proactive preparation, allocating resources to areas most likely to face imminent attack. Big data platforms make this possible by processing petabytes of heterogeneous security-relevant information in real time, drawing insights that human analysts alone can never uncover. The challenge will lie in balancing predictive power with accuracy, ensuring that organizations do not become overwhelmed by false forecasts or misallocated priorities.

In parallel with predictive modeling, the future of vulnerability and risk assessment is increasingly tied to the principle of threat-informed defense. The integration of the MITRE ATT&CK framework into assessment and remediation workflows is a pivotal development in this direction. MITRE ATT&CK provides a globally recognized knowledge base of adversary tactics, techniques, and procedures (TTPs), mapping how attackers operate in real-world scenarios. By aligning vulnerability data with this framework, organizations can move beyond generic severity scores and evaluate vulnerabilities in terms of how adversaries are actually exploiting them in the wild. This contextualization allows for more intelligent prioritization, where remediation is guided not only by technical severity but also by threat relevance. For example, a medium-severity vulnerability that directly aligns with a technique actively used by a known adversary group targeting the organization's sector may warrant higher remediation urgency than a critical vulnerability that lacks evidence of active exploitation. Incorporating MITRE ATT&CK also enhances red teaming and penetration testing, as defenders can simulate real-world attack paths to test the exploitability of vulnerabilities under adversarial conditions. The result is a more dynamic, threat-informed approach to risk assessment that closes the gap between theoretical weaknesses and practical attack scenarios.

Perhaps the most transformative trend on the horizon is the rise of automated remediation and self-healing systems. Current vulnerability management often falters at the remediation stage, where the discovery of weaknesses is not matched by timely fixes. Delays in patching and misconfigurations remain among the most common root causes of breaches. Emerging systems aim to close this gap by enabling infrastructure to repair itself in real time. Self-healing technologies draw on concepts from autonomic computing, enabling systems to detect anomalies, apply corrective patches, roll back unstable configurations, and restore services without human intervention. In containerized and cloud-native environments, where workloads are ephemeral and infrastructure is codified, these capabilities are increasingly feasible. For example, if a vulnerability is detected in a microservice, the orchestration platform may automatically replace the affected container with a patched version, ensuring continuity with minimal disruption. Similarly, endpoint systems equipped with self-healing agents may automatically restore critical files, reconfigure security controls, or isolate themselves from the network to contain damage. While full autonomy remains aspirational, incremental advances in automated remediation are already reducing mean time to patch (MTTP) and limiting the window of exposure. Nevertheless, questions of trust, accountability, and fail-safe mechanisms remain unresolved. Organizations must consider how much autonomy to grant machines in making remediation decisions that can impact critical operations.

The final major direction shaping the future of vulnerability and risk assessment is the movement toward regulatory convergence and the global harmonization of risk frameworks. Today, organizations face a patchwork of compliance obligations, from the European Union's GDPR and the United States' NIST Cybersecurity Framework to sector-specific standards like HIPAA and emerging national cybersecurity acts in Asia, Africa, and Latin America. This fragmentation complicates vulnerability management, as organizations operating globally must reconcile overlapping and sometimes conflicting requirements. There is growing recognition that a more harmonized approach is necessary to streamline compliance and enhance collective security. International organizations, such as the International Organization for Standardization (ISO) and the World Economic Forum, have begun advocating for greater cross-border alignment of cybersecurity standards. Similarly, regulatory convergence is being driven by the recognition that cyber threats do not respect national boundaries and that inconsistent standards create weak links in global supply chains.

A harmonized framework would not only simplify compliance but also facilitate more standardized reporting of vulnerabilities and risks, making it easier for regulators, insurers, and industry partners to evaluate security postures. However, geopolitical tensions, divergent legal traditions, and the uneven distribution of cybersecurity capacities across nations present formidable barriers to achieving such harmonization in practice.

Taken together, these emerging trends point toward a future where vulnerability and risk assessment becomes more predictive, contextualized, automated, and globally coherent. Predictive analytics promise to anticipate threats rather than merely react to them, while frameworks like MITRE ATT&CK embed adversarial realism into prioritization. Automated remediation offers the possibility of reducing human bottlenecks and accelerating recovery, and global harmonization of regulatory standards seeks to create a more consistent foundation for managing cyber risk at scale. Yet these trends also introduce new challenges—ranging from the reliability of predictive models to the governance of self-healing systems and the politics of international standardization. The trajectory of progress will therefore depend not only on technological innovation but also on organizational adaptability, legal frameworks, and international cooperation. What is clear is that vulnerability and risk assessment will no longer be a static exercise of cataloging weaknesses; it is evolving into a dynamic, adaptive discipline that must keep pace with the speed and complexity of the digital world.

Conclusion

This chapter has traced the evolution and practical implementation of vulnerability and risk assessment, emphasizing its centrality to modern cybersecurity strategy. At its core, the discipline involves not only the technical detection of weaknesses but also the structured processes of scoring, prioritization, and integration into organizational workflows. The effectiveness of these processes depends on how well raw technical findings are transformed into actionable intelligence that aligns with business objectives. Scoring frameworks, such as CVSS, remain foundational, but their value increases significantly when contextualized with environmental factors, threat intelligence, and business-criticality measures. By doing so, organizations move beyond theoretical severity ratings and develop a more nuanced understanding of which vulnerabilities truly represent material risks.

Prioritization emerges as the linchpin of effective vulnerability management. Given the sheer scale of vulnerabilities in modern hybrid infrastructures, no enterprise can remediate all weaknesses simultaneously. Instead, meaningful prioritization allows security leaders to focus resources on the threats most likely to be exploited and the assets most critical to organizational continuity. The process of prioritization therefore acts as a bridge between technical scoring models and practical remediation efforts. Without it, organizations risk wasting resources on low-impact vulnerabilities while leaving high-impact risks unaddressed. In practice, prioritization requires not only algorithms and automation but also human expertise to ensure that unique contextual factors are recognized.

Integration with development and operational lifecycles represents the third major theme of this chapter. Vulnerability and risk assessment cannot remain siloed within security teams; it must become part of the daily fabric of IT and DevOps operations. Embedding security testing within Agile and DevOps pipelines ensures that vulnerabilities are detected early, when remediation is faster and less disruptive. Similarly, integration with Security Orchestration, Automation, and Response (SOAR) platforms and Governance, Risk, and Compliance (GRC) systems allows vulnerability data to be operationalized in real time, enabling both technical teams and executives to act on a common understanding of organizational risk posture. Integration, therefore, represents the pathway through which scoring and prioritization are converted into tangible outcomes—reduced mean time to remediation, greater compliance alignment, and more resilient digital services.

Throughout these discussions, one recurring insight stands out: data is the foundation of modern risk assessment. The completeness, accuracy, and timeliness of data directly shape the quality of risk decisions. Incomplete or biased data can distort scoring models;

excessive false positives can overwhelm prioritization efforts; and weak data pipelines can hinder integration with operational workflows. Conversely, when data collection is comprehensive, continuously updated, and enriched with contextual threat intelligence, organizations are able to make decisions that are not only technically sound but also strategically relevant. As infrastructures expand into cloud, mobile, and IoT domains, building resilient data foundations will be critical for sustaining effective vulnerability and risk management practices.

For practitioners, the action points are clear. First, invest in processes and tools that strengthen the integrity and scope of vulnerability data, whether through improved scanning coverage, diverse threat intelligence sources, or continuous monitoring. Second, adopt prioritization strategies that combine quantitative scoring with contextual insights, thereby ensuring that remediation aligns with both the evolving threat landscape and business imperatives. Third, work toward embedding vulnerability management within existing operational pipelines, particularly DevOps and cloud orchestration systems, so that security becomes an enabler of agility rather than an obstacle. Finally, maintain a balance between automation and human expertise: automation provides scale and speed, but human judgment ensures contextual accuracy and accountability.

Key Terms

1. Vulnerability Assessment – The process of identifying, classifying, and analyzing weaknesses in digital systems.
2. Risk Assessment – Evaluation of potential threats and their impact on organizational assets.
3. Common Vulnerabilities and Exposures (CVE) – A public database of disclosed software vulnerabilities.
4. Common Vulnerability Scoring System (CVSS) – An industry-standard framework for quantifying the severity of vulnerabilities.
5. False Positive – An alert that incorrectly identifies a benign condition as a vulnerability or threat.

6. Alert Fatigue – The desensitization of security analysts caused by overwhelming volumes of alerts.
7. SIEM (Security Information and Event Management) – A platform that collects, aggregates, and analyzes security event data.
8. SOAR (Security Orchestration, Automation, and Response) – Tools that automate security workflows and incident responses.
9. GRC (Governance, Risk, and Compliance) – Systems aligning security management with regulatory and business objectives.
10. Open-Source Scanners – Free, community-driven tools for vulnerability scanning (e.g., OpenVAS, Nmap).
11. Commercial Scanners – Vendor-supported vulnerability scanners (e.g., Nessus, Qualys, Rapid7).
12. Cloud-Native Security Tools – Security services integrated into cloud platforms (e.g., AWS Inspector, Azure Security Center).
13. AI/ML-Driven Assessment – Use of artificial intelligence to predict, prioritize, and detect vulnerabilities.
14. Predictive Risk Assessment – Anticipating vulnerabilities and threats before exploitation occurs using big data and AI.
15. MITRE ATT&CK Framework – A knowledge base mapping adversary tactics and techniques used in real-world attacks.
16. Automated Remediation – Systems that apply patches or mitigations without human intervention.
17. Self-Healing Systems – Infrastructure capable of autonomously detecting and correcting vulnerabilities or misconfigurations.
18. Regulatory Harmonization – Global efforts to align cybersecurity standards and compliance requirements.
19. Mean Time to Remediate (MTTR) – A key metric measuring how quickly vulnerabilities are fixed after detection.
20. Shift-Left Security – Integrating security testing earlier in the software development lifecycle.

21. Threat Intelligence - Data and insights about current and emerging adversary activities.
22. Hybrid Cloud - An infrastructure model combining on-premises systems with public and private cloud services.
23. Data Completeness - The extent to which vulnerability datasets cover all potential weaknesses.
24. Prioritization - The process of ranking vulnerabilities based on business impact and exploitability.
25. Risk-Informed Decision-Making - Using vulnerability data and contextual intelligence to guide strategic security actions.

Review Questions

1. Define vulnerability assessment and explain how it differs from risk assessment.
2. Why is CVSS widely used, and what limitations does it have in practical environments?
3. How do open-source scanners differ from commercial vulnerability scanners in terms of cost, customization, and support?
4. Discuss the role of SIEM systems in supporting vulnerability and risk assessment.
5. In what ways do SOAR platforms reduce analyst workload in vulnerability management?
6. How do GRC platforms translate technical vulnerabilities into governance-level insights?
7. What challenges arise from incomplete or biased vulnerability data? Provide examples.
8. Explain the concept of false positives in vulnerability assessment and how they contribute to alert fatigue.
9. Why is the cybersecurity skills gap a significant limitation in implementing vulnerability assessment programs?
10. What does it mean to balance automation with human expertise in vulnerability management?
11. How do cloud-native security tools address the challenges of dynamic cloud infrastructures?

12. Provide an example of how AI/ML can predictively assess vulnerabilities before they are exploited.
13. What advantages does integrating the MITRE ATT&CK framework bring to vulnerability prioritization?
14. Describe how automated remediation and self-healing systems change the vulnerability management lifecycle.
15. Why is regulatory convergence important for multinational enterprises?
16. How can predictive analytics using big data improve vulnerability prioritization decisions?
17. In the case study presented, how did integrating vulnerability management into DevOps pipelines improve MTTR?
18. What measurable outcomes did the multinational enterprise achieve after embedding end-to-end risk assessment practices?
19. Why is data considered the foundation of modern risk assessment?
20. How can organizations reduce the impact of alert fatigue on security analysts?
21. Discuss the importance of prioritization in environments with thousands of vulnerabilities.
22. What risks emerge if an organization relies exclusively on automation for vulnerability remediation?
23. How does shift-left security contribute to cost reduction in vulnerability management?
24. In what ways can regulatory fragmentation create challenges for global enterprises?
25. Summarize the key themes of scoring, prioritization, and integration as they are applied to end-to-end vulnerability and risk assessment.

CHAPTER 10

The Future of Data-Centric Cybersecurity

Learning Objectives

By the end of this chapter, readers will be able to:

1. Explain the concept of data-centric cybersecurity and differentiate it from traditional perimeter- or network-centric approaches.
2. Analyze emerging threats in the digital ecosystem that necessitate a data-first security paradigm, including cloud adoption, IoT proliferation, AI-driven attacks, and advanced persistent threats.
3. Evaluate future trends in protecting data across its lifecycle—from creation and storage to transmission, processing, and disposal.
4. Identify the role of advanced technologies such as artificial intelligence, machine learning, blockchain, and homomorphic encryption in shaping next-generation data protection strategies.
5. Assess the implications of regulatory and compliance frameworks (e.g., GDPR, CCPA, and evolving global data protection laws) on future cybersecurity practices.
6. Critically discuss challenges and opportunities in balancing data privacy, security, usability, and innovation in a hyper-connected digital economy.
7. Formulate forward-looking strategies for organizations to transition from infrastructure-focused to data-centric cybersecurity models.

8. Anticipate the socio-technical impact of future data-centric security, including ethical considerations, workforce adaptation, and cross-border governance.

Overview

The history of cybersecurity has always been shaped by the evolution of computing and the ways in which societies use information. In its earliest form, cybersecurity was largely about protecting physical systems—mainframes housed in secured rooms, guarded by access badges and passwords. As networks emerged, the emphasis shifted toward perimeter security, with firewalls and intrusion detection systems acting as the digital equivalent of fortress walls. With the rise of the internet, mobility, and cloud computing, those perimeters dissolved, ushering in what many experts now call the data-centric era of cybersecurity. This transformation reorients the discipline away from infrastructure as the focal point and places data itself—the asset most valuable to businesses, governments, and individuals—at the center of protection strategies.

The rationale for this shift is simple yet profound: data has become the primary currency of the digital economy. It drives artificial intelligence systems, informs national policy, enables medical breakthroughs, and fuels innovation across industries. Unlike physical infrastructure, data is intangible, replicable, and mobile. It can cross borders within seconds, stored in decentralized clouds or distributed ledger systems. At the same time, it is vulnerable to theft, misuse, surveillance, and manipulation on a global scale. The stakes are evident in the headlines of recent decades: massive breaches exposing millions of identities, ransomware paralyzing hospitals, and cyber-espionage campaigns targeting intellectual property. In all these cases, it is not the servers or the networks per se that adversaries seek—it is the data residing within them.

Recognizing this shift, modern cybersecurity frameworks increasingly advocate for approaches that view data not just as an object to be shielded but as the foundation around which security architectures must be designed. This perspective is evident in regulatory regimes such as the European Union's General Data Protection Regulation (GDPR), which enshrines the principle of "privacy by design," and in architectural paradigms such as zero trust, which assumes that no data transaction is inherently trustworthy without verification. Similarly, technological innovations such as privacy-enhancing technologies (PETs), homomorphic encryption, and secure multi-party computation (MPC) are emerging to ensure that data can be used, shared, and analyzed without ever being fully exposed.

To appreciate the magnitude of this shift, it is useful to contrast the old and new paradigms. Traditional approaches to cybersecurity placed infrastructure—servers, endpoints, and networks—at the heart of protection. Access controls, patching regimes, and monitoring tools were designed to safeguard these assets. While effective in limited contexts, this model struggled as computing became distributed and dynamic. A company's data may today reside partially in its on-premises servers, partially in multiple public clouds, and partially in employees' personal devices. In such an environment, securing the perimeter is a near-impossible task.

The data-centric model, by contrast, begins with a different set of assumptions. It acknowledges that data will inevitably move across platforms and that adversaries will attempt to exploit that mobility. Security must therefore travel with the data, employing encryption, tokenization, and access control mechanisms that remain effective regardless of where the data is stored or processed. Moreover, because organizations increasingly depend on data analytics for decision-making, data must remain usable even while being protected. This dual requirement—protecting data without stifling its utility—forms the intellectual core of data-centric cybersecurity.

A useful illustration of this transformation comes from the healthcare sector. Under the infrastructure-centric model, a hospital might focus on securing its servers, firewalls, and electronic health record systems. Yet breaches often occur not because the infrastructure fails, but because data is shared with third parties—insurers, research institutions, or cloud providers—without adequate safeguards. A data-centric model instead emphasizes encryption of medical records, anonymization for research use, and rigorous tracking of data flows. This ensures that the value of the data can be harnessed without compromising patient privacy.

The growing centrality of data has also transformed it into a strategic geopolitical resource. Governments recognize that control over data streams confers economic, military, and political advantages. For example, the US and the European Union have repeatedly clashed with other powers over data sovereignty, leading to frameworks such as the EU–US Data Privacy Framework (2023). Similarly, adversarial nation-states have launched campaigns of data exfiltration to acquire intellectual property, personal information, and sensitive defence data.

This strategic dimension is compounded by the rise of artificial intelligence (AI). Training AI models requires vast quantities of high-quality data, which has made large datasets both extremely valuable and highly targeted. A breach that exposes millions of health records or financial transactions is not only a privacy catastrophe but also a potential boon for adversaries seeking to train their own AI systems. Thus, the protection of data is no longer just a corporate responsibility—it is a matter of national security.

As cybersecurity becomes data-centric, it is not enough to deploy new technologies; governance frameworks must evolve in tandem. Regulations such as GDPR, the California Consumer Privacy Act (CCPA), and China's Personal Information Protection Law (PIPL) all reflect the recognition that citizens must have rights over their personal data. At the same time, compliance with these regulations imposes significant challenges for organizations, which must build systems capable of respecting user consent, enabling data portability, and ensuring timely breach notification.

Technology is responding to these pressures. For example, homomorphic encryption enables computations on encrypted data, allowing datasets to be shared across organizations without exposing sensitive details. Federated learning enables machine learning models to be trained across multiple decentralized datasets, reducing the need for centralized collection. Together, these innovations make it possible to reconcile the often competing goals of data utility and data privacy.

Privacy-Enhancing Computation

Conceptual Foundations

The transition to a data-centric cybersecurity paradigm has created a profound tension between two imperatives: the need to extract value from data and the obligation to protect it from misuse. Modern organizations rely on vast datasets to drive innovation, optimize operations, and deliver personalized services. Governments analyze citizen data to shape public policy, while scientists use massive research datasets to make discoveries in medicine, climate science, and energy. Yet, every time data is shared, aggregated, or analyzed, it risks exposure. The paradox is clear: data is most valuable when widely used, but its use increases the surface for abuse.

Privacy-enhancing computation (PEC), often referred to broadly as privacy-enhancing technologies (PETs), emerges as the solution to this paradox. PETs represent a family of techniques and tools designed to maximize the utility of data while minimizing the disclosure of sensitive information. Rather than relying solely on access controls or post-hoc anonymization, PETs embed privacy-preserving mechanisms directly into the process of computation. The aim is to make it possible for organizations to collaborate on data, run computations, and derive insights without ever exposing the underlying raw data.

This capability is increasingly critical in today's regulatory environment. Frameworks such as the General Data Protection Regulation (GDPR) in Europe and the California Consumer Privacy Act (CCPA) in the United States emphasize principles of data minimization and user consent. PETs provide the technical means to comply with these legal mandates while still harnessing the power of data-driven insights. For example, GDPR requires that personal data processing be limited to what is "necessary and proportionate." Traditional data sharing—where entire datasets are exchanged between entities—rarely satisfies this requirement. PETs, such as secure multi-party computation (MPC) or federated learning, instead allow computations to be conducted collaboratively while raw data never leaves its original custodian, aligning neatly with regulatory principles.

Historically, the development of PETs can be traced to advances in cryptography and secure systems design. Concepts such as homomorphic encryption, which allows computation on encrypted data, emerged from theoretical research in the late 20th century but remained impractical due to computational overhead. Similarly, multi-party computation was once confined to academic discussions but is now being deployed in financial services and healthcare. What distinguishes the present moment is the convergence of necessity and feasibility: as data volumes and regulatory pressures increase, and as computing power becomes more affordable, PETs are moving from research labs into mainstream cybersecurity strategies.

PETs in the Ecosystem of Data-Centric Cybersecurity

It is helpful to situate PETs within the broader ecosystem of data-centric security. Traditional tools like encryption and tokenization primarily protect data at rest or data in transit. PETs extend protection to the third, often neglected domain: data in use. This is the state in which data is actively being processed—when a machine learning algorithm trains on patient records, or when a fraud detection system analyzes credit card transactions. Protecting data in use ensures that even during computation, sensitive attributes remain confidential.

This is a profound shift in the philosophy of cybersecurity. Conventional models assumed that once data was decrypted for processing, it was necessarily exposed to risk. PETs challenge this assumption by enabling secure computation environments, where even operators and administrators cannot view the raw data. Consider, for example, a consortium of banks collaborating to detect money-laundering patterns. Under traditional approaches, they would need to pool customer transaction records into a central repository, raising significant privacy and compliance risks. With PETs, each institution can keep its data local, while joint analytics are performed in a distributed or encrypted fashion, ensuring that no party gains access to another's raw records.

Applications Driving PET Adoption

The appeal of PETs becomes evident when viewed through practical applications. In healthcare, the potential to share data across hospitals and research institutes is enormous for accelerating drug discovery and personalized medicine. Yet privacy regulations and ethical concerns often make such data sharing impossible. PETs like federated learning allow AI models to be trained across hospitals without any raw data leaving institutional boundaries. In finance, institutions can use PETs to conduct joint risk analyses or credit scoring while keeping proprietary and sensitive client data private. Governments, too, are exploring PETs for purposes ranging from cross-border law enforcement collaboration to national census processing.

The common thread across these examples is that PETs enable collaboration without compromise. They represent a technical embodiment of the idea that privacy and utility need not be zero-sum. For this reason, PETs are increasingly viewed as a cornerstone of future cybersecurity architectures, bridging the gap between stringent privacy requirements and the data-driven imperatives of modern society.

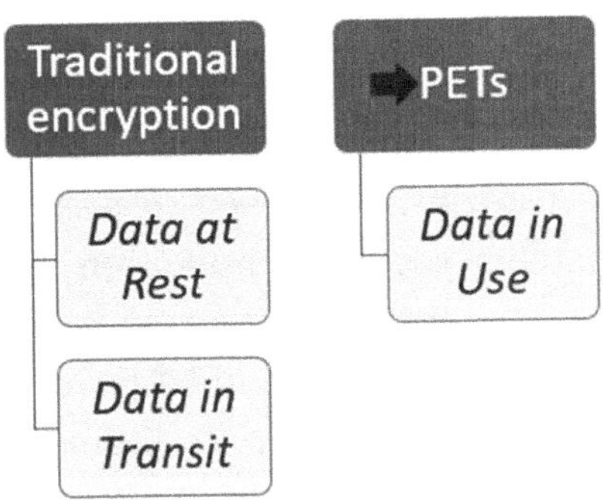

Figure 10.1: The Role of PETs in Data Lifecycle Security

Homomorphic Encryption

The idea of homomorphic encryption (HE) stands as one of the most transformative innovations in modern cryptography. At its core, it promises something once thought impossible: the ability to perform computations directly on encrypted data without first decrypting it. The output of such computation, once decrypted, yields the same result as if the operations had been performed on the plaintext data. This capability is revolutionary for data-centric cybersecurity because it means that organizations can outsource computation, share analytics, or collaborate on sensitive datasets without ever exposing the underlying information.

To illustrate the concept, consider a simple analogy. Imagine that data is a set of delicate jewels locked inside a strongbox. Traditional encryption protects the jewels by locking the box, but to use them—say, to appraise their value—the box must be opened, exposing its contents to potential theft. Homomorphic encryption changes the rules: it allows the appraiser to shake or weigh the locked box and still derive meaningful insights, all without ever opening it. The jewels remain secure, but their utility is not lost.

Mathematical Foundations

The theoretical basis for homomorphic encryption lies in algebraic structures that allow operations to be mirrored between plaintext and ciphertext spaces. In mathematical terms, let *Enc(x)* represent the encryption of some plaintext *x*. A homomorphic encryption scheme ensures that:

- $Enc(x) \quad Enc(y) = Enc(x + y)$
- $Enc(x) \quad Enc(y) = Enc(x \times y)$

Here, ⊕ and ⊗ represent operations in the encrypted domain, corresponding to addition and multiplication in plaintext. Depending on the scheme, the encryption may allow only one of these operations (partially homomorphic) or both in unlimited succession (fully homomorphic).

The concept of partially homomorphic encryption (PHE) has been known since the late 1970s, with the RSA cryptosystem enabling multiplicative homomorphism and the Paillier cryptosystem supporting additive homomorphism. However, the dream of fully homomorphic encryption (FHE)—supporting both operations without limit—remained elusive until 2009, when Craig Gentry proposed the first feasible FHE scheme. Though initially impractical due to computational overhead, this breakthrough opened the door to a new era of research.

Types of Homomorphic Encryption

Homomorphic encryption schemes can be broadly categorized into three classes:

1. **Partially Homomorphic Encryption (PHE):** Supports one operation (addition or multiplication) repeatedly. For instance, the Paillier cryptosystem allows encrypted numbers to be added, making it useful for applications such as voting systems and aggregated statistics.
2. **Somewhat Homomorphic Encryption (SHE):** Supports both addition and multiplication, but with a limited number of operations before noise overwhelms the ciphertext. This is more versatile than PHE but constrained in depth.
3. **Fully Homomorphic Encryption (FHE):** Supports unlimited operations of both types. FHE enables arbitrary computations, effectively allowing encrypted data to be treated like plaintext in computational processes.

Practical Applications

The implications of HE are far-reaching across industries. In healthcare, HE can enable research institutions to collaboratively analyze patient datasets without compromising patient privacy. For example, hospitals in different countries can collectively train a diagnostic model on encrypted data, ensuring compliance with strict cross-border privacy laws.

In finance, homomorphic encryption can secure outsourced computations to cloud providers. A bank can send encrypted financial transactions to a third-party service for fraud detection. The cloud provider performs the computations without ever seeing the plaintext transactions, and the bank receives decrypted results that flag suspicious patterns.

In the realm of government and defense, HE offers possibilities for intelligence sharing between allied nations. Sensitive data such as biometric identifiers or classified communications can be processed jointly without either side exposing raw data to the other.

A concrete case study comes from the collaboration between Microsoft Research and health organizations, where homomorphic encryption has been applied to secure genomic data processing. Genomic information is among the most sensitive forms of personal data, yet its analysis is essential for advancing personalized medicine. Homomorphic encryption ensures that research insights can be generated without revealing raw genomes to external processors.

Limitations and Challenges

Despite its promise, HE is not without challenges. The most significant limitation lies in its computational overhead. Operations on encrypted data are orders of magnitude slower than those on plaintext. For example, while adding two plaintext integers might take microseconds, performing the same operation homomorphically can take milliseconds or seconds, depending on the scheme. This overhead makes HE impractical for real-time applications, such as interactive web services or high-frequency trading systems.

Another challenge is ciphertext expansion. Homomorphic encryption schemes produce ciphertexts much larger than the plaintexts they represent, creating storage and bandwidth burdens. For large-scale data, such as medical imaging or financial transaction logs, this overhead can be prohibitive.

Additionally, while FHE supports arbitrary computations in theory, the complexity of building efficient circuits for real-world algorithms remains a research frontier. The process of designing, optimizing, and maintaining homomorphic circuits requires deep expertise and careful engineering.

Recent Advances

Encouragingly, recent years have seen significant progress. Companies such as IBM and Microsoft, as well as startups such as Zama, are investing heavily in making FHE practical. The introduction of optimized libraries such as HElib (IBM) and SEAL (Microsoft) has made it possible to experiment with HE in applied contexts. Hybrid approaches are also emerging, combining HE with other PETs such as secure multi-party computation or trusted execution environments to balance performance and privacy.

A notable example is the use of leveled FHE, where computations are restricted to a limited depth but are sufficient for many practical machine learning tasks. For instance, training a linear regression model on encrypted data can often be achieved without requiring unlimited homomorphic operations. This compromise makes FHE more usable today while researchers continue to push toward full efficiency.

Homomorphic Encryption in the Data-Centric Future

The role of homomorphic encryption in the future of data-centric cybersecurity is both symbolic and practical. Symbolically, it demonstrates that the once impossible goal of "using data without seeing it" is no longer a dream. Practically, it equips organizations with a tool to reconcile the competing demands of data utility, privacy, and regulatory compliance. As computing resources grow cheaper and algorithms more efficient, HE may well become a default component of secure data infrastructures, enabling encrypted cloud computing, privacy-preserving AI, and cross-border collaboration without compromise.

Secure Multi-Party Computation (MPC)

Secure Multi-Party Computation (MPC) is another cornerstone of privacy-enhancing computation, complementing homomorphic encryption by allowing multiple entities to jointly compute a function over their private inputs without revealing those inputs to one another. The fundamental idea is deceptively simple but profoundly powerful: parties collaborate to obtain a collective result, such as an aggregated statistic or a machine learning prediction, while ensuring that each participant's raw data remains confidential.

The origins of MPC can be traced back to Andrew Yao's seminal work in the 1980s, known as *Yao's Millionaires' Problem*. Yao posed the question of whether two individuals could determine who was wealthier without disclosing their actual net worth. The solution involved cryptographic protocols that provided a proof-of-concept for computing arbitrary functions securely between distrustful parties. Over the decades, this work matured into a general framework of protocols under the umbrella of MPC, and today it forms a practical foundation for privacy-preserving collaboration in finance, healthcare, and even governmental data exchanges.

At its core, MPC operates by splitting each party's private data into **shares** using techniques such as *secret sharing*. Instead of transmitting the original data, each participant distributes mathematically obfuscated fragments across all collaborating parties. No single fragment reveals useful information, but when combined through the protocol, these fragments reconstruct the intended computation. A canonical example is Shamir's Secret Sharing, in which data is represented as coefficients of a polynomial; only when enough shares are collected can the polynomial be solved and the secret revealed. This property ensures that partial leaks do not compromise the overall confidentiality of the inputs.

Consider a healthcare consortium where hospitals across different regions want to compute an aggregated survival rate for patients undergoing a new treatment. Regulatory restrictions, such as HIPAA or GDPR, may prohibit sharing raw patient records across institutions. Using MPC, each hospital can encode its patient outcomes into secret shares and contribute them to a distributed protocol. The final computation delivers the aggregate survival rate without any hospital learning the sensitive details of another's dataset. Such workflows demonstrate how MPC resolves the tension between collaboration and compliance in highly regulated industries.

Another illustrative example can be drawn from the financial services industry. Competing banks may wish to jointly train a fraud-detection model that benefits from broader behavioral data. None of the institutions, however, is willing to expose client transaction histories due to confidentiality agreements and competitive risk. By leveraging MPC, they can securely pool their training data into a federated protocol that outputs a model without revealing individual transaction logs. This creates an ecosystem of collaborative defense while preserving customer privacy.

MPC can be realized through several paradigms. One is garbled circuits, where computations are represented as encrypted Boolean circuits; each party evaluates the circuit without learning intermediate values. Another is additive secret sharing, often used for arithmetic operations, where each party holds random "slices" of the data that add up to the true value. Protocols differ in performance trade-offs: garbled circuits are versatile but computationally heavy, while secret sharing offers efficiency in linear algebra-type tasks, making it especially useful in machine learning contexts.

Despite its promise, MPC faces challenges in scalability and efficiency. Secure protocols typically introduce significant computational and communication overhead compared to standard centralized computation. While recent advances in hardware acceleration and cryptographic libraries have made MPC more practical, it remains resource-intensive for real-time, large-scale applications. A trade-off often emerges: stronger security guarantees can slow down processing, while more efficient protocols may provide weaker resilience against adversarial models.

To aid comprehension, textbooks often use diagrams to show how data flows in MPC systems. A useful teaching diagram can depict three organizations (e.g., hospitals) each holding private datasets. These datasets are split into encrypted shares and sent across the network to all other participants. The shares travel through a secure computation layer where the joint function—say, the average recovery time—is computed. Finally, only the aggregate output is revealed, while no organization ever learns the others' raw inputs. This visualization reinforces the principle that MPC enables *collective insight without individual disclosure*.

As regulatory and ethical requirements for data privacy tighten globally, the role of MPC will continue to expand. Its applications now extend beyond academic proofs into industrial adoption: privacy-preserving advertising in big tech firms, collaborative research in genomics, and even secure electronic voting. The trajectory suggests that MPC is not merely a cryptographic curiosity but an operational necessity in data-centric cybersecurity. By embedding MPC into data pipelines, organizations can collaborate across silos, advance shared defenses, and comply with stringent data protection laws—all without betraying the trust of their data subjects.

Trusted Execution Environments (TEEs)

Trusted Execution Environments (TEEs) represent a hardware-centric strand of privacy-enhancing technology, designed to secure computation by carving out isolated regions within a processor. Unlike software-only methods such as homomorphic encryption or multi-party computation, which focus on mathematical transformations, TEEs rely on trusted hardware enclaves to provide a controlled environment where code and data can be executed with confidentiality and integrity guarantees.

The most prominent industrial implementations of TEEs are Intel's Software Guard Extensions (SGX) and ARM's TrustZone. Intel SGX, available on x86 platforms, allows developers to create "enclaves"—secure areas in memory where sensitive computations can occur, shielded from the rest of the system. ARM TrustZone, widely deployed in mobile and embedded devices, establishes two "worlds": a secure world, dedicated to sensitive operations, and a normal world for general tasks. By separating execution domains, TrustZone ensures that critical applications such as digital wallets or biometric authentication remain protected even if the broader operating system is compromised.

The key advantage of TEEs lies in performance efficiency. Whereas fully homomorphic encryption can slow computation by orders of magnitude, TEEs allow near-native processing speeds because data is decrypted and processed within the enclave using conventional methods. This makes them particularly attractive for cloud computing, where sensitive data—ranging from genomic records to financial transactions—must often be analyzed on third-party infrastructure. By deploying workloads inside TEEs, organizations can ensure that cloud providers cannot access plaintext data, even though the providers supply the hardware and operating system.

However, TEEs are not without risks. A major concern lies in side-channel attacks, which exploit indirect information leaks such as cache timings, page faults, or speculative execution behavior to infer what occurs inside the enclave. Research has demonstrated that even highly isolated TEEs, such as Intel SGX, can be vulnerable to carefully orchestrated side-channel exploits, challenging the perception of hardware enclaves as impenetrable fortresses. Moreover, TEEs shift a portion of the trust model from mathematics to hardware supply chains: organizations must place confidence in chip manufacturers to design, implement, and update secure architectures.

In practice, TEEs are being deployed across a range of domains. In digital rights management, enclaves safeguard media decryption keys from user tampering. In finance, TEEs protect cryptographic wallets and ensure the integrity of high-frequency trading algorithms. In cloud environments, enterprises leverage confidential virtual machines (VMs) built on SGX or TrustZone to analyze sensitive workloads while maintaining strong confidentiality assurances. These applications highlight the value proposition of TEEs: they make privacy-preserving computation practical at an industrial scale without the prohibitive cost of software-only PETs.

Yet, the vulnerabilities of TEEs remind us that no solution is absolute. Security researchers continue to discover novel enclave attacks, prompting rapid cycles of patches and architectural redesigns. Thus, while TEEs offer a performance-efficient path to secure computation, they must be viewed as one layer in a broader defense-in-depth strategy rather than a silver bullet.

Dimension	**Trusted Execution Environments (TEEs)**	**Software-Only PETs (HE, MPC, DP)**
Underlying Mechanism	Hardware enclaves isolate code and data from the OS and hypervisor.	Mathematical techniques transform or obfuscate data during computation.
Performance	Near-native execution speed.	Significant computational overhead (10x–1000x slower for HE/MPC).

Dimension	Trusted Execution Environments (TEEs)	Software-Only PETs (HE, MPC, DP)
Trust Model	Relies on hardware vendors (Intel, ARM) and secure chip design.	Relies on provable mathematical guarantees, independent of hardware vendors.
Deployment Complexity	Requires hardware support and enclave-enabled CPUs.	Software-based; can run on commodity hardware.
Resistance to Attacks	Vulnerable to side-channel and micro-architectural attacks.	Resistant to hardware exploits, but may leak statistical or structural info.
Scalability	Highly scalable for real-time workloads (e.g., cloud, IoT).	Scalability limited by computational and communication costs.
Applications	Cloud confidential computing, DRM, financial trading, secure wallets.	Secure analytics, federated learning, anonymized databases, census data.

Table 10.1: Trusted Execution Environments (TEEs) vs. Software-Only PETs

Federated Learning

Federated Learning (FL) extends the principles of privacy-preserving computation into the realm of distributed machine learning. Traditional machine learning relies on aggregating all training data into a central server, where algorithms learn from the pooled dataset. This model, while effective, introduces profound privacy, regulatory, and security concerns—particularly when dealing with sensitive domains such as healthcare, finance, or mobile device usage. Federated learning challenges this paradigm by keeping data localized and instead moving the model to the data. In doing so, it decentralizes training while still enabling powerful global models.

The essential mechanism of federated learning is relatively straightforward but conceptually transformative. Multiple clients (such as smartphones, hospitals, or banks) each hold private datasets.

Instead of sharing this data with a central authority, each client downloads a shared model architecture and trains it locally. The updates to the model—typically in the form of gradients or weight adjustments—are then transmitted back to a coordinating server. The server aggregates these updates, often through a method known as federated averaging, and updates the global model accordingly. Crucially, only the model parameters are shared, never the raw data.

For instance, consider Google's deployment of federated learning in its Gboard keyboard application. Millions of users generate typing data that improves predictive text algorithms, but sending raw keystroke logs to Google's servers would create intolerable privacy risks. Instead, each device trains the model locally on the user's keystrokes. The updates are then aggregated to refine the shared prediction model without Google ever seeing the raw input. Similarly, in the medical domain, hospitals can use federated learning to collectively build diagnostic models from patient scans, while ensuring that no sensitive patient data leaves institutional boundaries.

Federated learning does not operate in isolation. It is often coupled with secure aggregation protocols to ensure that even model updates cannot be reverse-engineered to reveal private data. Moreover, differential privacy can be applied to gradients before they are shared, further protecting individuals' contributions. In effect, federated learning creates a layered privacy-enhancing framework in which sensitive information remains local, updates are cryptographically secured, and outputs are noise-hardened against adversarial inference.

A suggested diagram for teaching this section can show three hospitals training local models on patient data. Each sends only parameter updates to a central server, which then aggregates them into a single improved model. No patient data crosses institutional boundaries, visually reinforcing the principle that "the model moves, not the data."

Despite its promise, federated learning faces significant challenges. Communication overhead is substantial because model updates must be exchanged repeatedly across participants. Data heterogeneity also poses problems: not all clients have datasets that are equally distributed, leading to potential biases in the global model. Moreover, adversarial participants can attempt to poison the system by submitting manipulated gradients, which underscores the need for robust anomaly detection and trust mechanisms.

Still, federated learning represents a major step forward in reconciling the power of machine learning with the imperatives of privacy and security. Its growing adoption by technology companies, healthcare research consortia, and even governmental initiatives demonstrates that it is no longer a niche concept but a practical tool for real-world problems. By enabling collaboration without centralization, federated learning offers a vision of machine learning that is both inclusive and privacy-respecting—qualities essential for data-centric cybersecurity in the future.

Case Applications of PETs

The practical significance of privacy-enhancing technologies (PETs) becomes clearest when viewed through their application in real-world domains where data sensitivity and regulatory oversight intersect. Industries such as healthcare, financial services, and government administration are all characterized by high-value datasets that, if exposed, can compromise individual rights, corporate confidentiality, or national interests. PETs enable these sectors to strike a balance between utility and privacy, allowing data to be shared, analyzed, and acted upon without surrendering control over sensitive information.

Healthcare: Genomic Research and Patient Privacy

Healthcare is at the forefront of PET adoption due to the highly sensitive nature of medical and genomic data. Genomic sequencing, for instance, provides unparalleled opportunities for precision medicine, yet it also carries the risk of irrevocable privacy loss—since genetic data uniquely identifies individuals and their families. Here, PETs such as homomorphic encryption and secure multi-party computation (MPC) allow researchers from multiple institutions to collaborate on large-scale genomic studies without exposing raw patient data.

For example, instead of centralizing genomic datasets in a single location, institutions can use MPC protocols to compute aggregate risk factors across distributed datasets. Homomorphic encryption enables algorithms to be trained on encrypted genomes, producing useful predictive models without ever accessing the underlying genetic code. This not only satisfies privacy requirements under regulations like HIPAA and the GDPR, but also builds patient trust, which is critical for voluntary participation in genomic research initiatives.

Financial Services: Collaborative Anti-Money Laundering (AML)

Financial institutions also leverage PETs to manage the tension between regulatory compliance and data confidentiality. Anti-money laundering (AML) investigations require banks to share transactional data across borders and institutions in order to detect suspicious patterns of behavior. Yet, such sharing can conflict with competition law, client confidentiality, and data residency requirements.

Using MPC frameworks, banks can jointly analyze distributed transaction ledgers to identify suspicious entities or transaction flows without revealing details about legitimate customers. Similarly, differential privacy can be applied to enable the exchange of aggregate risk indicators while ensuring that individual client data remains protected. By reducing the risk of overexposure, PETs facilitate the cross-institutional cooperation demanded by global regulators while safeguarding proprietary financial data.

Government: Privacy-Preserving Census and Demographic Analysis

Governments face a unique challenge in balancing statistical accuracy with individual privacy. National censuses, for example, generate datasets that are indispensable for policymaking, funding allocation, and demographic analysis. Yet, the more granular the data provided, the higher the risk of re-identification, especially when cross-referenced with other public or private databases.

The US Census Bureau's 2020 release was one of the first to incorporate differential privacy as a systematic safeguard. Instead of reporting exact population counts for each small district, the Bureau introduced calibrated noise to ensure that no single household could be reverse-engineered from published results. This decision sparked significant debate within academia and policymaking circles: while some researchers expressed concern over reduced accuracy for small geographic units, the move underscored the growing consensus that privacy must be built into data governance at the national scale.

Zero Trust and Continuous Monitoring

From Perimeter Security to Zero Trust

For decades, enterprise cybersecurity revolved around the notion of a secure perimeter, often described metaphorically as a "castle-and-moat" architecture. In this model, organizations erected strong defenses around their networks—firewalls, intrusion detection systems, and secure gateways—while largely trusting all traffic and actors inside the boundary. The assumption was simple: if adversaries could be kept out, then the internal environment could be treated as safe.

This paradigm worked reasonably well in an era of centralized IT infrastructures, where most resources resided in corporate data centers, employees worked on-site, and external connections were limited. However, the model began to erode as cloud computing, mobile workforces, and third-party integrations reshaped enterprise IT. Once virtual private networks (VPNs), software-as-a-service platforms, and supply chain connectivity blurred the perimeter, attackers quickly learned to exploit trusted internal access. Insider threats—whether malicious or accidental—further undermined the security assumptions of perimeter-based defense.

The Zero Trust model emerged in the late 2000s as a direct response to these failures. Coined and formalized by analyst John Kindervag at Forrester Research, Zero Trust turns the perimeter model on its head. Instead of assuming that anything inside the network is safe, Zero Trust asserts: "Never trust, always verify." Under this philosophy, every access request, whether originating from inside or outside the organization, must be authenticated, authorized, and continuously validated based on real-time data.

Traditional Perimeter vs. Zero Trust Model

To illustrate the contrast, Figure 10.10 (below) presents a side-by-side diagram. On the left, the castle-and-moat model shows a strong perimeter wall protecting an interior where users and services interact with implicit trust. On the right, the Zero Trust model represents a distributed architecture in which each user, device, and application is independently authenticated, policies are enforced in context, and continuous monitoring ensures that access cannot be abused once granted.

Dimension	Perimeter Model (Castle & Moat)	Zero Trust Model
Trust Assumption	Inside = trusted, outside = untrusted	No implicit trust; every entity must be verified
Boundary	Clear network edge (firewalls, VPNs)	Dynamic, identity- and resource-centric
Access Control	Single-time verification at entry	Continuous authentication and authorization
Threat Response	Reactive: prevent external intrusion	Proactive: assume breach, minimize lateral movement
Adaptability	Poor fit for cloud, mobile, hybrid environments	Designed for distributed, cloud-native infrastructures

Table 10.2: Key Contrasts between Traditional Perimeter Security and the Zero Trust Model

Core Principles of Zero Trust

While implementations vary, several core principles define the Zero Trust philosophy.

1. **Never Trust, Always Verify**: Unlike perimeter security, which automatically trusts internal actors, Zero Trust treats every request as potentially hostile. Access to resources is only granted once identity, device health, and contextual

signals are validated. For example, an employee connecting from a corporate laptop in the office might be subject to the same scrutiny as one connecting remotely on a personal device.

2. **Least Privilege Access**: Users and systems are granted the minimum access necessary to perform their roles. This reduces the blast radius of a compromise. If an attacker gains control of a marketing user's account, Zero Trust ensures they cannot pivot into financial databases or administrative consoles.
3. **Continuous Authentication and Monitoring**: Access decisions are not static. Instead, Zero Trust enforces continuous evaluation of trustworthiness. If a user suddenly attempts to download large volumes of sensitive files, their session may be revalidated, restricted, or terminated—even if they initially passed authentication.
4. **Microsegmentation and Lateral Movement Prevention**: Zero Trust architectures divide networks into smaller zones where traffic is tightly controlled. Even if a breach occurs in one zone, microsegmentation ensures attackers cannot easily move laterally to compromise more critical assets.

Practical Implications

In practice, moving from a perimeter-based security model to Zero Trust requires significant organizational change. It involves:

- **Identity as the new perimeter**: Identity and access management (IAM), multi-factor authentication (MFA), and single sign-on (SSO) become foundational.
- **Device trust**: Endpoints must be continuously evaluated for compliance, patching, and threat indicators.
- **Policy-driven access**: Access control decisions increasingly rely on contextual signals such as geolocation, time of day, device health, and behavioral baselines.
- **Real-time analytics**: Data from logs, sensors, and user behavior analytics feeds continuous verification loops.

Major cloud providers and security vendors now embed Zero Trust capabilities directly into their platforms, making it possible to enforce policies across hybrid and multi-cloud infrastructures. For instance, Microsoft's Azure Active Directory integrates conditional access policies based on device compliance, while Google's BeyondCorp architecture pioneered large-scale enterprise adoption of Zero Trust by eliminating VPN reliance altogether.

Identity as the New Perimeter

As organizations transition away from the traditional perimeter model, identity has emerged as the primary control point for modern cybersecurity. In distributed architectures where users, devices, and services interact across cloud environments, corporate networks, and third-party platforms, the notion of a fixed boundary becomes obsolete. Instead, the digital identity of a user or device now functions as the new perimeter, defining who or what is allowed to access enterprise resources.

The Role of Identity Providers (IdPs)

At the heart of this identity-centric model are Identity Providers (IdPs), services responsible for authenticating and validating users across multiple applications and systems. IdPs enable single sign-on (SSO) and federated identity management, ensuring that a verified identity can securely traverse different domains without the need for repeated credential entry. Popular enterprise IdPs include Microsoft Azure Active Directory, Okta, Ping Identity, and Google Identity Platform.

The shift toward IdPs reflects two core realities: first, users increasingly access corporate resources through cloud-based applications outside the traditional perimeter; second, attackers disproportionately target identity credentials as the fastest route into enterprise systems. By centralizing and strengthening identity verification, IdPs have become the linchpin of Zero Trust implementations.

Multifactor Authentication (MFA)

While passwords remain the most common authentication factor, they are notoriously weak. Phishing, credential stuffing, and password reuse make them easily exploitable. For this reason, Multi-factor Authentication (MFA) has become a cornerstone of Zero Trust. MFA requires users to provide at least two of the following categories of evidence:

- Something you know: passwords, PINs.
- Something you have: hardware tokens, mobile apps, smart cards.
- Something you are: biometric identifiers like fingerprints or facial recognition.

By combining these factors, MFA dramatically reduces the probability of account compromise. Even if a password is stolen, an attacker would still need access to a second factor—often a one-time code or a registered device. Many enterprises now enforce MFA across all critical services, and regulatory frameworks such as the Payment Services Directive 2 (PSD2) in the European Union mandate its use for online financial transactions.

Adaptive Authentication

Beyond static MFA, enterprises are increasingly adopting adaptive (or risk-based) authentication. Adaptive systems adjust the level of authentication required based on contextual risk signals. For example, a user logging in from a familiar device at a typical time of day may only need a password and a token, while the same user attempting to access from a new country at midnight may be prompted for biometric verification or denied access altogether.

Adaptive authentication leverages machine learning and behavioral analytics to evaluate signals such as device posture, geolocation, IP reputation, and user behavior patterns. This approach aligns closely with Zero Trust's principle of continuous verification, ensuring that identity validation is not a one-time event but an ongoing assessment of trustworthiness.

Implications for Security Strategy

The elevation of identity to the role of perimeter has profound strategic implications. It requires organizations to invest heavily in:

- **Strong IdP platforms** that can scale across hybrid environments.
- **Universal MFA adoption**, reducing reliance on passwords alone.
- **Integration of adaptive policies,** so authentication is dynamic rather than rigid.
- **Identity governance and lifecycle management**, ensuring that access rights are continuously aligned with organizational roles.

Failures in identity management have already demonstrated catastrophic consequences. Breaches such as the SolarWinds supply chain attack (2020) and the Okta support system compromise (2023) highlight that compromised identities can be used as stepping stones for lateral movement and privilege escalation. By treating identity as the new perimeter, organizations can significantly reduce these risks while enabling seamless, secure access across the modern digital ecosystem.

Continuous Monitoring and Data Analytics

If identity is the new perimeter of cybersecurity, then continuous monitoring is the operational backbone that ensures trust is never static. In Zero Trust environments, granting access once and assuming continued legitimacy is not sufficient; verification must be ongoing, adaptive, and informed by contextual data. Continuous monitoring provides the necessary visibility to enforce Zero Trust principles by observing user behavior, device status, application interactions, and data access patterns in real time.

Real-Time Behavioral Monitoring

Modern cyber defense assumes that breaches are inevitable. Therefore, the goal is not only to prevent initial access attempts but also to detect and respond quickly to abnormal behaviors that may indicate compromise. Real-time monitoring involves collecting telemetry from multiple layers of the digital ecosystem:

- **Users**: login frequency, time of access, geolocation, and behavioral baselines (e.g., typing cadence, navigation patterns).
- **Devices**: operating system health, patch status, antivirus results, and evidence of jailbreaking or rooting.
- **Applications**: patterns of API calls, unusual query volumes, or attempts to bypass standard workflows.
- **Data**: access to sensitive files, unusual download spikes, or anomalous database queries.

For example, an employee who typically accesses HR files during business hours in London might suddenly attempt to download gigabytes of customer financial data from a server in Singapore at 3:00 a.m. Even if this employee passed multifactor authentication, the deviation from their baseline behavior would trigger additional verification or incident response.

AI and Machine Learning in Anomaly Detection

The vast volume of monitoring data exceeds the capacity of human analysts to review manually. This is where artificial intelligence (AI) and machine learning (ML) play a central role. Algorithms can establish baselines of normal behavior across thousands of users and devices, then flag deviations that may indicate threats.

- **Supervised learning models** can be trained on historical incidents to recognize known malicious patterns, such as lateral movement or credential stuffing.
- **Unsupervised learning models** detect anomalies without prior labels, clustering behaviors and identifying outliers that deviate significantly from established norms.
- **Probabilistic models** such as Bayesian inference can assign confidence scores to unusual events, helping security teams prioritize the most suspicious activities.

These models not only improve detection accuracy but also reduce false positives — a major challenge in traditional security operations centers (SOCs). By automating pattern recognition, AI-driven monitoring allows analysts to focus on strategic response rather than sifting through alert fatigue.

Integration into Zero Trust Architectures

Continuous monitoring is not a standalone process; it is tightly woven into the verification gates of Zero Trust architectures. At each layer—user, device, application, and data—real-time analytics determine whether access should be maintained, escalated, or revoked. This dynamic enforcement prevents attackers who gain initial footholds from exploiting trust to move laterally or exfiltrate data.

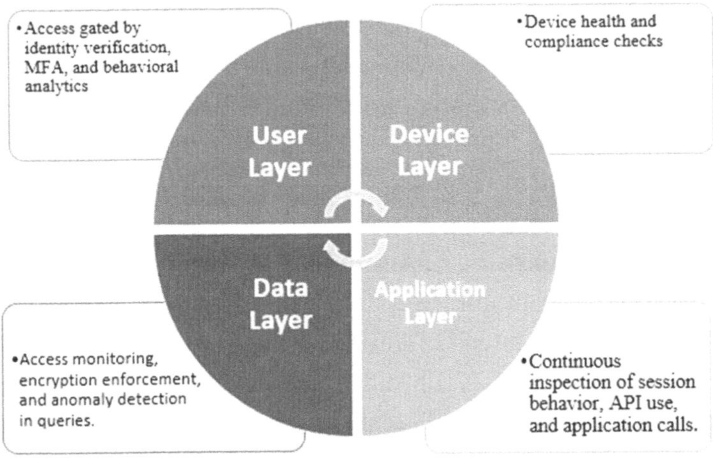

Figure 10.2: Zero Trust Architecture Layers with Verification Gates

Strategic Implications

Continuous monitoring enables organizations to transition from reactive security—responding after damage has been done—to proactive resilience, where anomalies are detected before they escalate into breaches. It also provides critical data for compliance reporting under regulations such as GDPR, HIPAA, and PCI DSS, which increasingly require organizations to demonstrate not only access control but also ongoing oversight of data use.

However, continuous monitoring also raises challenges. Privacy concerns arise when behavioral analytics involve invasive data collection. Organizations must therefore implement strong governance, transparency, and data minimization practices. Additionally, the deployment of AI/ML models requires careful tuning to avoid bias or blind spots that attackers can exploit.

Despite these challenges, continuous monitoring powered by data analytics is indispensable in realizing the "never trust, always verify" ethos of Zero Trust. By embedding intelligence at every layer, organizations can detect the faint signals of compromise and respond before attackers achieve their objectives.

Zero Trust in Cloud and Hybrid Environments

As enterprises increasingly migrate workloads to the cloud while maintaining critical on-premises systems, cybersecurity strategy must adapt to the reality of hybrid and multi-cloud environments. In these distributed architectures, resources are no longer confined to a single data center or controlled by a single vendor. Instead, organizations orchestrate services across AWS, Microsoft Azure, Google Cloud, and private clouds, while legacy applications may remain on local infrastructure. This fragmentation introduces profound challenges to implementing Zero Trust principles, as the boundaries of control are blurred and each platform has its own identity, security, and monitoring frameworks.

Challenges of Multi-Cloud and Distributed Systems

One of the central difficulties lies in identity federation. Each cloud provider offers its own native identity and access management (IAM) system—AWS IAM, Azure Active Directory, Google Cloud Identity—which do not always interoperate seamlessly. Enterprises often find themselves managing multiple identity silos, increasing the risk of misconfigurations, orphaned accounts, and inconsistent enforcement of least privilege. A Zero Trust architecture requires a unifying layer, often in the form of a centralized identity provider (IdP) that integrates with all cloud and on-premises systems.

A second challenge involves policy consistency. Security policies such as conditional access rules, encryption requirements, and monitoring standards may vary across platforms. Without harmonization, attackers can exploit the weakest link in the ecosystem, bypassing controls by targeting workloads deployed on less secure providers. For example, a misconfigured storage bucket in one cloud platform can undermine the protections applied elsewhere. Zero Trust in hybrid environments requires policy orchestration tools that enforce uniform standards across providers.

Finally, there is the issue of visibility. Traditional monitoring tools struggle in distributed architectures where workloads dynamically scale, shift regions, or run as ephemeral containers. Without continuous observability, organizations may fail to detect anomalous behavior, such as lateral movement between microservices or data exfiltration via misconfigured APIs. To overcome this, modern Zero Trust implementations embed cloud-native monitoring tools, AI-driven anomaly detection, and centralized log aggregation to maintain situational awareness across all platforms.

Integration with DevSecOps Pipelines

Zero Trust in cloud and hybrid settings also intersects with the rise of DevSecOps, the integration of security practices directly into development and operations workflows. Traditional approaches often treated security as an afterthought, introduced at the end of the software development lifecycle. In contrast, DevSecOps embeds security testing, monitoring, and enforcement throughout the code development lifecycle, from the earliest phases through deployment and maintenance.

In this model, Zero Trust principles guide how code is built, deployed, and executed:

- **Shift-left security testing** ensures that vulnerabilities are identified early, before they reach production. Static application security testing (SAST) and software composition analysis (SCA) tools run during build phases to detect insecure code or libraries.
- **Dynamic and runtime monitoring** extend Zero Trust into deployed applications. Dynamic application security testing (DAST) and runtime application self-protection (RASP) continuously validate

application behavior, ensuring that anomalous actions cannot bypass policies.

- **Policy-as-code** integrates Zero Trust into infrastructure automation. Using tools such as HashiCorp Sentinel or Open Policy Agent, organizations define security policies in code repositories, allowing enforcement to scale across multi-cloud deployments automatically.
- **Continuous verification loops** ensure that every change to infrastructure, container, or application is revalidated against Zero Trust principles before deployment. This prevents insecure updates from creating gaps in the defense posture.

A **case example** illustrates the convergence of Zero Trust and DevSecOps: a financial institution deploying microservices across AWS and Azure integrates its CI/CD pipeline with an IdP that enforces least privilege access for each containerized workload. As code is built, automated scans check for vulnerabilities; when deployed, the microservices communicate only through service meshes that enforce encryption and authentication at every call. Monitoring tools continuously evaluate traffic flows and terminate sessions that deviate from expected patterns. Here, Zero Trust ensures both the integrity of the code and the security of the execution environment.

Strategic Importance

The extension of Zero Trust into cloud and hybrid environments is no longer optional. With enterprises facing rising risks from supply chain attacks, misconfigured APIs, and cloud-native threats, static, perimeter-based approaches cannot suffice. Zero Trust provides a framework to unify fragmented infrastructures under a common set of principles: verify identity continuously, enforce least privilege, and monitor relentlessly.

However, achieving this vision requires more than technology. It demands organizational change: cross-team collaboration between developers, operations staff, and security analysts; governance frameworks that align security policies with business objectives; and ongoing investments in monitoring, automation, and training. The organizations that succeed will be those that recognize that, in the cloud era, security is not a boundary but a continuous validation process across every platform and every stage of development.

Case Studies of Zero Trust in Action

Theoretical models of Zero Trust provide a powerful conceptual framework, but their value becomes fully apparent when applied in real-world organizational contexts. Case studies demonstrate both the opportunities and challenges of adopting Zero Trust in practice, offering insights into implementation strategies, technology choices, and the cultural transformations required. This section examines three prominent case applications: Google's BeyondCorp, Microsoft's Zero Trust framework, and the US Federal Zero Trust Strategy. Each case highlights how Zero Trust principles translate into operational environments, providing lessons for enterprises of different scales and sectors.

Case Study 1: Google BeyondCorp

Google's BeyondCorp initiative is often cited as the seminal model of Zero Trust in action. Launched in response to the 2009 Aurora cyberattacks, BeyondCorp emerged from the recognition that perimeter-based defenses were insufficient in an era of distributed workforces and persistent threats. Rather than relying on VPNs or static firewalls, BeyondCorp placed identity and device trustworthiness at the center of access control.

In practice, this meant that an employee working from home, a café, or Google's campus would access corporate resources under the same rules: every request was verified through strong authentication and device health checks, regardless of network location. The architecture eliminated the distinction between "inside" and "outside," embodying the core Zero Trust principle of "never trust, always verify."

The BeyondCorp case illustrates the scalability of Zero Trust. Supporting tens of thousands of employees globally, Google proved that decentralized, identity-driven architectures could enhance security while improving usability by removing reliance on clunky

VPNs. However, the transition required massive investment in infrastructure, device management, and organizational change, underscoring that Zero Trust is not a product to buy but an architecture to build.

Case Study 2: Microsoft's Zero Trust Framework

Microsoft has operationalized Zero Trust as both a strategic internal practice and a customer-facing framework integrated into its cloud platforms. Unlike Google's single-enterprise approach, Microsoft's model is designed to scale across diverse industries and regulatory environments, making it especially relevant for organizations adopting Azure and Microsoft 365.

Microsoft emphasizes three guiding principles: verify explicitly, use least-privilege access, and assume breach. These principles manifest in Azure Active Directory's conditional access policies, which evaluate user location, device health, and behavior before granting access. For example, a user logging in from an unusual location may be prompted to enable multifactor authentication or be restricted entirely until further review.

Additionally, Microsoft integrates Zero Trust into cloud-native monitoring through Azure Sentinel (SIEM) and Defender (XDR), enabling continuous anomaly detection and automated remediation. The framework also incorporates policy-as-code, allowing customers to define and enforce consistent access rules across hybrid environments.

Dimension	Google BeyondCorp	Microsoft Zero Trust
Origin and Motivation	Developed internally after the 2009 Aurora attacks to secure Google's global workforce.	Designed as a commercial framework to serve diverse customers adopting Azure and Microsoft 365.
Scope of Deployment	Single-enterprise model tailored for Google employees and contractors.	Broad platform intended for enterprises across industries, governments, and SMEs.
Access Control Approach	Device and identity-based verification for every request; VPNs eliminated.	Conditional access policies integrating identity, location, device health, and risk-based signals.

Dimension	Google BeyondCorp	Microsoft Zero Trust
Architecture Focus	Employee usability and security through decentralized, device-centric access.	Hybrid and cloud-native integration across multiple tenants, applications, and infrastructures.
Tooling and Ecosystem	Proprietary internal systems, not packaged as a customer product.	Commercial suite including Azure AD, Microsoft Defender, Sentinel, and Intune.
Scalability	Proven at Google scale (tens of thousands of employees) but not exported as a service.	Designed for global adoption, supporting millions of enterprise users across cloud ecosystems.
Business Model	Internal security transformation; not sold externally.	Vendor-driven model, integrated into subscription and licensing offerings.
Key Limitation	Not easily replicable outside Google without significant engineering effort.	Risk of vendor lock-in; organizations may become overly dependent on Microsoft ecosystem.

Table 10.3: Comparison between Google BeyondCorp and Microsoft Zero Trust

The Microsoft case underscores how Zero Trust can be commercialized and standardized, offering tools and guidance for organizations lacking Google's engineering resources. Yet, it also raises questions of dependency: adopting vendor-driven Zero Trust architectures risks vendor lock-in, requiring enterprises to balance ease of integration with long-term flexibility.

Case Study 3: U.S. Federal Zero Trust Strategy

In 2022, the US federal government formalized its Zero Trust Strategy, directing all federal agencies to implement core principles by 2024. This initiative reflects the growing consensus that traditional perimeter defenses are untenable for protecting sensitive government data against nation-state adversaries and supply-chain threats.

The strategy emphasizes five pillars: identity, devices, networks, applications, and data. Agencies are required to adopt multifactor authentication, encrypt data in transit and at rest, segment networks to reduce lateral movement, and apply continuous monitoring across all layers. Importantly, the federal approach highlights data-centric

Zero Trust, requiring agencies to treat data as a protected resource independent of location.

This case illustrates the governance dimension of Zero Trust. Unlike corporate implementations driven by efficiency and innovation, the federal model is motivated by national security imperatives, requiring coordination across hundreds of agencies and contractors. The scale of the challenge is immense, but the federal mandate establishes a benchmark for public sector adoption, pushing even resource-limited agencies toward modern architectures.

Lessons Learned Across Cases

Taken together, these case studies demonstrate several recurring themes. First, identity and access management is universally central, whether through Google's device-health checks, Microsoft's conditional access, or the federal mandate for multifactor authentication. Second, successful Zero Trust adoption requires integration with cloud-native monitoring and analytics to enable continuous verification in dynamic environments. Third, organizational transformation is as critical as technology: Google restructured its internal IT, Microsoft built customer ecosystems, and federal agencies redefined compliance requirements.

At the same time, challenges persist. Costs of adoption remain high, interoperability across platforms is uneven, and cultural resistance to change can undermine implementation. The path to Zero Trust is therefore incremental, requiring sustained investment, executive leadership, and cross-team collaboration.

Operationalizing Zero Trust

While the principles of Zero Trust are conceptually compelling, their value lies in how they can be operationalized within the daily workflows of security teams. Translating "never trust, always verify" into measurable processes requires well-defined metrics, robust toolchains, and alignment with established frameworks such as NIST Special Publication 800-207. By grounding Zero Trust in concrete operational practices, organizations move from theory to a sustainable security posture that can withstand evolving threats.

Metrics for Zero Trust Effectiveness

The success of Zero Trust implementations depends heavily on the ability to measure performance and outcomes. Two of the most critical metrics are:

- **Mean Time to Detect (MTTD):** The average time it takes to identify a security incident from the moment it occurs. In a Zero Trust context, continuous monitoring, AI-driven anomaly detection, and identity analytics should drive this number down significantly compared to perimeter-based approaches.
- **Mean Time to Respond (MTTR):** The average time required to contain and remediate a security incident after detection. A mature Zero Trust architecture—especially one integrated with automated response mechanisms—should demonstrate shorter MTTR, preventing lateral movement and limiting damage.

For example, a financial institution adopting Zero Trust with automated identity checks and behavioral monitoring reduced its MTTD from 27 hours to under 3 hours, and its MTTR from days to minutes through integration with Security Orchestration, Automation, and Response (SOAR) platforms.

Beyond MTTD and MTTR, organizations also track metrics such as policy enforcement rates (the percentage of requests verified against Zero Trust policies), false-positive rates in anomaly detection, and privileged access session duration (ensuring least privilege is time-bound and continuously verified).

Toolchains for Zero Trust Operations

Zero Trust cannot be operationalized without the right technology stack that integrates identity, monitoring, and automated response. Among the core components are:

- **Security Information and Event Management (SIEM):** Platforms, such as Splunk or Azure Sentinel, aggregate and analyze logs from across users, devices, applications, and networks. In Zero Trust, SIEM functions as the central nervous system, correlating events for real-time detection.

- **Security Orchestration, Automation, and Response (SOAR):** Tools such as Palo Alto Cortex XSOAR or IBM SOAR automate incident response. For instance, if anomalous login behavior is detected, a SOAR playbook can automatically revoke credentials, isolate devices, and notify analysts.
- **Extended Detection and Response (XDR):** Unifies endpoint, network, and cloud telemetry to provide contextual insights. XDR platforms, such as Microsoft Defender or CrowdStrike Falcon, complement Zero Trust by continuously verifying activities across diverse environments.
- **Data Lakes and Analytics Pipelines**: At the foundation, organizations increasingly rely on centralized data repositories to store massive volumes of security telemetry. Data lakes integrated with AI/ML models enable **predictive security**, identifying risky behaviors before they escalate into incidents.

Collectively, these tools operationalize the Zero Trust principle of continuous monitoring and adaptive enforcement, ensuring that access decisions are not static but dynamic and context-aware.

Mapping Zero Trust Controls to NIST 800-207

The US National Institute of Standards and Technology (NIST) formalized Zero Trust guidance in SP 800-207, which has become the de facto reference for aligning architectures and practices. To operationalize Zero Trust effectively, organizations should map their chosen controls and technologies to the NIST guidelines. The table below demonstrates *how technologies such as IAM, SIEM, SOAR, and microsegmentation embody formal principles.*

Zero Trust Control	Operational Mechanism	Mapped NIST 800-207 Principle
Identity and Access Management (IAM)	Strong authentication, conditional access policies	Subject and resource authentication and authorization
Continuous Monitoring	SIEM/XDR logging, real-time behavioral analytics	Continuous diagnostics and mitigation
Microsegmentation	Network segmentation, service mesh architectures	Policy enforcement close to the resource
Automated Incident Response (SOAR)	Automated playbooks for credential revocation, isolation	Dynamic and adaptive trust evaluation
Data Security Controls	Encryption, tokenization, differential privacy	Protecting data independent of network location
Policy-as-Code	Codified enforcement of access and compliance rules	Consistent, automated policy enforcement

Table 10.4: Mapping Zero Trust Controls to NIST SP 800-207 Guidelines

Strategic Perspective

Operationalizing Zero Trust is not about deploying a single product or tool, but about creating an ecosystem of interdependent technologies and processes that reinforce the principles of explicit verification, least privilege, and continuous monitoring. Metrics such as MTTD and MTTR allow organizations to measure progress; toolchains such as SIEM, SOAR, XDR, and data lakes provide the infrastructure to enforce and adapt policies. When mapped to NIST's guidelines, these operational elements ensure compliance with a recognized standard, offering both accountability and interoperability.

Ultimately, organizations that succeed in operationalizing Zero Trust move beyond slogans into measurable, adaptive defenses that reflect the realities of cloud, hybrid, and mobile environments.

Case Studies

While Zero Trust has become a widely accepted security paradigm, its implementation looks very different across industries. Each sector presents unique risks, regulatory requirements, and technological landscapes that shape how Zero Trust principles are applied. By examining concrete case studies in the financial sector, healthcare, and government, it becomes possible to understand both the adaptability and the challenges of Zero Trust in practice.

Zero Trust in the Financial Sector: Digital Banking

The financial services industry provides one of the clearest examples of why Zero Trust is essential in modern cybersecurity. Banks and fintech firms face continuous attacks targeting online banking platforms, mobile payment services, and core transaction systems. The traditional model of securing internal networks with firewalls and VPNs proved increasingly inadequate once customers began accessing accounts from personal devices, often over unsecured networks. Furthermore, the rise of open banking and third-party application programming interfaces (APIs) created new opportunities for attackers to exploit weak links between interconnected services.

To respond, leading banks have begun embedding Zero Trust directly into their digital banking platforms. Every transaction request, regardless of whether it originates from a known customer device or from within the bank's own internal systems, must be authenticated and authorized dynamically. This means that a customer logging in from their usual smartphone may encounter a streamlined experience, while the same login attempt from a new location or device triggers step-up verification through multifactor authentication. Similarly, internal bank employees accessing high-value systems such as payment processing platforms are continuously monitored, with permissions restricted to the minimum necessary for their role and revoked immediately after use.

The impact of these measures is both technical and regulatory. From a technical perspective, banks that deploy Zero Trust significantly reduce fraud and account takeover incidents because stolen credentials alone are not sufficient to grant access. From a compliance perspective, aligning security practices with Zero Trust supports adherence to regulations such as the Payment Services Directive 2 (PSD2) in Europe, which mandates strong customer authentication, and the Gramm-Leach-Bliley Act (GLBA) in the United States, which requires financial institutions to protect consumer data. The financial case study demonstrates that Zero Trust not only mitigates cyber risk but also enables institutions to meet legal obligations in a landscape of growing digital interconnectedness.

Zero Trust in Healthcare: Securing IoT Medical Devices

Healthcare presents an entirely different challenge. The rapid adoption of Internet of Things (IoT) devices in hospitals—ranging from infusion pumps and heart monitors to connected imaging equipment—has expanded the attack surface in ways that traditional perimeter defenses cannot control. Many of these devices run outdated software, lack built-in encryption, or cannot be patched easily due to regulatory restrictions on altering medical equipment. As a result, attackers can exploit these endpoints as entry points into hospital networks, threatening both patient safety and sensitive medical records.

Zero Trust offers a path forward by reframing how hospitals view device trust. Rather than assuming that all devices connected to a hospital's internal network are safe, Zero Trust requires that every device be continuously verified. In practice, this involves microsegmentation of networks so that an infusion pump, for instance, can only communicate with its designated control server and not with unrelated hospital systems. Machine learning analytics monitors normal device behavior and generates alerts if unusual activity is detected, such as a medical imaging device suddenly transmitting large volumes of data to an unfamiliar destination.

The benefits extend beyond technical containment. By applying Zero Trust, healthcare organizations meet strict regulatory requirements under the Health Insurance Portability and Accountability Act (HIPAA), which mandates strong protections for patient health information. Moreover, they strengthen resilience against ransomware attacks, which have increasingly targeted hospitals in recent years. In one notable case, a large healthcare system implemented Zero Trust microsegmentation across its IoT environment and successfully prevented an attempted ransomware infection from propagating beyond a single compromised imaging machine. This example illustrates how Zero Trust directly protects patient safety, preserves the integrity of medical data, and enhances organizational resilience in an environment where downtime can be life-threatening.

Zero Trust in Government: U.S. Federal Strategy

The most ambitious application of Zero Trust is unfolding at the national level through the United States federal government's Zero Trust Strategy. In January 2022, the Office of Management and Budget (OMB) released a memorandum directing all federal agencies to implement Zero Trust principles by the end of fiscal year 2024. This mandate was driven by a series of high-profile breaches, including the SolarWinds supply chain compromise, which demonstrated the inadequacy of perimeter defenses against sophisticated nation-state adversaries.

The federal approach emphasizes five key areas: identity, devices, networks, applications, and data. In practice, this means that agencies must implement multifactor authentication for all employees and contractors, continuously monitor device compliance, segment networks to minimize lateral movement, encrypt data in transit and at rest, and apply dynamic access controls for applications. Unlike in the private sector, where adoption may be driven by risk appetite and business objectives, the federal initiative is codified as a requirement, making it one of the most comprehensive and large-scale Zero Trust implementations in the world.

The challenges, however, are considerable. Federal agencies vary widely in their technical maturity, resources, and mission-critical systems. Some agencies operate modern cloud-native platforms that align readily with Zero Trust principles, while others still rely on decades-old legacy systems that are difficult to integrate. The scale of the transition also raises procurement and workforce challenges, as thousands of employees must be retrained and hundreds of contracts renegotiated to align with Zero Trust requirements.

Despite these hurdles, progress has been visible. Agencies such as the Department of Defense and the Department of Homeland Security have already reported improvements in incident response and threat visibility. By enforcing continuous verification across identity and data access, agencies are better able to detect insider threats and prevent adversaries from moving laterally within sensitive systems. The federal Zero Trust strategy not only raises the baseline of US government cybersecurity but also sets a precedent for governments worldwide, many of which are now developing their own Zero Trust roadmaps.

Across these three cases, a pattern emerges. The financial sector demonstrates Zero Trust as a defense against fraud and compliance risk in digital banking. Healthcare illustrates its role in protecting patient safety by securing vulnerable IoT devices. Government shows how Zero Trust can be scaled into a national mandate, addressing systemic threats at the highest level. Taken together, these examples highlight that Zero Trust is not a one-size-fits-all solution but a flexible architecture that adapts to different risk landscapes while remaining anchored in the core principles of explicit verification, least privilege, and continuous monitoring.

Career Opportunities at the Intersection of Data and Security

The Evolving Cybersecurity Workforce

The transformation of cybersecurity into a data-driven discipline has reshaped the nature of the workforce that sustains it. Historically, cybersecurity careers were dominated by roles that focused on managing infrastructure, enforcing perimeter defenses, and ensuring compliance with established security frameworks. Security administrators monitored firewalls and intrusion detection systems, network engineers segmented traffic to protect sensitive resources, and compliance officers documented adherence to regulatory standards. These traditional roles were essential in an era where security revolved around well-defined organizational boundaries and relatively static infrastructures. However, as enterprises moved to cloud-native architectures, mobile workforces, and global supply chains, the skills once sufficient to defend corporate networks no longer addressed the complexity of modern threats.

In today's environment, the rise of data-centric cybersecurity has elevated the importance of roles that combine technical defense with deep analytical capability. Instead of simply responding to alerts or managing access lists, modern professionals are expected to interpret vast quantities of telemetry, logs, and contextual data to make real-time risk decisions. The security analyst of the past might have reviewed packet captures to identify a suspicious pattern, but the analyst of today is expected to leverage machine learning models, anomaly detection systems, and behavioral analytics to identify subtle signals of compromise hidden in terabytes of streaming data. This shift has transformed cybersecurity into a field where fluency in data science, statistics, and automation is as valuable as traditional networking or systems knowledge.

The workforce transformation is particularly visible in the redefinition of the security operations center (SOC). Where SOC analysts once triaged alerts manually, contemporary SOCs are increasingly augmented by Security Information and Event Management (SIEM) platforms, Security Orchestration, Automation, and Response (SOAR) tools, and Extended Detection and Response (XDR) ecosystems. Analysts must now understand how to configure, tune, and interpret these data-driven platforms, ensuring that automated pipelines reduce false positives without overlooking genuine threats. This requires not only technical skills but also a mindset attuned to iterative improvement, since machine learning models and detection rules must be continually retrained on new datasets.

The evolution of roles is also shaped by the growing **interdisciplinarity of cybersecurity**. Data-centric defense draws on insights from behavioral psychology, economics, and organizational science, since understanding how attackers exploit trust or manipulate user behavior often requires more than technical acumen. Similarly, the demand for professionals who can bridge the gap between compliance and analytics has surged. Regulations such as the General Data Protection Regulation (GDPR) and the California Consumer Privacy Act (CCPA) require organizations not only to protect data but also to demonstrate, through auditable evidence, that protections are effective. As a result, roles such as privacy engineers and data protection officers are increasingly aligned with cybersecurity teams, bringing legal and ethical considerations into technical decision-making.

The changing workforce landscape is amplified by a widening skills gap. Numerous industry reports indicate that millions of cybersecurity positions remain unfilled worldwide, with the gap especially pronounced in roles requiring advanced data analytics expertise. Organizations struggle to find professionals who can write detection algorithms, train AI models, or operationalize advanced telemetry for threat-hunting exercises. The shortage is compounded by the fact that many traditional security professionals are themselves in transition, seeking retraining to adapt from network- or compliance-centric positions into data-driven ones. Universities, training programs, and industry certifications are responding by designing curricula that combine cybersecurity fundamentals with data science, cloud computing, and automation, but the demand continues to outpace supply.

The surge in demand is particularly acute in sectors undergoing rapid digitalization. Financial services, for instance, require specialists in fraud analytics who can apply machine learning to detect abnormal transaction patterns. Healthcare demands professionals capable of securing patient data while enabling secure research on sensitive genomic information. Government agencies seek experts in adversarial machine learning who can defend against data poisoning or evasion attacks targeting AI systems. Each of these roles extends beyond the scope of traditional firewalls or endpoint protection, requiring professionals to be comfortable working at the intersection of cybersecurity, big data, and artificial intelligence.

Beyond technical ability, the evolving workforce must also embody adaptive and collaborative skills. In hybrid cloud environments where assets span multiple providers, no single individual can master all configurations, policies, and risk factors. Cybersecurity has therefore become a highly collaborative profession in which teams must integrate diverse expertise, from cryptography specialists designing secure multiparty computation systems to analysts interpreting the outputs of behavioral monitoring models. Success depends not only on individual technical excellence but also on the ability to work within multidisciplinary teams that bring together developers, operations staff, compliance officers, and business leaders.

The reorientation of the cybersecurity workforce reflects a broader cultural shift. The old perimeter-based mentality cultivated a defensive posture centered on building walls and reacting to intrusions. The new data-centric workforce embodies a proactive, analytical mindset, emphasizing prediction, prevention, and continuous validation. This evolution mirrors broader trends in digital society: as data becomes the most valuable resource in both business and governance, protecting it demands professionals who are as comfortable working with algorithms and datasets as they are with firewalls and encryption protocols.

Emerging Roles

The rapid expansion of data-centric cybersecurity has given rise to a new generation of professional roles that did not exist a decade ago, or that have evolved significantly in their responsibilities. These emerging careers are shaped by the twin pressures of protecting data as a critical resource and defending increasingly complex digital infrastructures that rely heavily on artificial intelligence, cloud computing, and global data exchanges. Unlike traditional roles, which were largely reactive and infrastructure-bound, these new positions demand a forward-looking skill set rooted in proactive defense, privacy engineering, and continuous innovation.

One of the most visible roles to emerge in this landscape is that of the Data Privacy Engineer. This professional serves as the bridge between legal and technical domains, tasked with embedding privacy by design into digital products and services. In practice, data privacy engineers must translate abstract regulatory requirements, such as those found in GDPR or HIPAA, into concrete system configurations and software architectures. They design data minimization frameworks, implement anonymization protocols, and validate that systems comply with user consent requirements. In sectors such as healthcare or finance, the privacy engineer ensures that sensitive datasets can be analyzed for research or fraud detection while preserving the confidentiality of individuals. Their role highlights the growing importance of ethical considerations in technical practice, as they must anticipate not only compliance failures but also reputational risks stemming from the misuse of personal information.

Equally significant is the role of the AI/ML Security Specialist, a career born from the convergence of artificial intelligence and cybersecurity. As machine learning models are increasingly deployed to detect threats, manage identities, and even automate security operations, they themselves become targets for adversaries. Attacks such as data poisoning, adversarial inputs, and model extraction have proven that AI is not inherently secure. Specialists in this field, therefore, focus on safeguarding both the integrity of training data and the resilience of deployed models. They build adversarially robust algorithms, develop red-teaming exercises against AI systems, and design monitoring tools that can detect anomalous outputs indicative of manipulation. Beyond defending the models, these specialists also ensure that AI-driven cybersecurity tools produce explainable and trustworthy results, reducing the "black box" risk that often undermines stakeholder confidence.

The migration of enterprises to multi-cloud and hybrid infrastructures has also generated demand for the Cloud Security Data Analyst. Unlike traditional network security analysts, these professionals must manage the unique challenges of securing distributed, elastic and rapidly changing cloud environments. Their responsibilities include interpreting telemetry from diverse cloud providers, correlating logs across environments, and identifying misconfigurations that can expose sensitive data. They often work closely with DevSecOps teams to integrate automated vulnerability detection and compliance validation into cloud-native pipelines. For instance, when a new containerized application is deployed, the analyst ensures that it inherits secure defaults, that runtime monitoring is active, and that anomalous behavior is logged and analyzed in real time. The complexity of cloud ecosystems requires analysts to be proficient not only in cybersecurity fundamentals but also in data analytics and platform-specific architectures.

Another emerging career path is that of the Privacy-Preserving Data Scientist, whose work exemplifies the fusion of advanced analytics with privacy-enhancing technologies. Unlike conventional data scientists, who may work freely with large datasets, these professionals are trained to operate in environments where direct access to raw data is restricted for ethical or legal reasons. They leverage tools such as secure multiparty computation, federated learning, and homomorphic encryption to conduct meaningful analyses without exposing sensitive information. For example, a privacy-preserving data scientist might develop machine learning models that predict disease outbreaks using hospital data across multiple institutions, without any party ever sharing patient-level details. Their expertise ensures that the insights generated from data do not come at the cost of individual privacy, making their role critical in a world where the demand for analytics collides with the imperative of data protection.

These emerging roles share several characteristics. They are highly interdisciplinary, requiring expertise that cuts across cybersecurity, data science, legal frameworks, and ethics. They also demand continuous learning, as the underlying technologies evolve at a pace that often outstrips formal training programs. Importantly, these roles highlight the premium placed on professionals who can not only secure data but also enable its safe and responsible use. This is a key distinction from earlier generations of cybersecurity careers, which often focused solely on defense and restriction. Today, organizations seek specialists who can unlock the potential of data while ensuring compliance, trust, and resilience.

To provide students and practitioners with a structured view of these new roles, the following table summarizes their defining characteristics, required skill sets, relevant certifications, and typical salary ranges based on recent industry surveys. While salary bands vary significantly by region and industry, the table reflects global averages to illustrate the premium placed on these specialized skills.

Role	Core Responsibilities	Required Skills	Common Certifications	Average Salary Range (USD)
Data Privacy Engineer	Embed privacy-by-design into systems; implement anonymization and consent frameworks.	Regulatory knowledge (GDPR, HIPAA), cryptography, systems design	CIPP/E, CIPT, ISO 27701	$95,000 – $135,000
AI/ML Security Specialist	Defend ML models from adversarial attacks; secure training data; ensure AI explainability.	ML/AI algorithms, adversarial ML, secure coding, red-teaming	CSA AI Security, Offensive AI Cert (OAI)	$110,000 – $160,000
Cloud Security Data Analyst	Monitor multi-cloud environments; detect misconfigurations; enable secure DevSecOps.	Cloud platforms (AWS, Azure, GCP), SIEM, automation, analytics	CCSP, AWS Security Specialty, CompTIA CASP+	$100,000 – $140,000
Privacy-Preserving Data Scientist	Apply PETs for analytics; federated learning; secure computations across datasets.	Differential privacy, MPC, federated learning, data science	TensorFlow Privacy Certs, PETs workshops	$105,000 – $150,000

Table 10.5: Emerging Data-Centric Cybersecurity Roles

Skills and Training Pathways

The emergence of data-centric cybersecurity careers has brought with it the challenge of preparing professionals with the right mix of technical, analytical, and ethical competencies. Traditional computer science or information security degrees alone are no longer sufficient. Instead, aspiring professionals must develop hybrid skill sets that draw from cybersecurity, data science, cryptography, and legal compliance. The pathways for developing these skills include formal academic programs, professional certifications, and practical engagement with open-source tools that shape real-world innovation.

Universities around the world are beginning to adapt their curricula to meet this demand. Whereas older programs in cybersecurity often emphasized defensive network operations, intrusion detection, and cryptographic theory in isolation, newer academic pathways are increasingly interdisciplinary. Joint programs in cybersecurity and data science are becoming more common, equipping students with training in machine learning alongside advanced security practices. For example, a master's program may include coursework in adversarial machine learning, federated analytics, and governance frameworks, ensuring graduates can both design secure systems and evaluate the ethical risks of data-driven solutions. Institutions in North America and Europe have already launched specialized tracks in privacy-enhancing technologies (PETs), where students experiment with secure multi-party computation or homomorphic encryption within applied lab settings. This academic shift reflects the recognition that tomorrow's professionals must be fluent in both protecting and leveraging data.

Alongside university education, professional certifications remain critical for validating expertise and signaling readiness to employers. Established credentials such as the CISSP (Certified Information Systems Security Professional) continue to be valued, particularly for their broad coverage of cybersecurity principles and governance. However, the growing emphasis on data privacy has made certifications such as the CIPP (Certified Information Privacy Professional) and CIPT (Certified Information Privacy Technologist) increasingly sought after. These validate not only knowledge of privacy law but also the technical implementation of compliant systems. Meanwhile, cloud-focused certifications like the CCSP (Certified Cloud Security Professional) or platform-specific credentials from AWS, Google Cloud, and Microsoft Azure allow practitioners to demonstrate their ability to secure multi-cloud environments where most modern data infrastructures now reside. The value of these certifications lies in their specificity: they bridge the gap between theoretical security knowledge and the unique architectures shaping enterprise ecosystems.

Beyond academic and certification pathways, the open-source ecosystem has become a vital training ground for aspiring professionals. Tools such as TensorFlow Privacy, which provides libraries for implementing differential privacy in machine learning, enable learners to experiment with real-world models under controlled privacy constraints. Similarly, PySyft offers an accessible framework for exploring federated learning and secure computation, allowing students to simulate multi-institutional data analysis without direct data sharing. Libraries for homomorphic encryption, once considered too complex for practical use, are now open-sourced by companies such as Microsoft (SEAL) and IBM (HELib), lowering the barrier to experimentation with fully encrypted computation. By engaging with these tools, learners can translate theoretical concepts into applied practice, gaining hands-on skills that align directly with the needs of emerging industries.

A particularly important advantage of working with open-source tools is exposure to collaborative problem-solving. Many projects thrive on contributions from distributed communities of researchers, engineers, and policy experts. For students and early-career professionals, participation in such ecosystems is not only a way to develop technical expertise but also a means of building professional networks. For example, contributing to a federated learning project on GitHub or participating in open challenges hosted by organizations like the OpenMined community provides visibility and demonstrates practical competence to potential employers.

Ultimately, the skills and training pathways for data-centric cybersecurity careers cannot be static. The rapid evolution of both threats and defense mechanisms ensures that lifelong learning is an inherent requirement of the profession. Whether through formal graduate programs, professional certifications, or continuous engagement with open-source technologies, practitioners must cultivate adaptability. Employers are increasingly aware that technical knowledge must be complemented with soft skills such as ethical reasoning, regulatory awareness, and the ability to communicate technical risks to non-technical stakeholders. This broadening of the skill profile reinforces the reality that careers at the intersection of data and security are as much about enabling trust and innovation as they are about defending against threats.

Conclusion

The future of cybersecurity is inseparable from the future of data. As this chapter has explored, the convergence of privacy-enhancing technologies, zero trust architectures, continuous monitoring, and a transformed professional workforce marks a decisive shift in how organizations conceptualize digital defense. No longer can security be framed solely as a defensive barrier against external threats; it must now be understood as a framework for ensuring that data—arguably the most valuable and contested resource of the twenty-first century—is protected, governed, and leveraged responsibly.

The central challenge lies in balancing innovation with privacy and trust. Organizations are under constant pressure to innovate, whether through AI-driven personalization, large-scale analytics, or real-time decision-making in sectors such as finance, healthcare, and government. At the same time, they face a regulatory and societal demand for rigorous privacy protections. If innovation is pursued without security, the result is fragile systems vulnerable to exploitation, leading to reputational damage and legal consequences. Conversely, if privacy and security are implemented as rigid barriers, they risk stifling the very innovation that drives economic and social progress. The task for cybersecurity professionals, therefore, is not to choose between innovation and security, but to design frameworks where they reinforce each other. Privacy-enhancing technologies, for example, illustrate how computation can proceed on encrypted or federated data without compromising confidentiality, proving that innovation and protection are not mutually exclusive.

A second theme that emerges is the necessity of trust as the foundation of modern cybersecurity. Trust is no longer implicit, as it was in the perimeter-based security models of the past. Instead, trust must be earned and verified continuously, whether in the authentication of identities, the verification of device health, or the assurance of compliance with legal frameworks. Zero trust architectures encapsulate this principle by operationalizing the maxim "never trust, always verify." When coupled with continuous monitoring and advanced analytics, these architectures provide the resilience required in a landscape where breaches are assumed rather than treated as rare anomalies.

Finally, this chapter has emphasized the need to treat data as a first-class citizen in cybersecurity strategy. Historically, defenses were built around networks, endpoints, or applications, with data often considered a secondary concern. Yet as cloud computing, distributed infrastructures, and machine learning systems dominate the digital ecosystem, data itself becomes the primary target, the medium of innovation, and the object of regulation. To elevate data to first-class status means embedding its protection into every layer of defense, every compliance initiative, and every product design. It also means equipping the workforce with the skills and ethical awareness to navigate the delicate trade-offs between utility and confidentiality.

Looking forward, the organizations that succeed will be those that not only defend their assets but also create ecosystems of trust. They will recognize that robust cybersecurity is not merely a technical function but a strategic enabler of innovation, competitiveness, and societal confidence in digital systems. The professionals leading this transformation will need to be interdisciplinary, agile, and grounded in both technical and ethical literacy. For students, researchers, and practitioners alike, the imperative is clear: to build a cybersecurity future where privacy, trust, and innovation are not opposing forces, but complementary pillars of resilience.

Key Terms

1. Privacy-Enhancing Technologies (PETs): A class of tools such as homomorphic encryption, secure multi-party computation, and differential privacy that enable computation or analysis without exposing raw data.
2. Homomorphic Encryption (HE): A cryptographic method that allows computations to be performed directly on encrypted data.
3. Secure Multi-Party Computation (MPC): A cryptographic protocol enabling multiple parties to compute joint functions over their inputs while keeping those inputs private.

4. Differential Privacy: A mathematical technique that adds statistical noise to datasets or queries to prevent re-identification of individuals while preserving overall trends.
5. Trusted Execution Environments (TEEs): Hardware-based enclaves that protect sensitive computations from external interference, such as Intel SGX or ARM TrustZone.
6. Zero Trust Model: A cybersecurity framework that assumes no implicit trust, requiring continuous verification of every user, device, and application.
7. Continuous Monitoring: The ongoing process of observing user and system behavior to detect anomalies and threats in real time.
8. Identity Provider (IdP): A service that manages digital identities and authentication across systems, critical in Zero Trust frameworks.
9. Adaptive Authentication: A form of authentication that adjusts its stringency based on contextual factors such as device health, location, or user behavior.
10. SIEM (Security Information and Event Management): A system that collects and analyzes log data for threat detection and compliance.
11. SOAR (Security Orchestration, Automation, and Response): A platform for automating incident response workflows in cybersecurity operations.
12. XDR (Extended Detection and Response): An integrated approach that consolidates security data across endpoints, networks, and cloud for unified defense.
13. PETs in Healthcare: Use of privacy-preserving computation methods for medical research without violating patient confidentiality.
14. BeyondCorp: Google's internal implementation of Zero Trust, designed after the Aurora attacks to eliminate VPN dependence.
15. NIST 800-207: The US National Institute of Standards and Technology's publication providing guidelines for Zero Trust architecture.

16. Federated Learning: A machine learning approach where models are trained across multiple decentralized devices or institutions without centralizing raw data.
17. Differentially Private Census: Use of differential privacy in government data collection, such as the US Census Bureau's approach to protect individual respondents.
18. Shift-Left Security: Integrating security testing early in software development cycles to minimize remediation costs.
19. Data Privacy Engineer: An emerging career role focusing on embedding privacy-by-design principles into technical systems.
20. AI/ML Security Specialist: A professional focused on defending machine learning models from adversarial attacks and data poisoning.
21. Cloud Security Data Analyst: A role responsible for analyzing telemetry across hybrid and multi-cloud environments for misconfigurations and threats.
22. Privacy-Preserving Data Scientist: A data scientist skilled in PETs who conducts analytics without exposing raw sensitive data.
23. Post-Quantum Cryptography: Cryptographic algorithms resistant to attacks from quantum computers, a growing future career domain.
24. Mean Time to Detect (MTTD): A key performance metric measuring how quickly an organization identifies a potential breach.
25. Mean Time to Respond (MTTR): A key metric reflecting the time taken to remediate or contain a cybersecurity incident.

Review Questions

1. What are Privacy-Enhancing Technologies (PETs), and why are they central to the future of data-centric cybersecurity?
2. Explain the difference between Partially, Somewhat, and Fully Homomorphic Encryption. Which applications are most suitable?

3. How does Secure Multi-Party Computation (MPC) enable collaboration across organizations while preserving data privacy?
4. In what ways does differential privacy prevent re-identification in large-scale datasets, and what are its limitations?
5. Describe the function of Trusted Execution Environments (TEEs) such as Intel SGX. What risks do they still face?
6. Compare and contrast the traditional perimeter security model ("castle and moat") with the Zero Trust framework.
7. What are the core principles of Zero Trust, and how do they address the limitations of perimeter-based models?
8. Why is identity now considered the new perimeter in modern cybersecurity?
9. How does adaptive authentication differ from multifactor authentication, and why is it vital for Zero Trust?
10. Discuss the role of continuous monitoring and data analytics in detecting anomalies across users, devices, and applications.
11. How can artificial intelligence and machine learning be applied in continuous monitoring, and what risks might they introduce?
12. What unique challenges does Zero Trust face in cloud and hybrid environments compared to traditional enterprise networks?
13. How do Google's BeyondCorp and Microsoft's Zero Trust models differ in terms of scope, architecture, and scalability?
14. Explain how SIEM, SOAR, and XDR platforms contribute to operationalizing Zero Trust strategies.
15. According to NIST 800-207, what are the essential components of a Zero Trust architecture?
16. Provide an example of how Zero Trust has been applied in the financial sector to secure digital banking.
17. What are the particular challenges of applying Zero Trust in healthcare, especially concerning IoT medical devices?
18. Summarize the US federal government's Zero Trust strategy and its importance for national cybersecurity.

19. How do academic programs in cybersecurity and data science prepare students for data-centric security careers?
20. Which professional certifications are most relevant for careers that combine cybersecurity and privacy, and why?
21. Describe how open-source tools such as TensorFlow Privacy or PySyft provide practical training in PETs.
22. What distinguishes a Data Privacy Engineer from a Privacy-Preserving Data Scientist in terms of skills and responsibilities?
23. Why is the role of an AI/ML Security Specialist increasingly important in defending against adversarial attacks?
24. How does the concept of "data as a first-class citizen" reshape organizational cybersecurity strategies?
25. Looking ahead, what interdisciplinary opportunities will shape careers at the intersection of cybersecurity, law, ethics, and policy?

GLOSSARY OF TERMS

1. Access Control – The practice of limiting system and data access to authorized entities.
2. Access Logs – Records that capture user and system activities, enabling auditability.
3. Advanced Persistent Threat (APT) – A prolonged, targeted cyberattack where intruders maintain an undetected presence.
4. AES (Advanced Encryption Standard) – An NIST-standardized symmetric encryption algorithm widely used in securing communications.
5. Algorithmic Bias – Unintended bias in AI/ML models, often due to flawed training data.
6. Anomaly Detection – Identifying unusual patterns that deviate from normal behavior, often used for intrusion detection.
7. Anonymization – The process of irreversibly removing identifiers from datasets.
8. API Gateway – A security layer that manages and monitors API traffic between clients and services.
9. Application Programming Interface (API) – A set of rules enabling communication between software components.
10. Asset Valuation – The process of assigning business value to IT systems or data for prioritization in risk assessment.
11. Asymmetric Encryption – A cryptographic system using a public/private key pair.
12. Attribute-Based Access Control (ABAC) – A policy-based model where access depends on attributes such as role, device, or time.
13. Audit Trail – A documented sequence of activities providing evidence of system operations.
14. Authentication – Verifying the identity of users or devices.
15. Authorization – Granting permissions to authenticated users or systems.

16. Availability – The assurance that systems and data are accessible when required.
17. Backdoor – A hidden method of bypassing authentication or encryption in software.
18. Bayesian Risk Model – A statistical approach applying Bayesian inference to risk calculations.
19. Blockchain – A decentralized ledger used for secure, immutable transaction records.
20. Botnet – A network of compromised devices controlled remotely by attackers.
21. Brute Force Attack – An attack that systematically tries all possible password or key combinations.
22. Business Continuity Plan (BCP) – A framework ensuring critical business functions can continue during a disruption.
23. Business Impact Analysis (BIA) – Identifying and evaluating how system failures affect organizational operations.
24. Certificate Authority (CA) – A trusted PKI entity issuing digital certificates.
25. CIA Triad – Confidentiality, Integrity, Availability — the foundation of cybersecurity.
26. Cloud Access Security Broker (CASB) – A tool enforcing security policies across cloud services.
27. Cloud Security – Practices and technologies securing cloud-hosted systems and data.
28. Compliance – Conformance with legal, regulatory, or industry-specific cybersecurity requirements.
29. Confidential Computing – Using Trusted Execution Environments (TEEs) to secure data during processing.
30. Confidentiality – Protecting information from unauthorized disclosure.
31. Continuous Authentication – Verifying users' identities throughout sessions using behavior or biometrics.
32. Continuous Monitoring – Real-time, automated oversight of networks and systems.
33. Critical Infrastructure – Essential systems such as energy, healthcare, and transportation, requiring heightened cybersecurity.

34. Cross-Site Scripting (XSS) – A web vulnerability allowing attackers to inject malicious scripts into webpages.
35. Cryptanalysis – Methods for breaking or weakening cryptographic systems.
36. Cryptography – The science of securing communications through algorithms and keys.
37. Cyber Kill Chain – A model describing stages of a cyberattack, from reconnaissance to exfiltration.
38. Cyber Threat Intelligence (CTI) – Knowledge about threats used to inform defensive decisions.
39. Data Breach – Unauthorized access, theft, or disclosure of sensitive data.
40. Data-Centric Security – Security strategies that directly protect data wherever it resides.
41. Data Classification – Categorizing data by sensitivity, value, and regulatory requirements.
42. Data Correlation – Combining data from multiple sources to identify patterns and attacks.
43. Data Exfiltration – The unauthorized transfer of data from a system.
44. Data Governance – Frameworks ensuring secure, compliant, and accountable data handling.
45. Data Integrity – Ensuring data accuracy, consistency, and trustworthiness.
46. Data Leakage – Unauthorized transmission of data outside organizational boundaries.
47. Data Masking – Concealing sensitive information with substitute values.
48. Data Minimization – Collecting only the minimum necessary personal or business data.
49. Data Pipeline – Structured processes for transferring and analyzing data.
50. Data Privacy – The protection of individuals' personal information against misuse.
51. Data Protection – Mechanisms that safeguard data against loss, corruption, or unauthorized access.
52. Data Residency – Geographic location of stored data, with legal implications.

53. Data Sovereignty – Data being subject to the laws of the jurisdiction where it resides.
54. Data Tokenization – Replacing sensitive values with random tokens.
55. Data Utility – The usefulness of data in analytics or operations, balanced with privacy.
56. Database Activity Monitoring (DAM) – Tools monitoring database traffic for suspicious activity.
57. Decryption – The process of converting ciphertext into readable plaintext.
58. Defense-in-Depth – Multiple, layered security measures to reduce risks.
59. Denial-of-Service (DoS) Attack – An attack that overwhelms systems, making them unavailable.
60. DevSecOps – Embedding security into DevOps processes for secure software delivery.
61. Differential Privacy – A privacy technique that adds statistical noise to data or queries.
62. Digital Certificate – An electronic credential proving ownership of a public key.
63. Digital Forensics – Investigating cyber incidents by collecting and analyzing digital evidence.
64. Digital Signature – Cryptographic assurance of authenticity and integrity in data.
65. Distributed Denial of Service (DDoS) – Coordinated DoS attacks from multiple compromised devices.
66. Elliptic Curve Cryptography (ECC) – A compact, secure form of asymmetric cryptography.
67. Encryption – Transforming plaintext into ciphertext to secure it.
68. Endpoint Detection and Response (EDR) – Tools for monitoring and responding to endpoint-level threats.
69. Exploit – Code or methods that take advantage of system vulnerabilities.
70. Federated Identity – Authentication that spans multiple organizations or domains.
71. Federated Learning – Training ML models across decentralized data sources without moving the data.
72. Firewall – A security system that filters network traffic by rules.

73. Fully Homomorphic Encryption (FHE) – A technique enabling computation on encrypted data.
74. General Data Protection Regulation (GDPR) – EU law governing data privacy and protection.
75. Honeypot – A decoy system used to attract and study attackers.
76. Identity and Access Management (IAM) – Policies and tools for managing digital identities.
77. Identity Federation – Enabling a single digital identity across multiple platforms.
78. Incident Response (IR) – Coordinated actions to detect, contain, and remediate security incidents.
79. Information Security (InfoSec) – The discipline of protecting digital and physical information.
80. Integrity – Ensuring accuracy and trustworthiness of data.
81. Intrusion Detection System (IDS) – A tool that alerts on suspicious network or host activity.
82. Intrusion Prevention System (IPS) – A tool that blocks threats in real time.
83. Key Escrow – Secure storage of cryptographic keys for lawful or recovery purposes.
84. Key Lifecycle Management – Managing cryptographic keys from generation to destruction.
85. Keylogger – Malicious software capturing keystrokes to steal credentials.
86. Least Privilege – Granting users the minimum access necessary to perform their roles.
87. Machine Learning (ML) – Algorithms that learn from data to make predictions or detect anomalies.
88. Malware – Malicious software including viruses, worms, trojans, and ransomware.
89. Man-in-the-Middle (MitM) Attack – An attacker intercepting communications between two parties.
90. Multi-Factor Authentication (MFA) – Requiring multiple credentials (e.g., password + fingerprint).
91. Multi-Party Computation (MPC) – A protocol enabling secure joint computation without revealing inputs.
92. Network Segmentation – Dividing networks into segments to limit attack spread.

93. NIST Cybersecurity Framework (NIST CSF) – US framework providing standards, guidelines, and practices for cybersecurity.
94. Penetration Testing (Pentesting) – Simulated attacks to identify vulnerabilities in systems.
95. Phishing – Deceptive attempts to obtain sensitive data by impersonating trusted entities.
96. Public Key Infrastructure (PKI) – A system of trust using digital certificates and keys.
97. Quantum Cryptography – Cryptographic techniques leveraging quantum mechanics for security.
98. Quantum-Resistant Cryptography – Algorithms resistant to quantum computing attacks.
99. Ransomware – Malware that encrypts files and demands payment for decryption.
100. Red Teaming – Simulated adversary testing to identify security weaknesses.
101. Residual Risk – The level of risk remaining after mitigation efforts.
102. Risk Assessment – Evaluating the likelihood and impact of security risks.
103. Risk Matrix – A visualization tool mapping risk likelihood against impact.
104. Role-Based Access Control (RBAC) – Permissions assigned to users based on organizational role.
105. Runtime Application Self-Protection (RASP) – Application-embedded defenses detecting and blocking attacks in real time.
106. Security Information and Event Management (SIEM) – Platforms for aggregating and analyzing security events.
107. Shift-Left Security – Integrating security testing earlier in software development.
108. Single Sign-On (SSO) – Authentication allowing users access to multiple systems with one login.
109. SOAR (Security Orchestration, Automation, and Response) – Platforms automating security workflows and response.
110. Social Engineering – Manipulative tactics exploiting human psychology to breach systems.
111. Supply Chain Security – Protecting software and hardware components from tampering and malicious code.

112. Symmetric Encryption – Encryption using a single shared key for both operations.
113. Threat Actor – An individual or group responsible for malicious activity.
114. Threat Hunting – Proactive search for hidden threats within systems.
115. Threat Intelligence – Insights into current and emerging threats.
116. Tokenization – Replacing sensitive data with non-sensitive placeholders.
117. Two-Factor Authentication (2FA) – An authentication process requiring exactly two credentials.
118. Vulnerability – A weakness in software, hardware, or processes.
119. Vulnerability Assessment – Systematic identification and evaluation of vulnerabilities.
120. Zero-Day Exploit – Attacks exploiting unknown vulnerabilities before patches exist.
121. Zero Trust – A model requiring continuous verification for every access request.

REFERENCES

1. Mohamed, N., Al-Jaroodi, J., Jawhar, I., & Kesserwan, N. (2020). Data-Driven Security for Smart City Systems: Carving a Trail. IEEE Access, 8, 147211–147230. https://doi.org/10.1109/ACCESS.2020.3015510
2. Rawat, D. B., Doku, R., & Garuba, M. (2021). Cybersecurity in Big Data Era: From Securing Big Data to Data-Driven Security. IEEE Transactions on Services Computing, 14(6), 2055–2072. https://doi.org/10.1109/TSC.2019.2907247
3. Tan, S., De, D., Song, W. Z., Yang, J., & Das, S. K. (2017, January 1). Survey of Security Advances in Smart Grid: A Data-Driven Approach. IEEE Communications Surveys and Tutorials. Institute of Electrical and Electronics Engineers Inc. https://doi.org/10.1109/COMST.2016.2616442
4. Duzenci, A., Kitapci, H., & Gok, M. S. (2023). The Role of Decision-Making Styles in Shaping Cybersecurity Compliance Behavior. Applied Sciences (Switzerland), 13(15). https://doi.org/10.3390/app13158731
5. Jalali, M. S., Siegel, M., & Madnick, S. (2019). Decision-making and biases in cybersecurity capability development: Evidence from a simulation game experiment. Journal of Strategic Information Systems, 28(1), 66–82. https://doi.org/10.1016/j.jsis.2018.09.003
6. Sarker, I. H., Kayes, A. S. M., Badsha, S., Alqahtani, H., Watters, P., & Ng, A. (2020). Cybersecurity data science: an overview from a machine learning perspective. Journal of Big Data, 7(1). https://doi.org/10.1186/s40537-020-00318-5
7. Sanjuan, E. B., Cardiel, I. A., Cerrada, J. A., & Cerrada, C. (2020). Message Queuing Telemetry Transport (MQTT) Security: A Cryptographic Smart Card Approach. IEEE Access, 8, 115051–115062. https://doi.org/10.1109/ACCESS.2020.3003998
8. Cugini, F., Scano, D., Giorgetti, A., Sgambelluri, A., De Marinis, L., Castoldi, P., & Paolucci, F. (2023). Telemetry and AI-based security P4 applications for optical networks [Invited]. Journal of Optical

Communications and Networking, 15(1), A1–A10. https://doi.org/10.1364/JOCN.470118

9. Sivanathan, A., Habibi Gharakheili, H., & Sivaraman, V. (2020). Managing IoT Cyber-Security Using Programmable Telemetry and Machine Learning. IEEE Transactions on Network and Service Management, 17(1), 60–74. https://doi.org/10.1109/TNSM.2020.2971213
10. Skopik, F., Landauer, M., & Wurzenberger, M. (2022). Online Log Data Analysis with Efficient Machine Learning: A Review. IEEE Security and Privacy. Institute of Electrical and Electronics Engineers Inc. https://doi.org/10.1109/MSEC.2021.3113275
11. Tao, Y., Li, M., & Hu, W. (2020). Research on Knowledge Graph Model for Cybersecurity Logs Based on Ontology and Classified Protection. In Journal of Physics: Conference Series (Vol. 1575). Institute of Physics Publishing. https://doi.org/10.1088/1742-6596/1575/1/012018
12. Rücker, N., & Maier, A. (2022). FlexParser—The adaptive log file parser for continuous results in a changing world. Journal of Software: Evolution and Process, 34(3). https://doi.org/10.1002/smr.2426
13. Gupta, V., Paupério, J., Burgin, J., Jayathilaka, S., & Cochrane, G. (2022). The ENA Source Attribute Helper: An API for improved biological source data. Biodiversity Information Science and Standards, 6. https://doi.org/10.3897/biss.6.91118
14. Correndo, A. A., Moro Rosso, L. H., & Ciampitti, I. A. (2021). Retrieving and processing agro-meteorological data from API-client sources using R software. BMC Research Notes, 14(1). https://doi.org/10.1186/s13104-021-05622-8
15. Holmgren, W., W. Hansen, C., & A. Mikofski, M. (2018). pvlib Python: a Python package for modelling solar energy systems. Journal of Open Source Software, 3(29), 884. https://doi.org/10.21105/joss.00884
16. Theodoropoulos, T., Rosa, L., Benzaid, C., Gray, P., Marin, E., Makris, A., ... Tserpes, K. (2023, December 1). Security in Cloud-Native Services: A Survey. Journal of Cybersecurity and Privacy. Multidisciplinary Digital Publishing Institute (MDPI). https://doi.org/10.3390/jcp3040034
17. Soldani, D., Nahi, P., Bour, H., Jafarizadeh, S., Soliman, M. F., Di Giovanna, L., ... Risso, F. (2023). E-BPF: A New Approach to Cloud-Native Observability, Networking and Security for Current (5G) and

Future Mobile Networks (6G and Beyond). IEEE Access, 11, 57174–57202. https://doi.org/10.1109/ACCESS.2023.3281480

18. Shih, C. C., Chen, J., Lee, A. S., Bertin, N., Hebrard, M., Khor, C. C., ... Dorajoo, R. (2023). A five-safes approach to a secure and scalable genomics data repository. IScience, 26(4). https://doi.org/10.1016/j.isci.2023.106546
19. Tavakoli, P., Yitmen, I., Sadri, H., & Taheri, A. (2024). Blockchain-based digital twin data provenance for predictive asset management in building facilities. Smart and Sustainable Built Environment, 13(1), 4–21. https://doi.org/10.1108/SASBE-07-2023-0169
20. Birch, K., Cochrane, D. T., & Ward, C. (2021). Data as an asset? The measurement, governance, and valuation of digital personal data by Big Tech. Big Data and Society, 8(1). https://doi.org/10.1177/20539517211017308
21. Hellenborn, B., Eliasson, O., Yitmen, I., & Sadri, H. (2024). Asset information requirements for blockchain-based digital twins: a data-driven predictive analytics perspective. Smart and Sustainable Built Environment, 13(1), 22–41. https://doi.org/10.1108/SASBE-08-2022-0183
22. Yoo, J., & Kang, S. (2023). Class-Adaptive Data Augmentation for Image Classification. IEEE Access, 11, 26393–26402. https://doi.org/10.1109/ACCESS.2023.3258179
23. Zhao, J., Jing, X., Yan, Z., & Pedrycz, W. (2021). Network traffic classification for data fusion: A survey. Information Fusion, 72, 22–47. https://doi.org/10.1016/j.inffus.2021.02.009
24. Alomar, K., Aysel, H. I., & Cai, X. (2023). Data Augmentation in Classification and Segmentation: A Survey and New Strategies. Journal of Imaging, 9(2). https://doi.org/10.3390/jimaging9020046
25. Kaur, R., Shahrestani, S., & Ruan, C. (2024). Security and Privacy of Wearable Wireless Sensors in Healthcare: A Systematic Review. Computer Networks and Communications. https://doi.org/10.37256/cnc.2120243852
26. Lubua, E. W., & Pretorius, P. D. (2019). Cybersecurity policy framework and procedural compliance in public organizations. In Proceedings of the International Conference on Industrial Engineering and Operations Management (pp. 1847–1856). IEOM Society.

27. Rohman, H., Sumarna, S., Suwanda, S., & Leksmanawati, W. (2022). Collaboration of ministries/institutions and the private sector in handling cyber threats through the establishment of Computer Security Incident Response Team (CSIRT). Technium Social Sciences Journal, 38, 87–102. https://doi.org/10.47577/tssj.v38i1.7906
28. Henriques, J., Caldeira, F., Cruz, T., & Simões, P. (2023). A forensics and compliance auditing framework for critical infrastructure protection. International Journal of Critical Infrastructure Protection, 42. https://doi.org/10.1016/j.ijcip.2023.100613
29. Sawmar, A. A., & Mohammed, M. O. (2021). Enhancing zakat compliance through good governance: a conceptual framework. ISRA International Journal of Islamic Finance, 13(1), 136–154. https://doi.org/10.1108/IJIF-10-2018-0116
30. Darmayasa, I. N., Arsana, I. M. M., & Putrayasa, I. M. A. (2022). Reconstruction of the Slippery Slope Framework Tax Compliance Model. ACRN Journal of Finance and Risk Perspectives, 11(1), 19–32. https://doi.org/10.35944/JOFRP.2022.11.1.002
31. Bradford, L., Aboy, M., & Liddell, K. (2020). COVID-19 contact tracing apps: A stress test for privacy, the GDPR, and data protection regimes. Journal of Law and the Biosciences, 7(1). https://doi.org/10.1093/jlb/lsaa034
32. Corte-Real, A., Nunes, T., & da Cunha, P. R. (2024). Reflections about Blockchain in Health Data Sharing: Navigating a Disruptive Technology. International Journal of Environmental Research and Public Health, 21(2). https://doi.org/10.3390/ijerph21020230
33. Seun Solomon Bakare, Adekunle Oyeyemi Adeniyi, Chidiogo Uzoamaka Akpuokwe, & Nkechi Emmanuella Eneh. (2024). DATA PRIVACY LAWS AND COMPLIANCE: A COMPARATIVE REVIEW OF THE EU GDPR AND USA REGULATIONS. Computer Science & IT Research Journal, 5(3), 528–543. https://doi.org/10.51594/csitrj.v5i3.859
34. Afiansyah, H. G., & Kadarwati Febriyani, N. A. (2023). Penyusunan Kebijakan Pengamanan dan Pengelolaan Infrastruktur Operasi Keamanan Siber Menggunakan NIST CSF 2.0 dan ISO/IEC 27001:2022. Info Kripto, 17(3). https://doi.org/10.56706/ik.v17i3.81
35. Malatji, M. (2023). Management of enterprise cyber security: A review of ISO/IEC 27001:2022. In 2023 International Conference on Cyber Management and Engineering, CyMaEn 2023 (pp. 117–122). Institute of Electrical and Electronics Engineers Inc.

https://doi.org/10.1109/CyMaEn57228.2023.10051114

36. Putri, T. S., Mutiah, N. M., & Prawira, D. P. (2022). ANALISIS MANAJEMEN RISIKO KEAMANAN INFORMASI MENGGUNAKAN NIST CYBERSECURITY FRAMEWORK DAN ISO/IEC 27001:2013 (Studi Kasus: Badan Pusat Statistik Kalimantan Barat). Coding Jurnal Komputer Dan Aplikasi, 10(02), 237. https://doi.org/10.26418/coding.v10i02.54972
37. Hummel, P., Braun, M., Tretter, M., & Dabrock, P. (2021). Data sovereignty: A review. Big Data and Society, 8(1). https://doi.org/10.1177/2053951720982012
38. Calzada, I. (2021). Data co-operatives through data sovereignty. Smart Cities, 4(3), 1158–1172. https://doi.org/10.3390/smartcities4030062
39. Hudson, M., Carroll, S. R., Anderson, J., Blackwater, D., Cordova-Marks, F. M., Cummins, J., … Rowe, R. K. (2023). Indigenous Peoples' Rights in Data: a contribution toward Indigenous Research Sovereignty. Frontiers in Research Metrics and Analytics, 8. https://doi.org/10.3389/frma.2023.1173805
40. Lee, D., Hess, D. J., & Heldeweg, M. A. (2022). Safety and privacy regulations for unmanned aerial vehicles: A multiple comparative analysis. Technology in Society, 71. https://doi.org/10.1016/j.techsoc.2022.102079
41. Škrinjarić, B., Budak, J., & Rajh, E. (2019). Perceived quality of privacy protection regulations and online privacy concern. Economic Research-Ekonomska Istrazivanja, 32(1), 982–1000. https://doi.org/10.1080/1331677X.2019.1585272
42. Akanfe, O., Lawong, D., & Rao, H. R. (2024, June 1). Blockchain technology and privacy regulation: Reviewing frictions and synthesizing opportunities. International Journal of Information Management. Elsevier Ltd. https://doi.org/10.1016/j.ijinfomgt.2024.102753
43. Alangot, B., Szalachowski, P., Dinh, T. T. A., Meftah, S., Gana, J. I., Aung, K. M. M., & Li, Z. (2023). Decentralized Identity Authentication with Auditability and Privacy. Algorithms, 16(1). https://doi.org/10.3390/a16010004
44. Canning, M., O'Dwyer, B., & Georgakopoulos, G. (2019). Processes of auditability in sustainability assurance–the case of materiality construction. Accounting and Business Research, 49(1), 1–27. https://doi.org/10.1080/00014788.2018.1442208

45. Luo, Y., & Malsch, B. (2023). Re-Examining Auditability through Auditors' Responses to COVID-19: Roles and Limitations of Improvisation on the Production of Auditing Knowledge. Auditing, 42(3), 155–175. https://doi.org/10.2308/AJPT-2020-114
46. Jamil, A. H., Mohd Sanusi, Z., Yaacob, N. M., Mat Isa, Y., & Tarjo, T. (2022). The impact of COVID-19 on financial crime and regulatory compliance in Malaysia. Journal of Financial Crime, 29(2), 491–505. https://doi.org/10.1108/JFC-05-2021-0107
47. Njinyah, S., Asongu, S., & Adeleye, N. (2022). The interaction effect of government non-financial support and a firm's regulatory compliance on firm innovativeness in Sub-Saharan Africa. European Journal of Innovation Management, 26(7), 45–64. https://doi.org/10.1108/EJIM-07-2022-0352
48. Sarawa, D. I., & Mas'ud, A. (2020). Strategic public procurement regulatory compliance model with mediating effect of ethical behavior. Heliyon, 6(1). https://doi.org/10.1016/j.heliyon.2019.e03132
49. Wong, J., Henderson, T., & Ball, K. (2022). Data protection for the common good: Developing a framework for a data protection-focused data commons. Data and Policy, 4(5). https://doi.org/10.1017/dap.2021.40
50. Meurisch, C., & Mühlhäuser, M. (2022, March 31). Data Protection in AI Services. ACM Computing Surveys. Association for Computing Machinery. https://doi.org/10.1145/3440754
51. He, Z. (2022). When data protection norms meet digital health technology: China's regulatory approaches to health data protection. Computer Law and Security Review, 47. https://doi.org/10.1016/j.clsr.2022.105758
52. Naser, S. M. (2021). CRYPTOGRAPHY: FROM ANCIENT HISTORY TO NOW, ITS APPLICATIONS AND A NEW COMPLETE NUMERICAL MODEL. International Journal of Mathematics and Statistics Studies (Vol. 9, pp. 11–30). Retrieved from www.ea-journals.org
53. Davies, D. (1997). A brief history of cryptography. Information Security Technical Report, 2(2), 14–17. https://doi.org/10.1016/s1363-4127(97)81323-4
54. Mandal, P. C. (2012). Evaluation of performance of the Symmetric Key Algorithms : DES, 3DES, AES and Blowfish. Journal of Global Research in Computer Science, 3(8), 67–70.

55. Rahman, A. U., Miah, S. U., & Azad, S. (2014). Advanced Encryption Standard. In Practical Cryptography: Algorithms and Implementations Using C++ (pp. 91–126). CRC Press. https://doi.org/10.1201/b17707
56. Rusheng, D., & Li, W. (2017). A hybrid method for service identification of SSL/TLS-encrypted traffic. In 2016, the 2nd IEEE International Conference on Computer and Communications, ICCC 2016 - Proceedings (pp. 250–253). Institute of Electrical and Electronics Engineers Inc. https://doi.org/10.1109/CompComm.2016.7924703
57. Furrer, F. J. (2020). Roger A. Grimes. Cryptography Apocalypse: Preparing for the Day When Quantum Computing Breaks Today's Crypto. Informatik Spektrum, 43(1), 70–72. https://doi.org/10.1007/s00287-020-01239-6
58. Hughes, L. E. (2022). Pro Active Directory Certificate Services: Creating and Managing Digital Certificates for Use in Microsoft Networks. Pro Active Directory Certificate Services: Creating and Managing Digital Certificates for Use in Microsoft Networks (pp. 1–459). Apress Media LLC. https://doi.org/10.1007/978-1-4842-7486-6
59. Zheng, L. Y., McMahon, C. A., Li, L., Ding, L., & Jamshidi, J. (2008). Key characteristics of management in product lifecycle management: A survey of methodologies and practices. Proceedings of the Institution of Mechanical Engineers, Part B: Journal of Engineering Manufacture, 222(8), 989–1008. https://doi.org/10.1243/09544054JEM1045
60. Lahtinen, N., Mustonen, E., & Harkonen, J. (2021). Commercial and Technical Productization for Fact-Based Product Portfolio Management over Lifecycle. IEEE Transactions on Engineering Management, 68(6), 1826–1838. https://doi.org/10.1109/TEM.2019.2932974
61. Niu, X., Wang, M., & Qin, S. (2022). Product design lifecycle information model (PDLIM). International Journal of Advanced Manufacturing Technology, 118(7–8), 2311–2337. https://doi.org/10.1007/s00170-021-07945-z
62. Akotam, A. W., Kontoh, M. S., & Ansah, A. K. (2013). E-governance public key infrastructure (PKI) model. International Journal of Electronic Governance, 6(2), 133–142. https://doi.org/10.1504/IJEG.2013.058360

63. Lozupone, V. (2018). Analyze encryption and public key infrastructure (PKI). International Journal of Information Management, 38(1), 42–44. https://doi.org/10.1016/j.ijinfomgt.2017.08.004
64. Pal, O., Alam, B., Thakur, V., & Singh, S. (2021). Key management for blockchain technology. ICT Express, 7(1), 76–80. https://doi.org/10.1016/j.icte.2019.08.002
65. Wang, Z., Lin, J., Cai, Q., Wang, Q., Zha, D., & Jing, J. (2022). Blockchain-Based Certificate Transparency and Revocation Transparency. IEEE Transactions on Dependable and Secure Computing, 19(1), 681–697. https://doi.org/10.1109/TDSC.2020.2983022
66. Zhang, H., & Zhao, F. (2023). Cross-domain identity authentication scheme based on blockchain and PKI system. High-Confidence Computing, 3(1). https://doi.org/10.1016/j.hcc.2022.100096
67. Garba, A., Chen, Z., Guan, Z., & Srivastava, G. (2021). LightLedger: A Novel Blockchain-Based Domain Certificate Authentication and Validation Scheme. IEEE Transactions on Network Science and Engineering, 8(2), 1698–1710. https://doi.org/10.1109/TNSE.2021.3069128
68. Kumar, M. (2022). Post-quantum cryptography algorithms' standardization and performance analysis. Array, 15. https://doi.org/10.1016/j.array.2022.100242
69. Radanliev, P. (2024, December 1). Artificial intelligence and quantum cryptography. Journal of Analytical Science and Technology. Springer Science and Business Media Deutschland GmbH. https://doi.org/10.1186/s40543-024-00416-6
70. Balamurugan, C., Singh, K., Ganesan, G., & Rajarajan, M. (2021, December 1). Post-Quantum and Code-Based Cryptography—Some Prospective Research Directions. Cryptography. MDPI. https://doi.org/10.3390/cryptography5040038
71. Kumar, M. (2022). Post-quantum cryptography Algorithm's standardization and performance analysis. Array, 15. https://doi.org/10.1016/j.array.2022.100242
72. Radanliev, P. (2024, December 1). Artificial intelligence and quantum cryptography. Journal of Analytical Science and Technology. Springer Science and Business Media Deutschland GmbH. https://doi.org/10.1186/s40543-024-00416-6

73. Balamurugan, C., Singh, K., Ganesan, G., & Rajarajan, M. (2021, December 1). Post-Quantum and Code-Based Cryptography—Some Prospective Research Directions. Cryptography. MDPI. https://doi.org/10.3390/cryptography5040038
74. kumarGK, R., B Justus Rabi, D., & TN, M. (2012). A Study on Dynamic Data Masking with its Trends and Implications. International Journal of Computer Applications, 38(6), 19–24. https://doi.org/10.5120/4612-6828
75. Xiao, Y., Wang, B., Wang, Z., Zhou, Z., & He, J. (2023). One-Time Pad Strategy Combined with Dynamic Key Embedding and Multi-Level Chaotic Encryption for RoF. Journal of Lightwave Technology, 41(1), 41–47. https://doi.org/10.1109/JLT.2022.3210757
76. Issaoui, A., Örtensjö, J., & Islam, M. S. (2023). Exploring the General Data Protection Regulation (GDPR) compliance in cloud services: insights from Swedish public organizations on privacy compliance. Future Business Journal, 9(1). https://doi.org/10.1186/s43093-023-00285-2
77. Al-Zubaidie, M., Zhang, Z., & Zhang, J. (2019). PAX: Using pseudonymization and anonymization to protect patients' identities and data in the healthcare system. International Journal of Environmental Research and Public Health, 16(9). https://doi.org/10.3390/ijerph16091490
78. Scaiano, M., Middleton, G., Arbuckle, L., Kolhatkar, V., Peyton, L., Dowling, M., ... El Emam, K. (2016). A unified framework for evaluating the risk of re-identification of text de-identification tools. Journal of Biomedical Informatics, 63, 174–183. https://doi.org/10.1016/j.jbi.2016.07.015
79. Munjal, K., & Bhatia, R. (2023). A systematic review of homomorphic encryption and its contributions to the healthcare industry. Complex and Intelligent Systems, 9(4), 3759–3786. https://doi.org/10.1007/s40747-022-00756-z
80. Fang, H., & Qian, Q. (2021). Privacy-preserving machine learning with homomorphic encryption and federated learning. Future Internet, 13(4). https://doi.org/10.3390/fi13040094
81. Kiesel, R., Lakatsch, M., Mann, A., Lossie, K., Sohnius, F., & Schmitt, R. H. (2023). Potential of Homomorphic Encryption for Cloud Computing Use Cases in Manufacturing. Journal of Cybersecurity and Privacy, 3(1), 44–60. https://doi.org/10.3390/jcp3010004
82. Zhu, T., Ye, D., Wang, W., Zhou, W., & Yu, P. S. (2022). More than Privacy: Applying Differential Privacy in Key Areas of Artificial

Intelligence. IEEE Transactions on Knowledge and Data Engineering, 34(6), 2824–2843. https://doi.org/10.1109/TKDE.2020.3014246

83. Joseph, M., Roth, A., Ullman, J., & Waggoner, B. (2020). Local differential privacy for evolving data. Journal of Privacy and Confidentiality, 10(1), 1–29. https://doi.org/10.29012/jpc.718
84. Ataya, G. (2010). PCI DSS audit and compliance. Information Security Technical Report. Elsevier Ltd. https://doi.org/10.1016/j.istr.2011.02.004
85. Clapper, D., & Richmond, W. (2016). Small business compliance with PCI DSS. Journal of Management Information and Decision Sciences, 19(1), 54–67.
86. Abouelmehdi, K., Beni-Hessane, A., & Khaloufi, H. (2018). Big healthcare data: preserving security and privacy. Journal of Big Data, 5(1). https://doi.org/10.1186/s40537-017-0110-7
87. Yue, X., Wang, H., Jin, D., Li, M., & Jiang, W. (2016). Healthcare Data Gateways: Found Healthcare Intelligence on Blockchain with Novel Privacy Risk Control. Journal of Medical Systems, 40(10). https://doi.org/10.1007/s10916-016-0574-6
88. Shahid, J., Ahmad, R., Kiani, A. K., Ahmad, T., Saeed, S., & Almuhaideb, A. M. (2022, February 1). Data Protection and Privacy of the Internet of Healthcare Things (IoHTs). Applied Sciences (Switzerland). MDPI. https://doi.org/10.3390/app12041927
89. Berger, B., & Cho, H. (2019, July 2). Emerging technologies towards enhancing privacy in genomic data sharing. Genome Biology. BioMed Central Ltd. https://doi.org/10.1186/s13059-019-1741-0
90. (2023). EMERGING PRIVACY ENHANCING TECHNOLOGIES CURRENT REGULATORY AND POLICY APPROACHES (pp. 1–51). Retrieved from https://www.oecd.org/en/publications/emerging-privacy-enhancing-technologies_bf121be4-en.html
91. Tewari, A. (2023). mHealth Systems Need a Privacy-by-Design Approach: Commentary on "Federated Machine Learning, Privacy-Enhancing Technologies, and Data Protection Laws in Medical Research: Scoping Review." Journal of Medical Internet Research. JMIR Publications Inc. https://doi.org/10.2196/46700
92. Ometov, A., Bezzateev, S., Mäkitalo, N., Andreev, S., Mikkonen, T., & Koucheryavy, Y. (2018). Multi-factor authentication: A survey. Cryptography, 2(1), 1–31. https://doi.org/10.3390/cryptography2010001

93. Otta, S. P., Panda, S., Gupta, M., & Hota, C. (2023). A Systematic Survey of Multi-Factor Authentication for Cloud Infrastructure. Future Internet, 15(4). https://doi.org/10.3390/fi15040146
94. Epping, M., & Morowczynski, M. (2021). Authentication and Authorization. IDPro Body of Knowledge, 1(6). https://doi.org/10.55621/idpro.78
95. Rostami, G. (2023). Role-based Access Control (RBAC) Authorization in Kubernetes. Journal of ICT Standardization, 11(3), 237–260. https://doi.org/10.13052/jicts2245-800X.1132
96. Cruz, J. P., Kaji, Y., & Yanai, N. (2018). RBAC-SC: Role-based access control using a smart contract. IEEE Access, 6, 12240–12251. https://doi.org/10.1109/ACCESS.2018.2812844
97. Aghili, S. F., Sedaghat, M., Singelée, D., & Gupta, M. (2022). MLS-ABAC: Efficient Multi-Level Security Attribute-Based Access Control scheme. Future Generation Computer Systems, 131, 75–90. https://doi.org/10.1016/j.future.2022.01.003
98. Alohaly, M., Takabi, H., & Blanco, E. (2019). Automated extraction of attributes from natural language attribute-based access control (ABAC) Policies. Cybersecurity, 2(1). https://doi.org/10.1186/s42400-018-0019-2
99. Alohaly, M., Balogun, O., & Takabi, D. (2022). Integrating Cyber Deception Into Attribute-Based Access Control (ABAC) for Insider Threat Detection. IEEE Access, 10, 108965–108978. https://doi.org/10.1109/ACCESS.2022.3213645
100. Martín, A. G., Beltrán, M., Fernández-Isabel, A., & Martín de Diego, I. (2021). An approach to detect user behaviour anomalies within identity federations. Computers and Security, 108. https://doi.org/10.1016/j.cose.2021.102356
101. Beer Mohamed, M. I., Hassan, M. F., Safdar, S., & Saleem, M. Q. (2021). Adaptive security architectural model for protecting identity federation in service-oriented computing. Journal of King Saud University - Computer and Information Sciences, 33(5), 580–592. https://doi.org/10.1016/j.jksuci.2019.03.004
102. SSO (Single Sign On) Implementation. (2016). International Journal of Science and Research (IJSR), 5(6), 988–990. https://doi.org/10.21275/v5i6.nov164426
103. Subhash, K. B., & Kahate, S. A. (2016). Different Framework for Single Sign-On (SSO). International Journal of Computer Science and Mobile Computing, 51(1), 53–56.

104. Manoj, T., Makkithaya, K., & Narendra, V. G. (2022). A Blockchain-Based Decentralized Identifiers for Entity Authentication in Electronic Health Records. Cogent Engineering, 9(1). https://doi.org/10.1080/23311916.2022.2035134
105. Wang, J., Wang, Z., Song, J., & Cheng, H. (2023). Attribute and User Trust Score-Based Zero Trust Access Control Model in IoV. Electronics (Switzerland), 12(23). https://doi.org/10.3390/electronics12234825
106. Awan, S. M., Azad, M. A., Arshad, J., Waheed, U., & Sharif, T. (2023). A Blockchain-Inspired Attribute-Based Zero-Trust Access Control Model for IoT. Information (Switzerland), 14(2). https://doi.org/10.3390/info14020129
107. Kang, H., Liu, G., Wang, Q., Meng, L., & Liu, J. (2023, December 1). Theory and Application of Zero Trust Security: A Brief Survey. Entropy. Multidisciplinary Digital Publishing Institute (MDPI). https://doi.org/10.3390/e25121595
108. Jakimoski, K. (2016). Security techniques for data protection in cloud computing. International Journal of Grid and Distributed Computing, 9(1), 49–56. https://doi.org/10.14257/ijgdc.2016.9.1.05
109. Zhao, N. (2024). Improvement of Cloud Computing Medical Data Protection Technology Based on Symmetric Encryption Algorithm. Journal of Testing and Evaluation, 52(1). https://doi.org/10.1520/JTE2021-0456
110. Xu, R., Jin, W., & Kim, D. (2019). A microservice security agent based on an API gateway in edge computing. Sensors (Switzerland), 19(22). https://doi.org/10.3390/s19224905
111. Qazi, F. (2023). Application Programming Interface (API) Security in Cloud Applications. EAI Endorsed Transactions on Cloud Systems, 7(23), e1. https://doi.org/10.4108/eetcs.v7i23.3011
112. Asha, L. N., Huang, Y., Yodo, N., & Liao, H. (2023). A Quantitative Approach to Measuring Sustainability Risk in Pipeline Infrastructure Systems. Sustainability (Switzerland), 15(19). https://doi.org/10.3390/su151914229
113. Lord, N. (2019). Data Protection: Data in transit vs. Data at Rest. Digital Guardian's Blog. Retrieved from https://digitalguardian.com/blog/data-protection-data-in-transit-vs-data-at-rest
114. Sisodia, J., & Khan, M. (2022). Understanding the Shared Responsibilities Model in Cloud Services. In Real-World Resilience

(Vol. 68, pp. 46–50). Information Systems Audit and Control Association. Retrieved from https://www.isaca.org/resources/isaca journal/issues/2022/volume-3

115. Tank, D., Aggarwal, A., & Chaubey, N. (2022). Virtualization vulnerabilities, security issues, and solutions: a critical study and comparison. International Journal of Information Technology (Singapore), 14(2), 847–862. https://doi.org/10.1007/s41870-019-00294-x
116. Han, J., Zang, W., Yu, M., & Sandhu, R. (2021). Quantify Co-Residency Risks in the Cloud through Deep Learning. IEEE Transactions on Dependable and Secure Computing, 18(4), 1568–1579. https://doi.org/10.1109/TDSC.2020.3032073
117. Mangalagowri, R., & Venkataraman, R. (2023). Ensure secure data transmission during virtual machine migration over a cloud computing environment. International Journal of System Assurance Engineering and Management. https://doi.org/10.1007/s13198-022-01834-8
118. Kinyua, J., & Awuah, L. (2021). AI/ML in security orchestration, automation and response: Future research directions. Intelligent Automation and Soft Computing, 28(2), 527–545. https://doi.org/10.32604/iasc.2021.016240
119. Lee, M., Jang-Jaccard, J., & Kwak, J. (2022). Novel Architecture of Security Orchestration, Automation and Response in Internet of Blended Environment. Computers, Materials and Continua, 73(1), 199–223. https://doi.org/10.32604/cmc.2022.028495
120. Bridges, R. A., Rice, A. E., Oesch, S., Nichols, J. A., Watson, C., Spakes, K., ... Erwin, S. (2023). Testing SOAR tools in use. Computers and Security, 129. https://doi.org/10.1016/j.cose.2023.103201
121. Cheng, X., Zhang, J., & Chen, B. (2019). Cyber situation comprehension for IoT systems based on APT alerts and logs correlation. Sensors (Switzerland), 19(18). https://doi.org/10.3390/s19184045
122. Safana Hyder Abbas, Wedad Abdul Khuder Naser, & Amal Abbas Kadhim. (2023). Subject review: Intrusion Detection System (IDS) and Intrusion Prevention System (IPS). Global Journal of Engineering and Technology Advances, 14(2), 155–158. https://doi.org/10.30574/gjeta.2023.14.2.0031

123. Yang, L., Moubayed, A., & Shami, A. (2022). MTH-IDS: A Multitiered Hybrid Intrusion Detection System for Internet of Vehicles. IEEE Internet of Things Journal, 9(1), 616–632. https://doi.org/10.1109/JIOT.2021.3084796
124. Apicella, A., Isgrò, F., Pollastro, A., & Prevete, R. (2023). On the effects of data normalization for domain adaptation on EEG data. Engineering Applications of Artificial Intelligence, 123. https://doi.org/10.1016/j.engappai.2023.106205
125. Trung, D. D. (2022). Development of data normalization methods for multi-criteria decision making: applying the MARCOS method. Manufacturing Review, 9. https://doi.org/10.1051/mfreview/2022019
126. Wijnia, L., Noordzij, G., Arends, L. R., Rikers, R. M. J. P., & Loyens, S. M. M. (2024). The Effects of Problem-Based, Project-Based, and Case-Based Learning on Students' Motivation: A Meta-Analysis. Educational Psychology Review, 36(1). https://doi.org/10.1007/s10648-024-09864-3
127. Wu, F., Wang, T., Yin, D., Xu, X., Jin, C., Mu, N., & Tan, Q. (2023). Application of case-based learning in psychology teaching: a meta-analysis. BMC Medical Education, 23(1). https://doi.org/10.1186/s12909-023-04525-5
128. Delua, J. (2021). Supervised vs. Unsupervised Learning: What's the Difference? IBM Analytics, Data Science/Machine Learning, 1–9.
129. Joachims, T. (2007). Supervised vs. Unsupervised Learning Machine Learning, 1–5.
130. Yeboah-Ofori, A., Islam, S., Lee, S. W., Shamszaman, Z. U., Muhammad, K., Altaf, M., & Al-Rakhami, M. S. (2021). Cyber Threat Predictive Analytics for Improving Cyber Supply Chain Security. IEEE Access, 9, 94318–94337. https://doi.org/10.1109/ACCESS.2021.3087109
131. Guarascio, M., Cassavia, N., Pisani, F. S., & Manco, G. (2022). Boosting Cyber-Threat Intelligence via Collaborative Intrusion Detection. Future Generation Computer Systems, 135, 30–43. https://doi.org/10.1016/j.future.2022.04.028
132. Alotaibi, A., & Rassam, M. A. (2023, February 1). Adversarial Machine Learning Attacks against Intrusion Detection Systems: A Survey on Strategies and Defense. Future Internet. MDPI. https://doi.org/10.3390/fi15020062

133. Aloraini, F., Javed, A., Rana, O., & Burnap, P. (2022). Adversarial machine learning in IoT from an insider point of view. Journal of Information Security and Applications, 70. https://doi.org/10.1016/j.jisa.2022.103341
134. Anthi, E., Williams, L., Rhode, M., Burnap, P., & Wedgbury, A. (2021). Adversarial attacks on machine learning cybersecurity defenses in Industrial Control Systems. Journal of Information Security and Applications, 58. https://doi.org/10.1016/j.jisa.2020.102717
135. Fudenberg, D., Newey, W., Strack, P., & Strzalecki, T. (2020). Testing the drift-diffusion model. Proceedings of the National Academy of Sciences of the United States of America, 117(52), 33141–33148. https://doi.org/10.1073/PNAS.2011446117
136. Horsman, G., & Sunde, N. (2022). Unboxing the digital forensic investigation process. Science and Justice, 62(2), 171–180. https://doi.org/10.1016/j.scijus.2022.01.002
137. Casino, F., Dasaklis, T. K., Spathoulas, G. P., Anagnostopoulos, M., Ghosal, A., Borocz, I., … Patsakis, C. (2022). Research Trends, Challenges, and Emerging Topics in Digital Forensics: A Review of Reviews. IEEE Access. Institute of Electrical and Electronics Engineers Inc. https://doi.org/10.1109/ACCESS.2022.3154059
138. Al-Dhaqm, A., Ikuesan, R. A., Kebande, V. R., Razak, S. A., Grispos, G., Choo, K. K. R., … Alsewari, A. A. (2021). Digital Forensics Subdomains: The State of the Art and Future Directions. IEEE Access, 9, 152476–152502. https://doi.org/10.1109/ACCESS.2021.3124262
139. Ito, A., Hagström, M., Bokrantz, J., Skoogh, A., Nawcki, M., Gandhi, K., … Bärring, M. (2022, July 1). Improved root-cause analysis to support resilient production systems. Journal of Manufacturing Systems. Elsevier B.V. https://doi.org/10.1016/j.jmsy.2022.07.015
140. Peerally, M. F., Carr, S., Waring, J., & DIxon-Woods, M. (2017). The problem with root cause analysis. BMJ Quality and Safety, 26(5), 417–422. https://doi.org/10.1136/bmjqs-2016-005511
141. Soares Ito, A., Ylipää, T., Gullander, P., Bokrantz, J., & Skoogh, A. (2022). Prioritization of root cause analysis in production disturbance management. International Journal of Quality and Reliability Management, 39(5), 1133–1150. https://doi.org/10.1108/IJQRM-12-2020-0402
142. Jang, J., Oh, Y., Ryu, G., & Choi, D. (2023). Data Reconstruction Attack with Label Guessing for Federated Learning. Journal of Internet Technology, 24(4), 893–903.

https://doi.org/10.53106/160792642023072404007

143. Sun, Y., Leng, L., Jin, Z., & Kim, B. G. (2022). Reinforced Palmprint Reconstruction Attacks in Biometric Systems. Sensors, 22(2). https://doi.org/10.3390/s22020591
144. Su, Q., Wang, H., Sun, C., Li, B., & Li, J. (2022). Cyber-attacks against the security of cyber-physical power systems: State estimation, attack reconstruction, and defense strategy. Applied Mathematics and Computation, 413. https://doi.org/10.1016/j.amc.2021.126639
145. Ohmori, M. (2019). On automation and orchestration of an initial computer security incident response by introducing centralized incident tracking system. Journal of Information Processing, 27, 564–573. https://doi.org/10.2197/ipsjjip.27.564
146. Kinyua, J., & Awuah, L. (2021). AI/ML in security orchestration, automation and response: Future research directions. Intelligent Automation and Soft Computing, 28(2), 527–545. https://doi.org/10.32604/iasc.2021.016240
147. Oujezsky, V., Horvath, T., & Holik, M. (2022). Security Incident Response Automation for xPON Networks. Journal of Communications Software and Systems, 18(2), 144–152. https://doi.org/10.24138/JCOMSS-2022-0033
148. Goldsmith, M. R., Kroemer, J. A., Pokhrel, S., Chang, D. T., Fortin, G. M., & Deschenes, A. (2021). Toward Playbooks, Workflows and Federated Models for Agrochemical Discovery and De-risking. In ACS Symposium Series (Vol. 1390, pp. 181–200). American Chemical Society. https://doi.org/10.1021/bk-2021-1390.ch009
149. Elvas, L. B., Marreiros, C. F., Dinis, J. M., Pereira, M. C., Martins, A. L., & Ferreira, J. C. (2020). Data-driven approach for incident management in a smart city. Applied Sciences (Switzerland), 10(22), 1–18. https://doi.org/10.3390/app10228281
150. Walkowski, M., Oko, J., & Sujecki, S. (2021). Article vulnerability management models using a common vulnerability scoring system. Applied Sciences (Switzerland), 11(18). https://doi.org/10.3390/app11188735
151. Orru, K., Hansson, S., Gabel, F., Tammpuu, P., Krüger, M., Savadori, L., ... Rhinard, M. (2022). Approaches to 'vulnerability' in eight European disaster management systems. Disasters, 46(3), 742–767. https://doi.org/10.1111/disa.12481
152. Flanagan, B. E., Gregory, E. W., Hallisey, E. J., Heitgerd, J. L., & Lewis, B. (2020). A Social Vulnerability Index for Disaster

Management. Journal of Homeland Security and Emergency Management, 8(1). https://doi.org/10.2202/1547-7355.1792

153. Fairbrother, A., Wenstel, R., Sappington, K., & Wood, W. (2007). Framework for Metals Risk Assessment. Ecotoxicology and Environmental Safety, 68(2), 145–227. https://doi.org/10.1016/j.ecoenv.2007.03.015
154. Kandasamy, K., Srinivas, S., Achuthan, K., & Rangan, V. P. (2020). IoT cyber risk: a holistic analysis of cyber risk assessment frameworks, risk vectors, and risk ranking process. Eurasip Journal on Information Security, 2020(1). https://doi.org/10.1186/s13635-020-00111-0
155. Mell, P., Scarfone, K., & Romanosky, S. (2007). The Common Vulnerability Scoring System (CVSS) and Its Applicability to Federal Agency Systems. National Institute of Standards and Technology (p. 33).
156. Basya, F., Hardjanto, M., & Permana Putra, I. (2022). SHA512 and MD5 Algorithm Vulnerability Testing Using Common Vulnerability Scoring System (CVSS). Buana Information Technology and Computer Sciences (BIT and CS), 3(1), 1–4. https://doi.org/10.36805/bit-cs.v3i1.2046
157. Wang, Y., Yu, B., Yu, H., Xiao, L., Ji, H., & Zhao, Y. (2023). Automotive Cybersecurity Vulnerability Assessment Using the Common Vulnerability Scoring System and Bayesian Network Model. IEEE Systems Journal, 17(2), 2880–2891. https://doi.org/10.1109/JSYST.2022.3230097
158. Păunescu, C., Popescu, M. C., & Blid, L. (2018). Business impact analysis for business continuity: Evidence from Romanian enterprises on critical functions. Management and Marketing, 13(3), 1035–1050. https://doi.org/10.2478/MMCKS-2018-0021
159. Torabi, S. A., Rezaei Soufi, H., & Sahebjamnia, N. (2014). A new framework for business impact analysis in business continuity management (with a case study). Safety Science, 68, 309–323. https://doi.org/10.1016/j.ssci.2014.04.017
160. Ramaj, X., Sánchez-Gordón, M., Gkioulos, V., Chockalingam, S., & Colomo-Palacios, R. (2022, November 1). Holding on to Compliance While Adopting DevSecOps: An SLR. Electronics (Switzerland). MDPI. https://doi.org/10.3390/electronics11223707
161. Lee, W. T., & Liu, Z. W. (2023). Microservices-based DevSecOps Platform using Pipeline and Open Source Software. Journal of

Information Science and Engineering, 39(5), 1117–1128. https://doi.org/10.6688/JISE.202309_39(5).0007

162. Camacho, N. G. (2024). Unlocking the Potential of AI/ML in DevSecOps: Effective Strategies and Optimal Practices. Journal of Artificial Intelligence General Science (JAIGS) ISSN:3006-4023, 3(1), 106–115. https://doi.org/10.60087/jaigs.v3i1.72
163. Umeugo, W. (2023). SECURE SOFTWARE DEVELOPMENT LIFECYCLE: A CASE FOR ADOPTION IN SOFTWARE SMES. International Journal of Advanced Research in Computer Science, 14(01), 5–12. https://doi.org/10.26483/ijarcs.v14i1.6949
164. Tudela, F. M., Higuera, J. R. B., Higuera, J. B., Montalvo, J. A. S., & Argyros, M. I. (2020). On combining static, dynamic, and interactive security testing tools to improve OWASP Top 10 security vulnerability detection in web applications. Applied Sciences (Switzerland), 10(24), 1–26. https://doi.org/10.3390/app10249119
165. Thatikonda, V. K. (2023). Beyond the Buzz: A Journey Through CI/CD Principles and Best Practices. European Journal of Theoretical and Applied Sciences, 1(5), 334–340. https://doi.org/10.59324/ejtas.2023.1(5).24
166. Rangineni, S., & Bhardwaj, A. K. (2024). Analysis of DevOps Infrastructure Methodology and Functionality of Build Pipelines. ICST Transactions on Scalable Information Systems. https://doi.org/10.4108/eetsis.4977
167. Wettinger, J., Breitenbücher, U., Kopp, O., & Leymann, F. (2016). Streamlining DevOps automation for Cloud applications using TOSCA as a standardized metamodel. Future Generation Computer Systems, 56, 317–332. https://doi.org/10.1016/j.future.2015.07.017
168. Hasani, T., Rezania, D., Levallet, N., O'Reilly, N., & Mohammadi, M. (2023). Privacy-enhancing technology adoption and its impact on SMEs' performance. International Journal of Engineering Business Management, 15. https://doi.org/10.1177/18479790231172874
169. Safa, N. S., Mitchell, F., Maple, C., Azad, M. A., & Dabbagh, M. (2022). Privacy Enhancing Technologies (PETs) for connected vehicles in smart cities. Transactions on Emerging Telecommunications Technologies, 33(10). https://doi.org/10.1002/ett.4173

170. Shen, Y., & Pearson, S. (2011). Privacy-enhancing technologies: A review. HP Laboratories Technical Report.

171. Marcolla, C., Sucasas, V., Manzano, M., Bassoli, R., Fitzek, F. H. P., Aaraj, N., & Marcolla, C. (2022). Survey on Fully Homomorphic Encryption, Theory, and Applications. Proceedings of the IEEE, 110(10), 1572–1609. https://doi.org/10.1109/JPROC.2022.3205665

172. Acar, A., Aksu, H., Uluagac, A. S., & Conti, M. (2019). A Survey on Homomorphic Encryption Schemes. ACM Computing Surveys, 51(4), 1–35. https://doi.org/10.1145/3214303

173. Acar, A., Aksu, H., Uluagac, A. S., & Conti, M. (2019, September 30). A survey on homomorphic encryption schemes: Theory and implementation. ACM Computing Surveys. Association for Computing Machinery. https://doi.org/10.1145/3214303

174. Zhou, J., Feng, Y., Wang, Z., & Guo, D. (2021). Using secure multi-party computation to protect privacy on a permissioned blockchain. Sensors, 21(4), 1–17. https://doi.org/10.3390/s21041540

175. Lindell, Y., Pinkas, B., Smart, N. P., & Yanai, A. (2019). Efficient Constant-Round Multi-party Computation Combining BMR and SPDZ. Journal of Cryptology, 32(3), 1026–1069. https://doi.org/10.1007/s00145-019-09322-2

176. Ouadrhiri, A. E., & Abdelhadi, A. (2022). Differential Privacy for Deep and Federated Learning: A Survey. IEEE Access, 10, 22359–22380. https://doi.org/10.1109/ACCESS.2022.3151670

177. Rodríguez-Barroso, N., Stipcich, G., Jiménez-López, D., Ruiz-Millán, J. A., Martínez-Cámara, E., González-Seco, G., ... Herrera, F. (2020). Federated Learning and Differential Privacy: Software tools analysis, the Sherpa.ai FL framework and methodological guidelines for preserving data privacy. Information Fusion, 64, 270–292. https://doi.org/10.1016/j.inffus.2020.07.009

178. Yang, J., Chen, S., Wang, G., Wang, Z., Jie, Z., & Arif, M. (2024). GFL-ALDPA: a gradient compression federated learning framework based on adaptive local differential privacy budget allocation. Multimedia Tools and Applications, 83(9), 26349–26368. https://doi.org/10.1007/s11042-023-16543-y

179. Suzaki, K., Nakajima, K., Oi, T., & Tsukamoto, A. (2021). TS-Perf: General Performance Measurement of Trusted Execution Environment and Rich Execution Environment on Intel SGX, Arm

TrustZone, and RISC-V Keystone. IEEE Access, 9, 133520–133530. https://doi.org/10.1109/ACCESS.2021.3112202

180. Geppert, T., Deml, S., Sturzenegger, D., & Ebert, N. (2022, July 7). Trusted Execution Environments: Applications and Organizational Challenges. Frontiers in Computer Science. Frontiers Media S.A. https://doi.org/10.3389/fcomp.2022.930741

181. Sebastian, D. J., Agrawal, U., Tamimi, A., & Hahn, A. (2019). DER-TEE: Secure Distributed Energy Resource Operations through Trusted Execution Environments. IEEE Internet of Things Journal, 6(4), 6476–6486. https://doi.org/10.1109/JIOT.2019.2909768

182. Phiayura, P., & Teerakanok, S. (2023). A Comprehensive Framework for Migrating to Zero Trust Architecture. IEEE Access, 11, 19487–19511. https://doi.org/10.1109/ACCESS.2023.3248622

183. Syed, N. F., Shah, S. W., Shaghaghi, A., Anwar, A., Baig, Z., & Doss, R. (2022). Zero Trust Architecture (ZTA): A Comprehensive Survey. IEEE Access. Institute of Electrical and Electronics Engineers Inc. https://doi.org/10.1109/ACCESS.2022.3174679

184. Alagappan, A., Venkatachary, S. K., & Andrews, L. J. B. (2022). Augmenting Zero Trust Network Architecture to enhance security in virtual power plants. Energy Reports, 8, 1309–1320. https://doi.org/10.1016/j.egyr.2021.11.272

185. Hussain Al-Naji, F., & Zagrouba, R. (2022). CAB-IoT: Continuous authentication architecture based on Blockchain for the Internet of Things. Journal of King Saud University - Computer and Information Sciences, 34(6), 2497–2514. https://doi.org/10.1016/j.jksuci.2020.11.023

186. Baig, A. F., & Eskeland, S. (2021, September 1). Security, privacy, and usability in continuous authentication: A survey. Sensors. MDPI. https://doi.org/10.3390/s21175967

187. Ivy, J., Lee, S. B., Franz, D., & Crumpton, J. (2019). Seeding Cybersecurity Workforce Pathways with Secondary Education. Computer, 52(3), 67–75. https://doi.org/10.1109/MC.2018.2884671

188. Suvarna, M., Yap, K. S., Yang, W., Li, J., Ng, Y. T., & Wang, X. (2021). Cyber–Physical Production Systems for Data-Driven, Decentralized, and Secure Manufacturing—A Perspective. Engineering, 7(9), 1212–1223. https://doi.org/10.1016/j.eng.2021.04.021

189. Paicu, S. C. (2023). Data-Driven Security and Democratic Intelligence: Key Role of Critical Engagement by Academia. International Journal of Intelligence and CounterIntelligence, 36(3), 711–728. https://doi.org/10.1080/08850607.2022.2032494
190. Daniel, C., Mullarkey, M., & Agrawal, M. (2023). RQ Labs: A Cybersecurity Workforce Skills Development Framework. Information Systems Frontiers, 25(2), 431–450. https://doi.org/10.1007/s10796-022-10332-